JOHN KEATS AND
THE CULTURE OF DISSENT

JOHN KEATS
AND THE
CULTURE OF DISSENT

NICHOLAS ROE

CLARENDON PRESS · OXFORD
1997

Oxford University Press, Great Clarendon Street, Oxford OX2 6DP

Oxford New York

Athens Auckland Bangkok Bogota Bombay
Buenos Aires Calcutta Cape Town Dar es Salaam
Delhi Florence Hong Kong Istanbul Karachi
Kuala Lumpur Madras Madrid Melbourne
Mexico City Nairobi Paris Singapore
Taipei Tokyo Toronto

and associated companies in
Berlin Ibadan

Oxford is a trade mark of Oxford University Press

Published in the United States by
Oxford University Press Inc., New York

British Library Cataloguing in Publication Data

Data available

Library of Congress Cataloging-in-Publication Data
Roe, Nicholas.
John Keats and the culture of dissent / Nicholas Roe.
Includes bibliographical references (p.) and index.
1. Keats, John, 1795–1821—Political and social views.
2. Politics and literature—Great Britain—History—19th century.
3. Radicalism—Great Britain—History—19th century.   4. Political
poetry, English—History and criticism.   5. Social problems in
literature.   I. Title.
PR4838.P6R64   1996   821'.7—dc20   96–34554
ISBN 0-19-818396-8

1 3 5 7 9 10 8 6 4 2

Typeset by Best-set Typesetter Ltd., Hong Kong
Printed in Great Britain
on acid-free paper by
Biddles Ltd.,
Guildford and Kings Lynn

And now, as deep into the wood as we
Might mark a lynx's eye, there glimmered light
Fair faces and a rush of garments white,
Plainer and plainer shewing, till at last
Into the widest alley they all past,
Making directly for the woodland altar.
O kindly muse! let not my weak tongue faulter
In telling of this goodly company,
Of their old piety, and of their glee:
But let a portion of ethereal dew
Fall on my head, and presently unmew
My soul; that I may dare, in wayfaring,
To stammer where old Chaucer used to sing.

(*Endymion*, I. 122–34)

We live far from the world of letters,—out of the pale of a
fashionable criticism,—aloof from the atmosphere of a
Court; but we are surrounded by a beautiful country, and
love Poetry, which we read out of doors, as well as in.

(John Hamilton Reynolds, 'The Quarterly Review.—
Mr Keats', *Examiner* (11 Oct. 1818), 649)

Preface and Acknowledgements

> Reynolds has returned from a six weeks enjoyment in Devonshire, he is well and persuades me to publish my pot of Basil as an answer to the attacks made upon me in Blackwood's Magazine and the Quarterly Review. There have been two Letters in my defence in the Chronicle and one in the Examiner, coppied from the Alfred Exeter paper, and written by Reynolds—I do not know who wrote those in the Chronicle—This is a mere matter of the moment—I think I shall be among the English Poets after my death.[1]

KEATS'S letter of October 1818 wishfully abstracted his life as a writer from the literary warfare carried on in *Blackwood's Magazine* and the *Quarterly Review*, projecting his reception 'among the English Poets' into future years beyond his death. The Romantic notion of a 'posthumous life' was frequently aired at celebrations of Keats's bicentenary during 1995, an appropriate recognition of his achievement as an English poet which has also been given scholarly currency by Andrew Bennett's study of reading and audience in Keats's poetry.[2] In surveying the two centuries since Keats's lifetime one finds that by seeking to disconnect his literary reputation from the 'matter of the moment', Keats had anticipated the aesthetic view of his poetry which was adopted by generations of nineteenth- and twentieth-century readers. Certainly, many readers responded to Keats as a 'thing of beauty'—but by no means all of them did so: over the years Keats's numerous biographers and some of his critics have related the poems to the vexing circumstances of his life and times. More lately the historical investment of Romantic studies has been so thorough that Michael O'Neill, concerned to re-assert the uniqueness of the 'verbal world' created in Keats's

[1] Keats to George and Georgiana Keats, 14, 16, 21, 24, 31 Oct. 1818, *Letters*, i. 393–4.

[2] Andrew Bennett, *Keats, Narrative, and Audience: The Posthumous Life of Writing* (Cambridge, 1994).

poetry, has observed that 'though a poem emerges from a life it takes on a life of its own; often the two lives will not be straight-forwardly related'.[3] In 'The Posthumous Life of John Keats', a BBC radio programme marking Keats's bicentenary, Marilyn Butler reflected from a similar angle on recent approaches to Keats: 'when a poet is very whole and complete in himself, when he actually tries to create a world that is an aesthetic world, he does demand . . . a lot of attention to his text, his words—particularly to words—and to the way he chose to shape it. I think that side of Keats, Keats's artistry, is actually being neglected.'[4]

Perhaps New Historicist criticism has indeed overlooked the artistry of Keats's poems and the extent to which, as Helen Vendler says, each of the poems 'arises from art as well as from circumstance'.[5] Scholarly and critical interests change, and attention may now be turning to a reappraisal of the qualities of verbal art in Keats's writing. Yet, as Vendler goes on to remind us, the aesthetic world—whether of painting, sculpture, music, or poetry—is never entirely sealed off from the circumstances of life to constitute a separate, perfected unity; in pointing to the face Benjamin Haydon sketched for his painting *Christ's Entry into Jerusalem*, Vendler recognizes Keats's 'vivacity, and even his pugnacity . . . the spirited eagerness remarked on by all [Keats's] friends'.[6]

Like many of the faces in Haydon's painting, and as Virginia Woolf noted, a

new book is attached to life by a thousand minute filaments. Life goes on and the filaments break and disappear. But at the moment they ring and resound and set up all kinds of irrelevant responses. Keats was an apothecary and lived in Hampstead, and consorted with Leigh Hunt and the Cockneys.[7]

Hostile responses to Keats's books arose from prejudices which at the time were pressingly relevant to his life as a writer. The

[3] See ' "When this warm scribe my hand": Writing and History in *Hyperion* and *The Fall of Hyperion*', in *K&H* 147.

[4] 'The Posthumous Life of John Keats', first broadcast on BBC Radio 3, 29 Oct. 1995.

[5] 'John Keats, 1795–1821: John Keats, 1795–1995', in *John Keats 1795–1995: With a Catalogue of the Harvard Keats Collection* (Cambridge, Mass., 1995), 9.

[6] Ibid. 11.

[7] 'Lockhart's Criticism', *The Moment and Other Essays* (London, 1947), 62.

attacks were of course generated by the immediacy with which Keats spoke to his contemporaries but, as I argue in my introduction, critical hostility also initiated the disconnection of those 'filaments' which were sparklingly apparent at the first publication of his poems.

In this book I have set out to restore the vivacious, even pugnacious, voices of Keats's poetry, seeking in particular to trace those frequently unstraightforward ways in which his poems responded to and addressed matters of the moment. Reynolds's idea that Keats might publish *Isabella; or, The Pot of Basil* as a counterblast to the critics built upon his confident arrival on the literary scene in *Poems, by John Keats.* I have tried to show that, even in the case of a writer about whose life so much is now known, there is fresh information to be discovered which opens new perspectives on the poetry. My first two chapters explore the dissenting culture of Enfield School where Keats passed his formative years, showing how the school exercised a strong influence on Keats's imaginative life and his political radicalism. Imagination and politics are two themes which intertwine through the following chapters on Keats's friendship with Charles Cowden Clarke, his medical career, the 'Cockney' milieu in which his poems were written, and the original, controversial impact of his three collections of poetry. Because the aesthetic world of Keats's poetry is so intensely realized, I have been concerned rather less with the reconstruction of contexts for it (although these have their place in this study) than I have with attempting to retrieve the contemporary resonances of Keats's language, and tracing the semantic threads which attached the poems to the world in which they were written (and which loosened as Keats assumed a canonical appeal). This has entailed a form of close reading which might properly be called a literal archaeology, in that I have sought to return (so far as possible) to the original inflections of Keats's language, imagery, and poetic style in an endeavour to recover how his poems were once understood to be loaded with controversial meaning.

One method I have adopted involves relating the poems to contemporary events as these were reported in journals of the day, especially those which we know Keats read and in which his poems were published—the *Examiner*, the *Yellow Dwarf*, and the

Champion. This has the effect of highlighting the explicit topicality of numerous poems, and it also places the more subdued, intimate idiom of others (the verse epistles, for instance) in the wider cultural perspective which defined their social and political meanings. When read alongside the *Examiner* and the writings of individuals associated with that journal, *Poems, by John Keats, Endymion*, even 'To Autumn' abound with contemporary references and pointers. Keatsian themes and motifs such as pagan ceremony in *Endymion* and 'Ode on a Grecian Urn', and woodland verdure in 'Robin Hood' and 'Ode to a Nightingale', can be located within a broader revolutionary discourse which dated from the 1790s. In all of these ways the unsettling, modish textures of Keats's vocabulary and style (frequently stigmatized as the signs of his 'vulgarity') articulate once again their conspiratorial melodies as lyrical counterparts to—and departures from—Leigh Hunt's vigorous political journalism and literary criticism.

While this book offers fresh readings of some of Keats's best-known poems, I hope also that it will encourage further reassessment of Hunt's achievement as poet and journalist. As I argue in the introduction, Z's polemic in *Blackwood's Magazine* has had a lasting effect in damning 'Cockney' or 'suburban' culture right down to our own time. Keats, Hunt, and Hazlitt were the principal targets for Z's prejudice, and one purpose of this book is to explain how and why those 'bad' writers appeared as powerful advocates for dissent from the cultural orthodoxies of the day. Another of my concerns has been more broadly to rehabilitate the 'Cockney School': these writers formed a coterie which did much to initiate the democratization of literary and political culture which is our inheritance today. Hazlitt said rightly that Leigh Hunt 'improves upon acquaintance'; others in their Cockney circle, such as John Hamilton Reynolds, Horace Smith, and even Cornelius Webb—ridiculed by Z, and treated slightly by Keats—do so too.[8]

My research was supported by a grant from the British Academy, and by the award of a Leverhulme Research Fellowship

---

[8] *Spirit of the Age*, Howe, xi. 176. For Keats's remark that Webb was 'unfortunately . . . of our Party occasionally at Hampstead' see his letter to Benjamin Bailey, *Letters*, i. 180 and n.

which enabled me to complete the research and write this book. The School of English at St Andrews University provided me with a word processor, and has facilitated my work in various ways. I acknowledge all of this assistance with thanks, and wish also to express my gratitude to the staff of the following libraries and institutions: the Bodleian Library; the British Library; the Brotherton Library, Leeds University, especially Christopher Sheppard, Head of Special Collections; Edinburgh University Library; the Keats Collection in the Houghton Library, Harvard University, especially Susan Halpert and Leslie Morris, Curator of Manuscripts; Keats House, Hampstead, especially the Curator Christina Gee and Roberta Davis; Manchester Public Library; the National Library of Scotland, Edinburgh, especially Ian Cunningham and Iain G. Brown of the Manuscripts Division; St Andrews University Library; the Library of the Wellcome Institute, London, especially Keith Moore; Wills Medical Library at Guy's Hospital, London, especially the Acting Librarian Andrew Baster. I owe particular debts to Christine Gascoigne and Cilla Jackson of the Special Collections Department, St Andrews University Library; they have kindly and patiently helped with my enquiries over many years. Vincent Newey's splendid essays on Keats's poetry and politics opened the subject up for me. John Barnard and David Fairer of the School of English, Leeds University, have been closely involved with my work on Keats from the outset and have helped in many ways. Jack Stillinger read a draft of the book with the meticulous care characteristic of all of his scholarship, and his advice and suggestions have been invaluable. Jason Freeman at Oxford University Press encouraged my work on this book from an early stage. The following colleagues and friends have shared ideas, and offered support and encouragement: J. H. Alexander, Michael Alexander, Richard Allen, Richard Altick, Isobel Armstrong, Martin Aske, Andrew Bennett, Drummond and Vivian Bone, Frederick Burwick, Jeffrey Cox, Rachel Crawford, Robert Crawford, Lilla Crisafulli-Jones, Thomas Duncan, Douglas Dunn, James Engell, Kelvin Everest, Reg and Mary Foakes, Bruce Graver, Terence Hoagwood, Mimi Hotchkiss, Lawrence and Mary James, Anthony Johnson, Kenneth Johnston, Theresa Kelley, John Kerrigan, Peter Kitson, Greg Kucich, Beth Lau, Thomas McFarland, Peter Manning,

Raimonda Modiano, Andrew Motion, Pamela Norris, Michael O'Neill, Barbara Packer, Morton Paley, Jack and Janice Patten, Thomas Pfau, Ralph Pite, Alan Richardson, Robert Ryan, Grant Scott, Philip Shaw, Paul Sheats, Helen Small, Stuart Sperry, Simon and Jane Taylor, Nicola Trott, Heather Walker, Stephen Wall, Daniel Watkins, Reggie and Shirley Watters, Timothy Webb, Susan Wolfson, Alastair and Liz Work. The book is dedicated to the person whose wisdom and encouragement, generously given, have improved these pages at numberless points.

N.H.R.

Permissions

John Betjeman, *Summoned by Bells*, is quoted by permission of John Murray (Publishers) Ltd. Tony Harrison's 'Them & [uz]' from *Selected Poems* is quoted by permission of Tony Harrison. Philip Larkin's 'Toads Revisited' from *Collected Poems* and Seamus Heaney's 'Exposure' from *North* are quoted by permission of Faber and Faber Ltd. Part of Chapter 8 originally appeared as an essay entitled 'Keats's Lisping Sedition' in *Essays in Criticism* (Jan. 1992). I am grateful to the editors Stephen Wall and Christopher Ricks for permission to include material from the essay here.

Contents

LIST OF ILLUSTRATIONS xviii

ABBREVIATIONS xix

INTRODUCTION: JOHN KEATS IN THE
COCKNEY SCHOOL 1

1. A COCKNEY SCHOOLROOM: KEATS AND
THE CULTURE OF DISSENT 27

Dissenting Culture and Enfield School 27

*'Knowledge enormous': The Achievement of John Collett
Ryland* 29

'The Living Orrery': Keats's Education at Enfield School 33

A Republican Library 45

2. COSMOPOLITICS: HISTORY, CLASSICS,
AND PRETTY PAGANISM 51

Keats and History 51

Cockney Classics 60

The Politics of Pan, and Pretty Paganism 71

3. KEATS AND CHARLES COWDEN CLARKE 88

John Keats's Lost Years 88

*A Radical's Vade-mecum: Charles Cowden Clarke's
Commonplace Book* 93

An Era in his Existence: Keats and Leigh Hunt 105

4. 'SOFT HUMANITY PUT ON': THE POETRY
AND POLITICS OF SOCIALITY 1798–1818 111

'Home-born feeling': The Example of Coleridge 111

Keats, Hunt, and Sociality 116

5. SONGS FROM THE WOODS; OR, OUTLAW LYRICS 134

   The Chaucerian Key 134

   Through the Tangled Mazes of the Forest 140

   Ethereal Pigs and Airy Citadels 155

6. THE PHARMACOPOLITICAL POET 160

   The Wavering Apprentice 160

   Dresser to 'Billy' Lucas: A Cautionary Tale 163

   Meeting Astley Cooper 169

   Radical Medicine: Astley Cooper and John Thelwall 173

7. 'APOLLO'S TOUCH': THE PHARMACY OF IMAGINATION 182

   Where's the Poet? 182

   The Chemistry of Revolution 187

   'Effigies of Pain' 191

   A Sylvan Hospice: 'Ode to a Nightingale' 195

8. LISPING SEDITION: *POEMS*, *ENDYMION*, AND THE POETICS OF DISSENT 202

   A Cockney Bantling 202

   A Time when Pan is not Sought 208

   The Suburban School 212

EPILOGUE: JOHN KEATS'S COMMONWEALTH: THE 1820 COLLECTION AND 'TO AUTUMN' 230

   Negative Capability and its Backgrounds: Shakespeare, Politics, Theatre 230

   Sympathetic Imagination 239

   The Godwinian Inheritance 242

   A Godwin Perfectibility Man 245

   John Keats's Commonwealth 248

   A Serious Conspiracy in Manchester 253

The Calendar of Nature   257
'Who hath not seen thee?'   263
Postscript   266

APPENDIX: *Correspondence Relating to the 'Cockney
School' Essays, from the 'Blackwood Papers' in the National
Library of Scotland*   268

BIBLIOGRAPHY   277

INDEX   293

List of Illustrations

Between pp. 156 and 157

1. John Collett Ryland
2. John Keats's School at Enfield
3. Charles Cowden Clarke
4. James Henry Leigh Hunt
5. Frontispiece to *Poems, by John Keats* (1817)
6. *Manchester Heroes*

Abbreviations

Unless indicated otherwise, quotations from Keats's poetry will be drawn from *Poems of John Keats*, ed. Jack Stillinger (Cambridge, Mass., 1978).

AP	*The Poems of John Keats*, ed. Miriam Allott (London, 1970)
BLJ	*Byron's Letters and Journals*, ed. Leslie A. Marchand (12 vols., London, 1973–82)
DNB	*Dictionary of National Biography*
Howe	*The Complete Works of William Hazlitt*, ed. P. P. Howe (21 vols., London, 1930–4)
K&H	*Keats and History*, ed. Nicholas Roe (Cambridge, 1995)
KC	*The Keats Circle: Letters and Papers 1816–1878 and More Letters and Poems 1814–1879*, ed. Hyder Edward Rollins (2nd edn., 2 vols., Cambridge, Mass., 1965)
KCH	*Keats: The Critical Heritage*, ed. Geoffrey Matthews (London, 1971)
KHM	Jerome J. McGann, 'Keats and the Historical Method in Literary Criticism', *Modern Language Notes*, 94 (1979), rpt. *The Beauty of Inflections: Literary Investigations in Historical Method and Theory* (Oxford, 1985)
KP	'Keats and Politics: A Forum', ed. Susan Wolfson, *SIR* 25 (Summer 1986)
K–SJ	*Keats–Shelley Journal*
K–SMB	*Keats–Shelley Memorial Bulletin*
Letters	*The Letters of John Keats, 1814–1821*, ed. Hyder Edward Rollins (2 vols., Cambridge, Mass., 1958)
LLL	Richard Monckton Milnes, *Life, Letters, and Literary Remains, of John Keats* (2 vols., London, 1848).
NLS	The National Library of Scotland

OED	*The Oxford English Dictionary* (2nd edn., Oxford, 1989)
PMLA	*Publications of the Modern Language Association of America*
Recollections	Charles and Mary Cowden Clarke, *Recollections of Writers* (1878; Fontwell, 1969)
'Recollections of Keats'	'Recollections of John Keats' in *Recollections*
SIR	*Studies in Romanticism*
TLS	*Times Literary Supplement*

Introduction:
John Keats in the Cockney School

Oh! Mr Blackwood, Mr Blackwood, oh!
How could you serve my Pretty Cockneys so?
(H. Townsend to Christopher North
(John Wilson), 6 Dec. 1821)[1]

Autumn 1795 in England was a season of riots and rumoured conspiracies. Crop failures, inflation, bread shortages, and the threat of invasion contributed to the misery of a nation that had been at war with France for almost three years. Throughout the country protesters organized meetings, seeking reform of parliamentary representation and an end to the war. At one such meeting on 26 October a massive crowd of London's citizens gathered in Copenhagen Fields to hear John Thelwall denounce the government for abandoning the people to 'misery, neglect, and injustice', while employing informers and agents to foment conflict:

Yes, Citizens, conspiracies there are; but they are not the friends of liberty who are the conspirators, but the friends of the tottering cause of despotism and corruption. Those are the wretches who will conspire together, in the vain hope of making the friends of liberty, by plunging them into tumult and disorder, the instruments of their detestable machinations.[2]

By conspiring to provoke 'tumult and disorder' in a miserable populace, the 'friends of despotism' sought a pretext for introducing oppressive legislation to shore up the establishment—that 'tottering cause of despotism and corruption'. Three days afterwards, at the opening of parliament on 29 October, the King's carriage was surrounded in the street and its windows

---

[1] NLS, MS 4007, quoted by permission of the Trustees of the National Library of Scotland.

[2] John Thelwall, *Peaceful Discussion, and not Tumultuary Violence the Means of Redressing National Grievances* (London, 1795), 4, 7–8.

were smashed as the crowd roared 'Bread! Peace! Down with Pitt! No war! No king! Peace! Bread! Peace!' Within two months the 'Gagging Acts' were passed, extending the law of treason and curtailing the right of assembly and freedom of speech. At this critical time of famine, conspiracy, riots, repression, and impending revolution, John Keats was born at Moorfields, London, on 31 October 1795.

A child of the 1790s, Keats's early boyhood, his schooldays (1803–11), and his medical training (1811–17) extended from the French Revolution, through the Napoleonic era, to the unsettled post-war years in which, as Coleridge said, 'Peace [had] come without the advantages expected from Peace, and on the contrary, with many of the severest inconveniences usually attributable to War.'[3] Keats's career as a poet dated from 1814, and overlapped with the widespread revival of reformist activity generated by the economic depression and unemployment which accompanied peace. This resurgence gathered to a crisis when, on 16 August 1819, the militia intervened at a reform meeting in St Peter's Fields, Manchester, killing and wounding scores of people: the Peterloo Massacre.

From the peaceful mass meeting in Copenhagen Fields to the tragic violence at Peterloo, Keats's life spanned three decades of intense political ferment in England. Yet, until very recently, he was regarded as remarkably disengaged from social and political issues, a poet who had travelled so far in romance as to have quite forgotten the uproar and sad peace of his own times. Keats's first biographer, Richard Monckton Milnes, announced his subject as a figure of minimal worldly presence, 'one whose whole story may be summed up in the composition of three small volumes of verse, some earnest friendships, one passion, and a premature death'.[4] That story was repeated in numerous subsequent biographies, which elaborated and enriched Milnes's outline of the circumstances of his life. None of these studies entirely overlooked the contemporary historical dimensions of Keats's life, although these aspects of his career and creativity were often deemed to be of secondary importance to

[3] See *A Lay Sermon* (1817), in *Lay Sermons*, ed. R. J. White, Bollingen Collected Coleridge Series 6 (Princeton, 1972), 141.

[4] *LLL* i. 2.

understandings of a writer whose experiences were believed to have been 'mainly literary'.[5]

Sidney Colvin offered a typical profile in which Keats was said to have

shared the natural sympathy of generous youth for Hunt's liberal and kind-hearted view of things, and he had a mind naturally unapt for dogma; ready to entertain and appreciate any set of ideas according as his imagination recognised their beauty or power, he could never wed himself to any as representing ultimate truth.[6]

Readily displacing 'ideas' with imagined 'beauty or power', Colvin's account was representative in offering a sentimental image of a 'kindly' poet naturally sympathetic to but also 'naturally unapt' for political ideals or activity. In her bulky two-volume life of Keats, Amy Lowell conceded that Keats was 'a friend of reformers' like Leigh Hunt, although she reminded her readers that

active participation in such things was not his part; he commented in private, but said no word in print, as he might easily have done through the medium of the *Examiner*. That he felt no desire to air his views in public gives the measure of his interest in such subjects, which was, in truth, very slight.[7]

This last claim has a very dubious logic, although it is clear that Lowell, like Colvin, believed that politics were intellectually and practically of no interest to Keats. Of the three excellent biographies of Keats published in the 1960s, Walter Jackson Bate's magisterial study focused primarily on events in the poet's inner life and was hailed, rightly, as 'the definitive critical biography'.[8] Published within two weeks of Bate's book, Aileen Ward's *John Keats: The Making of a Poet* also set out to record the 'inner drama of [Keats's] creative life', and remains the nearest approach we have to a (Freudian) psycho-biography of the poet; her book was distinctive, too, in a number of lively episodes

[5] See Paul de Man, 'The Negative Road', in *Selected Poetry of John Keats* (New York, 1966); rpt. *John Keats*, ed. Harold Bloom, Modern Critical Views Series (New York, 1985).

[6] *John Keats: His Life and Poetry, his Friends, Critics, and After-Fame* (London, 1917), 51.

[7] *John Keats* (2 vols., London, 1925), ii. 109.

[8] See David Perkins's review in *K–SJ* 13 (Winter 1964), 97–100.

treating the social and political dimensions of Keats's life, works, and times. Five years later, Robert Gittings's biography also sought to place Keats's life in its historical context, and differed with Bate on some matters of dating—notably the tough problem of when precisely Keats left school to begin his medical apprenticeship.[9]

Modern biographies can hardly be said to have ignored Keats's relation to political issues although, as Vincent Newey rightly judged, the subject has been 'relatively neglected'.[10] More specialized studies of Keats have offered a glimpse of the poet that is markedly different from that encountered in the biographies. Prominent here was H. W. Garrod's fine short study which argued forcefully that Keats was a poet of the 'revolutionary idea', ambitious to write 'poetry which should startle princes from the sleep of circumstance'; yet Garrod said, 'Philosophy, politics, action, character—all these are for ever calling [Keats] from his proper effectiveness to regions of enterprise where he can be only inefficient and unhappy.'[11] Clarence De Witt Thorpe's essay 'Keats's Interest in Politics and World Affairs' explicitly identified Keats as a 'fervid republican', 'an unusually close observer of men and affairs, intently alert to the social, economic, and political conditions of his day'. Thorpe's Keats emerged from the poet's letters, and from contextual reconstruction; but like Colvin, Lowell, and Garrod he was unable to trace the 'steady strength' of Keats's convictions in the poetry, beyond a generalized humanitarianism. 'The instinct and the fire were there, as the letters show', he concluded, 'but sublimated, the poet habitually suppressing the reformer.'[12] Here, as in some accounts of Keats already noted above, his commitment to poetry is understood to have re-

[9] See pp. 14, 89, 90, 163–73 below, and Jack Stillinger's review of Gittings's biography in *K–SJ* 18 (1969), 107–11.

[10] See Vincent Newey, ' "Alternate uproar and sad peace": Keats, Politics, and the Idea of Revolution', in J. R. Watson (ed.), *The French Revolution in English Literature and Art*, Modern Humanities Research Association Yearbook of English Studies, 19, (London, 1989), 265.

[11] H. W. Garrod, *Keats* (Oxford, 1926), 26, 60. See also Herbert G. Wright, 'Keats and Politics', in *Essays and Studies*, 18 (1933), 7–23, which continues Garrod's argument by observing that Keats had 'a more active political conscience than has generally been recognised', and see June Q. Koch, 'Politics in Keats's Poetry', *Journal of English and Germanic Philology*, 71 (1972), 491–501.

[12] See *PMLA* 46 (1931), 1228–45.

quired him to be unfitted for, or insulated from, the contemporary world. The persistence of this view can be illustrated in Jack Stillinger's essay on Keats for the 1985 edition of the Modern Language Association's *English Romantic Poets: A Review of Research and Criticism*. Out of a total of fifty-two pages in Stillinger's admirable bibliography of Keats, work on the poet's 'political and social ideas' was sufficiently summarized in just thirteen lines.[13]

As everyone knows, Romantic studies during the 1980s were characterized by a turn towards the contextually informed criticisms associated with New Historicism and, for the first time, Keats's political and social imagination received detailed and sustained scholarly attention. In *Romantics, Rebels and Reactionaries* (1981), Marilyn Butler observed that *Hyperion, The Fall of Hyperion*, and 'To Autumn' were 'not now read as political poems', but she nevertheless went on to show how both *Hyperion* poems endeavour to 'represent historical change as the liberal habitually sees it' and concluded that it would be misleading to suggest that this poetry is 'in any important sense evasive' of contemporary life.[14] Two years afterwards, 'evasion' and 'escapism' emerged as crucial imaginative strategies in Jerome McGann's study *The Romantic Ideology* (1983). Romantic poetry's 'displacement efforts . . . its escape trails and pursued states of harmony and reconciliation' were cited by McGann as the 'dominant cultural illusions' of the age, 'illusions' in that poems were conditioned by the very historical circumstances they sought to avoid. In *The Romantic Ideology* and in his essay 'Keats and the Historical Method in Literary Criticism', McGann read Keats's poetry (and 'To Autumn' in particular) as fundamentally reactionary efforts 'to disguise the horror entailed in the maintenance and reproduction of the social structures—of the human life—[Keats] knew, to hide from the recognition of horror'.[15] The escapist, reactionary paradigm brought forward in McGann's work did much to set the agenda

---

[13] Jack Stillinger, 'John Keats', in Frank Jordan (ed.), *The English Romantic Poets: A Review of Research and Criticism: Fourth Edition* (New York, 1985), 693.
[14] Marilyn Butler, *Romantics, Rebels and Reactionaries: English Literature and its Background, 1760–1830* (Oxford, 1981), 151–4.
[15] Jerome J. McGann, *The Romantic Ideology: A Critical Investigation* (Chicago, 1983), 133–4, and KHM 48–65.

for the 1986 special issue of *Studies in Romanticism* devoted to 'Keats and Politics'; the essays contributed by Morris Dickstein, William Keach, David Bromwich, Paul Fry, and Alan Bewell agreed that Keats was indeed a 'radical' but differed markedly in their assessments of how Keats's radicalism affected his writing. William Keach found in Keats's loose, run-on couplets the stylistic signature of his liberal politics, whereas Paul Fry argued for the neutral atmosphere of 'To Autumn', the poem's disengaged preoccupation with 'the ontology of the lyric moment'.[16]

The *Studies in Romanticism* forum marked a watershed in Keats studies beyond which it has no longer been possible to view Keats as a poet wanting political interests, priorities, and commitments.[17] At the bicentenary of Keats's birth, recent studies of him have adopted a variety of social, political, and gender-based approaches.[18] Marjorie Levinson's *Keats's Life of Allegory: The Origins of a Style* (1988) interpreted Keats's writing and career through the disadvantages which were imposed, she argued, by his family background, social class, and upbringing. Economic and social deprivations excluded Levinson's Keats from participation in English culture, and were also definitive of his career and stylistic presence as a poet. The materialist critical formulations of her book have subsequently been resumed, with different emphases, in Daniel Watkins's *Keats's Poetry and the Politics of the Imagination* (1989), the governing premiss of which is that Keats's poetry 'from the beginning, is haunted by politics':

His complex and turbulent poetic articulation and reworking of traditional poetic topics, of myths and legends, and of contemporary and past history and politics are signs of intense anxiety—not simply the psychological anxiety that came of Keats's frequent questioning of his own capabilities, but also the historical anxiety of an age threatened by economic collapse, by the militarization of culture, bad harvests, stag-

---

[16] See William Keach, 'Cockney Couplets: Keats and the Politics of Style', and Paul H. Fry, 'History, Existence, and "To Autumn"', KP 182–96, 211–19.

[17] See in particular Vincent Newey's two impressive essays on Keats's poetry and politics, ' "Alternate uproar and sad peace"', and 'Keats, History, and the Poets', *K&H* 165–93.

[18] For an excellent assembly of contemporary approaches to Keats, see in particular the thirteen essays in *K&H*, which approach Keats through politics, social history, feminism, economics, historiography, stylistics, aesthetics, and mathematical and statistical theory.

geringly high unemployment, and by a fear both of bourgeois, industrial triumph and of a return to feudalism.[19]

Here Keats appears as the poet of a nation and culture in crisis,
his 'turbulent' imagination betraying intense personal tensions
and registering the distress caused by contemporary social, political, and economic upheavals. This is a dangerous Keats: a
poet who embodied and gave voice to the anxieties and insecurities of his times; a poet thus capable of challenging and unsettling the preconceptions of his readers; a poet whom the
establishment would be obliged to silence.

One argument of the present book is that the vigorous campaign to suppress John Keats, carried on in Tory journals of the
day, has had an enduring and malign influence on later approaches to his life and work, especially so in having prejudiced
understanding of his education and its effect on his poetry.
Modern biographers of Keats agree in their accounts of his
education at Enfield School. In *John Keats: The Making of a Poet*
Aileen Ward noted that the school was 'enlightened' and 'liberal', and that it offered a 'more modern and rounded curriculum than the public schools'. Robert Gittings found that the
school had a 'distinct tone' and that it shared the 'liberal and
progressive' curriculum offered at nonconformist schools.
Walter Jackson Bate had Enfield School providing Keats with 'a
fairly liberal education to students whose families were in trade
or in the less affluent professions'. The most recent biography
of the poet, by Stephen Coote, has noted the school's nonconformist background, and described its teaching as 'neither narrow nor merely utilitarian ... kindly and enlightened ...
benevolent [and] earnest if slightly eccentric'.[20] As I hope to
show in this book, the slightly patronizing tone apparent in all
of these descriptions represents a faint but noticeable contamination from the politicized attacks on Keats during his lifetime.

The primary source for information about Keats's school
education is Cowden Clarke's 'Recollections of John Keats'

[19] Daniel P. Watkins, *Keats's Poetry and the Politics of the Imagination* (London,
1989), 22–3.
[20] See Aileen Ward, *John Keats: The Making of a Poet* (London, 1963), 7–8; Robert
Gittings, *John Keats* (Harmondsworth, 1968), 44; Walter Jackson Bate, *John Keats*
(Cambridge, Mass., 1963), 10; Stephen Coote, *John Keats: A Life* (London, 1995),
11–12.

which, although it was written after the passing of many years, describes in heartfelt detail some aspects of Keats's schooldays and his early reading. As Richard Altick has emphasized:

In it occur all the observations and incidents which have become so familiar through constant retelling: the description of the boy's suddenly developing a passion for reading, after having been a completely unbookish child; Clarke's reminiscences of his adventures in Spenser with his promising former pupil; the classic story of the writing of the Chapman's Homer sonnet; the genesis of the friendship with Hunt; the story of Keats's 'passage at arms' with the butcher boy; and the spirited defence of Keats against the aspersions cast upon him by Haydon in his journals. The essay, instinct as it is with Clarke's undiminished affection for the poet, presents a view of Keats's character which the passage of more than eighty years, with all the attendant minute examination of evidence, has failed substantially to alter.[21]

Clarke's memoir is still the best guide to Keats's school years, especially so in that it resists the myth of 'poor Keats', the victim of hostile critics, and reminds us of how mentally and physically vigorous Keats actually was. According to Clarke, as a schoolboy Keats had been 'highly pugnacious', with an 'ungovernable' temper, and 'terrier courage'.[22] But Clarke's essay was certainly not fresh material when it was quarried by twentieth-century biographers. It had first appeared in the *Atlantic Monthly* (January 1861), then in the *Gentleman's Magazine, Littel's Living Age,* and *Every Saturday* (all 1874), and in 1878 appeared in its final form in Charles and Mary Cowden Clarke's *Recollections of Writers*. Keats's biographers all acknowledge the 'Recollections of John Keats', but the fact that Clarke's narrative played down the political and religious dissent of Enfield School has made it difficult to evaluate how those aspects of the academy at Enfield may have influenced Keats while he was a pupil there and in later life.

Clarke tells us that Keats used to read Hunt's *Examiner* at Enfield, and that this 'no doubt laid the foundation of his love of civil and religious liberty'. Yet he seems to have had particular difficulty in pursuing this subject in more detail. In a manuscript of the 'Recollections' at the Houghton Library, Harvard

---

[21] Richard D. Altick, *The Cowden Clarkes* (London, 1948), 207.
[22] 'Recollections of Keats', 123.

University, the brief passages which touch upon Keats's politics are heavily deleted, interlined, and revised to an extent which is not typical of Clarke's manuscript as a whole. By way of explaining the poor sale of *Poems, by John Keats*, for example, Clarke recalled the political animus directed at reformists in the years after Waterloo but, on the evidence of the manuscript, he did so with some unease:

The word had been passed that its author was a Radical; and, in those [*one word deleted; illegible*] days of 'Bible-Crown-and-Constitution' supremacy, he might [*one word deleted; illegible*] have had better chance of success [*half a line deleted; illegible*], had he [*two words deleted; illegible*] been an Anti-jacobin. Keats had [not; *interlined*] made [not; *deleted*] [the slightest; *interlined*] demonstration of political opinion . . .[23]

The passage that immediately follows in the manuscript recalls Keats's dedication of *Poems* to Leigh Hunt: '[having; *deleted*] he had dedicated his book to Leigh Hunt; [*one and a quarter lines deleted; illegible*] Editor of the "Examiner," [*one word deleted; illegible*] a radical and a dubbed'—but at this point Clarke tore out the remainder of the page, and pasted a new sheet over the passage just quoted (it remains visible through the thin paper).[24] This dedication to Hunt was of course very much a calculated demonstration of political opinion, reinforced by his admiring sonnet 'Written on the Day that Mr Leigh Hunt left Prison' and other poems which made approving references to Hunt as 'Libertas'. The political signal Keats gave to his first readers was singular and unmistakable, just as it would be if one were to dedicate a book today to a similarly controversial public figure (although, that said, contemporary public life in England may not present for ready comparison a political journalist and poet of Leigh Hunt's stature). Finally, towards the end of his manuscript, Clarke transcribed some 'New Matter' on the back of one sheet as a kind of afterthought:

---

[23] Charles Cowden Clarke, autograph 'Recollections of John Keats'. MS Keats 4.4.19, fo. 28[r], quoted by permission of the Houghton Library, Harvard University. The manuscript is dated '187?', and probably dates from *c.*1873–4 when Clarke was expanding his memoir for publication in the *Gentleman's Magazine.*

[24] Ibid., fo. 29[r]. Written out on the replacement page pasted into the manuscript is the sentence as published in the *Gentleman's Magazine* (Jan.–June 1874), 191, and 'Recollections of Keats', 140: 'he had dedicated his book to Leigh Hunt, Editor of the *Examiner*, a Radical, and a dubbed partisan of the first Napoleon.'

With regard to [his; *deleted*] Keats's political opinions; [one of his Critics has expressed no doubt that he would become; *deleted*] I have little doubt that his whole civil creed was comprised in the master-principle, of universal 'Liberty',—Viz: 'Equal, and stern justice;—from the Duke to the Dustman'.[25]

Clarke was I believe endeavouring to present an honest account of Keats's politics, admitting the 'rumour' that the author of *Poems, by John Keats* was a 'radical' (and implicitly associating 'radical' with 'Jacobin') while allowing, in his 'New Matter', that Keats had been a convinced liberal. In the period 1817–22, however, 'liberal' and 'radical' were virtually synonymous terms in political discourse: during 1822–3, 'Libertas', the 'radical' editor of the *Examiner*, was associated with a celebrated if short-lived journal entitled the *Liberal*.

Clarke's well-intentioned if cautious narrative in the 'Recollections' offers one explanation for the longevity of a misleading account of Keats's schooldays at Enfield. This misconception dates from the poet's lifetime and the 'Cockney School' essays published over the initial Z in *Blackwood's Edinburgh Magazine* from October 1817 onwards. The fourth of these essays was written, famously, by John Lockhart and it appeared in August 1818 after the publication of Keats's first two volumes, *Poems, by John Keats* and *Endymion*. The essay's social polemic reflected and contributed to the controversy surrounding educational practices during the Romantic period, recently documented by Alan Richardson,[26] and it has been a principal source for the myth of Keats's 'poor' education and 'lower-class' background. Z's purpose in the essay was to disempower Keats by making him look ridiculous, inventing and enforcing his ephemeral presence as a writer in terms of his youth, his social class, cultural status, and gender.[27] According to Z this 'young' man's burgeoning literary ambition far outstripped his intellectual capacity: Keats was the 'wavering apprentice', 'our youthful poet', an 'uneducated and flimsy

[25] Autograph 'Recollections of John Keats', fo. 59ᵛ.

[26] See in particular the first chapter in Alan Richardson, *Literature, Education, and Romanticism: Reading as Social Practice 1780–1832* (Cambridge, 1994), esp. 2, 25–33.

[27] See Kim Wheatley, 'The *Blackwood's* Attacks on Leigh Hunt', *Nineteenth-Century Literature* (June 1992), 1–31, for a related discussion of the ways in which Z created Hunt in the image of his own insecurities, then displayed 'the seemingly paranoid ability to be frightened by his own inventions'.

stripling'. He was 'without logic to analyse a single idea'; he lacked 'the smallest knowledge or feeling of classical poetry or classical history'; he knew 'Homer only from Chapman [and wrote] about Apollo, Pan, Nymphs, Muses, and Mysteries, as might be expected from [a person] of [his] education'.[28] At this period, of course, 'uneducated' people made up the majority of the population in England, the mass who were excluded from the political and cultural life of the country—the working classes, religious dissenters, and—especially—women. Z's Keats was a poet of 'negative capability' indeed, doubly debarred from legitimate participation: his poetry demonstrated that he was 'not capable of understanding', and in this last respect his intellect was shown to be unformed, sickly, and 'feminine' in character. As Mary Wollstonecraft had pointed out in her *Vindication of the Rights of Woman*, 'women . . . generally speaking, receive only a disorderly kind of education . . . in the education of women, the cultivation of the understanding is always subordinate to the acquirement of some corporeal accomplishment; even while enervated by confinement and false notions of modesty . . . education thus gives this appearance of weakness to females.'[29] Wollstonecraft was addressing the informal education then widely deemed appropriate for women, and perhaps replying in particular to Edmund Burke's influential account of woman's 'corporeal accomplishment' in his *Philosophical Inquiry into the Origin of our Ideas of the Sublime and the Beautiful.* There, women were said to affect traits of the 'weakness and imperfection' Burke identified with 'beauty',[30] and it was precisely this Burkean paradigm of 'effeminate' incapacity which Z's criticism detected in Keats's poetry and sought to enforce by way of defining his social and cultural marginality.

The mischief of the 'Cockney School' essays was virulent, and has endured to the present time as an influential factor in the construction of ideas about the 'Cockneys', and about Keats's

---

[28] 'The Cockney School of Poetry: No IV', *Blackwood's Edinburgh Magazine* (Aug. 1818), 519–24.

[29] See Mary Wollstonecraft, *A Vindication of the Rights of Woman: with Strictures on Political and Moral Subjects* (London, 1792) in *The Works of Mary Wollstonecraft*, ed. Janet Todd and Marilyn Butler (7 vols., London, 1989), v. 91–2.

[30] See Edmund Burke, *A Philosophical Enquiry into the Origin of our Ideas of the Sublime and the Beautiful,* ed. Adam Phillips (Oxford, 1990), 100. For a more extensive discussion of Keats and Burke, see Ch. 8, pp. 225–6.

life and his poetry. The series of essays as a whole was jointly authored by John Lockhart and John Wilson, and they were in no doubt about the malign effect of their essays on the reputations of Keats, Hunt, and Hazlitt. In a letter to John Murray written late in 1818, they observed that

the articles on the Cockney School are little if at all more severe than those in the Quarterly review, & that they give more offence to the objects of their severity, only on account of their superior keenness— above all that happy name which you & all the reviews are now borrowing—*the Cockney School*—a thorn which will stick to them & madden them & finally damn them.[31]

Their conceit was vindicated in the pejorative resonance of 'that happy name' in numerous nineteenth- and twentieth-century commentaries, but their essays also worked to obliterate Keats's worldly existence for later generations of readers and critics. With some help from Shelley's lament in *Adonais* for Keats's 'delicate and fragile' genius, and Byron's tart observation in *Don Juan* that Keats had been 'snuff'd out by an article', Z initiated the nineteenth-century tradition of Keats's boyish, 'uneducated' incapacity for the world. For many readers at that period Keats had come to be a figure of apathetic sublimity, as in this extraordinary account of him written by Stopford Brooke:

[Keats] has, in spite of a few passages and till quite the end of his career, no vital interest in the present, none in man as a whole, none in the political movement of human thought, none in the future of mankind, none in liberty, equality and fraternity, no interest in anything but beauty.[32]

Brooke's evacuation of Keats, who becomes a poet with 'no interest in anything', is remarkable for showing how far Z's campaign had succeeded. As a devotee of 'beauty', Keats's intellectual and political presence has been wholly effaced by the supposedly uncerebral category of the aesthetic: ' "Beauty is truth, truth beauty,"—that is all | Ye know on earth, and all ye need to know.' The chiasmus with which the 'Ode on a Grecian Urn' concludes was an appropriately enigmatic, introverted figure for the nineteenth-century image of Keats: utterly insu-

---

[31] John Lockhart and John Wilson to John Murray, late 1818. NLS, MS 4003, quoted by permission of the Trustees of the National Library of Scotland.
[32] Stopford A. Brooke, *Studies in Poetry* (London, 1907), 204.

lated from the world, Keats was truly, beautifully, an *autistic* poet, the 'foster-child of silence'. We should not forget that it had been the insolent volubility of Keats's poetry which had so unsettled Z and the others who had determined to suppress the 'young Cockney rhymester'.

Directly in line with Z's view of Keats are modern studies of him which have continued to emphasize how social and educational 'disadvantages' placed him beyond the pale of legitimate culture and the tradition of English poets which some would argue he aspired to join. Having glancingly observed that the 'facts of Keats's life are too familiar to bear recounting', Marjorie Levinson presses on to explain the development of Keats's poetic style in the following way:

To observe that Keats's circumstances put him at a severe remove from the canon is to remark not only his educational deficits but his lack of those skills prerequisite to a transparent mode of appropriation . . . He knew some French and Latin, little Italian, no Greek. His Homer was Chapman, his Dante was Cary, his Provençal ballads translations in an edition of Chaucer, his Boccaccio Englished. Keats's art education was largely by engravings and, occasionally, reproductions. His absorption of the accessible English writers was greatly constrained by his ignorance of the originals upon which they drew and by his nonsystematic self-education.[33]

By seeking to define Keats's social and cultural removal in terms of 'educational deficits' and constraining 'ignorance', Levinson's provocative account evidently recalls the terms and rhetorical strategies of Z's attack in *Blackwood's Magazine*.[34] The

---

[33] Marjorie Levinson, *Keats's Life of Allegory: The Origins of a Style* (Oxford, 1988), 7.

[34] Compare Wheatley, '*Blackwood's Attacks*', 4, who observes that Levinson's book and Jon Klancher's *The Making of English Reading Audiences, 1790–1832* (Madison, 1987) 'repeat the rhetorical moves of the early-nineteenth-century reviewers'. According to Wheatley, Levinson 'allegorizes Keats as the representative of an "entire class", and retells the reviewers' story of social, sexual, and stylistic aspiration and overreaching' (4–5). Whereas Levinson recognizes that Z was responding to the 'social offensiveness' of Keats's writing, Wheatley (5) identifies the perceived 'threat' of Keats and Hunt as a fiction invented by paranoid Tory reviewers. In the following pages I seek to recover Keats's insolent presence for his first readers, modifying Levinson's image of the social-literary 'entrepreneur' by relating Keats to the tradition of English dissenting republicanism and thus, I hope, also answering Wheatley's claim that Keats would never have been noticed by the periodicals 'had [he] not been associated with Leigh Hunt'.

claim that Keats had been 'greatly constrained by his ignorance' takes at face-value, and reinforces, Z's fiction that Keats was 'incapable of understanding'. Where Z had found that Keats's poetry was an affront to literary and social decorums, Levinson similarly emphasizes Keats's 'vulgar' and 'overwrought' poetic style as the expression of intellectual lack 'driven by the strongest desire for an authorial manner and means, and for the social legitimacy felt to go with it'.[35] This argument had been outlined at the beginning of E. P. Thompson's study *William Morris: Romantic to Revolutionary*. But whereas Thompson had identified Keats as a radical like Shelley, Henry Hunt, and Richard Carlile,[36] Levinson's Keats is a proto-capitalist, a lower-class 'literary entrepreneur' who was aggressively—*literally*—on the make and determined to write himself out of the obscurity to which he had been born.

I should emphasize that *Keats's Life of Allegory* has been a valuable stimulant to my own research into and thinking about the relationship between Keats's education and his poetry, and nowhere more so than in the points at which Levinson's argument replicates Z's original polemic. Where Z had found Keats's social status disabling to his poetic ambitions, Levinson reads his poetry as the signature of his marginality in Regency society and of the 'educational deficits' which may be traced to his years at Enfield School, 1803–11, before he left aged 15 years and 10 months to become apprentice to the surgeon Thomas Hammond at Edmonton.[37] I shall look in some detail at Keats's schooling in my first chapter. For the moment I want to suggest that the idea of Keats's deficient education, his 'ignorance', reveals the deeper anxiety compelling Z's essays, in that it is predicated on the assumption that a more orthodox grounding in literary culture (Harrow, Eton, Cambridge, Oxford) would have enabled Keats to become 'acceptable' as a writer. Certainly those establishments offered what Coleridge termed the ' "*sound book learnedness*," into which our old public schools still continue to initiate their pupils'; for Coleridge in

[35] Levinson, *Keats's Life of Allegory*, 4.

[36] See E. P. Thompson, *William Morris: Romantic to Revolutionary* (London, 1955, 1977), 10–21, and Levinson, *Keats's Life of Allegory*, 19.

[37] I follow Bate, *John Keats*, 30, 703–4, in dating Keats's departure from the school to summer 1811.

1816, 'soundness' was in direct proportion to the schools' efficiency in reproducing and perpetuating the dominant ideology
and established social order of the day, and in preparing a
learned class which he would later identify as the 'clerisy'.[38] As
Levinson rightly points out, these 'conformable bowers' of social advantage were not available to Keats—although it is said
that his parents had wished to send him to Harrow School. But
to bring forward his 'ignorance' as the corollary is to reiterate
the social and political prejudices which emerged so forcefully
in the Cockney School essays nearly two centuries ago. I want
instead to shift the emphasis over to a more positive view of
Keats's education, attending to Keats's eloquence as a representative voice of the most vital sector of contemporary English
culture: that is, the culture of dissent in which ideological opposition to and consequent exclusion from the establishment
formed the intellectual dynamic of enlightened progress in
political, religious, aesthetic, and educational matters.[39]

In the fourth 'Cockney School' essay, published in August
1818, Z sought to ridicule Keats by identifying him with a
number of stereotypes. First, his childishness, which was in
effect the consequence of his unorthodox education: 'this
young man', 'so young a person', 'the wavering apprentice',
'good Johnny Keats', 'our youthful poet', 'Johnny', 'a young
Cockney rhymester', 'a boy of pretty abilities', 'back to the shop
Mr John'.[40] That last remark, tagging Keats as a shopkeeper,
intersects with another stereotype Z endeavoured to (re-)
establish: the supposedly lower-class origins which necessarily

---

[38] See *The Statesman's Manual*, in *Lay Sermons*, 39. See also Alan Richardson's
discussion of relations between ideology and education in the theoretical writings of
Louis Althusser, Pierre Bourdieu, and Raymond Williams; *Literature, Education, and
Romanticism*, 25–33.

[39] In a recent essay Donald Goellnicht has taken issue with Marjorie Levinson's
reading of Keats in terms which parallel my own account of the dissenting motives
for Keats's ambitions. Goellnicht writes that Levinson 'casts Keats as a man on the
margins who longs to live at the urbane and sophisticated centre, who envies the
freedom granted Byron by birth and Wordsworth by claim. She fails to entertain
the possibility of Keats's harbouring genuinely revolutionary ambitions, of his holding an oppositional social perspective from within the historical structure, of his
desiring to destroy the very Tradition to which he wishes to belong.' See Donald
Goellnicht, 'The Politics of Reading and Writing: Periodical Reviews of Keats's
Poems (1817)', in D. L. Clarke and D. C. Goellnicht (eds.), *New Romanticisms: Theory
and Critical Practice* (Toronto, 1995), 101.

[40] 'Cockney School IV', 519–24.

also restricted him to the subordinate social position occupied by women. Keats was relegated to 'the Grub-street race'[41] of scribbling 'farm-servants and unmarried ladies...footmen [and] superannuated governess[es]', and he was identified as a 'bound apprentice...to a worthy apothecary in town'.[42] As a direct result of these unfortunate circumstances Keats was disenfranchised from high culture—and nowhere was this more evident, according to Z, than in his want of education.

As an example of 'very pretty raving' Z quotes the passage from *Sleep and Poetry* in which Keats foresees his poetic career:

> 'O for ten years, that I may overwhelm
> Myself in poesy; so I may do the deed
> That my own soul has to itself decreed.
> Then will I pass the countries that I see
> In long perspective, and continually
> Taste their pure fountains. First the realm I'll pass
> Of Flora, and old Pan: sleep in the grass,
> Feed upon apples red, and strawberries,
> And choose each pleasure that my fancy sees
> Catch the white-handed nymphs in shady places,
> To woo sweet kisses from averted faces,—
> Play with their fingers, touch their shoulders white
> Into a pretty shrinking with a bite
> As hard as lips can make it...'[43]

This passage epitomizes the 'heroic vulgarity' that John Bayley has identified with Keats's distinctive poetic personality: 'at his most characteristic Keats always disconcerts', Bayley says.[44] To understand Z's charge that Keats was 'raving', we need to respond to the full sense of 'disconcerts' in Bayley's remark—that is, from the old French *disconcerté*, 'disordered, confused, set awry', merging into the English senses: 'to put out of concert or harmonious action; to throw into confusion; disarrange, derange, spoil, frustrate' (*OED*). A look into the *Metamorphoses* will show that Ovid's nymphs usually disappear or change form long

---

[41] *The Dunciad*, I. 44, in *Pope: Poetical Works*, ed. Herbert Davis (Oxford, 1966).

[42] 'Cockney School IV', 519. See also Margaret Homans, 'Keats Reading Women, Women Reading Keats', *SIR* 29 (Fall 1990), 341–2.

[43] Quoted from 'Cockney School IV', 520.

[44] John Bayley, 'The Vulgar and the Heroic in "Bad Poetry"', in *The Uses of Division: Unity and Disharmony in Literature* (London, 1976), 115.

before an admirer is close enough for a love-bite; perhaps Keats's nymphs, with their 'fingers', 'shoulders white', and shadowy allure are more sensually realized than their mythical ancestors. But what really invigorates this piece of Cockney eroticism is the way in which the act of reading falls in with the sexual dalliance evoked by the poetry. The reader is led on by a narrative of apparently intensifying desire ('choose . . . Catch . . . woo . . . Play . . . touch . . .') although this does not gather to the 'rich anger' of sexual passion; the sequence culminates with 'a bite' which immediately withdraws its pressure, 'a bite | As hard as lips can make it'. For all the mounting intimacy of its cadences, this is an impotent encounter which finally settles for the mediated experience of literature,

> 'till agreed,
> A lovely tale of human life we'll read'.

Startlingly, this couplet brings into focus the reader's complicity in the preceding narrative of sensual enticement; we are suddenly aware 'not just that something [was] happening, but that something [was] being watched'.[45] This example of Keats's eroticism disconcerts to the extent that it exposes the reader's role in generating its effects. John Bayley observes: 'Now a mark of the man of poise and breeding is to object beyond all things to being disconcerted, and it was no doubt for this reason that Byron hated Keats.'[46] Perhaps the aristocratic temper of the poet of *Don Juan* was a significant factor in his claim that 'the grand distinction of the under forms of the new school is their *vulgarity*'.[47] But (as we have just seen) the power to disconcert also works to bring out energies and insecurities which are usually suppressed, or at least contained, by formalities of social

---

[45] See Christopher Ricks's fine discussion of the lines about Niobe (*Endymion*, I. 337–43), showing how the passage recognizes not only that 'the embarrassingness of acute grief makes it hard for us to evince a full sympathy' but also that 'though hard it can be done'; *Keats and Embarrassment* (Oxford, 1974), 8–9. While the Niobe passage demonstrates a difficult but attainable 'companionship with grief', the erotic passage from *Sleep and Poetry* might be said to uncover a voyeuristic readiness to gaze at sexual activity.

[46] Bayley, 'Vulgar and Heroic', 115.

[47] See Byron's remarks in 'Observations upon "Observations": A Second Letter to John Murray, Esq. on the Rev. W. L. Bowles's Strictures on the Life and Writings of Pope', in *The Works of Lord Byron* (17 vols., London, 1832–3), vi. 413.

or sexual behaviour: Byron's attacks on Keats arose from an uneasy sense of self-recognition in Keats's poetic manner.[48] As Marjorie Levinson has shown, it is telling that his Lordship sought to reassert his *social* virility against Cockney Keats by *sexual* slander that was calculated to fix the distance between them, intimating that 'Mankin' Keats's poetry was wholly self-directed, socially and culturally impotent: 'he is always f—gg—g his *Imagination*.'[49]

Z's response to Keats's poems, and to *Sleep and Poetry* in particular, is just as revealing about his own anxieties. In reacting to Keats's tease about neoclassical poets who 'sway'd about upon a rocking horse, | And thought it Pegasus' (186–7), Z writes:

our youthful poet passes very naturally into a long strain of foaming abuse against a certain class of English Poets, whom, with Pope at their head, it is much the fashion with the ignorant unsettled pretenders of the present time to undervalue. Begging these gentlemens' pardon, although Pope was not a poet of the same high order with some who are now living, yet, to deny his genius, is just about as absurd as to dispute that of Wordsworth, or to believe in that of Hunt. Above all things, it is most pitiably ridiculous to hear men, of whom their country will always have reason to be proud, reviled by uneducated and flimsy striplings, who are not capable of understanding either their merits, or those of any other *men of power*—fanciful dreaming tea-drinkers, who, without logic enough to analyse a single idea, or imagination enough to form one original image, or learning enough to distinguish between the written language of Englishmen and the spoken jargon of Cockneys, presume to talk with contempt of some of the most exquisite spirits the world ever produced, merely because they did not happen to exert their faculties in laborious affected descriptions of flowers seen in window-pots, or cascades heard at Vauxhall; in short, because they chose to be wits, philosophers,

---

[48] William Keach's paper 'Byron as a Reader of Keats', presented to the Keats Bicentenary Conference at the University of Bologna, Nov. 1995, argued that Keats's eroticism displayed a close affinity with Byron's, a 'common writerly impulse'. So Byron's admiration for *Hyperion* ('His Hyperion is a fine monument & will keep his name') was related to Keats's perceived turn away from a style which had seemed uncomfortably close to Byron's own. See *BLJ* viii. 163, and see also Paul Dawson's analysis of Shelley's and Byron's responses to Keats and Hunt in 'Byron, Shelley, and the "New School"', in Kelvin Everest (ed.), *Shelley Revalued: Essays from the Gregynog Conference* (Leicester, 1983), 89–108.

[49] Levinson, *Keats's Life of Allegory*, 16–19; *BLJ* vii. 225.

patriots, and poets, rather than to found the Cockney school of versification, morality, and politics, a century before its time.[50]

All of this to assert the authority of those '*men of power*' against
the 'young man', the 'wavering apprentice'—'Johnny Keats'. Z
was evidently disturbed by Keats's poems, recognizing that *Sleep
and Poetry* coincided with Hunt's celebration of 'the downfall of
the French school of poetry' in the 'Preface' to *Foliage* (published early in 1818): 'The notions about poetry can no longer
be controlled, like the fashions, by a coterie of town gentlemen,' Hunt had written, signalling his opposition to 'the world
of letters [which] still rested with men who sought to continue
the servile tradition of dependence upon aristocratic patronage'.[51] As William Keach demonstrates in his splendid essay on
'Cockney Couplets',[52] when read alongside the explicitly politicized commentary in Hunt's preface the loose versification of
Sleep and Poetry expressed a distinctly registered politics of style
forming part of a concerted, cocky challenge to the neoclassical
values of the literary and political establishments.

Z sought to externalize his discomfiture by framing Keats and
Leigh Hunt as partisans of the 'unsettled' party—and we should
not overlook the fact that 'unsettled' was a term which since the
1790s had been closely associated with Jacobin revolution. But
we can also sense that Z's mockery of the Cockneys overlay
worries which ran far, far deeper than the immediate matters of
poetic style and radical politics. In Keats's poetry—one could
almost say in Cockney rhyming—

> high suspended/life is ended
> hold my pen/denizen
> on, and on/cinnamon
> infant's force/rocking horse
> reverence bow/could reach? How!

---

[50] 'Cockney School IV', 520–1. Tea-drinking was one of the social intimacies
relished by Hunt; see for example his verse epistle 'To William Hazlitt', 'Then
tea . . . | an egg for your supper, with lettuces white, | And a moon and friend's arm
to go home with at night,' *Foliage; or, Poems Original and Translated* (London, 1818),
p. xciv. See also my discussion of Hunt and 'sociality' in Ch. 4.

[51] *Foliage*, 12, and Thompson, *William Morris*, 16. Hunt had introduced Keats in
his 'Young Poets' essay as one of the 'new school of poetry . . . which promises to
extinguish the French one that has prevailed among us since the time of Charles the
2d'; *Examiner* (1 Dec. 1816), 761.

[52] See Keach, 'Cockney Couplets', KP 182–96.

> pleasant sonnet/think upon it
> pleasant flow/portfolio
> nearer bliss/Felicity's abyss!
> cold thin feet/winding-sheet
> whirlwind writhen/one huge Python[53]

—Z heard a truculent English equivalent of the 'Marseillaise', the music of the democratic revolution which had been under way since the later eighteenth century and which continues as a force for change in our own time.

This brazen, jaunty music is figured in Z's essay as *metromanie*, the mania for writing poetry that allegedly accompanied the French Revolution and shared its democratic impetus. The word 'metromania' actually dates from the revolutionary decade, and William Gifford's *Baviad* of 1794: 'This pernicious pest, | This metromania, creeps thro' every breast' (*OED*); *metromanie*—rampant, demented scribbling—might be aligned readily with the virulent 'social disease' of disaffection signalled by Edmund Burke's perception of revolutionary France as the 'antagonist world of madness and discord, vice, confusion, and unavailing sorrow'.[54] At all stages of European history, medical metaphors have been employed to denote and stigmatize the deviant, the disenfranchised, the alienated. Z's pathological account of Keats's poetry as a 'malady', an 'infection', 'a violent fit', a 'disease', exactly conformed to this pattern while highlighting—with 'sorrow'—the particularly distressing case of an apprentice healer who had succumbed to infection and become the transmitter of sickness.[55]

[53] *Sleep and Poetry*, 35–6; 47–8; 117–18; 185–6; 273–4; 319–20; 337–8; and *Endymion*, III. 175–6; 195–6; 529–30. These few examples of Keats's rhyming also help to explain John Wilson Croker's charge in the *Quarterly Review* (Sept. 1818) that Keats 'seems to us to write a line at random, and then he follows not the thought excited by this line, but that suggested by the *rhyme* with which it concludes'. See *KCH* 112.

[54] See *Reflections on the Revolution in France*, ed. Conor Cruise O'Brien (Harmondsworth, 1968), 195. Many of the terms of Z's caricature of the Cockneys, and Keats and Hunt in particular, recall Edmund Burke's attack on the French Revolution; compare especially Z's remarks on the sexual content of Hunt's *Story of Rimini*, in Ch. 4 below. Verbal links also reinforce Z's common ground with Burke, in defending the political and cultural establishment as 'a fixed compact . . . which holds each in their appointed place', *Reflections*, 195.

[55] 'Cockney School IV', 519. The pathological agenda of Z's criticism was illuminated by George Rousseau's seminar 'W/D/W: Writing Disease, Diseased Writing', at St Andrews University, 1 Nov. 1995.

Although written from a very different political standpoint from Gifford's high Toryism, the 'Advertisement' to *Lyrical Ballads* (1798)—and Wordsworth's prefaces to later editions of that book—responded to the same perceived adulteration of contemporary literature, and sought to correct 'the gaudiness and inane phraseology of many modern writers' by presenting 'a natural delineation of human passions, human characters, and human incidents'.[56] Both Wordsworth and Coleridge continued to be preoccupied with this issue in later life, although the humane experimentalism of their 1798 volume had been succeeded by different priorities. In addressing 'the Learned and Reflecting of all Ranks and Professions, especially among the Higher Class',[57] Coleridge's *Statesman's Manual* (published in December 1816, and read by Lockhart soon afterwards) argued that political revolution was associated with the 'craving for novelty' which had also produced a democratization, and debasement, of literary culture.[58] One cancerous 'misgrowth' encouraged by metromania, or, as Coleridge termed it, the 'luxuriant activity' of writers, was 'a promiscuous audience . . . a READING PUBLIC' fed by 'circulating libraries and the periodical press':

Does the inward man thrive on this regime? Alas! If the average health of the consumers may be judged of by the articles of largest consumption; if the secretions may be conjectured from the ingredients of the dishes that are found best suited to their palates; from all that I have seen, either of the banquet or the guests, I shall utter my *Profaccia* with a desponding sigh. From a popular philosophy and a philosophic populace, Good Sense deliver us![59]

For Coleridge, as for laureate Southey, 'popular philosophy' encouraged the 'stirrings of mind, with all their restlessness'[60]

[56] See *The Prose Works of William Wordsworth*, ed. W. J. B. Owen and J. W. Smyser (3 vols., Oxford, 1974), i. 116.

[57] Coleridge's corrected title for the *Statesman's Manual* appears in his letter to George Frere, 5 Dec. 1816, *Collected Letters of Samuel Taylor Coleridge*, ed. E. L. Griggs (6 vols., Oxford, 1956–71), iv. 695. For Coleridge's worries about his readership, see Lucy Newlyn, 'Coleridge and the Anxiety of Reception', *Romanticism*, 1/2 (1995), 46–78, and Klancher, *Making of English Reading Audiences*, 4–5, 47–50.

[58] *Statesman's Manual*, 25. For Lockhart's campaign in *Blackwood's Magazine* against the 'excessive, artificial supply of "sources of sentiment"' in the 'plethora of books' then being published, see J. H. Alexander, '*Blackwood's*: Magazine as Romantic Form', *Wordsworth Circle*, 15/2 (Spring 1984), 57–68, esp. 59.

[59] *Statesman's Manual*, 36–9.   [60] Ibid. 39.

which had already led to revolution in France. By the same token a proliferating literary culture in Britain, dedicated wholly to popular consumption, might be one symptom of a ('tubercular') society which had weakened its intellectual, religious, and moral constitution and was about to devour itself in revolution.

When *Poems, by John Keats* appeared in March 1817 (coinciding with *A Lay Sermon*, Coleridge's sequel to the *Statesman's Manual*) it seemed to present the paradigmatic case of 'disorderly appetite': a degenerate, sickly, 'luxuriant' poet who was, additionally, 'uneducated', ill read, and given to 'foaming abuse'.[61] To Z, the 'case of Mr John Keats', apprentice physician turned poet, represented the 'phrenzy' of metromania at its critical stage; yet Z hoped that the 'invalid' may in 'some interval of reason' be 'in a fair way to be cured', medicining himself in the quarantine of his former trade and appropriate social station.[62] The medical analogy (which had also been adopted by Coleridge) brings forward as a 'cure' the reassertion of Z's cultural authority against febrile Cockney writing. But 'recovery', in other words the re-establishment of an 'educated' cultural consensus against the upstart Cockneys, was not a possible outcome. Z's vigorously caustic diagnosis was itself an admission of the Cockneys' power to disconcert, an acknowledgement that their poetry was a vigorous assault upon the 'lousy leasehold' of cultural exclusivity rather than a quest for 'social legitimacy' and conformity with the establishment.

The robust northern English 'Cockney' idiom of Tony Harrison's sonnet 'Them & [uz]' deliberately alludes to Keats in staging a comparable social-literary skirmish:

> 4 words only of *mi 'art aches* and . . . 'Mine's broken,
> you barbarian, T.W.!' *He* was nicely spoken.
> 'Can't have our glorious heritage done to death!'[63]

This scene of confrontation—between 'nicely spoken' master and 'barbarian' pupil Harrison, between *sound* 'RP' and an inglorious dialect—exactly parallels Z's quarrel with 'Cockney Keats' while also highlighting the social and cultural stakes contested: 'I played the Drunken Porter in *Macbeth*.' In 1818, as

---

[61] *Reflections*, 247.   [62] 'Cockney School IV', 519.
[63] Quoted from Tony Harrison, *Selected Poems* (2nd edn., London, 1987), 122.

at this end of the twentieth century, the schoolroom was 'the primary apparatus of social regulation'—the arena in which wider forces for cultural change came into conflict with received values.[64] Z's decision to ridicule Keats's unauthorized schooling and supposed intellectual deficiencies was not, therefore, simply an abusive rebuff to a 'young' poet who was also deemed socially unacceptable. The tactic revealed Z's dismayed understanding that the seemingly naïve verses in *Poems, by John Keats* and *Endymion* represented a fresh and thoroughgoing challenge to the social and cultural standing of the status quo: that 'coterie of town gentlemen', whether in Edinburgh or London, who—as Hunt said—had presumed to control 'notions about poetry'.

As a counterblast to an emergent Cockney culture, Z's essay coincided with Coleridge's agenda in his *Lay Sermons* in seeking to recuperate the establishment represented by the public schools at Harrow and Eton; the universities of Oxford and Cambridge; the Church of England; and canonical writers such as Alexander Pope (*dead* Catholic) and William Wordsworth (*ex*-Jacobin). His intention was to reassert the hegemony of establishment values (political, social, religious, educational, aesthetic) and to discredit an incipient reorientation of the literary and cultural life of the country. It is worth emphasizing that Z would never have noticed Keats had he been really the common, uneducated stripling caricatured in his essay. The association with Leigh Hunt and William Hazlitt rendered Keats suspect, although others in the same circle (Charles Cowden Clarke, Charles and Mary Lamb, John Hamilton Reynolds, James Rice, Horace Smith, and John Clare for example) were not singled out in the same way: it was Keats's unusual educational background, above all, which served as a focus for Z's animosity. But did Z know anything about Enfield School, and Keats's education there? and if so, why was he so alarmed by its values, in so far as these were reflected in Johnny Keats's poems?

John Lockhart had heard about Keats's family and education in a conversation with the poet's friend Benjamin Bailey at Bishop Gleig's house, near Stirling, in summer 1818. 'I fear

---

[64] See Richardson, *Literature, Education, and Romanticism*, 29.

Endymion will be dreadfully cut up in the Edinburgh Magazine (Blackwood's)', Bailey wrote to John Taylor, 29 August 1818: 'I met a man . . . who is concerned in that publication, & who abused poor Keats in a way that, although it was at the Bishop's table, I could hardly keep my temper . . . In Scotland he is very much *despised* from what I could collect.'[65] Bailey remembered this difficult encounter some three years afterwards,

[I] explained that Keats was of a [good; *deleted*] respectable family; & though he & his brothers & sister were orphans, they were left with a small but independent Patrimony. He had been brought up to the profession of medicine which he had abandoned for the pursuit of Literature.[66]

He recalled the same conversation, as a still more distant memory, in 1849:

[Keats] was a young man, to whom Mr Hunt had shewn kindness which called forth gratitude in so young & warm a bosom,—but that he himself mingled in no party-politics, & as I could confidently say, from his own lips, saw the weakness of his friend, & the impolicy of having his name mixed up with so decididly [*sic*] a party-man as Mr Hunt. I gave him an outline of Keats's history—that he had been brought up as a surgeon & apothecary; & though not highly, that he was respectably educated.[67]

From Bailey's accounts, it is evident that Keats's medical training was discussed and that there was talk about his family background and schooldays. The memoirs seem bland enough, yet, even though the conversation was being recalled after many years, there are perhaps traces of the provocations which had made it difficult for Bailey to retain his composure at the Bishop's table. In particular, his emphasis on the 'respectability' of Keats's upbringing, a term which invokes social coding as much as intellectual quality, reveals an awareness that on these

---

[65] *KC* i. 34. It is notable that the 19th-cent. epithet 'poor Keats' was current this early, and that it coincided with the attack on Keats in *Blackwood's* in Aug. 1818.

[66] 'Benjamin Bailey: Notes on his Conversation with Lockhart, 8 May 1821', *KC* i. 246. A further source of information was Lockhart's friend Jonathan Henry Christie, who had met Keats in company with John Hamilton Reynolds, Nov. 1817; see L. M. Jones, *The Life of John Hamilton Reynolds* (Hanover, 1984), 127–8, and *Letters*, i. 187 n.

[67] Bailey to Richard Monckton Milnes, 7 May 1849, *KC* ii. 287.

matters Keats had proved vulnerable to attack. According to the earlier passage Keats's political opinions were not mentioned; in the later reminiscence, however, Bailey claimed to have given Lockhart a sentimental account of the 'young' man's politics as the glow of a 'warm bosom' responding to Hunt's kindness: the poet had not 'mingled' in 'party-politics' at all.

Whatever Bailey had said to Lockhart in 1818, his report of this aspect of their conversation was mild invention—as Bailey was surely aware. But it does reveal how the idea of Keats's 'youthfulness' (targeted by Z) was employed after his death to efface his worldly presence and interests. Bailey was responding to Milnes's *Life, Letters, and Literary Remains, of John Keats*, published in 1848, at a period when it had become prudent to obscure or disavow political activities, sympathies, and involvements of former years. Comparable examples of this revision can be found during the nineteenth century, in Southey's later journalism; in Coleridge's *Friend* and *Biographia Literaria*; in Wordsworth's successive versions of *The Prelude* between 1805 and 1850; and in Leigh Hunt's *Autobiography*, where the editor of the *Examiner*, who in 1813 had been gaoled for libelling the Prince Regent, declared that his reformist politics 'were rather a sentiment . . . than founded on any particular political reflection'.[68] For Keats this refashioning of the past was undertaken by friends (such as Bailey and Cowden Clarke), by critics, and by successive generations of biographers.

Although, as we have already seen, Cowden Clarke's memoir is reticent in places, the following passage in his 'Recollections' deserves close attention for what it reveals—indirectly—about the political culture of the school and its influence on the schoolboy Keats:

in my 'mind's eye', I now see him at supper (we had our meals in the school-room), sitting back on the form, from the table, holding the folio volume of Burnet's 'History of his Own Time' between himself and the table, eating his meal from beyond it. This work, and Leigh Hunt's *Examiner*—which my father took in, and I used to lend to Keats—no doubt laid the foundation of his love of civil and religious liberty. He once told me, smiling, that one of his guardians, being

[68] *The Autobiography of Leigh Hunt* (3 vols., London, 1850), ii. 4.

informed what books I had lent him to read, declared that if he had
fifty children he would not send one of them to that school. Bless his
patriot head![69]

The disapproving response of Keats's guardian Richard Abbey
indicates clearly that Enfield School represented something
more unusual than 'a fairly liberal education to students whose
families were in trade or in the less affluent professions'.[70]
Richard Abbey was a prosperous tea-merchant in Pancras Lane,
a 'solid pillar of the established order', as Aileen Ward has aptly
described him, 'landowner and churchwarden in Walthamstow,
member of the Port of London Committee and the Honourable
Company of Girdlers, Steward of the City of London National
Schools Examination, and twice Master of the Honourable
Company of Patten Makers'.[71] No wonder, then, that Abbey
disapproved of his ward reading Hunt's *Examiner*, and of the
school in which, as Richard Altick has said, 'John and Charles
Clarke were able to expose their heterodox political opinions to
their pupils in perfect freedom'.[72] Obviously enough Enfield
School was regarded as a controversial establishment, and it
may have been that Bailey told Lockhart something about it as
part of Keats's 'history' even as he tried to emphasize that it was
a 'respectable' institution. Yet there seems to have been little
curiosity to find out more about Keats's school than Cowden
Clarke remembered towards the end of his long life. This book
begins with a new account of that formative scene in John
Keats's career as a poet.

---

[69] 'Recollections of Keats', 124.
[70] Bate, *John Keats*, 10. Notice how Z's condescending attitude to Keats's origins
may have infiltrated Bate's reference to 'families in trade'.
[71] Ward, *Making of a Poet*, 20.
[72] Altick, *The Cowden Clarkes*, 22.

CHAPTER ONE

A Cockney Schoolroom:
Keats and the Culture of Dissent

> It has carried me back to *Enfield*, . . . There the fields, the
> lanes, the brooks, the decayed stiles, the relics of cottages
> and barns, the mouldering walls, with all their associations,
> are far more interesting to me than the lofty mansions and
> splendid palaces of the metropolis.
>
> (William Newman, *Rylandiana*, 1835)[1]

Dissenting Culture and Enfield School

Enfield Academy grew out of the dissenting culture which in
the late eighteenth century was the motor of progressive intellectual and political life in England. In this stimulating environment the Unitarian Joseph Priestley was a representative figure,
with many interests embracing experimental chemistry and
physics, the grammar of the English language, philosophical
materialism, civil and parliamentary reform, and biblical history
and translation. Charles Cowden Clarke remembered with evident pride that among his father's friends were some of the
most prominent reformists and dissenters of the day. John
Clarke had been an 'intimate' friend of Priestley; he knew the
veteran reformist Major Cartwright, whom Cowden Clarke recalled meeting at the house of Holt White, nephew of Gilbert
White of Selborne. John Clarke 'took a peculiar interest' in
biblical translations by the Catholic scholar Alexander Geddes,
and those by the great classicist, Unitarian, and reformist
Gilbert Wakefield. George Dyer was an old friend; in the 1780s
they had worked together as schoolteachers, and in later years
Dyer visited the Clarke family at Enfield. Dyer, whom Cowden

---

[1] William Newman, *Rylandiana: Reminiscences Relating to the Rev. John Ryland, A.M.
of Northampton* (London, 1835), p. vii.

Clarke remembered merely as 'eccentric', was acquainted from the 1790s with Samuel Taylor Coleridge, William Godwin, Mary Wollstonecraft, John Thelwall, William Wordsworth, Robert Southey, and Charles Lamb. One of the most active and best-known reformists, he was a figure of considerable stature in the radical intellectual circles of London in the 1790s and, unlike those contemporaries, he maintained his reformist politics in later years.[2]

John Clarke's circle of friends shows that his intellectual, political, and religious allegiances went as far as the radical intelligentsia of Britain at the time of the French Revolution. This is what his son meant, presumably, in describing him as 'independent-minded far in advance of his time', and what tea-merchant Abbey objected to in Enfield School. Richard Altick has said further that John Clarke

shared to the full the political tendencies which were so intimately associated with religious dissent in his day. A friend of Holt and Cartwright and even of Dr Priestley, he was of the breed of radicals who had refused to follow men like Wordsworth down the long bitter path of disenchantment after 1793. He clung to his republican ideals with undiminished fervour, and when Leigh Hunt began *The Examiner* in 1808 he immediately subscribed. The long weekly discussions between father and son of the stirring political articles by Mr Hunt, whose views they invariably approved, were a vital part of Charles Cowden Clarke's education.[3]

In this account, John Clarke and his son had maintained their reformist and republican opinions throughout the French Revolution and the Napoleonic era, undismayed by contemporary events and the repressive political climate in Britain. It was from the Clarkes that John Keats inherited the dissenting ideology of Priestley, Wakefield, Cartwright, and Dyer, as well as the longer radical tradition stemming from the seventeenth-century republicans of the English Revolution: Milton, Hampden, Sydney, and Vane. Against this background, we can hear Keats's early poems announce more clearly and more coherently the oppositional values of dissenting culture: 'On

[2] For John Clarke's acquaintances, see *Recollections*, 5–13; for Dyer more particularly, see my study *The Politics of Nature: Wordsworth and Some Contemporaries* (Basingstoke, 1992), 17–35.

[3] *Recollections*, 4; Altick, *The Cowden Clarkes*, 19.

Peace', 'Lines Written on 29 May', 'Written on the Day that Mr Leigh Hunt left Prison', 'To Hope', the epistles to George Felton Mathew, George Keats, Charles Cowden Clarke, the sonnet 'To Kosciusko', *Sleep and Poetry*, and *Endymion*, especially the 'Hymn to Pan' and the opening of Book III. In the longer term republicanism and religious dissent nourished Keats's thinking about politics, history, ideal beauty, and his quest for knowledge as the sublime of poetic achievement. But to understand more precisely how the Clarkes and Enfield School embodied dissenting culture for Keats, we must look more closely at the history of the school itself.

'Knowledge enormous': The Achievement of John Collett Ryland

One autumn morning [John Ryland] called up the whole school to see the departure of the swallows, which had clustered in surprising numbers on the roof of the building. His presence and zealous manner of explaining their migration has made this departure of the swallows a frequent occasion of bringing my worthy tutor to remembrance . . .

(James Culross, *Three Rylands* (London, 1897), 40)

And Gather'd Swallows twiter in the Skies—
('To Autumn', draft)

The founder of Enfield School was John Collett Ryland, eminent Baptist minister, progressive educationalist, and republican, 'at all times the ardent friend of liberty and the advocate of the oppressed' (see Fig. 1).[4] In all accounts, Ryland was a humane person of enormous energy which he directed into evangelical preaching, teaching, and numerous religious and educational publications. He was remembered as a figure of resounding presence, 'unwearied diligence and anxiety', who

possessed a vigorous understanding, various learning, a vivid imagination, and a range of talents that rendered him one of the most popular preachers of the day; for zeal and fidelity he had few equals, and none could surpass the bold and daring nature of his eloquence.

[4] J. W. Morris, *Biographical Recollections of the Rev. Robert Hall, A.M.* (London, 1833), 31.

His eccentricities were numerous and remarkable, his piety unquestionable; to a stranger his manners were sufficiently terrific, though in reality no man possessed more genuine kindness, or more enlarged and disinterested benevolence. With all his failings, and without any written memorial of his life and labours, he was one of the brightest ornaments of the last century.[5]

This powerful, enlightened individual was to be a presiding spirit in Keats's education at Enfield.

John Ryland was born at Bourton-on-the-Water, Gloucestershire, 12 October 1723, the son of Freelove Collett and a prosperous farmer Joseph Ryland. He discovered his spiritual calling as minister and teacher at an academy in Bristol, where he proved 'an excellent classical scholar, a better mathematician, and a very good Hebraist'.[6] His learning would later extend to English grammar, optics, mechanics, astronomy, biology, gardening, and ornithology—a diversity that invites comparison with Joseph Priestley. Ryland's many interests informed the teaching at his schools and the well-stocked school library at Enfield in which, eventually, John Keats discovered Ryland's works.

Ryland took up his first ministry at Warwick in 1745, where he started a boarding school in the Parsonage House. Under the Test and Corporation Acts, which applied 'to every schoolmaster and tutor, public and private', Ryland would have been obliged to conform to the extent of acquiring a certificate to prove 'that the person had actually received the sacrament according to the usage of the Church of England'.[7] The Test Acts denied dissenters the right to civil and religious liberties, and demonstrated the urgent need for a reform in the parliamentary system of representation. Like Joseph Priestley, and like the Unitarian Coleridge of the mid-1790s, Ryland's intellectual life and his religious belief were integral to his political aspirations as a reformist. At Warwick his reputation as preacher and schoolmaster was considerable, and his popularity explains why he should have been invited to move his ministry and school to the Baptist meeting-house at College Lane, North-

[5] J. W. Morris, 30.
[6] James Culross, *The Three Rylands: A Hundred Years of Various Christian Service* (London, 1897), 15–16.
[7] For Ryland at Warwick, see ibid. 21–7.

ampton, where he settled on 5 October 1759. He remained in Northampton for twenty-six years and, as at Warwick, Ryland's energy electrified his new congregation and community:

Northampton was illuminated with the full blaze of his ardour and activity for six and twenty years. The school flourished—the church increased—the congregation was overflowing—the meeting house in College Lane (now College Street) was twice enlarged, by the blessing of God, which eminently rested upon him. With the assistance of George Dyer, and others, he introduced the gospel into more than twenty neighbouring villages.[8]

Ryland's assistants, who were recruited to help with teaching and missionary work in Northampton, were destined to have an influential bearing on two English poets: Coleridge and Keats.

In June 1782 George Dyer had arrived at Northampton from Oxford, where he had been preaching as a Baptist. Dyer's own recollection suggests that Ryland had invited him to the school out of kindness because his ministry at Oxford had produced 'no very happy results'. Dyer, whose preaching must have been impeded by his stammer, recalled that Ryland's academy was 'open house "to all the vagrant train"'. He was at first 'a sort of supernumerary' in the school, there being no immediate need for teaching assistance when he arrived, although he 'found the situation very favourable to his own *prevailing pursuits*' as a scholar of classical literature and divinity.[9] In due course he became 'fellow-usher' (assistant teacher) with another young tutor in Ryland's school: John Clarke. Charles Cowden Clarke described in his *Recollections* how his father had joined Ryland's staff; like Dyer, he had found the school a welcome refuge:

---

[8] See Newman, *Rylandiana*, 11. For Ryland's career at Northampton, see also Morris, *Recollections of Hall*, 30–2; Culross, *Three Rylands*, 34–58; *Bicentenary History of College Street Church, Northampton* (Northampton, 1897), 23–33; W. T. Whitley, 'J. C. Ryland as Schoolmaster', *Baptist Quarterly*, NS 5 (1930–1), 141–4; E. A. Payne, *College Street Chapel Northampton, 1697–1947* (London, 1947); Altick, *The Cowden Clarkes*, 11–13.

[9] For Dyer's recollections of Ryland and Northampton, see *Mirror of Literature, Amusement, and Instruction* (13 Nov. 1841), 311–12, and E. V. Lucas, *The Life of Charles Lamb* (2nd edn., 2 vols., London, 1905), i. 144–9. See also E. A. Payne, 'The Baptist Connections of George Dyer', *Baptist Quarterly*, NS 10 (1940–1), 260–7, and E. A. Payne, 'The Baptist Connections of George Dyer: A Further Note', *Baptist Quarterly*, NS 11 (1942–5), 237–8; Altick, *The Cowden Clarkes*, 11–13, and *Recollections*, 2.

As a youth [John Clarke] was articled to a lawyer at Northampton; but from the first he felt a growing repugnance to his profession, and this repugnance was brought to unbearable excess by his having to spend one whole night in seeking a substitute for performing the duty which devolved upon him from the sheriff's unwillingness to fulfil the absent executioner's office of hanging a culprit condemned to die the following morning. With success in finding a deputy hangman at dawn, after a night of inexpressible agony of mind, came his determination to seek another profession, and he finally found a more congenial occupation by becoming usher at a school conducted by the Rev. John Ryland, Calvinistic minister in the same town. My father's fellow-usher was no other than George Dyer . . . the one being the writing-master and arithmetical teacher, the other the instructor in classical languages. Each of these young men formed an attachment for the head-master's step-daughter, Miss Ann Isabella Stott; but George Dyer's love was cherished secretly, while John Clarke's was openly declared and his suit accepted.[10]

With Dyer and Clarke as assistant teachers, Ryland's school flourished at Northampton until November 1785. Dyer remembered that Ryland's 'hand was apt to be liberal beyond his means': his generosity, and zeal for publishing pamphlets, eventually left him so short of money that he was obliged to close the school.

At this point, Dyer left for Cambridge where he lived as tutor in the house of the Baptist minister Robert Robinson. He joined the wider dissenting community in town and University, making the acquaintance of William Frend, who was at that time Fellow in Mathematics at Jesus College. A few years later, Frend became a hero to the undergraduate Coleridge, when in 1793 he was prosecuted and banished from the University for publishing his pamphlet *Peace and Union*. A little further in the future, Dyer, Frend, and Coleridge would coincide with Wordsworth in the London radical circles where William Godwin, Thomas Holcroft, John Thelwall, Mary Wollstonecraft, and other English Jacobins could also be found in 1795, the year of Keats's birth. At this period Dyer was in regular correspondence with Coleridge, discussing literature, politics, religion, and encouraging Coleridge's earliest publications including *The Fall of Robespierre*. He was also a frequent visitor at the school in Enfield where his old friend John Clarke now lived.

[10] *Recollections*, 1–2.

In November 1785 Ryland and Clarke had been obliged to quit Northampton for London 'to the deep regret of nearly all the older members of the Church and congregation'.[11] The following year, however, they moved once again, this time to Enfield, where Ryland founded a 'greatly enlarged' boarding school. As principal of this new establishment, and at 63 years old, Ryland's activity was undiminished: 'the whole family was sometimes nearly fourscore in number ... while the literary departments of the school were under the able direction of Mr Clarke, Mr R. devoted himself chiefly to the religious improvement of the pupils.' The new school at Enfield prospered, until it attained 'a still higher reputation than the school in Northampton'.[12] In Charles Cowden Clarke's recollection, the school house was 'airy, roomy, and commodious, the grounds sufficiently large to give space for flower, fruit and vegetable gardens, playground, and paddock of two acres affording pasturage for two cows that supplied the establishment with abundant milk' (see Fig. 2 for a nineteenth-century engraving of the school).[13] No wonder John Ryland should have 'frequently expressed the hope that his house would be used as a school "till the day of judgement"'.[14] That wish was typical of Ryland's indomitable spirit, and it suggests something of the generous and humane community Keats entered when in August 1803 he came to Enfield School as a pupil. By that time, however, John Ryland had been dead for ten years; yet in John Clarke and his family, in the library and classroom routines of the school itself, Ryland's remarkable presence and achievement lived on: as one memoir puts it, 'all of them in after days kept up the traditions [Ryland] implanted'.[15]

'The Living Orrery': Keats's Education at Enfield School

Card 12.
'I represent stupendous Saturn. My diameter is 78,000 miles. I move round the Sun in $29\frac{1}{2}$ years at the distance of

---

[11] *Bicentenary History of College Street Church, Northampton*, 33.
[12] Newman, *Rylandiana*, 14–19, gives an account of John Ryland at Enfield school; see also Culross, *Three Rylands*, 58–60.
[13] *Recollections*, 2–3.
[14] Culross, *Three Rylands*, 59–60.
[15] Whitley, 'J. C. Ryland as Schoolmaster', 144.

907,000,000 miles, and at the rate of 22,000 miles an hour'.

('The Living Orrery', in *Rylandiana*, 121)

'Look up, and tell me if this feeble shape
Is Saturn's; tell me, if thou hear'st the voice
Of Saturn . . .'

(*Hyperion*, I. 98–100)

John Ryland believed fervently that education had a spiritual imperative, and that it depended upon liberty of conscience; the pursuit of knowledge and his dissenting faith were therefore united in the progressive, liberal curriculum at his schools. John Clarke concurred with Ryland's views, and he took over as headmaster of Enfield School following Ryland's death in 1792. So it was that the 'fundamental principles' of dissent came to exercise a formative influence on Keats, to Richard Abbey's considerable dismay.

Since he believed in the evidences of God's existence in the created universe, Ryland held learning to be a quest for spiritual understanding—'from thoughts of the visible world, to a rational thought of GOD'.[16] Like his preaching, his school teaching was inspired with an evangelical fervour and conviction: 'An atheist', he wrote, 'is not an honest enquirer after truth: he is a wretch of a sickly and vitiated understanding; he will not make use of those ideas of the visible creation which are in his mind to enable him to discern the being of GOD.'[17] Like his religious writings, Ryland's lessons were a celebration and demonstration of God's presence in the universe; in seeking to prove 'evidences' of divine wisdom and design, he adopted teaching methods which were strongly empirical and practical:

A sponge will teach the rise of water in capillary tubes. A syringe, or a squib, or sucking with a reed or a wheaten straw, will show the nature of pump-work. A school-boy's jews-harp will serve to teach us those tremulous motions which are the cause of sounds; and a glass prism and soap bubbles*, a looking-glass and an ox's eye from the butcher's,

[16] John Ryland, *Contemplations on the Beauties of Creation* (3rd edn., 3 vols., London, 1777–82), i. 4 (the first volume only is the third edition). Cf.: 'The most simple and easy method of proof, with respect to the existence of GOD, is by making use of ideas, drawn from all the visible objects in the creation; the agreement of which ideas, with the idea of a wise, powerful, good being, is instantly and unavoidably seen by the mind in the whole process of its operations and reasonings'; ibid. 3.

[17] Ibid. 5 n.

will be a happy foundation for optics. A few hoops, from the cooper's shop, placed with skill, will shew the grand circles of the sphere; viz. the horizon, the meridian, and equinoctial line, the ecliptic or the sun's path, the two tropics and the polar circles.[18]

As this passage indicates, Ryland's teaching was imaginative and resourceful; the simple practical demonstrations mentioned here were reinforced by his knowledge of the latest developments and discoveries in a wide range of subjects. Indeed for Ryland, as for Joseph Priestley, the vindication of religious faith through progressive knowledge was apparent in contemporary scientific and astronomical discoveries, revealing 'the whole beautiful structure' of God's creation: 'Do not the uses of the SUN demonstrate a GOD? . . . the Comets lay open to our view amazing scenes of the omnipotence of GOD . . . The GLOBE of our EARTH, in all its PARTS, proclaims an infinite, powerful, and glorious GOD.'[19]

William Herschel's discovery in March 1781 of the 'new planet' or *Georgium Sidus* (the 'Georgian Star', or Uranus[20]) greatly impressed Ryland as proof of humankind's enlarging knowledge of the universe and of God's purposes. He visited this 'greatest of all practical Astronomers' at his house in Datchet, 9 May 1785, and recalled that Herschel had assured him

that he had seen, with his grand telescope, 116,000 stars in the space of fifteen minutes. He has likewise observed, in his letter to the Royal Society, that the Georgium Sidus, or the new planet, which he discovered, is eighteen hundred millions of miles distant from the sun.[21]

Ryland's close interest in modern astronomy made for lively and memorable lessons on the subject at Northampton and Enfield schools. As in all subjects that he taught, Ryland's method was to simplify information by writing it onto cards for his pupils to learn—educating them, as he said, 'by

[18] Newman, *Rylandiana*, 116. At the asterisk, Ryland added a footnote: 'Let the man that laughs at this be told that Sir Isaac Newton made a fine improvement in Optics, by seeing some boys blow up soap bubbles in the air.'

[19] Ryland, *Contemplations*, i. 7, 10, 13.

[20] By 1822 the name 'Uranus' had been 'almost universally adopted' instead of 'Georgium Sidus'; *Encyclopaedia Metropolitana* (1822), cited in *OED*.

[21] John Ryland, *The Character of the Rev. James Hervey, M.A.* (London, 1791), 190n. For Ryland and Herschel see also Newman, *Rylandiana*, 119.

recreation'.[22] He demonstrated the movements of planets and moons in the solar system by encouraging pupils to create a 'living orrery' (as he termed it) in the school playground. Individual pupils were given a card identifying one of the planets or a moon, and listing some information to be learned. Here are two examples:

Card 18.

'I represent the grand Georgium Sidus, discovered by Dr Herschel, March 13, 1781. Above 4,000 times as big as the Earth, I move round the Sun in about 83 years, and at the distance of 1,800,000,000 miles. My diameter is 34,000 miles.'

Card 19.

'I represent the inner Moon of the Georgium Sidus, whom I have the honour to illuminate.'[23]

With their cards, the pupil-planets and moons took up their stations in an appropriate circle of orbit around the classmate representing 'the great Sun'. The 'living orrery' was then set in motion,

giving each boy a direction to move from west to east; Mercury to move swiftest, and the others in proportion to their distances, and each boy repeating in his turn the contents of his card, concerning his distance, magnitude, period, and hourly motion. Half an hour spent in this play once a week, will, in the compass of a year, fix such clear and sure ideas of the solar system, as they can never forget to the last hour of life; and probably rouse some sparks of genius, which will kindle into a bright and beautiful flame in the manly part of life.[24]

This ingenious exercise in learning through play indicates something of the imaginative yet practical teaching offered to Keats at Enfield School. Indeed, the 'living orrery' may have contributed more to Keats's creative life than his celebrated prize copy of John Bonnycastle's *Introduction to Astronomy*. To take just one obvious example, the rapt attentiveness of these two lines from 'On First Looking into Chapman's Homer',

[22] Compare the strictly prescriptive tuition at Eton and other public schools, discussed on pp. 66–7 below.

[23] Newman, *Rylandiana*, 122. For Ryland's teaching methods, and the 'living orrery', see ibid, 117–22, and John Ryland, *An Easy Introduction to Mechanics* (London, 1768), pp. xix–xxii.

[24] Newman, *Rylandiana*, 118–19.

> Then felt I like some watcher of the skies
> When a new planet swims into his ken (9–10)

—comprehends a sense of awesome disclosure, much as John Ryland had recognized the image of divine power in 'the least sight of these immensely distant worlds'.[25] Compare John Bonnycastle's laconic account of Herschel's investigation of the night sky,

pursuing a design which he had formed of observing, with telescopes of his own construction, every part of the heavens, discovered, in the neighbourhood of H Geminorum, a star, which, in magnitude and situation, differed considerably from any that he had before observed, or found described in the catalogues.[26]

Bonnycastle has frequently been cited as the 'source' of Keats's reference to 'a new planet' in the sonnet.[27] But, on reflection, it seems unlikely that the desiccated prose of the *Introduction to Astronomy* should have quickened the marvellous vision of sidereal motion in Keats's poem.[28] More plausible, I think, is the possibility that Keats's imagination was feeding on the memory of discoveries made at Enfield while playing in the 'living orrery' or gazing at a planet's bright image through the school telescope. If this was indeed the case, 'On First Looking into Chapman's Homer' was a compliment for Charles Cowden Clarke (to whom Keats sent the sonnet) that extended beyond the 'golden realms' of Keats's reading to acknowledge more broadly the formative richness of his schooldays. Moreover, given Ryland's friendship with Herschel it is not unlikely that Keats would have discovered in the school library some of Herschel's own, intensely lyrical descriptions of the night sky:

I remember, that after a considerable sweep with the 40 feet instrument, the appearance of Sirius announced itself, at a great distance, like the dawn of the morning, and came on by degrees, increasing in brightness, till this brilliant star at last entered the field of view of the

---

[25] Ryland, *Contemplations*, i. 11.

[26] John Bonnycastle, *An Introduction to Astronomy: In a Series of Letters from a Preceptor to his Pupil* (4th edn., London, 1803), 409.

[27] See for example AP 62.

[28] Cf. the effects of 'cold philosophy' in reducing the 'awful rainbow once in heaven' to 'the dull catalogue of common things'; *Lamia*, II. 230–3.

telescope, with all the splendour of the rising sun, and forced me to take the eye from that beautiful sight.[29]

This extraordinary description of Sirius rising—'came on by degrees, increasing in brightness, till this brilliant star at last entered the field of view'—parallels Keats's use of intensities of light in tracing the celestial revolutions of *Hyperion*. The 'bright Titan' Hyperion is compelled by 'the sorrow of the time',

> And all along a dismal rack of clouds,
> Upon the boundaries of day and night,
> He stretch'd himself in grief and radiance faint (I. 302–4)

—whereas his successor, Apollo, assumes divinity as a figure of brilliant incandescence:

> At length
> Apollo shriek'd;—and lo! from all his limbs
> Celestial . . . (III. 134–6)

This climactic moment is framed as a revelation which the reader is invited to witness: 'and lo! from all his limbs | Celestial . . .' Apollo is invoked as a physical presence with 'limbs', although the celestial meaning of 'limb' (denoting the luminous edge of the sun's disc) also suggests the awesome radiance emanating from the new god of the sun—a luminosity which forces Keats, mortal poet and astronomer, to 'take [his] eye from that beautiful sight' and break off his poem.[30] The faculties of observation and recognition, or their failure, are repeatedly invoked in *Hyperion* as fundamental to an understanding of the Gods' dynastic struggle; 'Saturn, look up!' (I. 52); 'Look up, and tell me if this feeble shape | Is Saturn's' (I. 98–9); 'Have ye beheld the young God of the Seas, | My dispossessor?' (II. 232–3). *King Lear* was an important influence on *Hyperion*, in Keats's conception of the 'poor old King' Saturn (I. 52) and his concern with sight and looking, but in other respects astronomical observation was integral to the poem's meanings too. While the mythic action of *Hyperion* was invigorated by Keats's knowledge

[29] See William Herschel, 'On the Power of Penetrating into Space by Telescopes', *Philosophical Transactions, of the Royal Society of London. For the Year MDCCC. Part I* (London, 1800), 54.

[30] But compare also Hunt's 'Portrait of Apollo' extracted from *The Feast of the Poets* and published in the *Examiner* (13 Mar. 1814), 170: 'A figure sublim'd above mortal degree; | His limbs the perfection of elegant strength . . .'

of astronomy, the astronomer's inability to gaze upon a brilliant object was a reminder of the human frailties experienced by Apollo in assuming his powers as god of the sun, of poetry, and medicine. While medicine has frequently and rightly been cited as a deep influence on Keats's calling as a poet, *Hyperion* suggests that astronomy was an important factor too in the making of a poet intensely aware of human limitations, for whom the sublime of artistic achievement was appropriately figured by solar radiance in eclipse: 'A sun—a shadow of a magnitude' ('On Seeing the Elgin Marbles', 14). At the very least, we might conjecture that the poet who in *Hyperion* Book I could imagine the voice of a Titan in utter defeat might first have assumed that role in the schoolyard orrery at Enfield: 'I represent stupendous Saturn . . .'

The culture of progressive knowledge fostered by Ryland and the Clarkes transformed Keats with the intensity of a religious conversion and, as I have already indicated, subsequently encouraged his developing sense of calling as a poet. Keats was not alone in having been powerfully affected in this way. The Baptist minister Robert Hall was educated by Ryland at his Northampton school, and he had been invigorated by Ryland's tuition. I cite Hall's example by way of illuminating Keats's similar experience at Enfield:

The senior Mr Ryland, to stimulate the exertions of his pupils, gave them subjects on which to write, and the best composition carried off the prize. This placed young Robert in a state of direct competition, and roused his dormant faculties, which in this new situation had met with no particular excitement. No sooner was he forced into the ranks for this species of literary fame, than he produced a theme which not only surpassed the efforts of all his competitors, but afforded great delight to his tutor.[31]

Ryland's example described here was continued by John Clarke, and it seems to have worked a comparable change in Keats's studies at Enfield. Charles Cowden Clarke recalled how Keats's 'highly pugnacious spirit' as a schoolboy had been directed very successfully into studious competition:

My father was in the habit, at each half-year's vacation of bestowing prizes upon those pupils who had performed the greatest quantity of

---

[31] Morris, *Recollections of Hall*, 32.

voluntary work; and such was Keats's indefatigable energy for the last two or three successive half-years of his remaining at school, that, upon each occasion, he took the first prize by a considerable distance. He was at work before the first school-hour began, and that was at seven o'clock; almost all the intervening times of recreation were so devoted; and during the afternoon holidays, when all were at play, [Keats] would be in the school—almost the only one—at his Latin or French translation; and so unconscious and regardless was he of the consequences of so close and persevering an application, that he never would have taken the necessary exercise had he not been sometimes driven out for the purpose by one of the masters.[32]

Here, Clarke traced in prize-competitions at Enfield School the awakening of Keats's extraordinary tenacity of intellect and imagination. Keats's 'indefatigable energy' to succeed at his studies would subsequently drive his powerful ambition in writing *Endymion* as 'a test, a trial of [his] Powers of Imagination and chiefly of [his] invention'.[33]

As we have seen already, though, the school also favoured a method of education 'by recreation', alongside a more competitive approach to stimulating the pupils' studies. It might appear that these two techniques, of play and competition, ran directly counter to one another; that the imaginative resourcefulness of the one was cancelled by the more directed attention required in the other. Curiously, however, we find a synthesis of both in Keats's attitude to *Endymion*: while regarding the poem as a 'test, a trial', he also viewed it as a space for the mental recreation of readers (indicating the manner in which he read longer poems himself). After outlining his plan for composition of the '4,000 Lines' of *Endymion*, Keats continued:

I have heard Hunt say and may be asked—why endeavour after a long Poem? To which I should answer—Do not the Lovers of Poetry like to have a little Region to wander in where they may pick and choose, and in which the images are so numerous that many are forgotten and found new in a second Reading: which may be food for a Week's stroll in the Summer?[34]

Keats's disciplined 'endeavour' in the creation of a 'little Region' for his readers' refreshment strikingly recalls the

---

[32] 'Recollections of Keats', 122.
[33] *Letters*, i. 169.   [34] Ibid. 170.

competitive-recreative pattern of school life at Enfield—but also the physical layout of the establishment too. In his letter to Bailey quoted above Keats refers to the long poem as a garden, in which the reader may 'pick and choose' and 'stroll'. He was certainly thinking of *The Faerie Queene* (which at this time, 8 October 1817, was his most admired example of the longer poem) but probably also of the large garden surrounding Enfield School where he had first read Spenser's poem in company with Charles Cowden Clarke.[35] Alan Bewell has perceptively described Keats as 'a poet-nurseryman', who understood 'a poem as being a textual equivalent of a garden', while the garden figured 'not only how readers should read his poetry, but how he himself read other poets'.[36] Without wishing to enforce a literal, biographical context for Bewell's remarks, I think it likely that Keats's association of poetry and the 'gardencroft' may be traced to his years at Enfield and the period immediately thereafter when he returned to the school to borrow books and to read poetry, as Cowden Clarke remembered, 'in an arbour at the end of a spacious garden'.[37] Keats's 'trial' in writing *Endymion*, a narrative which like many of his early poems is a 'region' containing floral bowers and retreats, suggests that the classroom (associated with directed effort) and the gardenground (associated with recreation) were formative intellectual and physical environments which were subsequently transformed into the imaginative terrain of Keatsian romance. In *Sleep and Poetry*, for example, his resolution to fulfil his self-imposed 'decree' as a writer is projected as a leisurely, self-indulgent sojourn in a fruit garden:

> First the realm I'll pass
> Of Flora, and old Pan: sleep in the grass,
> Feed upon apples red, and strawberries,
> And choose each pleasure that my fancy sees . . . (101–4)

Similarly, although Endymion's quest for Diana is conceived as a passionate pursuit the course of their romance proves extremely dilatory and it is protracted throughout the four books

---

[35] See *Recollections*, 2–3, quoted pp. 39–40 above.
[36] See Alan Bewell, 'Keats's "Realm of Flora"', in David L. Clark and Donald C. Goellnicht (eds.), *New Romanticisms: Theory and Critical Practice* (Toronto, 1995), 74–5.
[37] 'Recollections of Keats', 125.

and 4,050 lines of the poem. In this respect the 'Poetic Romance' as a whole is dramatically appropriate to Keats's celebration of love as 'ardent listlessness' (I. 825), while that oxymoron works very finely as an intensification of the seemingly contradictory aspects of Keats's intellectual experience at Enfield School.[38]

A comparable, lasting effect of the school derived from Keats's voracious reading in his last terms there. This foreshadowed his determined quest for the 'knowledge' that would enable him to write a humane, philosophical poetry. 'I find that I can have no enjoyment in the World but continual drinking of Knowledge,' Keats wrote to John Taylor, 24 April 1818:

I find there is no worthy pursuit but the idea of doing some good for the world—some do it with their society—some with their wit—some with their benevolence—some with a sort of power of conferring pleasure and good humour on all they meet and in a thousand ways all dutiful to the command of Great Nature—there is but one way for me—the road lies th[r]ough application study and thought. I will pursue it and to that end purpose retiring for some years.[39]

Keats's plan to retire for 'study and thought' acknowledged his wish in *Sleep and Poetry* to understand all that the celestial charioteer 'writes with such a hurrying glow' (154). The charioteer's descent (and subsequent flight 'Into the light of heaven') accompanied Keats's determination to write poetry that would express 'the agonies, the strife | Of human hearts' (124–5), a 'sense of real things' (157), thereby 'sharpening [his] vision into the heart and nature of Man'.[40] In the letter to John Taylor quoted above, Keats associated his programme of learning with 'the command of Great Nature'. Yet if one substitutes 'God' for 'Great Nature', Keats's ambition can be seen to resemble John Ryland's belief that the quest for knowledge was a divine ordinance for humankind: 'The idea of a soul feeling an insuppressible ardour after more knowledge every day and every hour,

---

[38] The recreative and competitive aspects of Keats's Enfield schooling, which I describe here, emerged in the course of a general discussion at the one-day Keats Conference in the Centre for English Studies, University of London, on 24 Feb. 1995. I am grateful in particular to Professor Isobel Armstrong for her response to my paper on Keats at Enfield.

[39] *Letters*, i. 271.

[40] Letter to J. H. Reynolds, 3 May 1818, ibid. 281.

agrees with the idea of GOD.'[41] Indeed, Ryland's *Contemplations on the Beauties of Creation* offers a remarkable vision of imaginative sublimity, in a passage that may have had some bearing on Keats's poems and thought.

'The powers of man's mind shew him to be almost a divine existence,' Ryland begins:

He thinks—he is conscious of internal acts—he forms ideas of all things—he reasons on his thoughts—he perceives an infinite variety of objects—he reflects on these images of things in his mind—he recollects his thoughts, and surveys their agreement with objects, and their difference from each other—he brings all past ages and time present to his mind, and views the transactions of men, and revolutions of empires for thousands of years—he can recollect a thousand, ten thousands, a million of facts almost at once—or he makes them pass in a quick succession before the eyes of his mind—he marks the different nature and tendency of men's actions—sees how one kind have a direct influence upon his peace and happiness, while others issue in ruin, devastation, and death.

He commands the future time to the present view of his vast and mighty mind; looks into future years and ages; foretels the consequences of actions to individuals, and to the societies of men; penetrates the dark veil of future ages, and dives into the condition of the human nature for ten thousand years to come, yea for ten thousand millions in hell and heaven.

He pursues a mental tour round the earth, and ranges in his thoughts all over the skies; he roves from planet to planet, from sun to sun, from world to world, almost to infinity! he views one system of worlds after another with infinite speed and velocity; and after all can form in his imagination, and grasp in his thoughts, millions of worlds more than ever existed.

He sees the eternal difference between moral good and evil; and in spite of pride, in spite of hell, is forced to confess the beauty of the one, and the deformity of the other; the destructive consequences of vice, and the infinite advantages and transcendent joys of virtue.[42]

The 'strange journey' of the charioteer in *Sleep and Poetry* was Keats's first representation of the visionary faculty that 'ranges all over the skies' and contemplates the historical and moral 'tendency of men's actions'. *Sleep and Poetry* offers but a momentary glimpse of this sublime figure of the imagination, although Keats concluded:

[41] Ryland, *Character of Hervey*, 202.   [42] Ryland, *Contemplations*, i. 21–2.

> I will strive
> Against all doubtings, and will keep alive
> The thought of that same chariot, and the strange
> Journey it went. (159–62)

The living thought of his ambition as a poet endured, and in *Hyperion* and *The Fall of Hyperion* Keats returned to the ideal of universal knowledge as the foundation for poetic achievement. *Hyperion* Book III celebrates knowledge in the 'wondrous lesson' which initiates the deification of Apollo:

> 'Knowledge enormous makes a God of me.
> Names, deeds, gray legends, dire events, rebellions,
> Majesties, sovran voices, agonies,
> Creations and destroyings, all at once
> Pour into the wide hollows of my brain,
> And deify me . . .' (III. 113–18)

In the *Fall of Hyperion* this passage is refigured in terms of the poet-dreamer's own sublime aspiration:

> there grew
> A power within me of enormous ken
> To see as a God sees, and take the depth
> Of things as nimbly as the outward eye
> Can size and shape pervade. (I. 302–6)

John Ryland had written that 'an insuppressible ardour after more knowledge . . . agrees with the idea of GOD', and he had sought to encourage that zeal in his pupils. These two climactic passages from the *Hyperion* poems reaffirm Ryland's testament, albeit as the 'enormous ken' of poetic ambition appropriately represented in *Hyperion* by the god of poetry, Apollo.

But to postulate Ryland as a 'source' for Keats's deification of Apollo, or his idea of his poetic calling, would ultimately be limiting and unhelpful. I have no doubt that Keats had at least looked into Ryland's works when he 'exhausted' the Enfield School library; these books were most important, though, in that they were representative of his wider education at Enfield. It was in this more general sense that Ryland's vision was transmitted to Keats, influencing his ambition for 'continual drinking of Knowledge . . . in pursuit of doing some good for the world'. Crucially, Ryland's celebration of knowledge may have counted less in this respect than the radical politics associated with Enfield School from an early date.

A Republican Library

> Washington spoke: 'Friends of America, look over the Atlantic sea;
> A bended bow is lifted in heaven . . .'
>
> (William Blake, *America*, Plate 3, 6–7)

In 1776 dissenters and reformists in Britain united as zealous supporters of the American cause during the war of independence. John Ryland was among them and one of his pupils at the Northampton School, Robert Hall, remembered how the schoolmaster had expressed his views on the American crisis. Hall's anecdote offers a further instance of Ryland's vigorous personality, and suggests how his outspoken republicanism established the political tone of his schools:

My father . . . warmly advocated the American cause. When I was a little boy, he took me to the school of Mr Ryland at Northampton . . . this Mr Ryland was very eccentric, and a violent partizan of the Americans; it was in the hottest period of the war . . . and many persons were indignant at the conduct of the English government. That war . . . was considered as a crusade against the liberty of the subject and the rights of man. The first night we arrived at Northampton . . . the two old gentlemen (my father and Mr Ryland) talked over American politics until they both became heated on the same side of the question. At length, Mr Ryland burst forth in this manner: 'Brother Hall, I will tell you what I would do if I were General Washington'. 'Well', said my father, 'what would you do?'. 'Why, brother Hall, if I were General Washington, I would summon all the American officers; they should form a circle around me, and I would address them, and we would offer a libation with our own blood, and I would order one of them to bring a lancet and a punch-bowl; and he should bleed us all, one by one, into this punch-bowl; and I would be the first to bare my arm: and, when the punch-bowl was full, and we had all been bled, I would call upon every man to consecrate himself to the work, by dipping his sword into the bowl, and entering a solemn covenant engagement, by oath, one to another, and we would *swear by Him that sits upon the throne, and liveth for ever and ever,* that we would never sheathe our swords while there was an English soldier in arms remaining in America; and that is what I would do, brother Hall'.[43]

Eccentric, heated, violent: certainly. John Ryland was nevertheless a man of 'true liberty principles' whose opinions, as a friend of America, resembled William Blake's. His sanguinary libation to 'liberty . . . and the rights of man' was sufficiently extreme, but also a forceful assertion of the liberal and republican ideals he shared with Keats's schoolmaster John Clarke at Enfield School. At the beginning of the French Revolution in 1789, Ryland's excitement echoed the rapturous welcome from contemporaries such as Richard Price and Joseph Priestley: 'we may . . . hope that the astonishing revolution in France will be attended with the most happy consequences to the world at large . . . The Revolution . . . will highly tend to preserve the liberties and rights of us Englishmen.'[44] Ryland's pamphlet quoted here is indicative of the environment of dissenting radicalism in which Keats's imaginative and political identity was formed after 1803: the Clarkes' tuition, and Keats's reading in the school library, stirred his republicanism from an early date. Following Keats's departure from the school, his friendship with Charles Cowden Clarke ensured that this influence continued at the period when he was writing his earliest poems—as will appear in Chapter 3.

Like everything else at Enfield School, the library was remarkable. William Newman, an assistant tutor at the school in 1789, wrote that in the school library he had 'greater advantages for seeing, reading, and hearing of good books than thousands of youths of my age, in English, French, Latin, Greek, and Hebrew'.[45] It was this library that Keats read through in his last months at the school, obliging him to borrow further books from the Clarkes. According to Cowden Clarke, 'the quantity that [Keats] read was surprising' in that it embraced 'voyages and travels . . . Mavor's collection [*A Historical Account of the most Celebrated Voyages and Discoveries*], also his "Universal History"; Robertson's histories of Scotland, America, and Charles the Fifth; all Miss Edgeworth's productions, together with many

[43] John Greene, *Reminiscences of the Rev. Robert Hall, A.M.* (London, 1832), 92–3.
[44] John Ryland, *A Tribute of Honour to the Great and Good Men in France* (London, 1790), 6–7.
[45] See George Pritchard, *Memoir of the Rev. William Newman* (London, 1837), 18.

other works equally well calculated for youth'. Keats's 're-current sources of attraction were Tooke's "Pantheon", Lempr-ière's "Classical Dictionary", . . . and Spence's "Polymetis"': these three books, Clarke remembered, were 'the store whence he acquired his intimacy with the Greek mythology'.[46]

Keats's debt to these classical textbooks has been thoroughly explored by generations of editors and commentators. My con-cern here is not to offer a further search for classical sources, allusions, and references, but rather to explore how the dissent-ing opinions of Ryland and the Clarkes were represented in the school library and in some of the books Keats is known to have read there. Common to the classical, historical, scientific, and travel literatures available to Keats was a strong liberal and republican bias. This demonstrably affected his imaginative re-sponse to Greek mythology, his thinking about history, as well as his attitudes to contemporary politics and public affairs. Once again, it is John Ryland who allows us a glimpse of some books not mentioned by Cowden Clarke, but which were certainly in the school library at Enfield in Keats's time.

In his essay 'On the Advancement of Learning by Various Modes of Recreation', prefaced to *An Easy Introduction to Mechanics*, Ryland recommended some texts on 'the grand science of society, government, and the laws of [the] country'. His choice of authors revealed his priorities as a dissenter. 'To assist you in your views', he wrote, 'read the best books that were ever written, since Britain existed, Milton, Sydney, Locke and Dr Campbell, Sydney's Treatise on Government, folio, 1696. Locke on Government, 8vo. Dr Campbell's Present State of Europe, 8vo 5th edition . . .'.[47] This short catalogue demon-strates that for Ryland 'the best books ever written' about society and government were emphatically republican, liberal, and tol-erant. Milton's writings, with Algernon Sydney's *Discourses Concerning Government*, constituted the republican foundations of Ryland's politics as an 'ardent friend of liberty'. Locke's appeal

[46] 'Recollections of Keats', 123–4.

[47] Ryland, *Introduction to Mechanics*, pp. xxvii–xxviii. Compare another list of Ryland's political and intellectual heroes: 'the names of Raleigh, Hampden, Pym, Hale, Russel, Sydney, Locke, Newton, and Marlborough, can never be mentioned but with distinguished veneration and esteem'; *The Life and Character of Alfred the Great* (London, 1784), p. vi. For further discussion of this pamphlet in relation to Keats, see Ch. 2.

to Ryland would have included his argument in the *Letter on Toleration* for religious and intellectual liberty. Dr John Campbell's *Present State of Europe* (like his *Present State of Britain*) detailed the political and commercial aspects of European countries, presenting an optimistic view of Britain's progress and future improvement.

Here, then, is a brief profile of some texts that are likely to have been in the library at Enfield School and available to Keats. Whether he read Milton, Sydney, and the other republican books there has to remain a matter of conjecture, but all the evidence suggests that he did. Certainly, his early verses celebrated the English republicans as representatives of a 'patriotic lore' that had been lost in the modern world:

> Infatuate Britons, will you still proclaim
> His memory, your direst, foulest shame,
> >   Nor patriots revere?
> Ah! when I hear each traitorous lying bell,
> 'Tis gallant Sydney's, Russell's, Vane's sad knell,
> >   That pains my wounded ear.
> >   ('Lines Written on 29 May, the
> >   Anniversary of Charles's Restoration')

This curious and in some respects slight lyric is nevertheless an unequivocal expression of Keats's sympathies, aligning the patriot republican tradition of Algernon Sydney, Lord William Russell, and Sir Henry Vane against 'infatuated', 'shameful', 'traitorous' monarchists. What I want particularly to emphasize is that Enfield School placed Keats in direct continuity with English radicalism of the 1790s, with the dissenters of the later eighteenth century, and with the republicans of the seventeenth century. When George Felton Mathew remembered that in 1815 Keats had been 'of the sceptical and republican school. An advocate for the innovations which were making progress in his time. A faultfinder with everything established,'[48] he defined a political identity which was already fully formed when Keats met Leigh Hunt in October 1816. Hunt and his circle subsequently provided a base for Keats's literary ambitions and political opposition, at the period when he dropped his medical training to devote himself to poetry; but in a longer perspective

[48] See *KC* ii. 185–6.

this was just one stage in a career which shows remarkable consistency from his earliest years at school through to autumn 1819, and the great letter to George and Georgiana (17–27 September) in which Keats surveys 'progress' in European history from the time of the Normans to the French Revolution to the present day.[49]

The strong likelihood must be, therefore, that Keats's republicanism sprang from his reading and tuition at Enfield School, and subsequently during his apprenticeship to Hammond, when he remained on friendly terms with the Clarke family, and with Charles Cowden Clarke in particular. Unlike John Ryland, though, Keats's idea of America was ambiguous, modified according to his brother George's changing fortunes 'over the Atlantic sea'. He had no warm regard for Benjamin Franklin and George Washington (who 'sold the very Charger who had taken him through all his Battles') as compared to his esteem for 'those our countrey men Milton and the two Sidneys'.[50] Ryland and the Clarkes would have agreed with Keats's idea of the English republicans' 'sublimity'; indeed, Keats's journal-letter of 14–31 October 1818 regrets that 'We have no Milton, no Algernon Sidney' and marks the lamentable contrast between 'the present Government and oliver Cromwell's'.[51] Here, Keats was echoing Wordsworth's sentiments in his republican sonnets of 1802:

> Great Men have been among us; hands that penned
> And tongues that uttered wisdom, better none:
> The later Sydney, Marvel, Harrington,
> Young Vane, and others who called Milton Friend. (1–4)

—and, closer still to Keats's sense of England's present decline,

> Milton! thou should'st be living at this hour:
> England hath need of thee ... (1–2)

These two sonnets, 'Great Men' and 'London, 1802', were among the three of Wordsworth's political sonnets of 1802 that Charles Cowden Clarke copied into the commonplace book which he used between 1810 and 1818.[52] As John Barnard has recently shown, there is evidence that Keats had access to the

---

[49] See *Letters*, ii. 193–4.   [50] Ibid. i. 397.   [51] Ibid. 396.
[52] Charles Cowden Clarke's commonplace book is discussed in detail in Ch. 3; for Wordsworth's sonnets, see in particular p. 95 and n. 20.

commonplace book and, at the very least, the book indicates the kind of republican literary and political texts read and discussed by Keats and his friend at Enfield School and during Keats's apprenticeship to Hammond.[53] After 1802, Wordsworth never again expressed such overt admiration for the English republicans of the seventeenth century: as Richard Altick has pointed out, the continuity of English republicanism at this period was represented by the Clarkes at Enfield and by their pupil John Keats. For them, as for Shelley, Hunt, and others, an immediate issue in the post-revolutionary world was the need to keep faith with the progressive improvement of humankind while acknowledging the seemingly contradictory facts of recent history. Keats discussed human progress in his journal-letter to George and Georgiana Keats, 17–27 September 1819, in the midst of the crisis precipitated by the Peterloo Massacre. In reasserting a broadly optimistic view of history at this moment, Keats was once again drawing upon material that had been familiar to him since his schooldays—as will appear in my next chapter.

[53] See John Barnard, 'Charles Cowden Clarke's "Cockney" Commonplace Book', *K&H* 65–87. Barnard points out that the three sonnets by Wordsworth ('Great Men', 'London, 1802', and 'It is not to be thought of') are 'Significantly . . . the only poems by which Wordsworth is represented in the commonplace book' (81).

CHAPTER TWO

Cosmopolitics:
History, Classics, and Pretty Paganism

Woe woe to the half fledged Bantam Bards of Cockaigne—
and woe! woe! to the bared necks, long tresses and square
toed *historical* shoes of the disciples of Ben. Haydon.
(Allan Cunningham to William Blackwood,
29 Sept. 1820)[1]

even the better schooled among us can no longer cope
with Greek and Latin.
(George Steiner, 'To Civilize our Gentlemen')[2]

Keats and History

In his journal-letter of 17–27 September 1819, Keats announced that he would write 'a little politics'. What followed
this remark, however, was a liberal account of history as progressive enlightenment, or, as Keats phrased it, 'a continual change
for the better':

Look at this Country at present and remember it when it was even
though[t] impious to doubt the justice of a trial by Combat—From
that time there has been a gradual change—Three great changes have
been in progress—First for the better, next for the worse, and a third
time for the better once more. The first was the gradual annihilation
of the tyranny of the nobles, when kings found it their interest to
conciliate the common people, elevate them and be just to them. Just
when baronial Power ceased and before standing armies were so dangerous, Taxes were few. [K]ings were lifted by the people over the
heads of their nobles, and those people held a rod over kings. The

---

[1] NLS, MS 4005, quoted by permission of the Trustees of the National Library of
Scotland.
[2] See George Steiner, *Language and Silence: Essays 1958–66* (London, 1985),
82.

change for the worse in Europe was again this. The obligation of kings to the Multitude began to be forgotten—Custom had made noblemen the humble servants of kings—Then kings turned to the Nobles as the adorners of the[i]r power, the slaves of it, and from the people as creatures continually endeavouring to check them. Then in every kingdom therre was a long struggle of kings to destroy popular privileges. The english were the only people in europe who made a grand kick at this. They were slaves to Henry 8th but were freemen under William 3rd at the time the french were abject slaves under Lewis 14th. The example of England, and the liberal writers of france and england sowed the seed of opposition to this Tyranny—and it was swelling in the ground till it burst out in the french revolution—That has had an unlucky termination. It put a stop to the rapid progress of free sentiments in England; and gave our Court hopes of turning back to the despotism of the 16 century. They have made a handle of this event in every way to undermine our freedom. They spread a horrid superstition against all inovation and improvement—The present struggle in England of the people is to destroy this superstition. What has rous'd them to do it is their distresses—Perpaps on this account the pres'ent distresses of this nation are a fortunate thing—tho so horrid in the[i]r experience. You will see I mean that the french Revolution put a temporry stop to this third change, the change for the better—Now it is in progress again and I thing in an effectual one. This is no contest between whig and tory—but between right and wrong.[3]

In this passage, Keats interprets English and European history from the Middle Ages as a 'gradual enlightenment' in the relationships between the aristocracy (king, court, nobles) and the people ('popular privileges'). He touches upon matters of justice, tyranny, commonwealth, military power, and taxation. In concluding, however, he approaches the recent phenomenon of the French Revolution and emphasizes its adverse effects for the 'progress of free sentiments in England' in that it had encouraged 'a horrid superstition against all inovation and improvement'. His idea that the Revolution was an organic germination from 'seed' planted by liberal writers during the eighteenth century was sufficiently commonplace. But his account of the Revolution's failure, its 'unlucky termination', surrendered the liberal progress of humankind to the rules of chance. By glossing the Terror and Napoleon's career as 'un-

---

[3] *Letters*, ii. 193–4, with some minor alterations to punctuation, but retaining Keats's spelling.

lucky' developments in their effects on British political life, Keats avoided enquiry into the causes of revolutionary defeat— an issue which had preoccupied an earlier generation of radicals and poets. He was correspondingly at liberty, however, to dwell on the 'present distresses' of the country, recently focused by the killings at Manchester which had been extensively reported in the columns of the *Examiner*. 'Did ever a whole nation cry out without a cause,—aye, without a goading cause? Distress, and a stronger conviction of mis-government are the causes now; but because the people did not cry so loud five years ago, is it any proof that there was no mis-government then?'[4] In the distressed weeks which followed the Peterloo Massacre on 16 August, Keats associated the resurgence of 'effectual' progress with a modern 'trial by combat', a 'contest' between fundamental issues of 'right and wrong'. By dismissing 'whig and tory' as superficial allegiances in this arena, he implied his support for the renewed call for parliamentary reform summarized by the *Examiner* in the following way: 'The demand of the manufacturers and the other classes who are stirring just now is for what the Anti-Reformers chuse to call exclusively a *Radical Reform*,—that is, Universal Suffrage, Annual Parliaments, and (with some) Vote by Ballot.'[5]

The letter of 17–27 September is remarkable as an expression of Keats's informed and optimistic view of current events, and also for showing the long historical perspective in which he sought to understand the dynamics of 'progress' and 'turning back' in recent history. As Keats knew, David Hume's *History of England* presented a similar interpretation of historical cycles, or 'great changes . . . in progress', although with a more sceptical account of the prospects for the improvement of humanity: 'There is an ultimate point of depression', Hume had written, 'as well as of exaltation, from which human affairs naturally return in a contrary progress, and beyond which they seldom pass either in advancement or decline.'[6] William Robertson

---

[4] 'Arguments of the Reformers: How Met by the Corrupt', *Examiner* (5 Sept. 1819), 563.

[5] *Examiner* (5 Sept. 1819), 563.

[6] David Hume, *The History of England, from the Invasion of Julius Caesar to the Accession of Henry VII* (6 vols., London, 1762), ii. 441. For a full and illuminating discussion of Keats's response to the 'major preoccupation' of historiographers in the 18th cent. and during the revolutionary period, the 'question of progress

discussed this passage from Hume in his *History of the Reign of the Emperor Charles V*, which we know Keats had read at Enfield.[7] Hume had interpreted history as a pattern of 'natural return' from extremes of 'depression' and 'exaltation'. For Robertson, on the other hand, history presented a cumulative improvement in society, and in this respect his book offers a pattern for the unillusioned but nevertheless optimistic view outlined by Keats in his letter of September 1819. As with Keats's republicanism, his thinking about political and social history was initiated by his reading at Enfield School and through discussions with the Clarkes. Yet, given this generous and liberal background, it is notable that in some of his poems history and the imagination coincide in a more combative, imperious vision of human progress.

The Scottish theologian, scholar, and historian William Robertson was 'an avowed optimist of the eighteenth-century type . . . a champion of liberalism' (*DNB*). Of Robertson's many works, Charles Cowden Clarke remembered that besides the *History of Charles V*, Keats had also read Robertson's *History of Scotland*, and *The History of America*.[8] In all three histories Robertson was concerned to demonstrate universal progress in the fields of politics, society, commerce, the arts, and science. Like John Ryland, Joseph Priestley, and other liberals of their generation, Robertson welcomed the American Revolution as a promise of the 'future condition' of the world: 'The attention and expectation of mankind are now turned towards their future condition,' he wrote, 'a new order of things must arise in North America, and its affairs will assume another aspect.'[9] Sentiments such as these were sufficient to guarantee John Ryland's esteem for Robertson, and space for his books in the school library. My concern here is not to trace detailed parallels between Keats's political and social views and Robertson's books, but to suggest how fully Robertson's histories comple-

or decline', see Greg Kucich, 'Keats's Literary Tradition and the Politics of Historiographical Invention', *K&H* 238–61.

[7] See William Robertson, *The History of the Reign of the Emperor Charles V* (3 vols., London, 1769), i. 21, and for Keats's reading of this book, 'Recollections of Keats', 124.

[8] 'Recollections of Keats', 124.

[9] William Robertson, *The History of America* (6th edn., 3 vols., London, 1792), i. p. v.

mented Keats's wider reading in the liberal and republican texts which were representative of the intellectual environment at Enfield School. In these respects, Robertson's progressive views coincided with those of Ryland and the Clarkes, and contributed to Keats's ideas of a 'gradual enlightenment' in human affairs. As one might expect, however, Keats's later expressions of those ideas in his poems and letters were not always consistent.

For example, Oceanus's explanation of historical change in *Hyperion*,

> 'As Heaven and Earth are fairer, fairer far
> Than Chaos and blank Darkness, though once chiefs;
> And as we show beyond that Heaven and Earth
> In form and shape compact and beautiful,
> In will, in action free, companionship,
> And thousand other signs of purer life;
> So on our heels a fresh perfection treads,
> A power more strong in beauty, born of us
> And fated to excel us . . .' (II. 206–14)

—combines a progressive view of history (albeit as perceived by those 'fated' to be superseded) with Ryland's idea of a gradual refinement of aesthetic response:

the exquisite sensibility of the soul to every fine impulse of beauty, truth, and goodness . . . is wrought up to perfection and delicacy by education, study, and devotion, whereby the mind becomes able to discern, with an intuitive rapidity, how much truth, beauty and pleasure every object in heaven and earth can give us.[10]

Ryland's celebration of the soul's 'exquisite sensibility' prefigures the conclusion of 'Ode on a Grecian Urn', and the serene association of beauty and truth which subsequently informed nineteenth-century responses to Keats—especially those of William Morris, Edward Burne-Jones, and the Pre-Raphaelites.[11] Yet, as E. P. Thompson noted, the Pre-Raphaelites also shared the determination and ambition to succeed which Keats had brought forward as a principal theme in *Hyperion*. The poem emphasizes the competitive power of imagination, 'the eternal law | That first in beauty should be

[10] Ryland, *Contemplations*, i. 66.　　[11] Thompson, *William Morris*, 10.

first in might' (II. 228–9), but also the painful, destructive effects of that law of progress; ideal beauty defines history in successive acts of conquest and usurpation, an imperial advance in the course of which Neptune triumphs over Oceanus:

> 'Have ye beheld the young God of the Seas,
> My dispossessor? Have ye seen his face?
> Have ye beheld his chariot, foam'd along
> By noble winged creatures he hath made?
> I saw him on the calmed waters scud,
> With such a glow of beauty in his eyes,
> That it enforc'd me to bid sad farewell
> To all my empire; farewell sad I took . . .' (II. 232–9)

According to the same eternal law, beautiful Apollo will enforce his succession to Hyperion. In each case, the 'transcendental cosmopolitics' of *Hyperion*, remarked by Leigh Hunt, are defined by militant activity rather than the contemplative passivity adopted by Oceanus.[12]

In *The Fall of Hyperion* this imperious vision is qualified by Moneta's admonition that the poet should 'think of the earth' (I. 169); think, that is, of the distresses of human beings, but also of the 'unlucky' excesses to which extreme idealism might lead. In this last respect, Keats's schooling in the benevolent and vicious potentials of the imagination resembled the experiences of Samuel Taylor Coleridge, Helen Maria Williams, Mary Wollstonecraft, and William Wordsworth during the 1790s, for whom Robespierre's Terror projected the lethal effects of imagination's 'horrible misapplication'.[13] To Keats at Enfield School, Robertson's *History of America* presented a compelling narrative about the Spanish conquests in the new worlds of the Caribbean and South America. As is well known, these passages from Robertson's book constitute the invigorating and chastening historical matter that shadows the golden realms of Keats's early sonnet, 'On First Looking into Chapman's Homer':

> Much have I travell'd in the realms of gold,
>   And many goodly states and kingdoms seen;

[12] Hunt, *Autobiography*, ii. 202.
[13] See S. T. Coleridge, 'Lecture on the Slave-Trade', in *Lectures 1795 on Politics and Religion*, ed. L. Patton and P. Mann, Bollingen Collected Coleridge Series 1 (London, 1971), 235–6, and my *Wordsworth and Coleridge: The Radical Years* (Oxford, 1988), 216–17.

> Round many western islands have I been
> Which bards in fealty to Apollo hold.
> Oft of one wide expanse had I been told
>   That deep-brow'd Homer ruled as his demesne;
>   Yet did I never breathe its pure serene
> Till I heard Chapman speak out loud and bold:
> Then felt I like some watcher of the skies
>   When a new planet swims into his ken;
> Or like stout Cortez when with eagle eyes
>   He star'd at the Pacific—and all his men
> Look'd at each other with a wild surmise—
>   Silent, upon a peak in Darien.

The sonnet encompasses poetry and history, in that Keats's first reading of Chapman's Homer is said to have 'felt like' Herschel's and Cortez's momentous discoveries. The felt kinship between poetic imagination and the revelation of new worlds (across the Atlantic, beyond the Pacific, at the edge of the solar system) is one of marvellous, unutterable possibility: 'a wild surmise— | Silent'. In the aspiration to 'goodly states and kingdoms', Keats's sonnet suggests that political history and poetic imagination coincide.[14]

In his recent account of William Robertson's importance to the sonnet, Daniel Watkins elucidates parallels between the poem and the discovery-narratives of Cortez and Balboa in the *History of America*. He suggests in particular that Keats aspires to unite poetry and history as 'a single enterprise', although the aesthetic mastery of his sonnet may be achieved 'at the expense of history itself'.[15] Robertson's description of the 'visionary ideas' of the explorers has not yet been discussed in this context, so far as I am aware. It offers an impressive analogue to the 'realms of gold' of Keats's imagining, and may permit a reintegration of history and imagination under the sign of imperial militarism—the 'conquest and command' that Vincent Newey has recently brought forward as the 'latent concern of

---

[14] For the aspiring and speculative qualities of Keats's sonnet, contrasted with the 'ontic' settlement of Wordsworth's sonnets, see John Kerrigan, 'Wordsworth and the Sonnet: Building, Dwelling, Thinking', *Essays in Criticism*, 35 (1985), 45–75, esp. 59–65. For the public resonance of the 'Chapman's Homer' sonnet as a 'challenge to prevailing ideas of order in Regency England', see John Kandl, 'Private Lyrics in the Public Sphere: Leigh Hunt's *Examiner* and the Construction of a Public "John Keats"', *K–SJ* 44 (1995), 90.

[15] Watkins, *Keats's Poetry*, 26–31.

Keats's sonnet'.[16] Here is the relevant passage from Robertson's *History of America*:

The Spaniards, at that period, were engaged in a career of activity which gave a romantic turn to their imagination, and daily presented to them strange and marvellous objects. A New World was opened to their view. They visited islands and continents, of whose existence mankind in former ages had no conception. In those delightful countries, nature seemed to assume another form; every tree and plant and animal was different from those of the ancient hemisphere. They seemed to be transported into ancient ground; and, after the wonders they had seen, nothing, in the warmth and novelty of their admiration, appeared to them so extraordinary as to be beyond belief. If the rapid succession of new and striking scenes made such an impression even upon the sound understanding of Columbus, that he boasted of having found the seat of Paradise, it will not appear strange that Ponce de Leon should dream of discovering the fountain of youth.[17]

Along with this 'romantic' account of discovery, in which a 'strange and marvellous' world and the imaginative power of 'admiration' were at one, Robertson also describes (and deplores) the Spaniards' vicious exploitation of human beings in the gold mines of Hispaniola—where 'the consumption of the human species [was] no less amazing than rapid'.[18] Keats's sonnet omits the tragic human cost of Spanish activities in the new world, and celebrates Cortez (all struggles past) gazing over the Pacific in a moment of solitary personal triumph. Yet in so doing the sonnet has located imperial military aggressiveness as a prerogative of the imagination 'Which bards in fealty to Apollo hold'. Thus, as Homer appropriated 'one wide expanse' which he 'ruled as his demesne', so in a later time the conqueror's 'eagle eyes . . . star'd at the Pacific'. Imagination and imperial power coincide in the appropriation of wonderful new worlds—'realms of gold', 'a new planet', 'the seat of Paradise', or 'the fountain of youth'.

As Keats knew, Cortez had claimed his new world for the king of Spain. In a comparable gesture of obeisance Herschel, 'as a subject of the best of Kings . . . and owing every thing to His unlimited bounty', gave 'the name Georgium Sidus . . . to a star,

---

[16] See Newey, 'Keats, History, and the Poets', *K&H* 184–5.
[17] Robertson, *History of America*, i. 282–3.   [18] Ibid. 262–3.

which (with respect to us) first began to shine under His auspi-
cious reign'.[19] For the poet such imperial 'glories' (although as
yet 'dim-conceived') were the measure of his own ambitions as
a writer, although his aspiration was fortunately tempered by a
compassionate humanity and a sense of his own limitations as a
person:

> My spirit is too weak—mortality
>   Weighs heavily on me like unwilling sleep,
>   And each imagined pinnacle and steep
> Of godlike hardship tells me I must die
> Like a sick eagle looking at the sky.
>   ('On Seeing the Elgin Marbles', 1–5)

From his schooldays, Keats's understanding and imagining of
history comprehended the liberal and progressive culture
of dissent, as well as the thrusting, competitive imperialism of
European activities in South America. Alongside these histories
may be placed Keats's lived experience of 'the agonies, the strife
| Of human hearts' (*Sleep and Poetry*, 124–5), appropriately
represented in 'On Seeing the Elgin Marbles' by the 'sick
eagle'. Keats's aspiration to the 'pinnacle' of universal wisdom
(the condition for Apollo's deification in Book III of *Hyperion*)
brought home the burden of 'weariness, fever, fret'—a contradiction which many of his poems, 'On Seeing the Elgin Marbles', 'Ode to a Nightingale', *The Fall of Hyperion*, seek to resolve.
So it is that the imaginative contours of Keats's poems reveal a
subjective terrain, and also the 'contrary progress' of history in
turning back from the forgetful plot of romance to the forlorn
country of distresses and 'horrid experience':

> Adieu! the fancy cannot cheat so well
>   As she is fam'd to do, deceiving elf.
> Adieu! adieu! thy plaintive anthem fades
>   Past the near meadows, over the still stream,
>   Up the hill-side; and now 'tis buried deep
>   In the next valley-glades:
>   Was it a vision, or a waking dream?
>   ('Ode to a Nightingale', 73–9)

[19] 'A Letter from William Herschel, Esq. F.R.S. to Sir Joseph Banks, Bart. P.R.S.',
*Philosophical Transactions, of the Royal Society of London. Vol. LXXIII. For the Year 1783.
Part I* (London, 1783), 2.

In the fading, plaintive requiem for the imagination with which the 'Ode to a Nightingale' concludes we hear too the undeceiving music of post-revolutionary consciousness. No longer entranced by ideal forms, the poet's disorientation ('Do I wake or sleep?') gives voice to the larger historical confusion which grew particularly acute in the post-Waterloo years: the apparent conflict between unworldly 'vision'ries [and] dreamers' and those who labour at practical change, seeking 'no wonder but the human face; | No music but a happy-noted voice' (*Fall of Hyperion*, I. 161–4).[20] This tension emerges throughout Keats's writings, figured variously as an opposition between sensual life and 'thoughts'; joy and philosophy; imagination and science; romantic love and capitalism; the liberties of the pagan world and the oppressive realities of 'a time when Pan is not sought'. Some of the ways in which Keats drew upon classical antiquity to confront and resolve the distresses of the modern world are the subject of the following section of this chapter.

Cockney Classics

> and what is there in Bristol Hunt and Cobbett . . . —Why our classical education alone—should teach us to trample on such unredeemed dirt as the *dis*honest bluntness—the ignorant brutality, the unblushing baseness of these two miscreants.
>
> (Lord Byron to John Cam Hobhouse, 22 Apr. 1820)
>
> There is something to us quite shocking in the idea of Hunt translating Homer.
>
> ('On the Cockney School of Poetry: No VI')
>
> As is well known, Keats knew no Greek.[21]

We saw in the Introduction that by tagging Keats as a 'Cockney' Z identified a complex of deficiencies—lower class, profane, vulgar, illegitimate, profligate, radical, *ignorant*. That last item of abuse was aimed directly at Keats's supposed lack of accom-

[20] See the quotation from and discussion of Watkins, *Keats's Poetry*, in the Introduction, pp. 6–7 above.
[21] See *BLJ* vii. 81; *Blackwood's Magazine* (Oct. 1819), 74; and M. L. Clarke, *Greek Studies in England, 1700–1830* (Cambridge, 1945), 171.

plishment in classical studies: 'His Endymion is not a Greek shepherd, loved by a Grecian goddess; he is merely a young cockney rhymester, dreaming a phantastic dream at the full of the moon.'[22] The moon-madness of 'Cockney Keats' | 'Endymion', and the second-hand knowledge of classical literature intimated by the 'Chapman's Homer' sonnet,[23] defined the poet's exclusion from the high culture of classical poetry and history:

From his prototype Hunt, John Keats has acquired a sort of vague idea, that the Greeks were a most tasteful people, and that no mythology can be so finely adapted for the purposes of poetry as theirs. It is amusing to see what a hand the two Cockneys make of this mythology; the one professes that he never read the Greek Tragedians, and the other knows Homer only from Chapman; and both of them write about Apollo, Pan, Nymphs, Muses, and Mysteries, as might be expected from persons of their education. . . . As for Mr Keats' 'Endymion', it has just as much to do with Greece as it has with 'old Tartary the fierce'; no man, whose mind has ever been imbued with the smallest knowledge or feeling of classical poetry or classical history, could have stooped to profane and vulgarise every association in the manner which has been adopted by this 'son of promise'.[24]

Keats's 'vague idea' of Greek literature and culture, which Z believed he shared with Hunt, was of a piece with the 'loose, nerveless versification, and Cockney rhymes' he had also adopted from 'the poet of Rimini'. Accordingly—and as William Keach has argued—Keats's unschooled and formally undisciplined poetry was not just a 'profane and vulgar' jargon; for Z, Keats's verse announced the liberal values of the 'Cockney School of Politics' and, similarly, his travesty of classical myth paralleled his disorderly, disaffected political ambitions.[25]

[22] 'Cockney School IV', 522.

[23] For the sonnet's disclosure of cultural belatedness, and the 'impossibility of a pure, *unmediated* return to [classical] origins', see Martin Aske, *Keats and Hellenism: An Essay* (Cambridge, 1985), 42. Aske suggests how the sonnet transforms 'a promise of "firstness"'—which for Z defined cultural election—into an acknowledgement of lateness, thus enacting the decline which Z perceived more widely in Keats's and Hunt's writings.

[24] 'Cockney School IV', 522. See Hunt: 'With the Greek dramatists I am ashamed to say I am unacquainted', 'Preface' to *The Story of Rimini: A Poem* (London, 1816), p. xvii. For 'old Tartary the fierce', see *Endymion*, IV. 262.

[25] On the politics of 'Cockney' poetic style, see in particular William Keach, 'Cockney Couplets', KP 182–96, and on the 'Chapman's Homer' sonnet more

While the political controversy surrounding Keats's association with Hunt gradually subsided or was deliberately obscured in the years after Keats's death, the myth of his ignorance of the classics persisted. A representative instance appeared in the first biography of the poet, Milnes's *Life, Letters, and Literary Remains, of John Keats*. Milnes was concerned to present Keats's school education as favourably as possible, yet, as frequently in nineteenth-century accounts of Keats, the reality of the poet's life merges with the 'enchanted world' of romance supposed to be typical of his poems:

The quantity of translations on paper he made during the last two years of his stay at Enfield was surprising. The twelve books of the 'Æneid' were a portion of it, but he does not appear to have been familiar with much other and more difficult Latin poetry, nor to have even commenced learning the Greek language. Yet Tooke's 'Pantheon', Spence's 'Polymetis', and Lemprière's 'Dictionary', were sufficient fully to introduce his imagination to the enchanted world of old mythology; with this, at once, he became intimately acquainted, and a natural consanguinity, so to say, of intellect, soon domesticated him with the ancient ideal life, so that his scanty scholarship supplied him with a clear perception of classic beauty, and led the way to that wonderful reconstruction of Grecian feeling and fancy, of which his mind became afterwards capable.[26]

Here, the otherwise negative attribute of 'scanty scholarship' is detached from the 'more difficult' requirements of (masculine) study, by allowing it to 'domesticate' Keats with the 'ideal life' of antiquity. The tacit suggestion is that Keats was self-educated, or home-taught, like women who did not (could not) attend the public schools and universities at Oxford and Cambridge. In the absence of formally prescribed study, a susceptible and feminized 'natural consanguinity' of mind transformed Keats's slender but 'sufficient' learning into the 'capable' imagination of 'feeling and fancy' represented by 'Ode on a Grecian Urn'. Milnes was echoing almost word for word the 'few memoranda of the early Life of John Keats' which Charles Cowden Clarke had sent him in March 1846 (*KC* ii. 147–8), but his feminizing of Keats (absent in Clarke's memoranda) was a

particularly, David Pirie, 'Keats', in D. Pirie (ed.), *The Penguin History of Literature: The Romantic Period* (London, 1994), 358.

[26] *LLL* i. 8.

strategy intended to accommodate the poet's unorthodox classical learning within the prevailing gendered definitions of education, thereby making Keats acceptable to a broad nineteenth-century readership.[27]

Milnes's effort to extend Keats's appeal in this way effectively reversed Z's criticisms in *Blackwood's*, where Keats's want of 'the smallest knowledge or feeling of classical poetry or classical history' had been invoked in order to banish him from literary society. As I suggested in the Introduction, Z had detected in Keats's poems evidence of a cultural change which he sought to oppose through ridiculing the poet as inadequately educated. Z was above all dismayed by the erosion of received values signalled by Keats's 'ignorant'—in other words, unlicensed—use of classical literature and mythology in his poetry; in this respect, Keats's poems focused an otherwise gradual alteration in classical scholarship and tuition dating from the latter eighteenth century. Worse than this, his poems reflected the polemical myth-making current in the circles associated with Leigh Hunt, John Hamilton Reynolds, Horace Smith, Percy Bysshe Shelley, and Thomas Love Peacock. To these writers ancient Greek mythology was the pattern for contemporary paganism, a radical ideological cult opposed to the patrician classicism (and Toryism) of Wordsworth's *Excursion* and, especially, his *Laodamia*, which was perceived to reinforce the ascetic and exclusive hegemony of the orthodox Christian establishment. As Linda Colley has recently shown, classical literature was presented in the public schools so as to remind 'the élite of its duty to serve and fight', thus encouraging the emergence of British national consciousness at this period: masculine, patriotic, imperial invocations of the classics 'could inspire without being in any way threatening' because the 'societies they represented were emphatically dead'. Cockney classicism, however, sought to revive the liberal values associated with classical culture, thus presenting an articulate alternative to the establishment's coding of the classics.[28]

[27] For a full discussion of the 'feminizing' of Keats in 19th-cent. biographies and criticism, see Susan J. Wolfson, 'Feminizing Keats', in Hermione de Almeida (ed.), *Critical Essays on John Keats* (Boston, 1990), 317–56.

[28] See in particular Butler, *Romantics*, 131, and Linda Colley, *Britons: Forging the Nation 1707–1837* (London, 1994), 168.

The alteration in the texture of classical scholarship mentioned above was typified by the pragmatic educational initia-
tives of dissenting academies (such as Enfield) in the later
eighteenth century, and it was continued beyond the turn of the
century by the rising mercantile and industrial classes. Their
values of utility and material progress were reflected in a practical school curriculum—'conducted in the vernacular'—in
which classics were taught alongside 'English, French, mathematics, history, geography, accounting'. Charles Dickens
would satirize these utilitarian ideals in Mr Gradgrind's dreadful school at Coketown, but it is clear that otherwise vigorous
and democratic educational developments coincided with a
period at which the great public schools, the instruments of
the establishment or 'ruling class', were comparatively 'degenerate and openly denigrated'.[29] As James Bowen has shown,
nineteenth-century reformers at the public schools (Thomas
Arnold at Rugby, Samuel Butler at Shrewsbury) actually resisted
change by intensifying their preoccupation with the classics,
especially classical Greece.[30] Keats was therefore representative
of the diversification in educational practice which emerged
from the dissenting culture of the eighteenth century, persisted
into the nineteenth century, and which is reflected in the
school systems and curricula in England today. One might accurately say that the modern academy in schools and universities
is a 'Cockney' invention—and all the better for being so.

The scholarly and literary effects of this change have been
outlined in the following manner:

When we turn from the eighteenth century to the nineteenth we are
conscious of a change in the relations between learning and literature.
There is an estrangement between them which had scarcely existed in
the previous century. . . . The scholars went their way and the poets
went theirs, and they had little contact with one another. In the
eighteenth century the poet and scholar were united in such a typical
figure as Thomas Warton; but there is little in common between
Elmsley and Dobree, on the one hand, and Keats and Shelley on the

[29] See James Bowen, 'Education, Ideology and the Ruling Class: Hellenism and
English Public Schools in the Nineteenth Century', in G. W. Clarke (ed.), *Rediscovering Hellenism: The Hellenic Inheritance and the English Imagination* (Cambridge,
1989), 161–2.
[30] Ibid. 162.

other. It is true that on both sides there is a love of ancient Greece, but it is a long way from the *Museum Criticum* to *Endymion* or *Hellas*.[31]

Described here in very general terms is a perceived rift between the standards of eighteenth-century classical scholarship (represented by Peter Elmsley, Peter Paul Dobree, and the journal of the Cambridge classicists *Museum Criticum*) and the imaginative myth-making of Keats's and Shelley's poetry. The point is not that Keats and Shelley were poor classicists (which would be nonsense), but that their poetry was representative of a modish, liberal cast of mind through which antiquity was, as Marilyn Butler has said, 'reinterpreted . . . misread, or substantially invented' for their own times and purposes.[32]

Hunt's preface to *Foliage* expresses concisely this new 'Cockney' approach to the classics and to translation: while deprecating the 'narrow sphere of imagination' in poetry of the 'French school', Hunt announces that although he is 'no great scholar' his translations will properly suggest 'the natural energy of the original' for 'the intelligent reader, who is no scholar'. And, again: 'Shakespeare . . . felt the Grecian mythology not as a set of school-boy commonplaces . . . but as something which it requires more than mere scholarship to understand.'[33] Evidently, Hunt's idea of classical translation differed from the strictly prescriptive methods widely characteristic of schools during the eighteenth century.[34] We have already seen that this issue was particularly vexed in Z's response to Keats's sonnet—a poem which unblushingly announced that the author knew 'Homer only from Chapman'. As a principal intellectual foundation of contemporary education, classical learning was associated directly with matters of social and political authority and the question of parliamentary reform.

William Godwin's pamphlet *Account of the Seminary* (1783) sought to ensure the future improvement of government through the reform of education today. He identified the 'noble freedom of mind that was characteristic of the republicans of Greece and Rome' and accordingly recommended an attentive

---

[31] Clarke, *Greek Studies in England*, 164.
[32] Marilyn Butler, 'Myth and Mythmaking in the Shelley Circle', *English Literary History*, 49 (1982), 50–72.
[33] See Hunt, *Foliage*, 11, 23–4, 31.
[34] See in particular Clarke, *Greek Studies in England*, 14–24.

but humane study of the 'ancient languages': 'Translation! what a strange word! To me I confess it appears the most unaccountable invention, that ever entered into the mind of man.'[35] In that translation was an 'estrangement' from the original, he claimed that it compromised 'a perfect system of education' designed to form 'a perfect character'—a concern that he would return to, at length, in his great treatise on the philosophical bases of reform *Political Justice* (1793).[36] While *An Account of the Seminary* does not go so far as the claims of that later work, Godwin did seek to improve present methods of teaching classical literature, smoothing the access to knowledge which the pedantic methods of many contemporary educationalists had, as he said, 'plant[ed] round with briars and thorns'.[37]

In the later eighteenth century Eton was the most influential model for the teaching of classical grammar and literature at many other schools in Britain. Some twenty-five editions of the 'Eton Latin Grammar' are known to have been printed before 1800, and this indicates the wide usage of the book in public and grammar schools of the period. The classical curriculum at Eton (and at other old-established public schools) was rigid and narrow; in the time of John Keate (headmaster of Eton, 1809–34) and of his predecessors, 'written translations into English were unknown'.[38] The 'Eton Latin Grammar', for example, was written almost entirely in Latin, ancient Greek was learnt after Latin, and the Greek grammars were written in Latin as well.[39] Given Eton's status in England as a model of educational practice which reflected social standing and—as Linda Colley has argued—British patriotism, a departure from its methods might

[35] William Godwin, *An Account of the Seminary*, in *The Political and Philosophical Writings of William Godwin*, ed. Mark Philp *et al.* (7 vols., London, 1993), v. 6–8.

[36] Cf. Shelley's observation about the 'deleteriousness of classical education' to Godwin, 29 July 1812: 'I do not perceive how one of the truths of Political Justice rest[s] on the excellence of ancient literature.' His emphasis on the value of 'ideas', rather than rote-learning of '*words*', reflects his concern to oppose 'prejudice' and perhaps also memories of classics teaching at Eton. *The Letters of Percy Bysshe Shelley*, ed. F. L. Jones (2 vols., Oxford, 1964), i. 316–17. See also Timothy Webb, *The Violet in the Crucible: Shelley and Translation* (Oxford, 1976), 21–2.

[37] Godwin, *An Account of the Seminary*, in *Political and Philosophical Writings*, v. 11.

[38] For the classical curriculum at Eton, and translation, see Clarke, *Greek Studies in England*, 17–18. For the 'debased condition' of the English public schools at the end of the 18th cent., see Bowen, 'Education, Ideology, and the Ruling Class', 166–8.

[39] See the 'Eton Latin Grammar', that is, *An Introduction to the Latin Tongue, for the Use of Youth* (Eton, 1768), and Clarke, *Greek Studies in England*, 14–15.

readily be perceived as culturally deficient, socially defiant, and politically disaffected.[40]

Cowden Clarke recalled that Keats had '*voluntarily* translated . . . a considerable portion' of the *Aeneid* and that his principal sources of classical knowledge were anthologies and reference books in English, Tooke's *Pantheon*, Lemprière's *Classical Dictionary*, and Spence's *Polymetis*. This evidently contrasted with tuition modelled on the practice at Eton, although it was not quite so unusual as the comparison may at first suggest. The popularity of such compilations is indicated by Horace Smith's satirical squib, 'The Poet among the Trees',

> Apollo crown'd with Bays gives laws
>   To the Parnassian Empyrean;
> And every schoolboy knows the cause,
>   Who ever dipp'd in Tooke's Pantheon.[41]

This verse was published in 1825, and the rhyme 'Empyrean | Pantheon' marks it out as a deliberate 'Cockney' jest by Smith; perhaps the schoolboy 'dipping' in Tooke's anthology may have been intended to recall Keats—'looking into Chapman's Homer'. Leigh Hunt's *Autobiography* recalls his own reading at Christ's Hospital of Ovid, Horace, Cicero, Demosthenes, Homer, and Virgil—but he adds, 'there were three books which I read in whenever I could, and which often got me into trouble. These were Tooke's *Pantheon*, Lemprière's *Classical Dictionary*, and Spence's *Polymetis*, the great folio edition with plates.'[42] Hunt's and Coleridge's 'very severe master' at Christ's Hospital, James Bowyer, was determined to prepare his students as 'excellent Latin and Greek scholars'.[43] This explains why reading translations got schoolboy Hunt into trouble, but there was an ideological dimension to the issue as well. Andrew Tooke prefaced his *Pantheon* with an address '*To the Reader*' in which he explained why his classical anthology was written in English:

As for the quotations out of the *Latin Poets*, it was considered a while whether they should be translated or not; but it was at last judged

---

[40] See Linda Colley's discussion of 'patrician education' at Eton, Harrow, Westminster, and Winchester in *Britons: Forging the Nation 1707–1837*, 167–8.

[41] See *Gaieties and Gravities: A Series of Essays, Comic Tales, and Fugitive Vagaries* (3 vols., London, 1825), ii. 327.

[42] Hunt, *Autobiography*, i. 130–1.

[43] See Coleridge's recollection of Bowyer in *Biographia Literaria*, ed. J. Engell and W. Jackson Bate, Bollingen Collected Coleridge Series 7 (2 vols., London, 1983), i. 8–11.

proper to print them in *English,* either from those who had already rendered them well, or, where they could not be had, to give a new translation of them; so that nothing of the whole Work might be out of the reach of the young scholar's understanding, for whose benefit chiefly . . . this version was intended.[44]

Tooke's *Pantheon*—like Spence's and Lemprière's books—gave the 'young scholar' direct access to classical myth through translation, avoiding the severer discipline of classical studies discussed already. This coincided with other aspects of teaching at Enfield School, forming part of the liberal curriculum which enabled Keats to write a distinctly modern classical poetry no longer dependent on prescriptive rules of 'correctness'.

'Tintern Abbey' has been claimed by Harold Bloom as '*the* modern poem proper . . . most good poems written in English since *Tintern Abbey* inescapably repeat, rewrite, or revise it'.[45] Whether or not this Wordsworthian influence was 'inescapable', Bloom begs the question as to whether 'good' poetry has indeed been limited to confessional lyricism patterned after 'Tintern Abbey'. In his belated appropriation of antiquity, Keats surely also has a claim to distinctive modernity. His licentious, imaginative response to classical literature and myth in *Endymion,* the *Hyperion* poems, *Lamia,* even the 'Chapman's Homer' sonnet, arguably helped open the way for the reinvention, or free interpretation, of classical myth and literature by writers as diverse as Tennyson, Pound, Joyce, and Walcott. Karl Kroeber's candid remark on modern readerly habits is also pertinent: 'the truth, which we mostly choose not to admit, is that usually we do read the great Greek poets in translation and are excited by works of which we have "oft been told".'[46]

[44] Andrew Tooke, *The Pantheon* (London, 1783), pp. iii–iv. Cf. John Hamilton Reynolds's letter of 4 Nov. 1811, announcing his determination to study Greek through English: 'I am going to learn Greek by a new method which is by using an English & Greek grammar instead of a Latin & Gk. one whereby the Rules are more easily understood and a person may learn Greek without understanding Latin it is certainly a clearer & shorter way and consequently the best.' *Letters from Lambeth: The Correspondence of the Reynolds Family with John Dovaston, 1808–1815,* ed. J. Richardson (Woodbridge, 1981), 70.

[45] Harold Bloom, 'Wordsworth and the Scene of Instruction', in *Poetry and Repression: Revisionism from Blake to Stevens* (New Haven, 1976), 59.

[46] Karl Kroeber, *Ecological Literary Criticism: Romantic Imagining and the Biology of Mind* (New York, 1994), 79.

Joseph Severn lived to see the effect of Keats's Cockney classicism on later poets; forty years after Keats's death, he remarked:

altho he knew no Greek & could only get at the greek legends thro translations, yet he penetrated deeper into it & realized a modern arcadian world, such as no greek scholars of modern time had done & such forms the ground work of poetry at the present time, for Keats's poetry has been an impulse to an intire new school . . . a mine of inexhaustible wealth wherein the modern poets may delve without limit, without exhaustion.[47]

Z saw things less generously. By 'touching the beautiful mythology of Greece' in *Endymion* without approved 'education', Keats had irresponsibly invoked the 'liberal views' of classical culture which for Godwin betokened 'love of truth . . . and the love of liberty', and for Hazlitt 'raise[d] us above that low and servile fear, which bows only to present power and upstart authority'.[48] The 'unsettled pretender' Keats thus signalled his confrontation with the establishment on broad political and cultural fronts. The 'profanity' and 'vulgarity' which Z reviled in Keats's poetry was an acknowledgement of its accessible, democratic idiom, in which classical myth formed part of a slick polemic directed against those 'who lord it o'er their fellow-men' (*Endymion*, III. 1).

In this last respect, Keats's poetry had given voice to the politically contentious associations of neoclassicism which had been current throughout the revolutionary decades. The close association between classical civilization and modern radicalism (implicit in Godwin's *Account of the Seminary*) acquired considerable force in the years following 1789. French neoclassicism pre-dated the Revolution, of course, for example in Jacques-Louis David's paintings *The Oath of the Horatii* (1785), *The Death of Socrates* (1787), and *Brutus* (1789).[49] As the Revolution

[47] Joseph Severn, 'On the Adversities of Keats's Fame', autograph manuscript dated 'Rome [25 Dec.] 1861'. MS Keats 4. 16. 2, quoted by permission of The Houghton Library, Harvard University.

[48] William Godwin, *The Enquirer* (1797), in *Political and Philosophical Writings*, v. 98; William Hazlitt, 'On Classical Education', in *The Round Table* (2 vols., Edinburgh, 1817), i. 26–7. For the radical social/sexual associations of Greece, see Pirie, 'Keats', 371–2. See also Richard Jenkyns, *The Victorians and Ancient Greece* (Oxford, 1980), 14–15.

[49] See Ronald Paulson, *Representations of Revolution (1789–1820)* (New Haven, 1983), 6, 28–36.

progressed, French republicans looked to ancient Rome and Greece as inspiring precedents for their own political and social ideals, to the extent that classicism and Jacobinism were closely identified together. The intersection of classical antiquity and contemporary revolution in France can be illustrated in numerous ways: by debates in the National Convention about whether Athens or Sparta was the more appropriate model for the present Revolution; by the fashion for naming babies after classical heroes; by the eradication of royalty from playing-cards, so that the four kings became four classical 'Sages' (Solon, Brutus, Cato, Plato); and by the vogue, originating in the 1780s, for classical styles of dress.[50]

The most visible manifestations of revolutionary neoclassicism were the elaborate *fêtes* staged at Paris to commemorate revolutionary events. Dress, statues, banners and flags, even landscaping at the *fêtes* were deliberately orchestrated to present the virtues of the classical world—political, philosophical, civic, artistic—as intrinsic to the Revolution. Here are some details from the procession at the *Fête de Châteauvieux*, 14 July 1791:

the chariot of Liberty . . . modelled on the antique, was an imposing construction. On one of its sides, the happy painter of the Revolution, M. David, had sketched the story of Brutus the elder . . . With steady step twenty democratic horses (if we may be permitted to use the adjective) drew the chariot of the sovereign of the French people; their progress had none of the insolence of those idle coursers fed in the stables of Versailles or Chantilly.[51]

And the *Fête de l'Être Suprême*, 8 June 1794:

An immense amphitheatre was erected in front of the centre pavilion of the Tuileries, before which were placed statues of Atheism, Discord and Egotism; after a quasi-religious service including a hymn to the Supreme Being, Robespierre set fire to the statues, and then headed a march to the Champ de Mars where a huge artificial mountain had been built. Robespierre led the members of the Convention, all dressed in blue coats with tricolour sash and plumed hat, to sit on the mountain; there were further hymns and salvos of artillery, and the people lifted up their children to consecrate them to the Supreme

[50] See Ronald Paulson, 13, 17–18, and Lynn Hunt, *Politics, Culture, and Class in the French Revolution* (London, 1984), 20.

[51] *Révolutions de Paris*, quoted in Mona Ozouf, *Festivals and the French Revolution* (Cambridge, Mass., 1988), 68.

Being. Each Paris *section* elected favoured citizens to sit on the mountain; matrons and young girls were dressed in white with a tricolour sash, children in white tunics crowned with violets, and men were either in the uniform of the National Guard, or in what various accounts describe as 'Roman' dress.[52]

This *Fête de l'Être Suprême* had been designed by David with an attention to articulate symbolic detail comparable to his 1791 sketch of Brutus. The white costumes, for example, expressed a classical simplicity and purity combined with the patriotism of the tricolour sash, as well as a calculated revolutionary appropriation of the colour of the Bourbon dynasty.[53] Lynn Hunt has said that David's revolutionary neoclassicism was high-minded to the point of élitism; an 'artist-intellectual-politician's' creation for the edification of the people, a 'bourgeois fantasy' of playing the classics.[54] But neoclassical virtues were also invoked in the pamphlet which circulated most widely among the mass of citizens in Britain, *The Rights of Man*: in praising 'the democracy of the Athenians', Paine had also said that, 'We see more to admire, and less to condemn, in that great, extraordinary people, than in any thing which history affords.'[55] In Britain the neoclassical style was to some extent adopted at mass gatherings of reformers, where it became less of a 'fantasy' than an eloquent statement of democratic political claims which, moreover, can be related to classical myth and imagery in Keats's poetry.

The Politics of Pan, and Pretty Paganism

> Hot was the chace
> Through the wilds of Thrace . . .[56]

In the years immediately following the Battle of Waterloo, mass demonstrations organized by the reformers employed some of the props formerly used in the revolutionary *fêtes*. Here is a

[52] See Aileen Ribeiro, *Fashion in the French Revolution* (London, 1988), 93–4.

[53] See Paulson, *Representations of Revolution*, 17, and, for the restoration of the Bourbon colours, *Examiner* (10 Apr. 1814), 225. For republican dress, see also Hunt, *Politics, Culture, and Class*, 75–86.

[54] Hunt, *Politics, Culture, and Class*, 76.

[55] Thomas Paine, *The Rights of Man, Part Two*, ed. H. Collins (Harmondsworth, 1969), 199.

[56] Horace Smith, *Amarynthus, the Nympholept*, III. i, from *Amarynthus, the Nympholept: A Pastoral Drama, in Three Acts: With Other Poems* (London, 1821), 112.

description of one contingent arriving to hear 'Orator' Henry Hunt speak at the mass meeting in St Peter's Fields, Manchester, 16 August 1819:

> The Reformers from Rochdale and Middleton marched to the sound of the bugle, and in very regular time, closing and expanding their ranks, and marching in ordinary and double quick time, according as it pleased the fancy of their leaders to direct them. They had two green banners, between which they had hoisted on a red pole a cap of liberty, crowned with leaves of laurel, and bearing the inscription, 'Hunt and Liberty'.[57]

The reformists' emblems combined the French cap of liberty on its red pole, and the laurel which was the Roman token of civic virtue, recently adopted in France as an emblem of revolutionary ideals. These were intended to express the reformers' libertarian ideals and their disciplined resolve to achieve them—although one can see readily enough that such military ranks might appear like a revolutionary army on parade. On 13 September 1819, one month after Peterloo, Henry Hunt entered London in a long procession which had been carefully planned as a welcome and also a symbolic statement of the reformers' political aspirations. The attention to colour and symbolism in the following description of the procession is significant:

> Some hundreds of footmen bearing large branches of oak, poplar, and various other trees.
> A footman, bearing the emblem of union—a bundle of sticks stuck on a pitchfork, supported by groups of men on horseback and on foot.
> The Committees bearing white wands, and all wearing knots of red ribband and laurel leaves in their hats.
> A green silk flag, with gold letters and Irish harp; inscription, 'Universal, civil, and religious liberty;' borne and supported by 6 Irishmen, and numerous other footmen.
> A band of music.
> Horsemen.
> A white flag, surmounted and bordered with crape; inscription in black, 'To the immortal memory of the Reformers massacred at Manchester, Aug. 16, 1819.'

---

[57] 'Dispersal of the Reform Meeting at Manchester by a Military Force', *The Times* (19 Aug. 1819).

Groups of horsemen and footmen.

A large tricoloured flag, red, white, and green, with the words 'England,
Scotland, and Ireland', in gold letters.

Groups of men bearing white wands and red favours.

The old red flag, with the inscription 'Universal Suffrage'.

Two barouches, in which were some friends of Mr. Hunt.

Two carriages, in which were some gentlemen connected with the press.

A sky blue flag; inscription 'The palladium of liberty, a free press'.

Groups of footmen.

A carriage containing Messrs. Watson, Thistlewood, and Preston,
and other friends of Mr. Hunt.

A scarlet silk flag; inscription in gold letters, 'Hunt, the heroic
Champion of Liberty'.

Groups of men on horseback and on foot.

A Band of Music.

Mr. HUNT,

Standing in a landaulet, drawn by six handsome bays, decorated
with scarlet ribands.

Behind the carriage stood a man, bearing a large red flag, which waved over
Mr. Hunt's head; inscription, 'Liberty or Death'.

Groups of Horsemen and Footmen.

A white Silk Flag; inscription, 'Trial by Jury'.

The article goes on to describe Hunt's appearance: he 'stood in
the landau . . . dressed in a black coat and waistcoat, and white
jean trowsers. His white hat he held for the most part in his
hand.'[58] The staging of this procession was not as elaborate as
the French *fêtes*, not so overtly classical in inspiration—but there
are similarities: the tricoloured flag, the bundle of sticks (the
fasces, denoting fraternity), the laurel leaves. Most striking, perhaps, is the frequency with which the colour white appears in
flags, on the wands, in Henry Hunt's dress: as in revolutionary
France, white was an expression of the reformers' untainted
ideals and motives which (like the laurel) invoked the precedent of the classical world.[59]

[58] 'Mr. Hunt's Entry into London', *The Times* (14 Sept. 1819). The offset quotation has been centred to reproduce its appearance in the columns of the *Times*.

[59] Cf. the order of procession at the chairing of Sir Francis Burdett, in *Examiner*
(12 July 1818), 436: 'Large white Flag, carried on horse-back; motto, "Purity of
Election".' Earlier in the 18th cent., white had been the signal of Jacobite opposition to the Hanoverian regime. See, for example, the 'splendid, almost shocking
mixture of chaste classicism and gloating violence' in Joseph Enzer's stucco decora-
tions in the House of Dun, described in *Britons: Forging the Nation 1707–1837*, 74.

In Leigh Hunt's *Descent of Liberty* (1815), his masque celebrating the end of the Napoleonic wars, the triumph of 'Liberty' and Peace' was celebrated in a great pageant of laurel-decked figures from classical religions, literature, and myth. His fusion of classical antiquity with modern politics closely resembled the pattern of the revolutionary *fêtes* in France (which had incorporated masques and dumb-shows) but also the processions at urban and suburban meetings and celebrations in England. A fine Cockney detail in the *Descent of Liberty* is Hunt's choice of 'A PLEASURE-GROUND in the suburbs of a great city laid out in a natural stile with wood and turf, the spires and domes appearing over the trees toward the side' as the setting for Liberty's pageant.[60] Since the 1790s the reformers had organised mass meetings in the suburbs surrounding London at Copenhagen Fields (1795) and Spa Fields (1816), and in St Peter's Fields at Manchester (1819). Hunt's intention was I think to imply a parallel between the fanciful and stylized procession in his masque, and contemporary mass meetings of citizens gathered to call for parliamentary reform. In the preface to the masque he claimed that 'the popular Spirit' in England, rather than individuals such as Wellington, had triumphed over 'the great Apostate from Liberty' Napoleon—and that this democratic spirit was now working to improve 'the social atmosphere of the world'.[61]

Keats read Hunt's masque with close attention, and when he incorporated a comparable pageant or procession at the opening of the first book of *Endymion* he too reminded his readers of revolutionary politics in France and England. The Latmians' procession to Pan's 'woodland altar' from *Endymion* Book I presents the ritual of a benevolent 'natural' religion popular in the contemporary literary fashion for Pan-worship: Horace Smith's pastoral drama *Amarynthus, the Nympholept* (1821), for example, also begins with a rustic sacrifice at 'Pan's festival' which was almost certainly patterned on Keats's poem. But a procession such as the one described by Keats also invoked the neoclassical imagery of David's revolutionary ceremonies at Paris.[62] Details such as 'little children garlanded' (110), 'gar-

[60] Leigh Hunt, *The Descent of Liberty, a Mask* (London, 1815), 23.
[61] Ibid., pp. v, viii, xvi.
[62] See Butler, *Romantics*, 131. For the ancient Greeks as representative of 'a happy, humane, politically enlightened society without recourse to Biblical reli-

ments white, | Plainer and plainer shewing' (124–5), 'a white wicker over brimm'd | With April's tender younglings' (137–8), 'a vase, milk-white, | Of mingled wine' (153–4), 'valley-lilies whiter still' (157), the priest's 'aged head, crowned with beechen wreath' (159), all closely resembled aspects of the revolutionary and reformist costumes and iconography detailed above. Such poetry adopted classical myth and religion—and the cult of Pan in particular—as the genial representation of the reformists' political and social aims, the promise of universal participation in the commonwealth of nature's plenty.

Given these similarities, David Pirie's claim is markedly persuasive: 'To the more paranoid Tories amongst the poem's first readers this colour scheme for such efficiently marshalled ranks might suggest the opposite of innocence: white was firmly associated with the reform movement.'[63] Indeed, the association dated from the 1790s, if not earlier. When John Thelwall visited William and Dorothy Wordsworth at Alfoxden House, in July 1797, the informer Thomas Jones (servant to the Wordsworths) thought it worthwhile to report to the authorities that this 'little Stout Man . . . wore a White Hat . . . [and] talked so loud and was in such a Passion'.[64] As a result of this information a government spy was dispatched from London to monitor the suspicious goings-on in that remote part of Somerset.

Two decades later, in the turbulent and distressed months following Peterloo, a short-lived radical journal appeared on the London bookstalls, entitled the *White Hat*. The introduction to this journal explains the title's emblematic significance:

The *White Hat*, worn by so many steady and decided patriots, battered by the bludgeons of special constables, slashed by the sabres of Yeomanry Cavalry, the horror of paid magistrates, and welcomed by the appealing shouts of hundreds of thousands of the people, is become a badge too explicit to be mistaken, too honourable to be neglected, and too formidable to be despised.[65]

gion', see Robert Ryan, 'The Politics of Greek Religion', in H. de Almeida (ed.), *Critical Essays on John Keats* (Boston, 1990), 261–79. For the association of woodland and ancient English liberties (rather than the classical world) see Ch. 5.

[63] Pirie, 'Keats', 365. For a more extended discussion of *Endymion* as a 'critique of society', see Newey, 'Keats, History, and the Poets', *K&H* 168–76.

[64] See Roe, *Wordsworth and Coleridge: The Radical Years*, 261.

[65] See *White Hat*, 1 (16 Oct. 1819), 2. Nine issues only of this journal were published; the last appeared on 11 Dec. 1819. See also *Poetry and Reform: Periodical Verse from the English Democratic Press*, ed. Michael Scrivener (Detroit, 1992), 226–7.

These associations for the colour scheme and iconography of Keats's 'Hymn to Pan' were so familiar as to be unmistakable by 1819, and they help to explain why 'Government critics' should have read *Endymion* in relation to the patriot cause of the reformists dating from the 1790s and earlier. The poem's controversial presence for its first readers is further substantiated by the publication on 9 May 1818 of an extract from the 'Hymn to Pan' (corresponding to *Endymion* I. 232–306) in John Hunt's ultra-radical journal the *Yellow Dwarf,* a conjunction which helps to explain the violence of the contemporary critical response to the poem as a whole. Hostile reviews may have ridiculed and dismissed *Endymion* as a 'flimsy', 'vulgar', 'unintelligible' production, but at the same time they perceived clearly its ideological design, denouncing the poem as 'impious', 'impure', 'immoral', 'jacobinical', and 'seditious'.[66] Keats's poetry, like Hunt's, was the disreputable contrary to Wordsworth's integrity as the 'purest, the loftiest, and . . . the most classical of living English poets'.[67]

Ironically, Keats's use of myth in *Endymion* (and, earlier, in *I stood tip-toe*) was stimulated by his admiration for Wordsworth's account of the origin of Greek mythology in *The Excursion* Book IV. There, the Wanderer reverts to the myths of 'pagan Greece' as creations of an intuitive, imaginative response to nature which, he argues, might offer a corrective to the modern, rational intellect:

> go, demand
> Of mighty Nature, if 'twas ever meant
> That we should pry far off yet be unraised;
> That we should pore, and dwindle as we pore,
> Viewing all objects unremittingly
> In disconnection dead and spiritless;
> And still dividing, and dividing still,
> Break down all grandeur, still unsatisfied
> With the perverse attempt, while littleness
> May yet become more little; waging thus
> An impious warfare with the very life
> Of our own souls![68]

---

[66] See *KCH* 81, 94, 104, 109, 111. [67] See 'Cockney School IV', 520.
[68] William Wordsworth, *The Excursion,* IV. 957–68; *Wordsworth Poetical Works,* ed. Thomas Hutchinson, rev. E. de Selincourt (Oxford, 1969).

The unrelenting deconstructive process of rational analysis re-calls the 'scrupulous and microscopic views' of Godwin's phi-losophy in *Political Justice* which, as described in *The Prelude* Book X, led to a personal crisis of 'despair' comparable to the Soli-tary's 'despondency'. In contrast the pagans were inspired by an 'all-pervading Spirit' in nature (IV. 969), and the Wanderer finds in their vitality of response an expression of the 'celestial spirit' (IV. 1071) in humankind, which may alleviate

> 'the encumbrances of mortal life,
> From error, disappointment,—nay, from guilt;
> And sometimes, so relenting justice wills,
> From palpable oppressions of despair'. (IV. 1074–7)

With this glimpse of consolation, we are told, the despondent Solitary 'was touched | With manifest emotion' (IV. 1078–9). Here in *The Excursion*, then, Wordsworth had shown how mod-ern poetry might invoke the animating, imaginative principles of Greek mythology in a way that would have an urgent mean-ing for the present. Yet, as a convinced Tory and Anglican (and therefore 'the most classical of living English poets'), Wordsworth requires his Wanderer to dismiss the ancient Greeks as 'unenlightened swains', 'those bewildered Pagans of old time' (IV. 850, 934), thereby leaving the way open for the radical imagination to appropriate paganism in confronting the political and religious establishment to which Wordsworth now subscribed. While Keats admired and set out to emulate the classical spirit of Wordsworth's poetry, he used Greek myth in a manner directly opposed to the ideology of *The Excursion*.

The strong association between classical myth and religion, Homeric Hymns, and the celebration of love as an ideal had flourished, Marilyn Butler has shown, in the Shelley circle that gathered at Marlow during the summer of 1817, so much so that Leigh Hunt 'in his sentimental way, equated the Marlow circle with paganism, and took its divinity to be the god Pan'.[69] Hunt's view was perhaps less sentimental than this allows, in that it reflected his knowledge as poet and journalist of the wider cultural perspective in which political radicalism, Greek culture, paganism, and the cult of Pan were by this time closely

[69] Marilyn Butler, *Peacock Displayed: A Satirist in his Context* (London, 1979), 103–9.

associated.[70] Thomas Love Peacock's *Rhododaphne*, published in February 1818, expressed the ideals of the 'Marlow summer' in its celebration of natural religion and sexuality; as Butler suggests, the poem was explicitly an attack on the solemn Christian morality of Wordsworth's *Laodamia* (1815) and, by extension, the oppression of the religious and political establishments. Given this background we can see how, three months later, the publication of Keats's 'Hymn to Pan' in the *Yellow Dwarf* was fully consistent with anti-clerical articles which were also regularly included in its columns. To the first readers of the *Yellow Dwarf* it would have been evident that Pan's benevolent ministry,

> Breather round our farms,
> To keep off mildews, and all weather harms . . . (I. 283–4)[71]

—was directly at odds with the priorities of 'a Divine . . . [who] calls us his flock, but . . . cares not if the wolf take us day by day, and by two and threes, so that he be not disturbed after his dinner'.[72] Elsewhere in the *Yellow Dwarf* the political resonances of Keats's 'Hymn', and the cult of Pan more generally, were made explicit by comparison with 'pious pastors of the people and accomplices of the governments [who] make use of their heavenly calling and demure professions of meekness and humility, as an excuse for never committing themselves on the side of the people . . . Their religion is incompatible with a common regard to justice or humanity; but it is compatible with an excess of courtly zeal.'[73] In the pagan clime of Keats's 'Hymn', Pan's 'mighty palace' was the 'impious' source of all the generous, loving, liberal principles that were denied by the 'courtly zeal' of Church and State as established by law in England.

[70] See in particular the discussion of Shelley's responsiveness to the Greek example in Timothy Webb, *Shelley: A Voice not Understood* (Manchester, 1977), esp. 196–7.

[71] Quoted from *Yellow Dwarf: A Weekly Miscellany* (9 May 1818), 152. The literary currency of the Pan cult is further suggested by the *Yellow Dwarf*'s publication, 10 Jan. 1818, of George Chapman's translation of Homer's 'Hymn to Pan'.

[72] 'Pulpit Oratory No. 1', *Yellow Dwarf* (7 Feb. 1818), 47. The author was Keats's friend John Hamilton Reynolds.

[73] 'On the Clerical Character', *Yellow Dwarf* (7 Feb. 1818), 45. Compare Hunt's references to 'jealous rage', 'passions and bigotries', in his sonnet 'To Percy Shelley, on the Degrading Notions of Deity', and the anti-clerical sentiments of Keats's sonnet 'Written in Disgust of Vulgar Superstition', in which the soft Grecian music of 'Lydian airs' is preferred to the church bells' 'melancholy sound'.

In moving now to consider Keats's 'Poetic Romance' as a whole, we can understand how pagan impiety and sexual immorality were readily traced by hostile readers to its erotic theme and manner—the 'amorous scenes' which, Z claimed, filled all four books of the poem. There are many passages that could be cited in this context, but the following passage from Book II is a representative example. Endymion has thrown himself on the 'smoothest mossy bed and deepest', where, 'Stretching his indolent arms, he took, O bliss! I A naked waist' belonging to the moon-goddess Diana:

> long time they lay
> Fondling and kissing every doubt away;
> Long time ere soft caressing sobs began
> To mellow into words, and then there ran
> Two bubbling springs of talk from their sweet lips.
> 'O known Unknown! from whom my being sips
> Such darling essence, wherefore may I not
> Be ever in these arms? in this sweet spot
> Pillow my chin for ever? ever press
> These toying hands and kiss their smooth excess?
> Why not for ever and for ever feel
> That breath about my eyes?' (II. 710–13; 734–45)

Conventional formulae such as 'sweet lips', 'bubbling springs', 'sweet spot', 'toying hands' are mingled here with with voluptuous coinages such as 'caressing sobs', 'darling essence', and 'smooth excess'.[74] Z noted that 'After all this . . . the "modesty", as Mr Keats expresses it, of the Lady Diana prevented her from owning in Olympus her passion for Endymion.'[75] Fondling dalliance, not passionate consummation, characterizes this encounter and all of the poem's teaseful narrative. Rather than gathering to a climax the passage is lingeringly detumescent, an adolescent tryst in which sexual energy is dissipated into 'talk' and questions which will remain unanswered for another two books of the poem.

This encounter between Endymion and Diana represented a

[74] Critics objected particularly to Keats's neologisms as 'the flimsy veil of words in which he would involve immoral images', *British Critic* (June 1818), *KCH* 94 (citing the passage quoted from Book II) and 'the new words with which, in imitation of Mr Leigh Hunt, he adorns our language', John Wilson Croker, *Quarterly Review* (Apr., Sept. 1818), *KCH* 114.
[75] 'Cockney School IV', 522.

type of pastoral eroticism which was also characteristic of the literary vogue for 'nympholepsy'—that is, the psycho-sexual extremity at which men 'adopt delusion for reality' ('O known Unknown!') and are 'supposed to be possessed by the Nymphs, and driven to phrenzy'.[76] In Book II, Endymion is distracted by his inability to identify his lover; is she a vision, a waking dream, or goddess indeed? This aspect of *Endymion* was a marked influence on Horace Smith's extraordinary and very funny pastoral drama *Amarynthus, the Nympholept* (1821). As Smith explained in his preface, 'nympholepsy' was a manifestation of

religious scepticism and excitement prevalent in Greece at the period to which he has assigned his drama . . . conflicting opinions, producing doubt upon all points rather than conviction upon any, stimulated that insatiable curiosity for prying into the mysteries of nature, of which it has been attempted to delineate a faint outline in the character of Amarynthus, the Nympholept.

Sceptical yet intensely imaginative, Amarynthus finds himself (like Endymion) unable to discriminate mundane and supernatural experiences, although he is offered the cryptic promise that he will be freed from this maddening enthralment when 'fancied visions [are] | Reliev'd by their reality'. Under the delusion that he is being persecuted by nymphic 'fury', he throws himself on the protection of Dryope, a woodland nymph whom he identifies (wrongly) as a mortal shepherdess. They fall in love and, as with Endymion and the Indian Maid/Diana, human love has a tempering influence in reconciling ideal forms and worldly realities—a final vindication of the narrator's claim in *Endymion* that 'earthly love has power to make | Men's being mortal, immortal' (*Endymion*, I. 843–4).[77]

'I am certain of nothing but of the holiness of the Heart's affections and the truth of imagination,' Keats had written to Benjamin Bailey, 22 November 1817, as he set about writing the last section of his poem:

[76] Horace Smith, preface to *Amarynthus*, pp. v, vii.
[77] See Jack Stillinger, 'On the Interpretation of *Endymion*: The Comedian as the Letter E', in *The Hoodwinking of Madeline and Other Essays on Keats's Poems* (Urbana, Ill., 1971), 14–30, esp. items 1, 3, and 4 in Stillinger's table of themes in the poem. See also Stuart Sperry, *Keats the Poet* (Princeton, 1973), 90–7 for discussion of the allegoric meaning of *Endymion*, particularly the poem's division between ideal and real experiences. Stillinger and Sperry both point to the influential treatment of this theme in Shelley's *Alastor, or the Spirit of Solitude* (1816).

—What the imagination seizes as Beauty must be truth—whether it existed before or not—for I have the same Idea of all our Passions as of Love they are all in their sublime, creative of essential Beauty—In a Word, you may know my favorite Speculation by my first Book . . . The Imagination may be compared to Adam's dream—he awoke and found it truth. (*Letters*, i. 184–5)

This great statement of imaginative faith represented a distillation of *Endymion*'s romantic theme, but the conjunction of imagination with truth also expressed the ideological force of the pagan cult of love and sexuality as 'an accepted challenge to orthodoxy over its whole range of influence, cultural, moral, and political'.[78] In a more particular sense, too, the vehement critical/political response to the poem may be explained by the provocative similarities between pagan ceremony and newspaper reporting of contemporary religious controversy.

In April 1817, the month when Keats began the first book of *Endymion*, pagan religion was extensively discussed in the columns of the *Examiner*. Keats read at least one of these articles, 'To the English People: Letter VI', and praised it in a letter to Hunt (who was then staying with the Shelleys at Marlow) as a 'Battering Ram against Christianity' (*Letters*, i. 137).[79] A Liverpool Unitarian, John Wright, had been charged with blasphemy, prompting Hunt to publish a series of vigorous leading essays on religion and freedom of conscience in which the present 'alliance of intolerance with exclusive faiths' appeared 'inferior . . . to the Pagans'. According to Hunt, '[t]he Greek poets and philosophers were very free in expressing their difference from the established religion . . . the government requiring nothing of them but what is a necessary and indeed the only necessary thing in all societies, the exercise of justice, or virtue'.[80] He lists the Greek and Roman philosophers and poets who had been comparatively free to express their views, and concludes with Lucretius, who set Epicurus' atheist philosophy

---

[78] See Butler, *Romantics*, 129–37.

[79] For further discussion see Stephen Coote's *John Keats: A Life*, 80–1. A strength of Coote's new biography is the tact with which he interweaves Keats's life with his times: 'In the tense political atmosphere of 1817 . . . any attack on Christianity could be viewed by conservatives as an attempt at subversion . . . In such a climate as this, a thing of beauty could not be politically neutral.'

[80] 'To the English People: Letter VI', *Examiner* (27 Apr. 1817), 259. See also Ryan, 'Politics of Greek Religion', 261–3.

'to music by his poetry, and sounding it forth harmoniously to posterity, was never disturbed, while he was thus playing the pipe which he had stolen from PAN'.[81] At the very moment when Keats was beginning work on *Endymion*, in the *Examiner* an ideal image of the classical world, paganism, and the cult of Pan were associated with the liberties demanded by the democratic reform movement. The *Examiner* article concludes by mentioning 'the particular spirit of the present times; which I venture to say will never rest satisfied, till governments allow a perfect freedom in speculation, and set an infinitely better example of virtue in practice'.[82]

Given this background the extract in the *Yellow Dwarf* from the Latmians' celebration of Pan's universal ministry,

> Dread opener of the mysterious doors
> Leading to universal knowledge—see,
> Great son of Dryope,
> The many that are come to pay their vows
> With leaves about their brows![83]

—might be read as a chorus to the reformists' demand for an extension of the franchise and liberty of conscience. Their cause was discussed week by week in the *Yellow Dwarf* under the title 'Universal Suffrage and Annual Parliaments', and (in the same issue that carried Keats's 'Hymn') John Hunt left his readers in no doubt as to the reformists' determination in the face of government opposition:

—persecute and murder away: you cannot kill us all; and if you will use the bayonet, we must make up our minds to the quantity of suffering you can inflict; we shall soon see whether brute force or mind shall triumph,—we have no fear for the result; and the good which must follow our successful resistance, will be an ample compensation to succeeding ages. We who may become the victims of tyranny have all

[81] *Examiner* (27 Apr. 1817), 259.

[82] Compare Joseph Severn's recollection in his 'Notes on *Adonais*', autograph manuscript dated 'Rome 30 August 1873': 'The old charge . . . of paganism I cannot but think was very unjust but it was the tendency of the time and attached itself to all liberals who strove to fight with the conservative party.' MS Keats 4. 16. 3, quoted by permission of The Houghton Library, Harvard University. Severn's notes were intended for a projected illustrated edition of *Adonais* to be published by Macmillan; see *John Keats 1795–1995: With a Catalogue of the Harvard Keats Collection* (Cambridge, Mass., 1995).

[83] Quoted from *Yellow Dwarf* (9 May 1818), 151–2.

the consolation, and shall receive more praise than ever has been bestowed, and which even you have been compelled to admit is properly bestowed on those who, in former times, used their talents and spent their blood in the same cause. That you will use the bayonet, we have not the smallest doubt; that by means of your spies, to plot and instigate, you will find some opportunities for its employment,—we fully expect:—this we lament; but we are not so ignorant, after all, as not to know, that in proportion as knowledge increases, your minds will be soured, and your conduct be more and more outrageous as a change approaches. It would be hopeless for us to expect these dispositions of yours will fail to do their mischief.[84]

Keats's 'Hymn to Pan' appeared on the page immediately opposite this cool assessment of the government's mischievous intentions, and the reformists' unabashed determination to succeed. Revolutionary violence, so clearly foreseen here, seems far from the 'humble pæan' extracted from the first book of *Endymion*. Yet the concluding lines of the 'Hymn' (which John Hunt chose not to republish) seem calculated as an ominous reminder of the unsatisfied 'spirit of the present times':

> Even while they brought the burden to a close,
> A shout from the whole multitude arose,
> That lingered in the air like dying rolls
> Of abrupt thunder . . . (I. 307–10)

When read alongside John Hunt's prophecy, these 'dying rolls' of thunder might well be harbingers of the storm that would soon break, in August 1819, on St Peter's Fields at Manchester: 'persecute and murder away: you cannot kill us all . . . we shall soon see whether brute force or mind shall triumph,—we have no fear for the result; and the good which must follow our successful resistance, will be an ample compensation to succeeding ages.'

When Wordsworth commented that the 'Hymn to Pan' in *Endymion* was 'a Very pretty piece of Paganism' (KC ii. 144), he slighted Keats's reading of his poem and, no doubt, sought to belittle *Endymion* through an implicit comparison with the classicism of *The Excursion* and *Laodamia*. Certainly, this encounter in December 1817 reinforced Hazlitt's references in *The Round Table* to Wordsworth's 'intense intellectual egotism', and

---

[84] *Yellow Dwarf* (9 May 1818), 150.

Wordsworth's remark may in time have contributed to Keats's diminishing estimation of him. But more was at stake than literary rivalry and—in any case—Keats's early acquaintance with Wordsworth seems to have been genial until a first 'note of disharmony' emerged in the letter to Reynolds of 3 February 1818.[85] In 'taking [the 'Hymn'] as a bit of Paganism for the Time' (Benjamin Haydon's words) the older poet acknowledged (and disparaged) the powerful radical and sexual associations of Keats's classicism (*KC* ii. 144).[86] The political charge of 'Paganism' is further corroborated in Joseph Severn's version of Keats's encounter with Wordsworth. Walter Jackson Bate points out that Severn had not been present on this particular occasion, but adds that his anecdote rings true in some respects and that it may draw upon another meeting of the poets.[87] My point, however, is that Severn was alert to the political inflection of Wordsworth's comment and sought to emphasize this in his retelling of the story.

As Severn has it, Keats's reading of the 'Hymn' had followed a discussion on 'the fashion of a vegetable diet which was then being pursued by many led on by the poet Shelley'.[88] The radical associations of vegetarianism had been apparent since the beginning of the French Revolution and these contributed, as Timothy Morton says, to a 'discourse of naturalness' in which 'diet, nature and rights' were linked together.[89] In his *Vindication of Natural Diet* (1813), for example, Shelley went so far as to argue that a vegetable diet would have prevented the 'brutal suffrage' of Robespierre's Terror and the 'desire of tyranny' which gave impetus to Bonaparte's bloodthirsty career: 'The advantage of a reform in diet, is obviously greater than that of

[85] 'It may be said that we ought to read our Contemporaries. that Wordsworth &c should have their due from us. but for the sake of a few fine imaginative or domestic passages, are we to be bullied into a certain Philosophy engendered in the whims of an Egotist' (*Letters*, i. 223). See Jack Stillinger, 'Wordsworth and Keats', in Kenneth Johnston and Gene Ruoff (eds.), *The Age of William Wordsworth: Critical Essays on the Romantic Tradition* (New Brunswick, NJ, 1987), 173–95, esp. 173–7.

[86] See also my article 'The Liberty Man', *Times Literary Supplement* (29 Sept. 1995), 21.

[87] See Bate, *John Keats*, 266.

[88] Joseph Severn, 'My Tedious Life', autograph manuscript dated 'Sept. 1863'. MS Keats 4. 16. 4, quoted by permission of The Houghton Library, Harvard University.

[89] See especially Timothy Morton, *Shelley and the Revolution in Taste: The Body and the Natural World* (Cambridge, 1995), 35–41 and 57–73.

any other. It strikes at the root of the evil.'[90] According to Severn, Wordsworth's response to talk of a 'natural diet' was to make a facetious observation, 'If by chance of good luck they ever met with a caterpillar, that they thanked their stars for this delicious morsel of animal food', which also established the tone of his subsequent dismissive remark to Keats:

> On this occasion Keats was requested by Haydon to recite his classical ode to Pan from his unfinishd poem of Endymion, which he did with natural eloquence & great pathos & being finishd we all look'd in silence to Wordsworth for his [remarks *del.*] praises on the young poet—After a moment's pause [the old *del.*] Wordsworth cooly remarked 'a very pretty piece of Paganism' and with this cold water thrown upon us we all broke up.

If Severn's reminiscence was not factually based on his presence in the company when Keats read his poem, it was nevertheless true to the spirit of the occasion in a different sense. Bringing together vegetarianism and Keats's recitation of the 'Hymn to Pan', Severn's anecdote places Wordsworth's remarks in a broader ideological frame in which 'natural diet' and the pagan cult of Pan were equally resonant aspects of radical discourse. Wordsworth's carnivorous appetite for 'animal food' projected the bloodthirsty disposition of the political establishment, which (as John Hunt saw) would not flinch to 'use the bayonet' to 'persecute and murder' its opponents. Surprisingly, perhaps, this violent prospect may be one of the legends which 'haunts about [the] shape' of 'Ode on a Grecian Urn'.

The great *fêtes* at Paris had celebrated ideals (liberty, equality, fraternity, reason, justice) which were also invoked, during 1793–4, to justify the mass executions of the Terror.[91] If one is prepared to grant that a complex of reformist and revolutionary images, emblems, and associations may infiltrate the 'pretty

---

[90] See *The Works of Percy Bysshe Shelley*, ed. R. Ingpen and W. E. Peck (10 vols., London, 1926–30, 1965), vi. 10–11, 15. Compare Shelley's letter to the Hunts, 30 June 1817, which offers a less idealistic account of innovations in diet, religion, and politics: 'Do not mention that I am unwell to your nephew; for the advocate of a new system of diet is held bound to be invulnerable by disease, in the same manner as the sectaries of a new system of religion are held to be more moral than other people, or as a reformed parliament must at least be assumed as the remedy of all political evils. No one will change the diet, adopt the religion, or reform parliament else.' *The Letters of Percy Bysshe Shelley*, i. 543.

[91] See Roe, *Wordsworth and Coleridge: The Radical Years*, 209.

Paganism' of devotions to Pan in the first book of *Endymion*, one might also allow that the Dionysian festival in the 'Ode on a Grecian Urn' is haunted by the mass killings which accompanied the *Fête de l'Être Suprême* during June 1794:

> Who are these coming to the sacrifice?
>   To what green altar, O mysterious priest,
> Lead'st thou that heifer lowing at the skies,
>   And all her silken flanks with garlands drest?
> What little town by river or sea shore,
>   Or mountain-built with peaceful citadel,
>   Is emptied of this folk, this pious morn?
> And, little town, thy streets for evermore
>   Will silent be; and not a soul to tell
>   Why thou art desolate, can e'er return. (31–40)

Here, once again, are images of Grecian antiquity which also evoke the neoclassical *fêtes*—the 'green altar', 'mysterious priest', 'garlands'. Here too is the procession of 'folk', the 'little town' emptied for the festival this 'pious morn'. Immediate but inaccessible, precise but also unspecific, the questions invite the reader to translate the urn's imagery through historical correspondences and associations while simultaneously resisting that process.[92] The events depicted on the surface of the urn may have taken place somewhere in the distant mythic past, 'In Tempe or the dales of Arcady', but they also happen here and now in the urgent, present questioning of the poet: 'Who are these coming . . . ? . . . What little town . . . | Is emptied of this folk . . . ?' As the citizens unpeople their town to attend the ceremony, they too are sacrificed to unconsoling eternity:

> And, little town, thy streets for evermore
>   Will silent be; and not a soul to tell
>   Why thou art desolate, can e'er return. (38–40)

In Keats's 'cold pastoral' pagan festival, no longer associated with the joyous celebration of sexual or religious freedom, is brought into juxtaposition with death and the wasting of generations past and 'other woe' yet to come. This bleak conjunc-

---

[92] See Cleanth Brooks's analysis of the 'suggestiveness' of history in the ode's fourth stanza, and particularly the 'mysterious desolation' of the town, in 'Keats's Sylvan Historian: History without Footnotes', *The Well Wrought Urn* (London, 1949), 147–8.

tion may 'tease us out of thought' until we long for the abiding beauty of the Grecian Urn. Yet his poem may also command attention as an unillusioned response to revolutions which had found in pagan antiquity a powerful inspiration for the renovation of the modern world,

when France called her children to partake her equal blessings beneath her laughing skies; when the stranger was met in all her villages with dance and festive songs, in celebration of a new and golden era ... The dawn of that day was suddenly overcast; that season of hope is past; it is fled with the other dreams of our youth, which we cannot recal, but has left behind it traces, which are not to be effaced by Birth-day and Thanks-giving odes, or the chaunting of *Te Deums* in all the churches of Christendom.[93]

[93] William Hazlitt, 'On Mr Wordsworth's "Excursion"', in *The Round Table*, ii. 111.

CHAPTER THREE

John Keats and Charles Cowden Clarke

> If I were rich enough I wd purchase the copy-right and
> send penny editions of it round to every member of the
> Unions; for I will yield to no one in love of true liberty.
> (Charles Cowden Clarke on *The Masque of Anarchy*)[1]

> By this, friend Charles, you may full plainly see . . .
> ('To Charles Cowden Clarke', 21)

John Keats's Lost Years

On 15 December 1846 Richard Monckton Milnes, then re-
searching his biography of Keats, wrote to Charles Cowden
Clarke:

I take the liberty of applying to you as one of the earliest of his friends
&, I believe, his instructor, for any information you can afford me. I am
particularly anxious to enquire whether any special circumstances
directed his mind to the beauties of Heathen mythology, & whether he
came to occupy his imagination so strongly with Pagan religion by an
intuitive sympathy or by much knowledge of the classical writings.[2]

In Milnes's *Life* (as in other nineteenth-century accounts of
Keats) 'intuitive sympathy' was invoked as a sentimental distraction from the unsettling associations of Keats's 'scanty' education and paganism. Thus, Milnes claimed that 'while the old
Gods rewarded [Keats] for his love with powers and perceptions
that a Greek might have envied', he also reassured his readers
that Keats had 'kept his affections high and pure above these

---

[1] 'Copy of a letter from C. C. Clarke to Leigh Hunt on the receipt of the
accompanying Poem'; dated '67 Frith Street, Novr 14th 1832'. Folded inside a
presentation copy of Shelley's *Masque of Anarchy* from Leigh Hunt to Vincent
Novello. The Brotherton Collection, Leeds University Library.

[2] Autograph letter pasted into a presentation copy of *LLL* from Milnes to Clarke,
'with the editor's compts. and thanks'. The Brotherton Collection, Leeds University
Library.

sensuous influences, and led a temperate and honest life in an ideal world that knows nothing of duty and repels all images that do not please'.[3] In other respects, however, Milnes went to considerable trouble in ensuring that his biography would be historically accurate. Three days after his first enquiry he wrote to Clarke again, requesting him to 'supply . . . the following *dates* in Keats's life'. Milnes's letter has survived, with Clarke's responses jotted down alongside the questions and reproduced here in italic:

When did he leave school? *1811*
When did you lend him the Faery Queen? *1811–12*
When did he leave the Hammonds? *1815*
When did he take his lodgings in the Poultry? *1816–17*[4]

This correspondence arose some thirty-five years after Clarke's friendship with Keats and, not surprisingly, his memory of dates was now uncertain. His formal reply to Milnes, which is now in the Keats collection at the Houghton Library, frankly admits as much:

I have the most fatal memory with regard to dates. It always was so with me. I used annually to incur my mother's displeasure because I forgot the precise date of my father's birth. Your letter therefore has put me to my wits' trumps, and I can only guess at the precise points of time you require in Keats's life. For instance; I know that he was born in 1796; and that at 14 he went to Hammond's in the summer of 1810. He was bound to be with him 5 years. In 1817 however, (by the date of the first edition) his little maiden book of poems was published; and I know that he then lived, and had lived for some time in the Poultry; for I was present when he wrote the Dedication to Leigh Hunt, and Ollier took it away with him that night. By these dates therefore, it should seem that Hammond had released him from his apprentice-ship before his time; and I have some vague recollection that such was the case, for they did not agree; Keats's tastes being totally opposed to his master's.[5]

The lapses of Clarke's 'fatal memory', evident here in mistakenly assigning Keats's birth to 1796, have resulted in considerable

---

[3] *LLL* i. 24.
[4] Autograph letter pasted into Clarke's copy of *LLL* (see n. 2 above) with this annotation: 'The figures are in the handwriting of Charles Cowden Clarke. [signed] Mary Cowden Clarke'. The Brotherton Collection, Leeds University Library.
[5] Charles Cowden Clarke to R. M. Milnes, 20 Dec. 1846, *KC* ii. 168–9.

problems in dating events in the poet's early years. Notice that Clarke gives two dates (1810 and 1811) for Keats's departure from Enfield School to begin his apprenticeship with Thomas Hammond. Modern biographers continue to disagree about when this decisive event took place. Walter Jackson Bate and Aileen Ward argued (Bate in considerable detail) for 1811 as the start of his apprenticeship; but Robert Gittings subsequently pointed to 1810 as the more likely date, explaining that when Keats enrolled at Guy's Hospital the new Apothecaries' Act of March 1815 was being stringently enforced and one of its requirements was that candidates must have served the full five-year term as apprentice.[6] During his attachment to Hammond, who practised in the village of Edmonton some two miles to the south of Enfield, Keats remained on close friendly terms with Charles Cowden Clarke and his father, frequently walking across the fields to the school for their conversation and companionship—and to borrow books. Keats's medical training will be my subject in Chapter 6. In what follows here, I explore the significance of Keats's relationship with Cowden Clarke in the 'lost years' 1810–15, a period for which, as Walter Jackson Bate has said, only 'meager details' of information have survived—most of them in Clarke's 'Recollections of John Keats'.[7]

As Clarke recalled, their continuing friendship was decisive in encouraging Keats's literary interests and first poems after his departure from Enfield School:

> The distance between our residences being so short, I gladly encouraged his inclination to come over when he could claim a leisure hour; and in consequence I saw him about five or six times a month on my own leisure afternoons. He rarely came empty-handed; either he had a book to read, or brought one to be exchanged. When the weather permitted, we always sat in an arbour at the end of a spacious garden, and—in Boswellian dialect—'we had good talk'.[8]

Clarke's 'Recollections' dwells primarily upon literary matters, particularly Keats's enthusiastic reading in Spenser's *Faerie*

[6] See Gittings, *John Keats*, 56; Bate, *John Keats*, 29–30, 703–4, and Ward, *Making of a Poet*, 21–2.

[7] Bate, *John Keats*, 32. Keats's earliest surviving letters (leaving aside his verse epistle 'To George Felton Mathew', Nov. 1815) date from 1816.

[8] 'Recollections of John Keats', 125.

Queene and his first poetic compositions including his 'Imitation of Spenser', 'Written on the Day that Mr Leigh Hunt left Prison', and 'O Solitude!' Furthermore, and as we saw in Chapter 1, many of the poems dating from 1814–16 also reveal how Keats had responded to the dissenting politics of Enfield School. Greg Kucich has shown that a broadly based 'radicalizing' of Spenser was characteristic of Romantic poets, who summoned the 'tension of reality and ideality' in his poetry as a way to comment upon oppression and deadlock in the contemporary political scene.[9] Certainly, the interweaving of Spenserian themes and motifs with current political interests is a characteristic of Keats's poetry from the outset—as in the sonnet 'Written on the Day that Mr Leigh Hunt left Prison', for example:

> What though, for showing truth to flatter'd state,
>> Kind Hunt was shut in prison, yet has he,
>> In his immortal spirit, been as free
> As the sky-searching lark, and as elate.
> Minion of grandeur! think you he did wait?
>> Think you he nought but prison walls did see,
>> Till, so unwilling, thou unturn'dst the key?
> Ah, no! far happier, nobler was his fate!
> In Spenser's halls he strayed, and bowers fair,
>> Culling enchanted flowers; and he flew
> With daring Milton through the fields of air:
>> To regions of his own his genius true
> Took happy flights. Who shall his fame impair
>> When thou art dead, and all thy wretched crew?

The sonnet contrasts Hunt's incarceration, 'shut in prison', with the freedom granted by the 'halls' and 'bowers fair' of Spenserian romance and the aspirant 'daring' of Milton. Poetry offers a route of ideal escape from political oppression yet it is clear that Hunt's 'fame', which will outlast the 'wretched crew' of despots, arises from his bravery in having confronted the reality of the world by 'showing truth to flatter'd state'. His imaginative elation is an immediate and welcome comfort in

---

[9] For an excellent account of how the Romantics 'radicalized' Spenser, and Keats's early creative response to Spenser more generally, see Greg Kucich, *Keats, Shelley, and Romantic Spenserianism* (University Park, Pa., 1991), 100–1, 137–83.

prison, but it is more strictly the counterpart—rather than the 'escapist' alternative—to his practical aims as a politician.[10] Moreover, Jack Stillinger has traced a comparable theme bearing on Keats himself in the arrangement of poems in the 1817 volume as a whole. In showing that the poems are linked as a narrative 'dealing with the question of Keats's career as a poet', Stillinger places *Sleep and Poetry* (which concludes the book) as a final response to issues raised by the dedicatory sonnet. *Sleep and Poetry* sets Keats's future course as a writer, Stillinger argues, progressing from 'visions of leafy luxury to a more serious confrontation of human problems and the events of the wide world'; it points the way 'not only toward restoring glory and loveliness but toward easing the pain—soothing the cares, and lifting the thoughts—of man. *Endymion* and the poems of 1818 and 1819 proceed from there.'[11]

Human problems and public events certainly informed Keats's enjoyable conversations in the bower at Enfield, as we will see in a moment, and Clarke would have told Keats of his visits to Horsemonger Lane Gaol where Hunt had decorated his apartment as a Spenserian bower.[12] A more extensive reconstruction of their dialogue may help further to illuminate an obscure period of Keats's life, and the radical yet humane inflection of his early poetry. As with the 'Hymn to Pan' from *Endymion*, which I discussed in the second chapter, it may be possible to recover a sense of how these poems were read by Keats's contemporaries, and why they elicited such a strong response in those readers. In particular I seek to explain why

---

[10] Cf. Newey's contention, in ' "Alternate uproar and sad peace" ', 269, that in the sonnet 'Keats gets a firm, even aggressive purchase on the immediate historical situation while writing out of, and reinforcing, a field of transhistorical value'.

[11] See 'The Order of Poems in Keats's First Volume', in *The Hoodwinking of Madeline*, 1–13.

[12] 'My father so entirely sympathized with my devoted admiration of Leigh Hunt, that when, not very long after I had made his acquaintance, he was thrown into Horsemonger Lane Jail for his libel on the Prince Regent, I was seconded in my wish to send the captive Liberal a breath of open air, and a reminder of the country pleasures he so well loved and could so well describe, by my father's allowing me to despatch a weekly basket of fresh flowers, fruit, and vegetables from our garden at Enfield. Leigh Hunt received it with his own peculiar grace of acceptance, recognizing the sentiment that prompted the offering, and welcoming it into the spot which he had converted from a prison-room into a bower for a poet by covering the walls with a rose-trellised papering, by book-shelves, plaster casts, and a small pianoforte.' See *Recollections*, 17–18.

some of the verses in Keats's first collection, *Poems*, described by a twentieth-century scholar as 'timidly written', 'shy beginnings', and 'tentative gropings',[13] should have given one reviewer a sense of 'the proud and repulsive aspects of misnamed humanity', and to another smacked of ambition which might readily turn to 'the malignity of *patriotism*'.[14]

A Radical's Vade-mecum: Charles Cowden Clarke's Commonplace Book

> Ah! had I never seen,
> Or known your kindness, what might I have been?
> What my enjoyments in my youthful years,
> Bereft of all that now my life endears?
> And can I e'er these benefits forget?
> And can I e'er repay the friendly debt?
> No, doubly no . . .
> ('To Charles Cowden Clarke', 72–8)

Keats's verse epistle 'To Charles Cowden Clarke', dated September 1816, is a tribute to Clarke's friendship, influence and generosity, which also tells of Keats's own eagerness to learn from him. In conversation he encouraged Keats's interest in reading and writing poetry ('all the sweets of song', 53), and 'pointed out the patriot's stern duty' to oppose tyranny (69–72). Musical evenings in company with the Clarkes had introduced Keats to 'divine Mozart', Arne, Handel, and Irish folk-song (110–12).[15] But, beyond this acknowledgement of 'friendly debt', is it possible to indicate more precisely what Clarke and Keats may have discussed on their walks 'through shady lanes', or on evenings 'among [Clarke's] books' (115, 118)? Fortunately, the commonplace book used by Clarke

---

[13] Bate, *John Keats*, 34, 35.

[14] See the unsigned review in *Edinburgh Magazine, and Literary Miscellany* (Oct. 1817) and Josiah Conder's review, *Eclectic Review* (Sept. 1817), rpt. in *KCH* 69–70, 73.

[15] Cf. 'Recollections of Keats', 143: 'In after-years, when Keats was reading to me the manuscript of "The Eve of St Agnes", upon the repeating of the passage when Porphyro is listening to the midnight music in the hall below . . . "that line", said he, "came into my head when I remembered how I used to listen in bed to your music at school".'

between 1810 and 1814—the period of his closest friendship with and influence on Keats—has survived, and it provides a fascinating documentary record of Clarke's interests: his reading, his political views, his own attempts at writing poetry.

John Barnard has recently published a full sequence of entries from the commonplace book, with an impressive analysis suggesting how the book 'documents the specific cultural matrix which shaped the young man who began writing poetry in 1814'.[16] A few years previously Joan Coldwell's discussion of literary entries in the commonplace book had found Clarke's poems 'somewhat suggestive . . . of Keats's later poetry', noting especially echoes of Clarke's 'The Nightingale' in 'Ode to a Nightingale' and Clarke's 'Sunset' in 'To Autumn'.[17] Barnard is, rightly, more cautious about the possibility of Keats's access to the commonplace book, indicating that he was familiar with some of the original poetry it contained and that it is 'hard to believe that Keats was not allowed' to see the contents.[18] On 9 October 1816 Keats wrote to Clarke anticipating the pleasure of being introduced to Leigh Hunt, adding 'I am anxious too to see the Author of the Sonnet to the Sun' (*Letters*, i. 113). Clarke and Horace Smith have been suggested as authors of this sonnet (*Letters*, i. 113 n. 2) but, as Barnard shows, Keats was more likely referring to Charles Ollier's 'Sonnet on Sunset'. He had presumably seen Ollier's sonnet in manuscript, but might equally well have seen the transcript copied out by Clarke in the commonplace book and dated August 1813.[19] The question as to whether Keats had looked into the commonplace book is intriguing, as these literary conjectures demonstrate, but ultimately perhaps not crucial to an assessment of the book's significance. Its principal value consists in providing abundant documentary evidence which indicates a range of topics the two friends might have discussed and the kinds of interests that they shared.

[16] See John Barnard, 'Charles Cowden Clarke's "Cockney" Commonplace Book', *K&H* 65–87. In the following notes ' "Cockney" Commonplace Book' refers to Barnard's text; 'CCC Commonplace Book' refers to my own transcription from NCC, MS 6, in The Brotherton Collection, Leeds University Library. Pagination for my transcriptions follows that in the manuscript volume.

[17] See Joan Coldwell, 'Charles Cowden Clarke's Commonplace Book and its Relationship to Keats', *K–SJ* 29 (1980), 83–95, esp. 92.

[18] ' "Cockney" Commonplace Book', 68.   [19] Ibid. 81, 85 nn. 7, 8.

Clarke's entries are, broadly, literary and political in character, although frequently the two categories overlap. In many instances he transcribed poetry that appealed to (and illustrated) his strongly liberal, republican, and oppositional views: some examples are Chatterton's 'Ode to Freedom' (the final 'Chorus' from *Goddwyn: A Tragedie*), Cowper's 'Yardley Oak', Hunt's 'Stanzas on the Death of General Moreau', and three of Wordsworth's republican sonnets of 1802.[20] Clarke's pacifism is represented by his transcription of a celebrated Jacobin poem dating from the 1790s, 'lines written by the Revd. William Crowe, public Orator at the University of Oxford . . . intended to have been recited by him at the Installation of the Duke of Portland [in 1793], but . . . suppressed by the Vice-Chancellor on account of the Sentiments contained in them':[21]

> In evil Hour, and with unhallow'd Voice
> Profaning the pure gift of Poesy
> Did he begin to sing, he first who sung
> Of arms and combats and the proud array
> Of Warriors on th'embattl'd Plain and rais'd
> Th'aspiring spirits to Hopes of fair renown
> By Deeds of Violence. For since that time
> Th'imperious victor oft unsatisfied
> With bloody spoil and tyrannous Conquest, dares
> To challenge fame and honor; and too oft
> The Poet, bending low to lawless Power
> Hath paid unseemly reverence; yea, and brought
> Streams clearest of th'Aonian fount to wash
> Blood-stain'd ambition. If the stroke of War
> Fell certain on the guilty Head, none else;
> If they who make the Cause, might taste th'effect,
> And drink themselves the bitter Cup they mix,
> Then might the Bard—tho' Child of Peace—delight
> To twine fresh Wreaths around the Conqu'ror's Brow;
> Or haply strike his high-ton'd Harp to swell
> The Trumpet's martial sound, and bid them on
> Whom Justice arms for Vengeance; but alas!
> That undistinguishing and Deathful Storm

---

[20] See 'CCC Commonplace Book': for Chatterton, 159–60; for Cowper, 49–57; for Hunt's poem, 274; for Wordsworth's sonnets, 265–7, and see also Ch. 1, p. 49 above.

[21] 'CCC Commonplace Book', 34. See also ' "Cockney" Commonplace Book', 70, item 9.

> Beats heaviest on th'exposed Innocent
> And they that stir its fury while it raves
> Stand at safe Distance; send their mandate forth
> Unto the mortal Ministers that wait
> To do their Bidding.—Ah! who then regards
> The Widow's tears, the friendless Orphan's cries,
> And Famine and the ghastly train of Woes
> That follow at the dogged Heels of War?
> They in the Pomp and Pride of Victory,
> Rejoicing o'er the desolated Earth
> As at an Altar wet with human Blood,
> And flaming with the fire of Cities burnt,
> Sing their mad hymns of Triumph, hymns to God
> O'er the Destruction of his gracious Works!—
> Hymns to the Father o'er his slaughter'd Sons!
> Detested be their Sword, abhorr'd their Name,
> And scorn'd the Tongues that praise them.[22]

Crowe's anti-war poem was typical of other protest poetry in the mid-1790s, with resemblances to Wordsworth's *Salisbury Plain* poems and Coleridge's *Religious Musings* and 'Fears in Solitude'. It was much admired by Southey, and Coleridge published this 'suppressed' text in his *Watchman* newspaper, 2 April 1796, recommending in a Latin epigraph 'Whoever has not read it should read it, who has read it should read it again'. The appearance of Crowe's poem in Clarke's commonplace book demonstrates his familiarity with and admiration for protest literature dating from the 1790s, and also the continuity of opposition to war in Europe during Keats's lifetime.

Elsewhere in the commonplace book are further extracts from radical and dissenting texts which first appeared in the 1790s. A representative example is the following extract from a 'Sermon by Mrs Barbauld for a Fast Day in 1794':

We must fix our Eyes, not on the Hero returning with Conquest nor yet on the gallant officer dying in the Bed of Honor, the subject of Picture and of Song, but on the private Soldier, forced into the service, exhausted by Camp-Sickness and fatigue; pale [and] emaciated; crawling to a hospital with the prospect of Life—perhaps a long life— blasted, useless and suffering. We must think of the uncounted Tears of her who weeps alone, because the only being who shared her

---

[22] 'CCC Commonplace Book', 34–6.

Sentiments is taken from her; no martial music sounds in unison with her feelings; the long Day passes and he returns not. She does not shed her Sorrows over his Grave for she has never learnt whether he ever had one. If he had returned, his Exertions would not have been remembered individually, for he only made a small imperceptible part of a human Machine called a Regiment. We must take in the long Sickness which no glory soothes, occasioned by Distress of Mind, anxiety, and ruined fortunes.[23]

Mrs Barbauld (Anna Letitia Aikin) was a notable educationalist, Unitarian, and reformist. Her sermon (which actually dated from 1793) was typical of the 'Paineite' anti-war literature encouraged by *The Rights of Man*. It also has striking affinities with Thomas Cooper's attack on impressing (forced recruitment) in his pamphlet *Reply to Mr Burke's Invective* (1792), and with the tragic narrative of Margaret and Robert in Wordsworth's *Ruined Cottage*; indeed, the latter may well be indebted to the passage in the sermon which attracted Clarke's attention.[24] Mrs Barbauld's verse particularly appealed to Clarke, and may well have done to Keats too. Elsewhere in his commonplace book Clarke copied out a large portion of her marvellous *Summer Evening's Meditation*, describing a visionary tour of the solar system and the 'trackless deeps' of the universe:

> From the green Borders of the peopled Earth,
> And the pale Moon, her duteous fair attendant;
> From solitary Mars; from the vast Orb
> Of Jupiter, whose huge gigantic Bulk
> Dances in Ether like the lightest Leaf;
> To the dim Verge, the Suburbs of the System,
> Where cheerless Saturn, midst his watery Moons,
> Girt with a lucid Zone, majestic sits
> In gloomy grandeur . . .[25]

[23] Ibid. 12–14; see also '"Cockney" Commonplace Book', 70, item 7. Mrs Barbauld's sermon was 'Sins of the Government, Sins of the Nation; or, A Discourse for the Fast, Appointed on April 19, 1793'; see *The Works of Anna Letitia Barbauld* (2 vols., London, 1825), ii. 402.

[24] For Cooper, *The Ruined Cottage*, and anti-war protest see my *Wordsworth and Coleridge: The Radical Years*, 129–32. For Wordsworth's familiarity with Mrs Barbauld's poetry, see Duncan Wu, *Wordsworth's Reading, 1770–99* (Cambridge, 1993), 157.

[25] 'CCC Commonplace Book', 4; see also Anna Letitia Barbauld, *Poems* (London, 1773), 131–8.

Given Keats's interest in astronomy, this impressive passage was calculated to have drawn his attention and stirred his imagination. Whether he read it in the commonplace book or from another source, the image of 'cheerless Saturn, midst his watery Moons | . . . [sitting] In gloomy grandeur' has some resemblance to the desolate scene of 'fallen divinity' at the opening of *Hyperion*:

> Upon the sodden ground
> His old right hand lay nerveless, listless, dead,
> Unsceptred . . . (I. 17–19)

A further remarkable demonstration of Clarke's interest in protest literature appears in the twenty-nine pages which he filled with a transcription of Richard Porson's satire dating from 1792: *A New Catechism for the Use of the Natives of Hampshire: Necessary to be Had in All Sties.*[26] Like Daniel Isaac Eaton's *Politics for the People; or, A Salmagundy for Swine*, Porson's title echoes Burke's infamous description of the 'swinish multitude' in *Reflections on the Revolution in France* (1790), and his text presents a satirical dialogue explaining how the swinish population of England are oppressed and exploited.[27] In this opening passage from the *Catechism*, Clarke's own marginal comment appears in square brackets:

Q. What is your name?
A. *Hog* or *Swine.*
Q. Did God make you a hog?
A. No; God made me a Man in his own image; the *Right Honourable Sublime and Beautiful* made me a *Swine.* [+Reflections, p. 117 ed. 1]
Q. How did he make you a Swine?
A. By muttering uncouth words and dark Spells. He is a dealer in the black Art.
Q. Who feeds you?
A. Our Drivers the only *real Men* in the *County.*
Q. How many hogs are you in all?
A. Seven or eight Millions.

---

[26] For the publication of Porson's satire, see M. L. Clarke, *Richard Porson: A Biographical Essay* (Cambridge, 1937), 42 and n.

[27] *Politics for the People; or, A Salmagundy for Swine* was published in London by Eaton from 9 Sept. 1793 until 25 Feb. 1795, and targeted the 'Swinish Herd' of English citizens as its readership.

Q. How many drivers?
A. Two or three hundred thousand.[28]

Hunt republished Porson's *New Catechism* in the *Examiner* (30 August 1818) and, as Barnard notes, he may have used Clarke's transcription in the commonplace book, which dated from 1811, as his source. The topicality of the satire in 1818 is further indicated by Richard Carlile's immediate reprint of it as a pamphlet, subtitled *'From the Examiner'*. One year later, Hunt made an indirect reference to the *New Catechism* in his 'Calendar of Nature' for September 1819, an article which very likely supplied some images for Keats's 'To Autumn': 'The oaks and beeches shed their nuts, which in the forests that still remain, particularly the New Forest in Hampshire, furnish a luxurious repast for the swine, who feast of an evening in as pompous a manner as any alderman, to the sound of the herdsman's horn.'[29] Wittily identifying the alderman's pomp with the 'luxurious repast' of the swine, Hunt deftly brings Porson's satirical argument full-circle by confounding the ruling class with the 'swinish multitude'. In Chapter 5 I will suggest that Keats's 'outlaw lyrics' of February 1818, 'Robin Hood' and 'Lines on the Mermaid Tavern', may form part of this 'Cockney' response to Burke. And the 'Epilogue' to the whole book, 'Keats's Commonwealth', argues that 'To Autumn' offers a further intervention in this dialogue with Burke. Keats's celebration of autumnal plenitude—'To swell the gourd, and plump the hazel shells | With a sweet kernel' (7–8)—presents images of natural abundance which answer and redress some of the ideological conflicts traced in Clarke's, Porson's, and Hunt's responses to Burke's reactionary and divisive invective in his *Reflections on the Revolution in France*.

Alongside these examples of protest from the 1790s the commonplace book included more recent oppositional texts, once again showing how Clarke's literary and political interests were complementary. A splendid example is his transcription of Byron's 'Windsor Poetics', that is, 'Lines, composed on the occasion of H.R.H. the P[rinc]e R[e]g[en]t being seen standing

---

[28] 'CCC Commonplace Book', 86–7; for further commentary, see ' "Cockney" Commonplace Book', 71–3.
[29] *Examiner* (5 Sept. 1819).

betwixt the coffins of Henry 8th and Charles 1st, in the royal vault at Windsor':

> Fam'd for contemptuous breach of sacred ties,
> By *headless Charles* see *heartless Henry* lies;
> Between them stands another sceptr'd thing,—
> It moves,—it reigns,—in all but name a King.
> *Charles* to his *People, Henry* to his *Wife*,
> In him the *double Tyrant* starts to life.
> Justice and death, have mixed their dust in vain,
> The royal Vampires join to breathe again.
> What now shall tombs avail since they disgorge
> The blood and dust of both to mould a George.[30]

'Windsor Poetics' dates from April 1813 and, as Barnard says, Clarke probably acquired the text on one of his visits to Hunt in Surrey Gaol, where Byron frequently visited Hunt from May 1813 until Hunt's release in February 1815. The vampiric (re-)conception of the Prince Regent out of the 'blood and dust' of Charles I and Henry VIII would have been an appropriate and amusing gift for Hunt, 'the wit in the dungeon',[31] who had of course been gaoled for libelling George in the *Examiner*. Keats's early sonnet 'To Lord Byron' is a conventionally sentimental response to Byron's popularity, paying tribute to his 'sweetly sad melody' rather than his satire, but 'Lines Written on 29 May, the Anniversary of Charles's Restoration' has a polemical vigour comparable to Byron's attack on the Prince Regent. The 'Lines' also return us to the English republicans of the seventeenth century who are well represented in Clarke's commonplace book.

As we have seen, many of the passages in Clarke's book are drawn from contemporary (or near contemporary) publications. Clarke evidently saw his politics in a longer perspective, however, for numerous extracts show that, like John Ryland (and Hunt in his *Examiner* articles), he drew inspiration from constitutional theorists and historians and from the

---

[30] See ' "Cockney" Commonplace Book', 78–9, and *Lord Byron: The Complete Poetical Works*, ed. Jerome McGann (7 vols., Oxford, 1980–93), iii. 86, 424–5. For the composition of 'Windsor Poetics', and its wide circulation, see Molly Tatchell, 'Byron's *Windsor Poetics*', *K–SMB* 25 (1974), 1–5. Byron's verse also appears in the commonplace book kept by William Pitter Woodhouse (brother to Richard Woodhouse) during July–Aug. 1827, now in the Houghton Library, Harvard University, MS Keats 3.13.

[31] Byron to Thomas Moore, 19 May 1813, *BLJ* iii. 49.

seventeenth-century English republicans. One theme to which he returns again and again is the constitutional liberty of England. He quotes Locke on liberal education and the 'supreme power' of the community; Bacon on the oppressive effects of a 'numerous Nobility'; Selden's *Table-Talk* on the 'contract' between a prince and the people; and Bolingbroke's *Letters on the Spirit of Patriotism; [and] on the Idea of a Patriot King*: '*Nothing can be more absurd*, in pure *speculation*, than a *hereditary right in any mortal to govern other men; and yet in practice*, nothing can be more absurd, than to have a king to chuse at every vacancy of a throne.'[32]

Clarke's admiration for the English republicans appears in an extract about the liberty of the press from William Hayley's *Life of Milton*, and in a transcription of one of Clarke's own sonnets 'Left on Milton's Tomb',

> him, whose daring pen (a gift divine!)
> Was urg'd mid 'evil tongues in evil days' . . . .[33]

William Penn's esteem for Algernon Sydney is cited with Clarke's approval in an extract from the *Examiner*, 25 October 1812. A sonnet 'To the Memory of John Hampden' is worth quoting in full as representative of the late eighteenth-century libertarianism that appealed to Clarke:

> O Hampden last of that illustrious Line,
> Which greatly stood in Liberty's dear Cause,
> Zealous to vindicate our trampled laws,
> And rights, which Britons never can resign!
> From the wild claim of impious right divine
> Then when fell tyranny with harpy claws,
> Had seized its prey, and the devouring jaws
> Of that seven headed monster at whose shrine
> The nations bow, threaten'd our swift decay.
> Neighbour and Friend, farewell!—but not with thee
> Shall die the record of thy House's Fame;
> Thy grateful country shall its praise convey
> From age to age, and, long as Britain's free
> Britons shall boast in Hampden's glorious name.[34]

---

[32] 'CCC Commonplace Book': for Locke, 204–6; for Bacon, 79–81; for Selden, 136–43; for Bolingbroke, 106–13, passage quoted from 111, with Clarke's emphases.

[33] Ibid. 262.   [34] Ibid. 158.

This memorial for the parliamentarian John Hampden, asserting 'laws' and 'rights' against 'impious right divine', was extracted from Francis Blackburne's *Memoirs of Thomas Hollis*— a source which offers further indication of Clarke's republicanism and his support for liberty and constitutional rights.[35] Thomas Hollis (1720–74) was a republican and commonwealthman, whose estate at Corscombe in Dorset was celebrated by another poet Clarke admired, William Crowe, in his topographical poem *Lewesdon Hill*:

> Fain would I view thee, Corscombe, fain would hail
> The ground where Hollis lies; his choice retreat,
> Where, from the busy world withdrawn, he lived
> To generous Virtue and the holy love
> Of Liberty, a dedicated spirit . . . .[36]

The variety and thematic consistency of entries in the commonplace book speak for Clarke as a comparably 'dedicated spirit', who was very well informed about the libertarian and republican traditions of the seventeenth and eighteenth centuries as well as more recent political writings. His 'Sonnet to Liberty' draws together some of the literary and political materials already discussed; it also indicates Clarke's literary ambitions at the time when he was frequently seeing Keats, who was writing his own first poems too:

> Oh thou! to whom the wretched toil-worn slave
> In anguish groans his daily prayer for aid:—
> Thou in whose shrine of adamant are laid
> The spoils, and hard-gain'd trophies of the brave
> Who tug for freedom. Spirit of Bliss! Oh save
> Those favour'd ones that have so long obey'd
> Thy mandates. And although they now have stray'd
> From thee; yet visit them again I crave.—

[35] See *Memoirs of Thomas Hollis* (2 vols., London, 1780), ii. 784. The sonnet appears in the *Memoirs* with two elegies for Algernon Sydney and a fragment celebrating Brutus' assassination of Caesar, extracted from Akenside's *Pleasures of the Imagination*. Keats may echo this sonnet, or at least Cowden Clarke's views on divine right, in his teasing reference to Clarke teaching him the 'sweets' of poetry, especially 'What swell'd with pathos, and what right divine'; 'To Charles Cowden Clarke', 55.

[36] William Crowe, *Lewesdon Hill: A Poem* (Oxford, 1788), 21–2. For a recent discussion of Thomas Hollis, William Crowe, and the English commonwealthmen, see John Williams, *Wordsworth: Romantic Poetry and Revolution Politics* (Manchester, 1989), 10–18.

> But come not Goddess as thou wont'st of yore,
>   In crimson war-car and with flaming brand;
> With bick'ring spear and poignard steep'd in gore;
>   In dreadful Justice visiting each land:—
>   But here in pity change thy wrathful hand:—
> Goddess! no more of blood—Oh, blood no more!—[37]

In celebrating those who have obeyed Liberty's 'mandates', rather than those who 'send their mandate forth' as a call to war, Clarke's sonnet opens a dialogue with William Crowe's suppressed lines which he had already copied out in the commonplace book. Both poems are self-consciously literary in reference: inflated diction—'he first who sung | Of arms and combats' (Crowe), 'shrine of adamant' (Clarke)—points in each case to an attempt at Miltonic sublimity, while Clarke's 'dreadful Justice visiting each land' recalls the abstract, apocalyptic manner of Coleridge's 'Ode to the Departing Year' and 'Fears in Solitude'. More particularly, Clarke aligns himself with Crowe's detestation of those poets who have 'paid unseemly reverence' to 'Blood-stain'd ambition': 'Goddess! no more of blood—Oh, blood no more!' That final flourish aims for an emphatic, elevated conclusion, and is an appropriate measure of Clarke's ambitions as a poet at this moment.[38]

The 'Sonnet to Liberty' is dated 'Jany. 1814'. Very shortly afterwards, perhaps in April 1814, Keats wrote his sonnet 'On Peace', addressing identical themes in the topical context of Napoleon's surrender (11 April) and his subsequent exile in Elba:

> Oh Peace! and dost thou with thy presence bless
>   The dwellings of this war-surrounded isle;
> Soothing with placid brow our late distress,
>   Making the triple kingdom brightly smile?
> Joyful I hail thy presence; and I hail
>   The sweet companions that await on thee;
> Complete my joy—let not my first wish fail,
>   Let the sweet mountain nymph thy favorite be,
> With England's happiness proclaim Europa's liberty.
> Oh Europe, let not sceptred tyrants see

---

[37] 'CCC Commonplace Book', 273.
[38] See ' "Cockney" Commonplace Book', 65, 84 for Clarke's ambitions as a writer, and how Keats's precociousness as a poet 'quickly left Clarke behind'.

> That thou must shelter in thy former state;
> Keep thy chains burst, and boldly say thou art free;
> Give thy kings law—leave not uncurbed the great;
> So with the horrors past thou'lt win thy happier fate.

Stylistically this sonnet reveals Keats's familiarity with Bowles's *Fourteen Sonnets,* Charlotte Smith's *Elegiac Sonnets,* and, in lines 10–14 especially, with the manner of Wordsworth's political sonnets of summer 1802. The last five lines also echo Hunt's speculations in the *Examiner* during March and April 1814, about the new French regime. On 10 April, for example, he tackled 'the question between Bonaparte and the Bourbons', giving a list of the 'sceptred tyrants' who might claim the French throne and disclosing 'the great secret, which really influences all those who are so ardent in favour of the old dynasty':

It is not for this man or the other that they are concerned, whatever may be their personal dislike to BONAPARTE as an enemy; it is for the re-establishment of an old dynasty *as* an old one,—for the restoration of the old privileged classes and the high aristocratic race;—for the return of prejudice, and mediocrity, and all sorts of dull supereminences, which are once more to consider themselves as taking natural place of desert;—in short, for the few as distinguished from the many,—for the family of crowned heads as opposed to the infinitely greater family who ought to have the disposal of crowns, for *power* as opposed to the *people*.[39]

Hunt kept this issue before his readers, welcoming the new French Constitution ratified in April 1814: 'That [Louis XVIII] will not have power to play the tyrant like some of his predecessors, his subjects will take care, if they remain true to their new charter.'[40] In calling for a legal 'curb' on 'the great', Keats and Hunt were voicing sentiments also expressed by Selden and Bolingbroke in passages from Clarke's commonplace book: 'The King's Oath is not security enough for our property, for he

---

[39] 'The Bourbons', *Examiner* (10 Apr. 1814), 228. The polemical abstraction 'dull supereminences' anticipates the similarly elliptical manner of Keats's invective at the opening of *Endymion* III; cf. Keats's 'prevailing tinsel', 'being's high account', 'their dull skies, their thrones' (III. 2, 14, 15).

[40] 'Louis XVIII.—The Emperor Napoleon', *Examiner* (1 May 1814), 273. This passage is quoted in AP 6n. as a context for the final three lines of 'On Peace' although as I suggest above the sentiments of Keats's sonnet have a broad resemblance to Hunt's *Examiner* articles about France at this time.

swears to govern according to *law*; now the *Judges* they *interpret the law*, and what *Judges can be made to do we know*,'[41] and: 'The ultimate end of all governments is the *good* of the *people, for whose sake* they were made, and *without whose consent*, they could not have been made.'[42] I do not wish to deny the contemporary relevance of 'On Peace' in April 1814, nor do I want to argue that Selden and Bolingbroke are 'sources' for Keats's sonnet. The parallels outlined here are most helpful, I think, in suggesting how through Clarke's conversation—if not more directly— the wealth of material represented in the commonplace book informed the imaginative currency of Keats's response to recent events. In this way, Keats's friendship with Cowden Clarke reveals the continuity between his years at Enfield School and his gravitation to the focus of radical activity in London represented by Leigh Hunt and the *Examiner* newspaper.

> And can I e'er repay the friendly debt?
> No, doubly no . . .

An Era in his Existence: Keats and Leigh Hunt

By the time *Poems* appeared in March 1817 Keats's association with Leigh Hunt and his circle was public knowledge. They had been introduced by Cowden Clarke in October 1816, and within two months Hunt's 'Young Poets' article in the *Examiner*, 1 December 1816, welcomed Keats into the 'new school of poetry' alongside Shelley and John Hamilton Reynolds:

The last of these young aspirants whom we have met with, and who promise to help the new school to revive Nature . . . is JOHN KEATS. He has not yet published any thing except in a newspaper; but a set of his manuscripts was handed us the other day, and fairly surprised us with the truth of their ambition, and ardent grappling with Nature.[43]

The poem which Keats had 'published . . . in a newspaper' was his sonnet 'O Solitude', which appeared in the *Examiner* on

---

[41] 'CCC Commonplace Book', 137, Clarke's emphases.The passage was extracted from 'The King' in Selden's *Table-Talk*.
[42] From *The Idea of a Patriot King*, 'CCC Commonplace Book', 111, Clarke's emphases.
[43] See *Examiner* (1 Dec. 1816), 761–2, and *KCH* 41–2.

5 May 1816, and Clarke had subsequently shown Hunt 'two or three poems which [he] had received from Keats'.[44] *Poems, by John Keats* was carefully presented to reinforce this link with Hunt, through imitation of Hunt's lyrical idiom but also in the way the collection as a whole was structured. An introductory sonnet dedicated the book to Hunt; the epigraph to the first poem, *I stood tip-toe*, was drawn from Hunt's *Story of Rimini*; three of the poems—'Specimen of an Induction', 'To My Brother George', and 'To Charles Cowden Clarke'—celebrated Hunt as 'Libertas', and 'Written on the Day that Mr Leigh Hunt left Prison' was included with the sonnets. The last poem in the book, *Sleep and Poetry*, concluded with an 'inventory' of the studio in 'a poet's house', Hunt's home at the Vale of Health, Hampstead.

To many later readers *Poems* has appeared a callow, derivative volume, valuable to the extent that it offers glimpses of the greater poetry Keats subsequently wrote. To its first readers and critics, however, the book was an outspoken poetic and political manifesto which on every page announced the author's kinship with the 'new school' of poetry and politics that Z would later brand as the 'Cockney School'.[45] In his 'Recollections' Clarke described (not without difficulty, as I pointed out in the Introduction) the controversial presence of Keats's book accurately, even as he tried to pretend that in reality Keats had no coherent political sympathies or opinions. Clarke begins by begging the question:

The word had been passed that its author was a Radical; and in those days of 'Bible-Crown-and Constitution' supremacy, he might have had better chance of success had he been an Anti-Jacobin. Keats had not made the slightest demonstration of political opinion; but with a conscious feeling of gratitude for kindly encouragement, he had dedicated his book to Leigh Hunt, editor of the *Examiner*, a Radical and a dubbed partisan of the first Napoleon; because when alluding to him, Hunt did not always subjoin the fashionable cognomen of 'Corsican Monster'. Such an association was motive enough with the dictators of the day to thwart the endeavours of a young aspirant who should presume to assert for himself an unrestricted course of opinion. Verily,

---

[44] 'Recollections of Keats', 132.
[45] See also Newey, ' "Alternate uproar and sad peace"', 266–72, and Goellnicht, 'The Politics of Reading and Writing' 105–7.

'the former times were *not* better than these'. Men may now utter a word in favour of 'civil liberty' without being chalked on the back and hounded out.

Poor Keats! . . . .[46]

That last, regretful exclamation was routine in nineteenth-century accounts of Keats,[47] but markedly uncharacteristic of Clarke's memoir taken as a whole. In appearing here, it emphasizes how in this passage Clarke was concerned to insulate 'poor Keats' from Hunt's radicalism by sentimentalizing their relationship in terms of 'gratitude for kindly encouragement' and 'the endeavours of a young aspirant'. Keats was grateful for Hunt's interest and friendship, to be sure, but to suggest that *Poems* 'had not made the slightest demonstration of political opinion' was untrue (as Clarke's hint that Keats had presumed to an 'unrestricted course of opinion' implies). George Felton Mathew, who had known Keats in 1815, later described his political opinions at that time with some astringency:

He was not one who thought it better to bear the ills we have, than fly to others we know not of. He was of the sceptical and republican school. An advocate for the innovations which were making progress in his time. A faultfinder with every thing established. I, on the contrary, hated controversy and dispute . . . But I respected Keats's opinions, because they were sincere . . . At this time Keats was on intimate terms with Leigh Hunt . . . .[48]

As Keats's epistle 'To George Felton Mathew' indicates, their acquaintance dated from *before* the meeting with Hunt (*KC* ii. 180n.), and this further underlines the extent to which Keats's 'sceptical and republican' views agreed with Cowden Clarke's opinions as revealed by the contents of his commonplace book. Furthermore, many of the poems in Keats's first collection owe as much to the formative environment at Enfield as to Hunt's example as a writer.

In closing *Sleep and Poetry* with a description of Hunt's studio, Keats noticed two 'sacred busts' which reminded him of Hunt's political ideals but also of earlier times at Enfield and Edmonton:

---

[46] 'Recollections of Keats', 140–1.

[47] See Susan J. Wolfson, 'Keats Enters History: Autopsy, *Adonais*, and the Fame of Keats', *K&H* 24–5, 31–2, 40n. 21.

[48] *KC* ii. 185–6.

> Great Alfred's too, with anxious, pitying eyes,
> As if he always listened to the sighs
> Of the goaded world; and Kosciusko's worn
> By horrid sufferance—mightily forlorn. (385–8)

Thaddeus Kosciusko, the Polish patriot, soldier, and revolutionary, had been a hero for British radicals since the 1790s, when Coleridge dedicated one of his 'Sonnets on Eminent Characters' to him. Twenty years later, Hunt published a sonnet to Kosciusko in the *Examiner* (19 November 1815) and hailed him as a consistent champion of liberty (unlike Coleridge) in an article on 12 January 1817. Keats followed with his own sonnet, composed December 1816 and published in the *Examiner* (16 February 1817), in which he again associated Kosciusko's 'name with Alfred's and the great of yore' (11). Kosciusko represented modern revolutionary ideals that Keats shared with Hunt, whereas King Alfred was traditionally held to have been the originator of English constitutional liberties. As Miriam Allott notes, Keats's interest in Alfred and other national heroes was 'fostered by Cowden Clarke'[49]—hence this tribute in the epistle 'To Charles Cowden Clarke',

> You too upheld the veil from Clio's beauty,
> And pointed out the patriot's stern duty;
> The might of Alfred, and the shaft of Tell;
> The hand of Brutus, that so grandly fell
> Upon a tyrant's head. Ah! had I never seen,
> Or known your kindness, what might I have been? (68–73)

Clarke's attendance on Clio, Muse of History, is substantiated by many entries in the commonplace book, as is his commitment to the 'patriot's stern duty' to rid the world of tyranny. Perhaps Keats was thinking more especially of Clarke's outlined essay in his commonplace book, where he touches on Alfred the Great's fame and his achievement as founder of the English constitution.[50] In his esteem for Alfred, however, Clarke belonged in the tradition of English liberalism represented by the reformist Society for Constitutional Information (dating from the later eighteenth century) and by the founder of Enfield School, John Ryland, in particular. In 1784 Ryland had published *The Life and Character of Alfred the Great* (which he dedicated to the

---

[49] See AP 100n.   [50] ' "Cockney" Commonplace Book', 76, item 27.

Constitutional Society), hailing the English republicans while also singling out Alfred: 'we owe to him all the great outlines of the good old BRITISH CONSTITUTION' as well as 'many of those advantages, which render our constitution dear to us: for instance, trials by juries'.[51]

Charles Cowden Clarke had drawn Keats's attention to Alfred as a figure representative of the liberal politics of Enfield School discussed in the first chapter of this book. Accordingly when Keats first met Hunt, and as the conclusion to *Sleep and Poetry* intimates, their friendship developed out of the political and literary interests he had previously shared with the Clarkes at Enfield. A mutual admiration for Alfred, and other republican and literary heroes, is suggested by the *Examiner*'s response to the proposed suspension of Habeas Corpus following the Spa Fields riots of December 1816:

FELLOW-COUNTRYMEN, Inheritors of Magna Charta and the Bill of Rights, Demanders of Constitutional Reform, Demanders of decent and commonly capable Ministers, Descendants of the ALFREDS, the RUSSELLS, the HAMPDENS, the SHAKESPEARES . . .[52]

While Keats's friendship with the Clarkes grew more distant during his training at Guy's Hospital 1815–17, 'the poet's house' in the Vale of Health became a new arbour from which he would return to his lodgings 'brimfull of the friendliness / That in a little cottage I have found' ('Keen, fitful gusts', 9–10).

The sense of cheerful community that Hunt encouraged through evenings of music and poetry was welcomed by Keats as 'an Era in [his] existence' (*Letters*, i. 113). Yet to hostile eyes these sociable gatherings at Hampstead, and the poetry of 'sociality' cultivated by Hunt and Keats at this time, were evidence of a new radical sect whose writings recalled the Jacobin poetry of humane sensibility dating from the 1790s.[53] When Z sneered at Keats's tribute to Hunt,

[51] Ryland, *The Life and Character of King Alfred the Great*, pp. vi, 7.

[52] See *Examiner* (2 Mar. 1817), 129, and Hunt's *Feast of the Poets, with Notes, and other Pieces in Verse, by the Editor of the Examiner* (London, 1814), 38–42, for an enthusiastic note on Alfred who 'established the foundation of . . . liberties' in England. Kandl, 'Private Lyrics', 96–8, discusses Hunt's and Keats's invocations of Alfred and Kosciusko in the context of public 'rhetorical' opposition to 'divine right'.

[53] See David Fairer, 'Baby Language and Revolution: The Early Poetry of Charles Lloyd and Charles Lamb', *Charles Lamb Bulletin* (Apr. 1991), 33–52.

> He of the rose, the violet, the spring,
> The social smile, the chain for freedom's sake
> ('Addressed to the Same', 5–6)

—by observing that 'The world has really some reason to look to its foundations!', his jest betrayed a tremor of genuine alarm.[54] The conjunction in these lines of floral and vernal imagery, social affability, and martyrdom 'for freedom's sake' was typical of 'Cockney' affectation, but also a precise example of the 'new school's' challenge to established literary and political values. What follows in the next chapter is, in part, an attempt to show why those seemingly bland images in Keats's tribute should have produced such a strong response from Z. As I have already suggested, one explanation may be traced in the politics and poetry of the 1790s, and the example of Coleridge in particular.

[54] 'Cockney School IV', 520.

CHAPTER FOUR

'Soft humanity put on': The Poetry and Politics of Sociality 1798–1818

> . . . some uncertain notice, as might seem,
> Of vagrant dwellers in the houseless woods . . .
> (William Wordsworth, 'Lines Written a Few
> Miles above Tintern Abbey', 1798)

> Is there a reader that has had any gratification from the writings of the present author, and would willingly give him a personal one in return? A single branch of ever-green put up somewhere, which would not have been put before, will be an ample one.
> (Leigh Hunt, *Examiner* (21 Dec. 1817), 801)

'Home-born feeling': The Example of Coleridge

In *Wordsworth and Coleridge: The Radical Years* I argued that during the later 1790s there was no 'generalized pattern of retreat from politics into retirement'.[1] Although Coleridge was living at Nether Stowey, miles from the centres of political activity at London and Bristol, he was 'markedly consistent' in maintaining his opposition to government policies. Many of Coleridge's poems written in the years 1795–8 seek to reconcile solitary experience,

> as on the midway slope
> Of yonder hill I stretch my limbs at noon
> Whilst thro' my half-clos'd eyelids I behold
> The sunbeams dance, like diamonds, on the main,
> And tranquil muse upon tranquillity . . .

—with social obligations to family, friends, and the larger cause of humankind: 'the bloodless fight | Of Science, Freedom, and

[1] *Wordsworth and Coleridge: The Radical Years*, 238–9.

the Truth in Christ'.[2] In 'Effusion XXXV' solitary reverie amid
nature's beautiful forms brings 'phantasies' of universal har-
mony, 'one intellectual Breeze, | At once the Soul of each, and
God of all'—yet these visions are all too quickly dispersed by
the 'mild reproof' of another person. By way of contrast, in
'This Lime-Tree Bower my Prison', Coleridge's solitude is, initially, the frustrating circumstance which isolates him from his
companions, 'friends, whom I may never meet again'. The
poem feelingly traces his friends' progress across the Quantock
landscape he knows so well and embraces their experience with
his own recollected joy, wakening him to the soothing pres-
ences of the bower and this recognition:

> Henceforth I shall know
> That Nature ne'er deserts the wise and pure,
> No scene so narrow but may well employ
> Each faculty of sense, and keep the heart
> Awake to love and beauty! And sometimes
> 'Tis well to be bereft of promis'd good,
> That we may lift the soul, and contemplate
> With lively joy the joys we cannot share.[3]

Here, responsiveness to nature redeems solitude with 'love and
beauty', keeping the heart alive to social feeling in the contemplation even of 'joys we cannot share'. In 'Fears in Solitude' a
comparable transformation takes place, enabling Coleridge to
come to terms with his harrowing vision of the retribution im-
minently to be visited on Britain:

> and lo! recall'd
> From bodings, that have well nigh wearied me,
> I find myself upon the brow, and pause
> Startled! And after lonely sojourning
> In such a quiet and surrounded scene,
> This burst of prospect, here the shadowy main,
> Dim-tinted, there the mighty majesty
> Of that huge amphitheatre of rich

---

[2] 'Effusion XXXV: Composed August 20th, 1795, at Clevedon, Somersetshire', in
Poems on Various Subjects (Bristol, 1796), and 'Reflections on Entering into Active
Life: A Poem, which Affects not to be POETRY', in *Monthly Magazine* (Oct. 1796).

[3] 'This Lime-Tree Bower my Prison: A Poem, Addressed to Charles Lamb, of the
India-House, London', in *The Annual Anthology* (2 vols., Bristol, 1799–1800), ii.
140–4.

And elmy fields, seems like society,
Conversing with the mind, and giving it
A livelier impulse, and a dance of thought;
And now, beloved STOWEY! I behold
Thy church-tower, and (methinks) the four huge elms
Clust'ring, which mark the mansion of my friend;
And close behind them, hidden from my view,
Is my own lowly cottage, where my babe
And my babe's mother dwell in peace! With light
And quicken'd footsteps thitherward I tend,
Rememb'ring thee, O green and silent dell!
And grateful, that by nature's quietness
And solitary musings all my heart
Is soften'd, and made worthy to indulge
Love, and the thoughts that yearn for human kind.[4]

This homecoming of the feeling heart, open and receptive to love and compassion, effects a natural reconciliation of self and community at a time of acute crisis—'the Alarms of an Invasion' noticed in the poem's subtitle. The 'beloved' village comprising the 'mansion of [his] friend' Thomas Poole, '[his] own lowly cottage', the 'babe', and its 'mother' represents the small, personal survival group in which E. P. Thompson and others have identified one resort of persecuted democrats in the latter 1790s. Such loving relationships might nurture, on a small scale, those 'thoughts that yearn for human kind' which were no longer permitted to find expression in active public life. Thompson went on to suggest that this modification of radical aspiration allows us to understand some of the forms of writing at this time: the interior monologue of the isolated individual (he cites Blake's prophetic books) but also 'the personal dialogue with one intimate friend [which] gives us *The Prelude*'.[5]

As I suggested above, Coleridge's poems written at this time repeatedly seek to integrate these two forms of discourse, notably in the 'conversation' poems such as 'This Lime-Tree Bower', 'Frost at Midnight', and 'The Nightingale', in order to orient the otherwise solitary, alienated self within a particular community. Some years ago Kelvin Everest argued that, in the midst of

---

[4] 'Fears in Solitude: Written, April 1798, During the Alarms of an Invasion' in *Fears in Solitude . . . To which are Added, France, an Ode; and Frost at Midnight* (London, 1798).
[5] E. P. Thompson, 'Disenchantment or Default? A Lay Sermon', in C. C. O'Brien and W. D. Vanech (eds.), *Power and Consciousness* (London, 1969), 162.

political crisis and social dislocation, Coleridge sought in this way to 'establish the presence of a sympathetic audience . . . to create relationship, a sense of connectedness, between men and women (and, especially important for Coleridge, between adults and children), and between man and his particular world'.[6] Coleridge was well aware that poetry celebrating the 'little platoon' and retired life might be understood as endorsing a loyal, local, Burkean conservatism,[7] or as a culpable abdication of responsibility, 'throw[ing] up all hopes of the amelioration of mankind, and . . . sinking into an almost epicurean selfishness, disguising the same under the soft titles of domestic attachment and contempt for visionary *philosophes*'.[8] Alternatively, we may understand poetic themes of relationship, family, friendship, marriage, children, home, retirement, the natural world, God, as continuations of the dissenting religious and political ideals which fired Coleridge's enthusiasm for the Pantisocracy community in 1794–5, and which formed the philosophic matter of his public lectures of 1795–6.

'The ardour of private Attachments makes Philanthropy a necessary *habit* of the Soul,' Coleridge had written to Southey, 13 July 1794,

I love my *Friend*—such as *he* is, all mankind are or *might be*! The deduction is evident—. Philanthropy (and indeed every other Virtue) is a thing of *Concretion*—Some home-born Feeling is the *center* of the Ball, that, rolling on thro' Life collects and assimilates every congenial Affection.[9]

Pantisocracy, a 'family of Love' to be established on the banks of the River Susquehannah in Pennsylvania, was to form a 'centre' of feeling to which benevolence would necessarily gravitate. The Pantisocracy scheme was short-lived,[10] but the philosophical, religious, and emotional ideals that it represented survived

---

[6] Kelvin Everest, *Coleridge's Secret Ministry: The Context of the Conversation Poems, 1795–8* (Hassocks, 1979), 10.

[7] See Burke, *Reflections*, 135, and Butler, *Romantics*, 85–6.

[8] Coleridge to William Wordsworth, c.10 Sept. 1799, *Collected Letters*, i. 527. For a related discussion of Charles Lamb's and Charles Lloyd's poetry celebrating 'the firm, tho' little band I Of those I love', indicating how 'conservatism' and 'radicalism' may be organised together, see David Fairer, 'Baby Language and Revolution', 35, 46–7.

[9] *Collected Letters*, i. 86.

[10] See 'Southey and the Origins of Pantisocracy', in my *Politics of Nature*, 36–55.

in Coleridge's lectures and poems of subsequent years. In his 'Introductory Address' to *Conciones ad Populum*, for example, Coleridge argued that the 'sympathetic passions', by effecting true 'Justice', will establish 'the universal fraternity of Love'; and, again, in his third lecture on revealed religion, 'the Love of our Friends, parents and neighbours lead[s] us to the love of our Country to the love of all Mankind. The intensity of private attachment encourages, not prevents, universal philanthropy.'[11]

In the public political arena during the years 1795–8 Coleridge's expression of sympathetic feeling in lectures and poems had an ambiguous resonance for contemporary readers. The *British Critic*, reviewing *Conciones ad Populum*, aligned Coleridge with the English Jacobins:

His tender and compassionate anxiety for the welfare of mankind, he dwells upon through many pages, and with that spirit of patriotism, which has frequently actuated the writers of his party, attempts to ascribe the murders of Robespierre, and all the horrors acted in France, to the obstinate hostility of this country. When shall we cease to see this nonsense repeated, which the best informed even of our French enemies have again and again contradicted?[12]

In this reader's view, solicitude for human welfare identified Coleridge as a 'patriot' in the cause of France and the Revolution, an apologist for 'the murders of Robespierre'. When in July 1797 Coleridge was joined at Nether Stowey by William and Dorothy Wordsworth, and 'Citizen' John Thelwall in his white hat, they excited suspicions that there was a 'Nest' of rascally democrats forming in the neighbourhood. As the 'Spy Nosy' episode demonstrated, in 1797 a life of rural retirement might readily be construed as a signal of 'disaffection' warranting the attentions of a government agent sent down from London to Somerset.[13] In direct contrast, however, the 'tender and compassionate' feeling expressed in 'Frost at Midnight' was welcomed by the *Monthly Review* as 'a pleasing picture of virtue and content in a cottage'. Given the acute political divisions of the country in 1798 the word *contentment*, as Paul Magnuson has shown, implied that Coleridge was inoffensive: a truly English

---

[11] See *Lectures 1795 on Politics and Religion*, 40, 163.
[12] *British Critic* (June 1796), in *Coleridge: The Critical Heritage*, ed. J. R. de J. Jackson (New York, 1970), 28.
[13] See *Wordsworth and Coleridge: The Radical Years*, 248–62.

'patriot' who was 'not ill-disposed to the existing state of society . . . not, therefore, seditious'.[14] Yet—like 'Fears in Solitude'—'Frost at Midnight' celebrates those 'thoughts that yearn for human kind' which had always been part of Coleridge's dedication to 'divinest liberty'—an ideal to which he redevotes himself in 'France; an Ode', with 'intensest love'.

In the latter 1790s, therefore, the various invocations of solitude, nature, community, and social feeling in Coleridge's poems were understood by readers to reflect the wider political controversies of the time. In many respects, these poems and critical responses prefigure the terms in which Keats's and Hunt's poetry was read in the post-Waterloo period, namely as the productions of 'writers of [a] party' with an oppositional agenda. Whereas in Coleridge's poems the discourse of compassion, benevolence, fraternity, and philanthropy was construed by Tory readers as 'Jacobin', in the 'Cockney School of Poetry' seemingly innocuous categories such as cheerfulness, sociality, the greenwood, pastoral bowers, suburban life, and even tea-drinking were received as suspect tokens of a resurgent radical community whose opinions were canvassed explicitly in the columns of newspapers such as the *Examiner* and the *Yellow Dwarf*.

Keats, Hunt, and Sociality

> Here too let friendship come, without its aid
> In vain this scene of happiness were made;
> The heart would languish 'mid the sweets alone . . .
> (John Hamilton Reynolds, *The Eden of
> Imagination*, 1814)

> That greenish coloured individual is an Advocate of Arras;
> his name is *Maximilien Robespierre*.
> (Thomas Carlyle, *The French Revolution*, 1837)

In his preface to *Foliage* (1818), Hunt announces that, following the 'downfall of the French school of poetry' and recent 'political convulsions in the world', 'notions about poetry can no

---

[14] *Monthly Magazine* (May 1799), in *Coleridge: The Critical Heritage*, 47, and Paul Magnuson, 'The Politics of "Frost at Midnight"', *Wordsworth Circle*, 22 (Winter 1991), 6–7.

longer be controuled, like the fashions, by a coterie of town gentlemen'.[15] He recalls Wordsworth's justification of *Lyrical Ballads* against 'pre-established codes of decision' and the disapproval of 'readers of superior judgment',[16] supplanting Wordsworth's ironic deference with a combative challenge to the prejudiced 'control' exercised by the metropolitan literary establishment. As Hunt's reference to revolutionary 'political convulsions' suggested, the liberation of poetry from 'a coterie of town gentlemen' was construed in terms of wider political and cultural change.[17] His alternative definition of poetry once again owed much to the prefaces to *Lyrical Ballads*: 'A sensativeness [*sic*] to the beauty of the external world, to the unsophisticated impulses of our nature, and above all, imagination, or the power to see, with verisimilitude, what others do not,—these are the properties of poetry.'[18] A little later in the preface Hunt related these 'properties of poetry' to what he termed his 'moral theories':

An unattractive creed, however the hypocritical or envious may affect to confound the cheerful tendencies of our nature with vicious ones, or the melancholy may be led really to do so, is an argument against itself . . . The depreciators of this world,—the involuntary blasphemers of nature's goodness,—have tried melancholy and partial systems enough, and talked enough of their own humility. It is high time for them, and for all of us, to look after health and sociality; and to believe, that although we cannot alter the world with an ipse dixit, we need not become desponding, or mistake a disappointed egotism for humility.[19]

In juxtaposing 'health and sociality' with desponding egotism Hunt recalled his remarks about Wordsworth in the notes to *The Feast of the Poets*; there, he regretted that Wordsworth 'lives too much apart, and is subject . . . to . . . solitary morbidities', and recommended 'a better acquaintance with society' as the

[15] See *Foliage*, 12.

[16] 'Advertisement' to *Lyrical Ballads, with A Few Other Poems* (London, 1798), pp. ii–iii.

[17] As the *Eclectic Review* (Nov. 1818), 484–5, noted, it was 'impolitic' of Hunt to refer to his 'religious creed [and] political opinion': 'What sentiments indeed can we look for but such as may comport with the creed of a heathen and the morals of a libertine?'

[18] *Foliage*, 13; other influences on Hunt's idea of poetry in *Foliage* may include Coleridge's *Biographia Literaria* (1817) and the first book of *The Excursion* (1814).

[19] *Foliage*, 15–16.

means for Wordsworth to fulfil the humane 'utility' of his poetry.[20] In other words, 'sociality' was a healthy antidote to
Wordsworth's rural solitude, and—by implication—to the Tory
politics Wordsworth had so emphatically announced in his
dedication of *The Excursion* to the 'illustrious Peer' the Earl
of Lonsdale.[21] In the two parties of 'them' and 'us' Hunt also
invokes the sharp divisions of contemporary political argument,
represented elsewhere by his oppositional journalism in the
Examiner. In the less polemical language of the preface to *Foliage*, however, political confrontation is resumed in terms peculiar to Hunt's poetic and critical discourse. Here, 'sensativity',
'unsophisticated impulses', 'beauty', 'cheerful tendencies',
'nature's goodness', 'health and sociality' are opposed to the
'vicious', 'melancholy', 'blasphemous', and 'desponding' effects of what Hunt calls 'partial systems'. A crucial word here is
partial, denoting the exclusive political establishment already
acknowledged in the 'coterie of town gentlemen' who presume
to control notions of poetry.[22] When Keats observed that 'there

[20]   *The Feast of the Poets*, 107–8.

[21]   Wordsworth's association with Lowther connected him with a peer who was,
according to the *Examiner*, 'the greatest boroughmonger in England' (*Examiner*, 22
Feb. 1818). When Keats inquired after Wordsworth on visiting Ambleside in late
June 1818, he found that he was 'canvassing for the Lowthers' in the Westmorland
election against the Whig candidate Henry Brougham: 'What think you of that—
Wordsworth versus Brougham!! Sad-sad-sad (*Letters*, i. 299). The scale of Wordsworth's diminishment for Keats was indicated a few days later in the *Examiner*'s
description of the Lowthers as 'an old family' now 'merged into mere courtiers and
boroughmongers, [and] are only felt through the medium of tax-gatherers,
tithesmen, attornies, and every species of humiliating intercourse, not excepting
that which looks kindliest; they are aristocratical usurpers and dictators of the
county, not leading gentry of it' (5 July 1818), 417. In 1818 Wordsworth was of
course one of the local 'tax-gatherers' and 'tithesmen', and his role in 'this contest
between sycophancy and independence' was exposed a few pages later in the same
issue of the *Examiner*: 'A certain Poet is said to have taken part in the literary
drudgery of the *patronage* side of the question, and in the division of labour, with a
view to that of the spoil—to have taken upon him to find out and expose the bad
grammar of his rustic and less classical opponents.' *Examiner* (5 July 1818), 427.

[22]   The pejorative resonances of 'partial' had been signalled by Richard Price
at the beginning of the French Revolution: 'When . . . representation is partial, a
kingdom possesses liberty only partially; and if extremely partial, it only gives a
semblance of liberty; but if not only extremely partial, but corruptly chosen, and
under corrupt influence after being chosen, it becomes a *nuisance*, and produces
the worst of all forms of government—a government by corruption—a government
carried on and supported by spreading venality and profligacy through a kingdom.
May heaven preserve this kingdom from a calamity so dreadful! It is the point of
depravity to which abuses under such a government as ours naturally tend, and the

are many Men like Hunt who from a principle of taste would like to see things go on better' (*Letters*, i. 396), he caught exactly the temper of the preface to *Foliage*, and indicated that Hunt's politics of 'taste' were representative of a group in which Keats had himself been numbered. In *Sleep and Poetry*, for instance, Keats had damned the neoclassical principles of the 'French School' as 'a schism | Nurtured by foppery and barbarism' (181–2). Unnatural, unfeeling, and circumscribed by 'musty laws' and 'wretched rule' like an oppressed nation, these poets displayed 'a poor, decrepid standard' bearing the name of a tyrant, the neoclassical poet and critic Nicholas Boileau (204–6).

For Hunt, too, the false 'taste' of the 'French School of wit and satire' was appropriate to an age of oppression:

It is bad taste of all sorts, and not good, which belongs to such a period of disease and imbecility;—gaudiness, gross intemperance, submission to ignorant tyranny, frivolous disputation,—a foresaking of real art and nature, not a love of them. The swords with which Harmodius and Aristogeiton slew the Grecian tyrant, were braided with myrtle.[23]

The downfall of the French School was effected by a revolution of 'taste' (which extended to radical vegetarianism) liberating the temperate, humane values of 'real art and nature' symbolized here by the evergreen leaves of the myrtle, emblem of love. '[C]old and artificial compositions have given way', Hunt writes, 'like so many fantastic figures of snow; and imagination breathes again in a more green and genial time.'[24]

Z's first 'Cockney School' essay acknowledged and sought to reverse Hunt's democratization of 'taste', pillorying him as 'a man . . . of extravagant pretensions in wit, poetry, and politics, and withal of exquisitely bad taste, and extremely vulgar modes of thinking and manners in all respects'.[25] His principal target was *The Story of Rimini*, in which Hunt had sought to inculcate a 'sense of justice . . . recommending men's minds to the consideration

last stage of national unhappiness.' See *A Discourse on the Love of our Country, Delivered on Nov. 4, 1789, at the Meeting House in the Old Jewry, to the Society for Commemorating the Revolution in Great Britain* (London, 1790), 33–4.

[23] *Foliage*, 20.
[24] Ibid. 9.
[25] 'On the Cockney School of Poetry: No I', *Blackwood's Edinburgh Magazine* (Oct. 1817), 38.

of *first* causes of misfortune [in] confounding forms with justice, [and] setting authorized selfishness above the most natural impulses'.[26] Hunt's narrative is developed from Dante's encounter in the *Inferno* with two 'wearied spirits' damned for adultery and incest: these are the lovers Paulo, Prince of Rimini, and Francesca, his brother's wife. In Hunt's retelling of their story, the emphasis has shifted from sin and damnation to a sympathetic understanding of their behaviour. An 'elaborate snare'[27] is created by Giovanni, Duke of Rimini, and Francesca's father Guido, Duke of Ravenna, to further their own financial interests. Francesca is betrothed to Giovanni without meeting him, and as part of this conspiracy she is courted by and falls in love with his young brother Prince Paulo—unaware that Paulo has been sent as Giovanni's proxy in the marriage ceremony. Paulo and Francesca marry but, because the wedding has been contrived as a 'holy cheat', Francesca is actually 'ensnared' as Giovanni's wife. Bitter disappointment follows her discovery of this 'virtue-binding sin':

> The shock, that told this lovely, trusting heart,
> That she had given, beyond all power to part,
> Her hope, belief, love, passion, to one brother,
> Possession (oh, the misery!) to another![28]

Isolated and ignored by her 'possessor' Giovanni, Francesca eventually meets once again with Paulo, this time in the 'garden green' which surrounds their palace at Rimini. There, while reading 'Launcelot of the Lake, a bright romance', and responding to 'the most natural impulses', they consummate their passion:

> Sacred be love from sight, whate'er it is.
> The world was all forgot, the struggle o'er,
> Desperate the joy.—That day they read no more.

At this moment we can, perhaps, just hear two echoes which add resonance to the lovers' desperate joy. The first comes from *Paradise Lost*, and the moment when Adam and Eve are cast out

---

[26] Hunt's explanation of his intentions in writing *The Story of Rimini* appears in the preface to *Foliage*, pp. ix–x.
[27] See *The Story of Rimini*, 28, and for the controversy surrounding Hunt's poem, Newey, 'Keats, History, and the Poets', *K&H* 168–9.
[28] *The Story of Rimini*, 44.

into wilderness: 'The world was all before them' (XII. 646), Milton had written, and it is a world well forgotten, Hunt implies, by Paulo and Francesca. The second, 'the struggle o'er', may be a semi-blasphemous allusion to Christ's crucifixion, refiguring his martyrdom at a climax of all too human passion.

As this short summary will suggest, Hunt intended his poem to recommend a sympathetic understanding of their transgression, affirming 'natural feeling' against the codes of 'authorized selfishness' which tragically bring about the lovers' deaths— and, in the *Inferno*, an eternity of torment. Paulo impales himself on his brother's sword in a duel, and Francesca subsequently dies broken-hearted. They are buried together 'under a tree . . . | In the green ground'.[29]

Predictably, Z was only too ready to yoke the sexual politics of *The Story of Rimini* to the radical programme of the *Examiner*, by way of denouncing both. Hunt's 'sour Jacobinism' as editor was inseparable from his 'extreme moral depravity' as a poet, qualities which together made up 'those glittering and rancid obscenities which float on the surface of Mr Hunt's Hippocrene': 'In Rimini a deadly wound is aimed at the dearest confidences of domestic bliss. The author has voluntarily chosen—a subject not of simple seduction alone—one in which his mind seems absolutely to gloat over all the details of adultery and incest.'[30] Z's patriarchal confidence might tolerate 'simple seduction', but not the more thoroughgoing challenge to sexual codes articulated by Hunt's poem. He returns to the theme repeatedly in subsequent essays, denouncing *The Story of Rimini* as 'a lewd tale of incest, adultery, and murder, in which the violation of Nature herself was wept over, palliated, justified, and held up to imitation, and the violators themselves worshipped as holy martyrs'.[31] Here, the damned souls in the *Inferno* have been consecrated 'holy martyrs'—Z has picked up those echoes from *Paradise Lost* and the Bible; seen how Hunt was using them to justify his liberal agenda; and now turns them back on Hunt by way of reinforcing the forms of a more conventional morality.

A later review of *Foliage* (which Z presented as a mock-obituary) damned Hunt as a writer who 'so largely dealt' in

[29] Ibid. 111.   [30] 'Cockney School I', 39, 40.

[31] 'The Cockney School of Poetry: No III', *Blackwood's Edinburgh Magazine* (July 1818), 453.

'licentiousness, sedition, and impiety'. In the circumstances, Hunt's dedication of *Foliage* to Sir John Swinburne (grandfather of Algernon Charles) could only be understood as 'a gross public insult, not to [Swinburne] alone, but to the country-gentlemen of England'.[32] It was, of course, precisely the codes of social-sexual power controlled by 'gentlemen' which Hunt's poem had brought into question. Ironically this was demonstrated by a letter in Hunt's defence, sent anonymously to William Blackwood from 'a gentleman of some consequence' who sought to vindicate the 'gentle' values of his class against the 'scurrilous blaggardism' of Z:

I have no sort of acquaintance with Leigh Hunt except through his writings, and from report of others; this libel, however, professes from his writings, to represent him as a man of most licentious and immoral private character, and in his editorial or rather authorial capacity as a pander to the basest and most depraved passions of *our nature*, I was going to say;—but this anonymous scribe goes even farther than all this, and charges him with being the wanton advocate of unnatural vice—such a flagitious accusation brought forward publicly against an individual by name . . . is I think altogether an unprecedented thing in the literay world [*sic*].[33]

By construing Z's 'unauthorized' public attack on Hunt as a libel, this letter—along with the 'Cockney School' essays—shows how *The Story of Rimini* was very finely calculated to unsettle the 'authorized' complacencies of Regency life. Hunt's poetry of sympathetic, natural justice in *The Story of Rimini*, of 'nature' and 'sociality' in *Foliage* ('a world that has friendships and flowers'[34]), was a lyrical expression of the *Examiner*'s oppositional politics—a connection that Z saw particularly clearly.[35] The continuity between Hunt's politics, literary productions, and poetic theories was symbolized by the myrtle

[32] 'Cockney School VI', 71.

[33] NLS, MS 4002, quoted by permission of the Trustees of the National Library of Scotland. Letter dated 16 Nov. 1817.

[34] 'To William Hazlitt', from *Foliage*, p. xciv.

[35] In his essay 'Christmas and Other Old National Merry-Makings Considered', Hunt refers to 'every new and kind sociality' as an ideal for the times. To a disapproving reader, '*kind* sociality' might be read as a euphemism for the (unacceptable) sexual liberalism associated with *The Story of Rimini*. See *Examiner* (21 Dec. 1817), 802, and *OED*. In his sonnet 'Written on the Day that Mr Leigh Hunt left Prison', Keats had referred to 'Kind Hunt . . . shut in prison' (2).

leaves around the Greek liberators' swords, by the 'garden green' at Rimini, and in the 'more green and genial clime' of imaginative and social renewal. Indeed, the 'dedication' to *Foliage* had announced that the book's object was 'to cultivate a love of nature out of doors, and sociality within' in the midst of 'this war and money-injured land'.[36] A similar entwining of poetic and political design was also characteristic of the verses in *Poems, by John Keats.*

In *Sleep and Poetry*, Keats hailed the promising aspect of contemporary poetry in a passage which deliberately echoed the terms of Hunt's editorials in the *Examiner* and the preface to *Foliage*:

> Yet I rejoice: a myrtle fairer than
> E'er grew in Paphos, from the bitter weeds
> Lifts its sweet head into the air, and feeds
> A silent space with ever sprouting green. (248–51)

The myrtle was a token of love sacred to the goddess Venus who was worshipped at Paphos (now Cyprus): classical allusions and vernal imagery work together to suggest the 'delightful hopes' Keats feels at the 'green' revival of English poetry. Less obvious for a modern reader, perhaps, is the association of such verdant emblems with the reform movement of the time.

Green had for centuries been the colour favoured by radical political and religious groups and sects in England and elsewhere, very probably following the Lincoln Green supposed to have been worn by the outlaw Robin Hood (although I suspect ancient and obscure ritualistic sources should also be invoked here). As Christopher Hill has shown, the sea-green colours and green aprons of the seventeenth-century English Levellers were adopted by later generations including the Whig Green Ribbon Club, the Quakers, the United Irishmen, and the Chartists.[37] Given the long continuity of green opposition down to the Environmental Movement of our own time, it comes as no surprise to find that green was the badge for reformists in Keats's lifetime. As we saw in Chapter 2, the procession

---

[36] *Foliage*, 8.
[37] See 'From Lollards to Levellers' in *The Collected Essays of Christopher Hill*, ii: *Religion and Politics in 17th Century England* (Brighton, 1986), 108, and 'Robin Hood' in Hill's *Liberty against the Law: Some Seventeenth-Century Controversies* (London, 1996), 75.

accompanying Henry Hunt's return to London in September 1819 displayed 'large branches of oak, poplar, and various other trees', green flags, and 'laurel leaves' so that, to the *Times* reporter, 'the approach of the procession seemed like that of a moving grove. The mixture of green boughs with the wands of the committees gave no faint idea of the approach of Birnam-wood to Dunsinane.' The reporter's allusion to the closing scenes of *Macbeth* invokes Shakespeare as an ally for the reformists, associating their procession entering London with the imminent downfall of tyranny: 'let every soldier hew him down a bough, | And bear't before him', Malcolm had ordered, 'thereby shall we shadow | The numbers of our host' (v. iv. 4–6).[38]

The carrying of branches was (and still is) a traditional folk custom on fair days and festivals. By the early nineteenth century, such celebrations were a reminder of better times in the past and consequently an appropriate emblem for those who sought to re-establish the liberties of England.[39] In his *Examiner* essay about 'Old National Merry-Makings', for example, Hunt alluded to *Macbeth*—and 'Birnam-wood' in particular—in evoking the 'universal leafiness' of old English folk culture, a time of 'simplicity, of cheerfulness, of benevolence, of justice, of poetry or the arts'.[40] And in *The Descent of Liberty* Hunt had located the pageant which accompanied Liberty's restoration in 'the best and greenest spot' of a city's suburbs, surrounded by 'heaps of leafiness on every side'. As Hunt explained, this imagery would function as a decorative distraction from political matters for 'those [readers] who might wish to meet with no politics at all', while remaining intrinsic to the

---

[38] 'Mr. Hunt's Entry into London', *The Times* (14 Sept. 1819). As Jonathan Bate points out, in George or Robert Cruikshank's cartoon of Peterloo, *Massacre at St Peter's or 'Britons Strike Home'!!!*, the Manchester Yeomanry are depicted with a banner reading ' "Be Bloody, bold and Resolute"—"Spur your proud Horses and Ride hard in blood"' thus associating them with two of Shakespeare's bloodiest tyrants, Macbeth (see IV. i. 79) and Richard III (see v. iii. 341). See *Shakespearean Constitutions: Politics, Theatre, Criticism 1730–1830* (Oxford, 1989), 97.

[39] See for example the decorating of signposts with 'green birch' on Midsummer Eve described in John Brand, *Observations on the Popular Antiquities of Great Britain* (3 vols., London, 1849), i. 307 and n. See also 'Christmas and Other Old National Merry-Makings Considered', 801–3, and 'Old May-Day', *Examiner* (10 May 1818), 289–91.

[40] 'Christmas and Other Old National Merry-Makings Considered', 801–3.

masque's contemporary meaning—both a cover for and symbolic expression of a libertarian message arising from the deep traditions of English radical and popular life.[41]

Read against this Cockney background, the frequent invocations of green imagery in *Poems, by John Keats* would have awakened associations comparable to those of the 'white' iconography in *Endymion*, discussed in the second chapter. Take the following, apparently innocuous details from *Poems*—'cool and green', 'light green brethren shoots', 'bowery green', 'green attire' (*I stood tip-toe*, 33, 39, 84, 136), 'laurels green' ('Specimen of an Induction', 54), 'green island', 'green hill', 'green robe', 'sprouting green', 'shady green' (*Sleep and Poetry*, 6, 77, 114, 251, 389). All of these 'greenings'—and there are many more that could be cited—disclose Keats's radical sympathies ambushed in an otherwise naïve, pastoral idiom comparable to that of Hunt's *Descent of Liberty*. When Keats adopted Hunt's line 'Places of nestling green for Poets made' as an epigraph for *I stood tip-toe*, his choice was more than a compliment for his new friend: the borrowing acknowledged their mutual commitment to renewal of poetry as the imaginative preparation for a renovation of society, 'blossoming with plenty and joy again . . . to do justice to the face both of the earth and of the human race'.[42] It was not an accident, in this respect, that Keats's epigraph was drawn from the most controversial section of *The Story of Rimini*: the third canto in which the poet's 'green nest' was neighbour to the bower where Paulo and Francesca consummated their love—an expression of natural human feeling against unjust social 'form' and 'virtue-binding sin'.[43]

That Keats initially responded warmly to Hunt's generous 'sociality' is evident from poems which date from their early friendship such as 'Keen, fitful gusts', 'On Leaving some Friends at an Early Hour,' and *Sleep and Poetry*. Hunt's cultivation of sociability was reflected in his poetry, most notably perhaps in his epistles to Byron, Moore, Hazlitt, Barron Field, and Lamb ('Home-lover, thought-feeder, abundant joke-giving'), but also in the sonnets addressed to Keats published in *Foliage*. 'To John Keats', for example, commends 'such a heart as Charles's, wise and warm', adding in a footnote, 'Charles

---

[41] *The Descent of Liberty*, pp. vii, 23, 32. [42] *Examiner* (21 Dec. 1817), 802.
[43] See *The Story of Rimini*, 68, 44.

C. C., a mutual friend'; the sonnet 'On the Same', marking the occasion when Keats had crowned Hunt with ivy, concludes:

> 'Tis what's within us crowned. And kind and great
> Are all the conquering wishes it inspires,—
> Love of things lasting, love of the tall woods,
> Love of love's self, and ardour for a state
> Of natural good befitting such desires,
> Towns without gain, and haunted solitudes.[44]

Here poetic sociality inspires Hunt's 'ardour' for 'natural good' as the crowning expression of all that is best in humanity. Significantly, he associates that good with the banishment of mercantilism ('Towns without gain'[45]) and the attractions of 'haunted solitudes'—'solitudes' that are visited frequently or habitually, perhaps in company. Paradoxically, the 'haunted solitude' becomes the resort of sociality, of community.[46] Appropriately, then, Hunt's characteristic territory is the suburban landscape of his sonnet 'Description of Hampstead':

> A steeple issuing from a leafy rise,
> With farmy fields in front, and sloping green,
> Dear Hampstead, is thy southern face serene,
> Silently smiling on approaching eyes.
> Within, thine ever-shifting looks surprise,
> Streets, hills, and dells, trees overhead now seen,
> Now down below, with smoking roofs between,—
> A village, revelling in varieties.
> Then northward what a range,—with heath and pond,
> Nature's own ground; woods that let mansions through,
> And cottag'd vales with pillowy fields beyond,
> And clump of darkening pines, and prospects blue,
> And that clear path through all, where daily meet
> Cool cheeks, and brilliant eyes, and morn elastic feet.

There are noticeable echoes of 'Frost at Midnight' and 'Tintern Abbey' here. Coleridge's evocation of hushed community,

> Sea, hill and wood,
> This populous village! Sea, and hill, and wood,
> With all the numberless goings on of life . . .

---

[44] *Foliage*, p. cxxvii.

[45] Compare the similar note struck in Keats's sonnet 'On Receiving a Laurel Crown from Leigh Hunt': 'Turbans and crowns, and blank regality' (12).

[46] Cf. 'Empty the haunted air', *Lamia*, II. 236.

—is overheard in Hunt's description of Hampstead's 'face serene':

> Streets, hills, and dells, trees overhead now seen,
> Now down below, with smoking roofs between,—
> A village, revelling in varieties.[47]

The effect of this relationship between the poems, however, is to emphasize that Hunt's terrain is neither the awe-inspiring sublime nature of Coleridge, nor the 'houseless woods' of Wordsworth, contemplated in solitude, but a populated suburban landscape that welcomes 'approaching eyes' (Z tagged Hunt's 'Description of Hampstead' 'an adventurous constitutional stroll'[48]). Unlike Coleridge at Stowey, or Wordsworth at the Wye, Hunt welcomes the proximity of 'Streets, hills, and dells', and the 'clear path' between the cultural attractions of town and the recreational spaces of the countryside:

> In the town, of the town,—in the fields, of the fields;
> In the one, for example, to feel as we go on,
> That streets are about us, arts, people, and so on;
> In t'other, to value the stillness, the breeze,
> And love to see farms, and to get among trees.[49]

To Z Wordsworth's genius was expressed in 'dignified purity of thought . . . patriarchal simplicity of feeling' and through 'pardonable' disdain for the world. In contrast to Wordsworth's classical austerity and aversion to community, Hunt was chattily familiar and only too ready to 'get among trees' on the outskirts of 'town'. As a consequence he was 'unacquainted with the face of nature in her magnificent scenes':[50] 'Suppose for a moment, Leigh Hunt at sea—or on the summit of Mont Blanc! it is impossible. No. Hampstead was the only place for him.'[51] Z's

---

[47] Compare also Hunt's 'smoking roofs' with Coleridge's 'thatch | Smokes in the sun-thaw'.

[48] See 'Cockney School VI', 74, and Elizabeth Jones's discussion of 'Cockney' suburban landscape in 'The Suburban School: Snobbery and Fear in the Attacks on Keats', *TLS* (27 Oct. 1995), 14–15.

[49] 'To William Hazlitt', from *Foliage*, pp. xci–xcii. Hunt's epistle was first published in *Examiner* (14 July 1816), 440–1, as part of a series, 'Harry Brown's Letters to his Friends: No III: To W.H. Esq'.

[50] 'Cockney School I', 40, 41.

[51] 'Cockney School VI', 72. For the currency of Z's argument in late 20th-cent. criticism, see Thomas McFarland's contention in *Romantic Cruxes: The English Essayists and the Spirit of the Age* (Oxford, 1987), 15–16, that Wordsworth and Coleridge

ridicule is a precise exposure of Hunt's limitations as a poet which also identifies his distinction as an originator of the 'suburban' idiom in modern literature, adopted with varying degrees of irony by John Betjeman,

> safe once more, we gained the leafy slope
> And buttered toast and 31 West Hill[52]

—and Philip Larkin:

> Walking around in the park
> Should feel better than work:
> The lake, the sunshine,
> The grass to lie on . . .[53]

But the fact that 'the only place' for Hunt was in the suburban neighbourhood of London also located him as a threat to the political and cultural establishment. The offices of the *Examiner* were directly accessible for the poet who lived at the Vale of Health and, apart from Hunt's oppositional activities, his ready mobility as a creature of the suburbs made it all the more urgently necessary to discredit him. In the mid-twentieth century, the calculated eccentricity of John Betjeman's persona in *Metroland* (which celebrates easy access from town to surrounding countryside) assumed the antic role Z had allotted to Hunt, but by way of rehabilitating the suburban landscape, architecture, and culture which Z had strenuously and successfully endeavoured to place beyond the pale of serious artistic or intellectual consideration.

'None of [the Cockneys] are men of genius', Z affirmed, '— none of them are men of solitary meditative habits; they are lecturers of the Surrey Institution [Hazlitt], and the editors of

---

stand as the 'dizzying elevations' of English Romanticism while Maria Edgeworth and Thomas Love Peacock (as treated in Marilyn Butler's *Romantics, Rebels, and Reactionaries*) represent the 'outlying foothills' of the same mountain range. Butler's response emphasizes the social community found among the 'foothills' of Romanticism: 'You get a great deal of interesting local activity around foothills, quite apart from the whole of human life actually existing at that level'; see Jennifer Wallace, 'The Sociable Revolutionary', *Times Higher Education Supplement* (15 Sept. 1995), 15, 19. Whereas McFarland scans the 'magnificent scenes' of Romantic sublimity, Butler dwells in the sociable terrain of 'arts, people, and so on' which Z firmly associated with the Hunt circle and 'Cockney' Romanticism.

[52] John Betjeman, 'Before MCMXIV', in *Summoned by Bells* (London, 1960), 5.
[53] Philip Larkin, 'Toads Revisited', in *The Whitsun Weddings* (London, 1964), 18.

Sunday papers [Hunt, Thelwall], and so forth.' Furthermore, the Cockneys had a numerous following: 'They have all abundance of admirers in the same low order of society to which they originally belong.' Hunt's popularity (a measure of his 'vulgarity') could be manipulated to make him look ridiculous, the 'Cockney Homer' who 'cannot be *at home* at Hampstead, without having his Johnny Keatses and his Corny Webbs to cram sonnets into his waistcoat pockets'.[54] But, as always in the Cockney School essays, the mockery overlay genuine unease. The fact that 'the most fierce democrat and demagogue of the day' was the focus of admiring attention was alarming. Worse still, the adulterous and incestuous *Story of Rimini* had been read (and reviewed) with what Z regarded as a regrettably 'dangerous sympathy'.[55] Hunt's suburban *sociality*, a focus of 'sensativity', 'unsophisticated impulses', 'cheerful tendencies', 'nature's goodness', was also the nurturing medium for a sect

[54] 'On the Cockney School of Poetry: No V', *Blackwood's Edinburgh Magazine* (Apr. 1819), 97. Among the papers of William Blackwood is a letter from Cornelius ('Corny') Webb, dated Sept. 1817, enclosing for publication three sonnets and a 'printed *Epistle to a Friend*'. The sonnets survive in manuscript, and were also published in Webb's *Sonnets, Amatory, Incidental, and Descriptive; with Other Poems* (London, 1820). But the *Epistle*—probably an exercise in Cockney sociality—has disappeared. It seems at least possible that this poem was passed to Z, and that it was the source for his epigraph to the 'Cockney School' essays, the first of which appeared a month after Webb sent his letter, in Oct. 1817:

> Our talk shall be (a theme we never tire on)
> Of Chaucer, Spenser, Shakespeare, Milton, Byron,
> (Our England's Dante)—Wordsworth—HUNT, and KEATS,
> The Muses' son of promise; and of what feats
> He yet may do.
>
> CORNELIUS WEBB.

NLS MS 4002, quoted by permission of the Trustees of the National Library of Scotland. See also *Blackwood's Edinburgh Magazine* (Oct. 1817), 38.

[55] 'Cockney School III', 453. *The Story of Rimini* had been well received by a range of journals: the *British Lady's Magazine* (Apr. 1816), 239, described the poem as 'a picture of guilty tenderness and penitential woe' and applauded 'the execution of a master'. The *Eclectic Review* (Apr. 1816), 383, suggested that the 'tenderness, the exquisite pathos . . . cannot fail, we think, to touch the heart of the most careless reader' and, in the same spirit, the *Literary Panorama* (Sept. 1816), 936, found the poem 'so lively, graceful, and applicable, that the reader shares with [Hunt] in the delight of his composition'. More alert to the seductive charm of Hunt's style, and the perils of reading his poem with a 'dangerous sympathy', was the *Monthly Review* (June 1816), 138: 'Though the scene, in which [Paulo and Francesca's] unhallowed intimacy is related, is as delicately touched as such subjects are capable of being touched, yet enough occurs to alarm the vigilant and perhaps fastidious supervisors of female reading in the present nice era.'

which was perceived by hostile eyes as vulgar, immoral, and seditious.

As we have seen, Keats's participation in this coterie was explicitly signalled by references to Hunt in *Poems*. Less obvious, perhaps, is Keats's own poetry of sociality in his epistles and sonnets to relatives and friends in which he dwells on mutual ideals and aims. As David Pirie has recently observed,[56] Keats's poetry of nature invokes a conventionally romantic 'loneliness, and wandering' (*I stood tip-toe*, 121), although nature is experienced as a 'haunted solitude':

> at *our* feet, the voice of crystal bubbles
> Charms *us* at once away from all *our* troubles:
> So that *we* feel uplifted from the world . . .
>   (137–9; my emphases)

The *Edinburgh Magazine* noted that Keats's poetry resembled Hunt's in that it was 'vivacious, smart, witty, changeful, sparkling', and that both writers 'appear as much alive to the socialities and sensual enjoyments of life, as to the contemplative beauties of nature'.[57] Keats's sonnet 'O Solitude!' anticipates a contemplative 'vigil' amid the forms of nature, but welcomes 'the highest bliss of human-kind, | When to thy haunts *two kindred spirits* flee' (13–14, my emphasis). Keats's three verse epistles 'To George Felton Mathew', 'To My Brother George', and 'To Charles Cowden Clarke' are affectionate fraternal tributes to 'a brotherhood in song' ('To George Felton Mathew', 2), which also celebrate an ideological kinship in the mutual admiration of patriotic heroes:

> We next could tell
> Of those who in the cause of freedom fell;
> Of our own Alfred, of Helvetian Tell;
> Of him whose name to ev'ry heart's a solace,
> High-minded and unbending William Wallace.
> While to the rugged north our musing turns
> We well might drop a tear for him, and Burns.
>   ('To George Felton Mathew', 65–71)

---

[56] 'Keats', 352.

[57] *Edinburgh Magazine, and Literary Miscellany* (Oct. 1817), in *KCH* 72. Compare the Cockney sociality of John Hamilton Reynolds's *The Eden of Imagination* (London, 1814) cited as the epigraph to this section. Reynolds's poem, and its companion piece, *A Recollection*, had a marked influence on *I stood tip-toe*.

Compare these lines from 'To Charles Cowden Clarke':

> The might of Alfred, and the shaft of Tell;
> The hand of Brutus, that so grandly fell
> Upon a tyrant's head. (70–2)

In both of these passages heartfelt libertarian sympathies, which Keats had absorbed during his days at Enfield School, now contributed to a poetry of 'social feeling' (or 'soft humanity') which had a markedly controversial relevance when published in *Poems* on 3 March 1817. To appreciate this aspect of Keats's first book, the context of its publication needs to be reconstructed in some detail.

In his review of *Poems* for the *Examiner*, Hunt's emphasis on the 'strong evidences of warm and social feelings'[58] typical of Keats's verse epistles was certainly intended to contrast with the betrayal of social confidence emphasized in a series of recent *Examiner* leaders on 'Informers':

[The Informer] presses the husband's hand, and thinks during the pressure how he shall get it manacled. He compliments the wife on her love for the husband, and thinks how he shall tear them asunder. He takes the little children on his knee, chucks them under the chin, dandles, and kisses them, and thinks how he shall ruin them and their parents.[59]

Given current fears about the activities of government spies and informers, Keats's expressions such as 'social thought', 'friendliness unquell'd', 'fraternal souls', and '[t]he social smile'[60] might be interpreted as guarantees of security against the 'jackals of despotism' (Hunt's phrase[61]) hired by a corrupt and oppressive establishment. A comparable, polemical thrust in Keats's poetry of social feeling emerged in his developing idea of the poet's calling. In his epistle 'To My Brother George' a dying poet looks forward to 'far posterity's award':

> 'What though I leave this dull, and earthly mould,
> Yet shall my spirit lofty converse hold

---

[58] *Examiner* (13 July 1817), 443, rpt. in *KCH* 61.

[59] 'Informers', *Examiner* (6 July 1817), 418. The second section of Hunt's review of Keats's *Poems* also appeared in this issue, and was concluded in the issue for 13 July; see preceding note.

[60] 'To My Brother George' (sonnet), 13; 'To a Friend who Sent me some Roses', 14; 'To My Brothers', 4; 'Addressed to the Same', 6.

[61] 'Informers', 417.

> With after times.—The patriot shall feel
> My stern alarum, and unsheath his steel;
> Or, in the senate thunder out my numbers
> To startle princes from their easy slumbers.' (71–6)

No doubt this shows Keats assuming a melodramatic pose to impress his brother George, who had been employed in the unglamorous surroundings of Richard Abbey's counting house. But there is an aspect of Keats's undaunted personality genuinely represented here, agreeable with his later assertion that he would be numbered 'among the English Poets after [his] death' (see *Letters*, i. 394). In all of these poems, sociality, friendship, and community are valued as a forum for 'green' sympathies, more or less explicitly expressed.[62] The reviews of Coleridge's poetry in the 1790s, and Z's attacks on Hunt's *Story of Rimini* and *Foliage*, showed how poetry of retirement and the natural world which may seem bland and uncontroversial to modern readers was perceived as immoral, seditious, and traitorous by some of its first readers. One reviewer, by no means ill disposed to Keats, associated the 'changeful', sociable features of his 'poetical philosophy' with 'misnamed humanity', much as Coleridge's 'tender and compassionate anxiety for the welfare of mankind' was formerly understood to endorse French terrorism. It was for similar reasons that another well-intentioned critic, Josiah Conder, argued that disappointed ambition might sour Keats, leading him to seek 'the plaudits of some worthless coterie, whose friendship consists in mutual flattery' or, same thing, 'community in crime . . . or in the malignity of *patriotism*'.[63] In the passage from 'To My Brother George' quoted above, 'lofty converse' and 'stern alarum' are perhaps closer to the austere republican spirit of Cowden Clarke's commonplace book than to the more amenable sociality of Hunt's poetry. Once again, this indicates the extent to which Enfield and the Clarkes had contributed to Keats's poetic identity in the period

---

[62] A notice of *Endymion* in the *Chester Guardian* remarked that Croker in the *Quarterly Review* had 'intended to put down the young aspirant, because, forsooth, his politics and friendships are not agreeable to the managers of that liberal vehicle'. See *Examiner* (1 Nov. 1818), 696.

[63] See *KCH* 69–70.

leading up to his meeting with Hunt. And as we shall see in the next chapter this tougher, more independent streak in Keats's poetic personality would eventually be a factor in his growing dissatisfaction with Hunt early in 1818.

CHAPTER FIVE

Songs from the Woods; or, Outlaw Lyrics

Hard by there is a secret greenwood nook . . .
'Twill soon be reached if we use willing speed;
Then let us hence . . .
> (Cornelius Webb)[1]

the real lords of the woods were pigs
> (Simon Schama)[2]

'Vert and venison! vert and venison!' exclaimed the baron.
'Treason and flat rebellion.'
> (Thomas Love Peacock, *Maid Marian*)[3]

The Chaucerian Key

In the preceding chapter we saw how verdant imagery in Keats's and Hunt's poems was associated with a complex of oppositional values represented in public life by the 'moving grove' of reformers in Henry Hunt's procession. The 'Places of nestling green, for poets made' in Canto III of Hunt's *Story of Rimini* were the resorts of natural feeling, justice, and imaginative life excoriated in *Blackwood's Magazine*; the 'leafy rise, . . . and sloping green' of the Hampstead landscape signalled 'health and sociality', and a community dedicated to the liberal politics of the *Descent of Liberty* and the *Examiner*. Some years later, Horace Smith's sonnet 'On a Green-House', published in his collection

---

[1] 'Sonnet 1', in Webb's letter to William Blackwood, Sep. 1820; NLS, MS 4002, quoted by permission of the Trustees of the National Library of Scotland. The sonnet was published in Webb's *Sonnets, Amatory, Incidental, and Descriptive; with Other Poems.*

[2] See 'The Liberties of the Greenwood', in Simon Schama, *Landscape and Memory* (London, 1995), 143.

[3] (London, 1822), 54.

Amarynthus, the Nympholept, made explicit reference to the politics of greenery:

> Here, from earth's dædal heights and dingles lowly,
>   The representatives of Nature meet;
> Not like a congress, or Alliance Holy,
>   Of kings, to rivet chains, but with their sweet
>   Blossomy mouths to preach the love complete,
> That with pearl'd misletoe, and beaded holly,
>   Cloth'd them in green unchangeable, to greet
> Winter with smiles, and banish melancholy.[4]

The vegetable eroticism of Smith's sonnet probably owed much to Erasmus Darwin's *Loves of the Plants,* and the democratic convention of these 'representatives of Nature' was an elaboration of 'unchangeable' / 'evergreen' natural rights theory which dated from eighteenth-century writings by Rousseau, Paine, and Wollstonecraft. Both of these themes—the erotic and the political—are present in the title poem of Smith's collection, the lyrical drama *Amarynthus, the Nympholept,* which was, I have already indicated, patterned on Keats's *Endymion.* Smith's poem is a quest for and celebration of the liberating power of human love, represented in the union of Amarynthus and the wood-nymph Dryope (like Endymion and the Indian Maid/Diana). At its conclusion the lovers Amarynthus and Dryope retreat into the primeval forest's 'wide and vast I Magnificence',

>   To stray
> Through colonnades of Doric trunks whose high
> O'er-arching boughs form temples dedicate
> To Pan. (III. v)[5]

As with Keats's treatment of the festival of Pan in the first book of *Endymion,* in Smith's drama Pan is summoned in terms which spoke directly to modern political concerns:

>   O joy above
> All joys, to feel that the benignant Pan,
> Who still renews these blessings, ne'er forsakes
> The world he made, nor lessens in his love.
>   . . . Let us but strive
> To love our fellow-men as Heaven loves us,

---

[4] Horace Smith, *Amarynthus, the Nympholept,* 212.
[5] *Amarynthus, the Nympholept,* 157.

> (Which is true piety,) and earth will seem
> Itself a heaven. (III. v)

Amarynthus, the Nympholept brings together themes which had also informed the 'Hymn to Pan' in *Endymion*—community; liberty; the universal, natural franchise of 'benignant Pan'. But Smith associates these ideals more particularly with a woodland of 'Older, and older, and still older trees'—the dim refuge of mythical beings which, like the forest scene at the opening of *Hyperion*,[6] 'the last | Of the Gods and Titans [had] made their glorious stage' (III. v). In so doing *Amarynthus, the Nympholept* represents a conjunction between the cult of Pan, which I discussed in Chapter 2, and the libertarian and mythic associations of the old English greenwood which also formed a significant theme in some of Keats's poems.[7]

In late February 1817 Keats wrote his sonnet 'This pleasant tale is like a little copse' in Charles Cowden Clarke's copy of Chaucer's *Poetical Works*, after the end of *The Floure and the Leafe*:

> This pleasant Tale is like a little Copse:
> The honied Lines do freshly interlace,
> To keep the Reader in so sweet a place,
> So that he here and there full-hearted stops;
> And oftentimes he feels the dewy drops

---

[6] One of the 'recollections of . . . ancient glory' voiced by an aged tree in Smith's drama evidently invokes Keats's fragmentary epic:

> 'beneath my shade
> Did hoary-headed Saturn sit and fold
> His hands in lonely thought. Hyperion,
> Far off, and yet beneath my boughs, hath laid
> His giant symmetry to sleep; and one
> Of the Titans, mightier still, Porphyrion,
> Tired of the chace, supported once his vast
> Huge-muscled back against my bending trunk.
> Sometimes I dream of elemental forms
> More ancient still, but dim, for they have past,
> Past all away, torn from me in the storms
> Of ages, that have left me bare, and shrunk
> Into a hollow nothing.'
> (*Amarynthus, the Nympholept*, 160)

[7] For recent discussion of 'the lore of the free greenwood', which mentions Keats in connection with the survival of a 'mythic memory of greenwood freedom . . . into the nineteenth century', see 'The Liberties of the Greenwood', in *Landscape and Memory*, 135–84, and Hill, 'Robin Hood' in *Liberty against the Law*, 81–2.

Come cool and suddenly against his face,
And by the wand'ring Melody may trace
Which way the tender-legged Linnet hops.

O what a power has white Simplicity!
What mighty power has this gentle story!
I, that do ever feel athirst for glory,
Could at this moment be content to lie
Meekly upon the grass, as those whose sobbings
Were heard of none beside the mournful Robins.[8]

Keats's sonnet—'a light thing', as Walter Jackson Bate described it[9]—likens the interlacing of rhyme royal stanzas in *The Floure and the Leafe* (then attributed to Chaucer[10]) to the cool, refreshing seclusion of a 'little copse'. The 'power of white Simplicity' refers to the emblematic coding of the encounter between maidens and knights in *The Floure and the Leafe*, in which white apparel is associated with chastity, and green with the 'noble' laurel's 'leaves aye lasting'. The maidens in white and the worthy knights are 'servaunts everichone | Unto the Leafe' (denoting evergreen virtue) unlike those who are devotees of the flower (emblem of ephemeral, worldly pleasures).[11] *The Floure and the Leafe* has delicacy and charm to which Keats's sonnet responds; but what was the 'mighty power' in 'this gentle story', subduing ambition to 'content' and 'meekness' like the ballad 'Two Children in the Wood'? Joseph Addison had written of this ballad as 'moving . . . natural . . . [and] tender', while 'the Circumstance of the *Robin-red-breast*' he described as 'a little

---

[8] Quoted from *Examiner* (16 Mar. 1817), 173. Keats had apparently written the sonnet during Cowden Clarke's visit to his lodgings at the Poultry, where Keats lived while a medical student at Guy's. Clarke recalled that he had 'called upon [Keats] and finding his young friend engaged, took possession of a sofa, and commenced reading, from his then pocket companion, Chaucer's "Flower and the Leaf". The fatigue of a long walk, however, prevailed over the fascination of the verses, and he fell asleep. Upon awaking, the book was still at his side; but the reader may conceive the author's delight, upon finding the . . . elegant sonnet written in his book at the close of the poem.' See Charles Cowden Clarke, *The Riches of Chaucer* (2 vols., London, 1835), i. 52–3.

[9] Bate, *John Keats*, 144.

[10] See for example Thomas Warton's attribution of the poem to Chaucer in his influential *History of English Poetry, from the Close of the Eleventh to the Commencement of the Eighteenth Century* (3 vols., London, 1774–81), i. 465–7.

[11] Quoted from the text of *The Floure and the Leafe* in *The Works of the English Poets from Chaucer to Cowper* (21 vols., London, 1810), i. 394–9.

Poetical Ornament' showing 'the Genius of the Author amidst all his Simplicity'.[12] *The Floure and the Leafe* was also a tender, decorative, even a moving poem, although another aspect of its 'mighty power' is evident, I think, from the wider circumstances of composition and publication of Keats's sonnet.

On 27 February 1817, possibly the day on which Keats wrote 'This pleasant tale', John Hamilton Reynolds composed his 'Sonnet to Keats—on Reading his Sonnet Written in Chaucer'. In this conversation, Reynolds adopts images from Keats's sonnet in fashioning a decorous compliment for his friend:

> Thy thoughts, dear Keats, are like fresh gathered leaves,
>   Or white flowers pluck'd from some sweet lily bed;
>   They set the heart a-breathing, and they shed
> The glow of meadows, mornings, and spring eves,
> Over the excited soul. Thy genius weaves
>   Songs, that shall make the age be nature-led
>   And win that coronal for thy young head
> Which Time's strange hand of freshness ne'er bereaves.
>
> Go on! and keep thee to thine own green way,
>   Singing in that same key which Chaucer sung:
> Be thou companion of the Summer day,
>   Roaming the fields and olden woods among:—
> So shall thy Muse be ever in her May,
>   And thy luxuriant Spirit ever young.[13]

Reynolds figures Keats's 'thoughts' and 'genius' by adopting the pastoral imagery of *The Floure and the Leafe* and Wordsworth's 'Immortality' ode—and, certainly, his sonnet would be a slight thing indeed but for the glowing, exciting power it acknowledges in Keats's poetry, and its urgent exhortation: 'Go on! and keep thee to thine own green way, | Singing in that same key which Chaucer sung.' Reynolds was not using a private code in his dialogue with Keats although it is perhaps difficult, now, to appreciate some of the resonances of language and imagery in his poem which Keats and others in their circle of

[12] 'Broadsides and "The Two Children in the Wood"', *Spectator* (7 June 1711), quoted from *Selections from the Tatler and the Spectator*, ed. Angus Ross (Harmondsworth, 1982), 361–4.

[13] Reynolds's 'Sonnet to Keats', dated 27 Feb. 1817, appears in two of Richard Woodhouse's commonplace books of poems in the Harvard Keats Collection, MSS Keats 3.1, fo. 15ʳ and 3.2, fo. 20ʳ (the text reproduced here). Quoted by permission of The Houghton Library, Harvard University.

friends would have understood. Why, for example, should 'fresh gathered leaves', the 'green way', and 'that same key which Chaucer sung' have been associated with the heart-stirring prospect of a lyrical revolution to be effected by 'Songs, that shall make the age be nature-led'?

A little while after Keats wrote his sonnet, Hunt printed it under a praising headnote in the *Examiner* (16 March 1817), noting the poem's 'exquisite' qualities but no doubt also pleased that it chimed with his own high regard for Chaucer as 'one of the great fathers of modern poetry'. Hunt had, in fact, celebrated Chaucer in the columns of the *Examiner* just the week before Keats's poem appeared—recommending him with Shakespeare and Milton as a great poet, but also as a political hero whose example might help rouse public opposition to suspension of the Habeas Corpus Act (4 March 1817):

You are descendants of CHAUCER, one of the great fathers of modern poetry, who was a Reformer in his day, and set his face both against priestly and kingly usurpation; and yet you are told that Reform is essentially a vulgar and foolish thing, and that it is much wiser to let kings and priests settle matters without you![14]

Hunt invokes an English tradition of intellectual and imaginative hostility to despotism springing from 'the great Alfred' and Chaucer, and he directs it against the 'disgraceful usurpations of ignorance' perpetrated by 'the servants of state monopoly':

Come forward then, Fellow-countrymen, every one of you who, to say nothing of sympathy with suffering, has the least respect for common sense and understanding. Every one of you, who knows any thing not merely of politics or taxes, but of prose or poetry,—or who values even the name of books, of conversation, of the intellectual celebrity of his countrymen,—should feel ashamed at neglecting any constitutional opportunity of putting an end to this oligarchy of the shallow. There is not a youth who walks out of doors with a book, not a single scholar who has got beyond his syntax, not a reader of newspapers or reviews, not an individual, young or old, who loves to go to the theatre and hear SHAKESPEARE ... that ought not to blush at seeing a nation, renowned for every species of literature and greatness, governed

[14] 'To the English People: Letter II', *Examiner* (9 Mar. 1817), 145. For Hunt's further references to Chaucer as a politician and a 'zealous' reformer, see *Examiner* (10 May 1818), 289 and Ch. 8, p. 209 and n. below.

'gainst its will by a junto who neither feel what is English, nor can even talk it.—Reform, Reform, Reform:—Petition, *Petition*.[15]

Whereas Hunt justified some of his literary productions with references to 'political convulsions of the world',[16] the passage above shows how in the *Examiner* he invoked literature to reinforce his attack on the government. Seven days later Hunt introduced the sonnet 'from the pen of the young poet (KEATS)', adding that Keats 'may already lay true claim to that title'. In locating a 'mighty power' in Chaucer 'at this moment', Keats's sonnet as published in the *Examiner* affirmed his Chaucerian lineage as a 'young poet', and, by implication, his cultivated support for the English liberties Hunt was championing elsewhere in the paper. More particularly, Keats's sonnet associated poetry and liberty with a 'sweet place' of woodland; the 'little copse' of English language and landscape in *The Floure and the Leafe*, and the simplicity of the 'Two Babes in the Wood'—an 'old Ballad' as Addison had described it, 'one of the Darling Songs of the Common People, and . . . the Delight of most *Englishmen* in some Part of their Age'.[17]

When published in the *Examiner*, 'This pleasant tale' was nothing less than an eloquent contribution to current debate about reform and renewal of the English constitution—a subtle, lyrical 'petition' for the changes Hunt sought to bring about. If one now turns back to the less public sonnet conversation between Reynolds and Keats, verbal and emblematic details such as the 'little copse', 'fresh gathered leaves', and the 'green way' of poetry make up a woodland chorus to the overtly political campaign carried on in the *Examiner*. As we shall see, early in 1818 the greenwood emblem would provide a comparable focus for Keats's imagining of the traditional liberties of old England as contrasted with the diminished freedoms of the present.

Through the Tangled Mazes of the Forest

Hunt's collection of poems *Foliage; or Poems Original and Translated* was published early in 1818, probably sometime between

[15] 'To the English People: Letter II', 145–6.
[16] See for example *Foliage*, 10.
[17] 'Broadsides and "The Two Children in the Wood"', 362.

4 February and 10 March.[18] At this period Keats was still a frequent visitor to Hunt's home in the Vale of Health; he had access to the poems Hunt was preparing for his collection, and no doubt discussed the book's purpose, 'to cultivate a love of nature out of doors, and sociality within', before its public appearance.[19] *Foliage* was divided into two sections; first, 'Greenwoods, or Original Poems', followed by translations from classical poetry in a section headed 'Evergreens; or Translations from Poets of Antiquity'. This design recalled Ben Jonson's publication of his poems under the titles 'The Forest' (1616) and 'Under-woods' (1640), a link reinforced by one epigraph to 'Greenwoods' drawn from Jonson's Sherwood pastoral *The Sad Shepherd; or, A Tale of Robin Hood*:

> I doe not know what their sharpe sight may see
> Of late, but I should thinke it mighte be,
> As 'twas, a happy age, when on the plaines
> The woodmen met the damsells.[20]

In Jonson's play, this speech expresses Robin Hood's celebration of greenwood life against the 'the sowrer sort | Of Shepherds . . . [who] . . . disclaime in all such sport' as degenerate '*Pagan* pastimes' (I. iv. 18–19, 36). The political meaning of Hunt's epigraph is evident from his discussion of *The Sad Shepherd* in the *Examiner*, where he observed that the play was 'singularly applicable to the present' in that it showed 'charitable times [that] had *no mistrust*' (I. iv. 55) as well as 'the whole history of the loss of our rural pleasures'.[21] The Sherwood pastoral represented the values of a 'happy age' which Hunt sought to revive in *The Story of Rimini, Foliage*, and in his four 'Songs of Robin Hood' published in the *Indicator*, Nov. 1820.[22] In

---

[18] See John Barnard, 'Keats, Reynolds and the "Old Poets"', *Proceedings of the British Academy*, 75 (Oxford, 1990), 196–7 and n. Hunt's sonnet 'The Nile', written 4 Feb. 1818 in competition with Keats and Shelley, was included in *Foliage*, p. cxxxiv.

[19] See *Foliage*, 8; for Keats's familiarity with Hunt's *The Nymphs* before publication in *Foliage*, see *Letters*, i. 126–7 and n., 138–9 and nn., 143 n., 224 and n.

[20] Quoted from *Foliage*. Cf. *The Sad Shepherd*, I. iv. 43, in *Ben Jonson*, ed. C. H. Herford and P. and E. M. Simpson (11 vols., Oxford, 1925–52), vii. 16. Hunt's epigraphs also quote Lorenzo de' Medici and Lodovico Paterno.

[21] 'Old May-Day', 290–1; the emphasis on '*no mistrust*' was Hunt's.

[22] See *Indicator* (15 and 20 Nov. 1820). Hunt's four poems, 'Robin Hood, a Child', 'Robin Hood's Flight', 'Robin Hood: An Outlaw', and 'How Robin and his Outlaws Lived in the Woods', are sentimental treatments of what Hunt termed 'this good old English subject'.

contrast, Keats's two poems dating from February 1818, 'Robin Hood: To a Friend' and 'Lines on the Mermaid Tavern', present Robin Hood's life as a vanished idyll, as distant from the moderns as the achievements of poets such as Jonson and Shakespeare. In other words, and as we shall see in a moment, early in 1818 the figure of Robin Hood focused growing tensions in Keats's relationship to Hunt and the circle of acquaintances associated with him.

Alongside the passage from *The Sad Shepherd*, two Shakespearian epigraphs evoke the greenwood values of Hunt's original poems in *Foliage*. One of these epigraphs—Lewis's melancholy observation that 'Bitter shame hath spoiled the sweet world's taste' (*King John* III. iii. 110)—is moderated by the cheerful invitation of Amiens's song in *As You Like It* (II. v. 1–7):

> Under the greenwood tree
> Who loves to lie with me,
> And tune his merry note
> Unto the sweet bird's throat,
> Come hither, come hither, come hither.
> Here he shall see
> No enemy.

Certainly, the Forest of Arden forms a romantic refuge for Duke Senior, who lives there as an exile, 'and a many merry men with him; and there they live like the old Robin Hood of England. They say many young gentlemen flock to him every day, and fleet the time carelessly as they did in the golden world' (I. i. 114–19). The 'careless' life in the Forest of Arden may indeed recall the 'golden world' of antiquity—a distant past that is also invoked, as we have seen, by Robin Hood in *The Sad Shepherd*. This was the 'adventurous and romantic' life of 'good living and good fellowship' which Hazlitt (in a lecture delivered at the Surrey Institution, February 1818) likewise associated with Robin Hood:

The archers green glimmer under the waving branches; the print on the grass remains where they have just finished their noon-tide meal under the green-wood tree; and the echo of their bugle-horn and twanging bows resounds through the tangled mazes of the forest, as the tall slim deer glances startled by.[23]

---

[23] Hazlitt, 'On Burns, and the Old English Ballads', Howe, v. 143.

But the idyllic greenwood, so frequently associated with 'truth, love, freedom . . . justice',[24] also disclosed a more sombre aspect in that the plot of *The Sad Shepherd* turned upon jealousy and cruel deception. Similarly, the Forest of Arden was the retreat of individuals forced into 'banishment' and 'voluntary exile' from Duke Frederick's 'new court' (i. i. 98–104), signalling the unhappy effects of oppression in a way that would have spoken directly to Hunt and his circle in 1817–18.

Shakespeare's allusion in *As You Like It* to 'the old Robin Hood of England' serves as a reminder that the greenwood was also the typical scene of *outlaw life*—the habitation of those who were 'put outside the law' and deprived of its 'benefit and protection' (*OED*). In Godwin's *Caleb Williams*, for instance, Caleb falls into company with thieves in a less 'romantic' greenwood, where he is taken to a ruin in 'the most uncouth and unfrequented part of the forest'.[25] Robin Hood might also be found in this vagrant company, according to Bishop Percy whose *Reliques of Ancient English Poetry* had traced this 'celebrated outlaw' to the oppressive years following the Norman Conquest:

The severity of those tyrannical forest-laws, that were introduced by our Norman kings, and the great temptation of breaking them by such as lived near the royal forests, at a time when the yeomanry of this kingdom were every where trained up to the long-bow, and excelled all other nations in the art of shooting, must constantly have occasioned great numbers of outlaws, and especially of such as were the best marksmen. These naturally fled to the woods for shelter, and forming into troops, endeavoured by their numbers to protect themselves from the dreadful penalties of their delinquency. The ancient punishment for killing the king's deer, was loss of eyes and castration: a punishment far worse than death. This will easily account for the troops of banditti, which formerly lurked in the royal forests, and from their superior skill in archery and knowledge of all the recesses of those unfrequented solitudes, found it no difficult matter to resist or elude the civil power.

Among these, none was ever more famous than [Robin Hood] . . .[26]

[24] See Schama, *Landscape and Memory*, 140.
[25] See *The Collected Novels and Memoirs of William Godwin*, ed. Mark Philp *et al.* (8 vols., London, 1992), iii. 190–1.
[26] *Reliques of Ancient English Poetry* (3rd edn., 3 vols., London, 1775), i. 81–2.

This passage from Percy's *Reliques* represented a traditional aspect of the 'matter of Robin Hood', the outlaw in conflict with 'tyrannical laws' and 'civil power'. From the first, Robin Hood had been associated with the just redress of social wrongs— especially those perpetrated by the Church—as for example in the very early ballad *A Lytell Geste of Robyn Hode*:

> Ther of no fors, sayd Robyn,
>   We shall do well ynough;
> But loke ye do no housbonde harm
>   That tylleth with his plough;
>
> No more ye shall no good yemàn,
>   That walketh by grene wode shawe,
> Ne no knyght ne no squyer,
>   That wolde be a good felawe.
>
> These byshoppes, and thyse archebysshoppes,
>   Ye shall them bete and bynde;
> The hye sheryfe of Notynghame,
>   Hym holde in your mynde.[27]

The ballad exemplified Percy's idea of Robin Hood's 'levelling principle of taking from the rich and giving to the poor' which 'in all ages rendered him the favourite of the common people'.[28] Drayton's *Poly-Olbion* (a source for Jonson's *Sad Shepherd*) offered a similar account of Robin's 'levelling' activities

> From wealthy Abbotts chests, and Churles abundant store,
> What often times he tooke, he shar'd amongst the poore.
>   (345–6)[29]

An identical figure of the folk-hero appeared in Thomas Love Peacock's Sherwood novel, *Maid Marian* (1822): 'your wild forester, Robin, cousin Robin; Robin Hood of Sherwood Forest, that beats and binds bishops, spreads nets for archbishops, and hunts a fat abbott as if he were a buck.'[30] But Peacock's novel

[27] Quoted from *Robin Hood: A Collection of all the Ancient Poems, Songs, and Ballads, now Extant, Relative to that Celebrated English Outlaw*, ed. Joseph Ritson (2 vols., London, 1795), i. 4–5.

[28] *Reliques*, i. 82. See Hill, 'Robin Hood', 74, for ballads about Robin as 'history from the commoners' point of view'.

[29] See 'The Sixe and Twentieth Song' in *Poly-Olbion, The Works of Michael Drayton*, ed. J. William Hebel (5 vols., Oxford, 1931–41), iv. 530. 'Churl' denotes a 'countryman, peasant, rustic, boor' (*OED* sense 4), usually in a disparaging sense, and here specifically with the sense 'One who is sordid, "hard", or stingy in money-matters; a niggard; a miser' (*OED* sense 6).

[30] Peacock, *Maid Marian*, 103–4.

also responded to a marked alteration in the significance of Robin and the 'matter of Sherwood', which accompanied the revolutions of the late eighteenth century. At this time, Robin Hood the 'good yemàn's' friend had been transformed into a revolutionary, a proto-Jacobin opposed to the social and political establishment.

In 1795 Joseph Ritson, political radical, antiquarian, and vegetarian published his two-volume anthology *Robin Hood: A Collection of all the Ancient Poems, Songs, and Ballads.*[31] As has frequently been pointed out, it was Ritson's book which was principally responsible for reconstructing Robin Hood as a radical hero for the 1790s,

> a man who, in a barbarous age, and under a complicated tyranny, displayed a spirit of freedom and independence, which has endeared him to the common people, whose cause he maintained, (for all opposition to tyranny is the cause of the people) and, in spite of the malicious endeavours of pitiful monks, by whom history was consecrated to the crimes and follies of titled ruffians and sainted idiots, to suppress all record of his patriotic exertions and virtuous acts, will render his name immortal.[32]

Ritson's Robin Hood has more to do with Paine's *The Rights of Man* than with the 'grene wode shawe'; his 'patriotic exertions and virtuous acts' represented an active commitment to social amelioration that was appropriate in an age of democratic revolution.[33] But times changed and such idealistic hopes were forgotten, disowned, or ridiculed by former partisans. As Marilyn Butler has said, when Peacock revived the Jacobin Robin in *Maid Marian* his purpose was to adapt Ritson's folk-hero as an opponent of the newly restored monarchies in Europe. But the ideological divide of the 1790s was no longer so clearly cut in the sceptical atmosphere of the post-revolutionary, post-war

---

[31] For Ritson, see in particular Morton, *Shelley and the Revolution in Taste*, 26–8; Butler, *Peacock Displayed*, 143–9; Schama, *Landscape and Memory*, 182–3; and Hill, 'Robin Hood', 75.

[32] Ritson's 'Life of Robin Hood' in *Robin Hood: A Collection*, i, pp. xi–xii. For Ritson's 'innovative' and scholarly approach to Robin Hood, and his reformist principles, see Stephen Knight, *Robin Hood: A Complete Study of the English Outlaw* (Oxford, 1994), 153–8. See also J. C. Holt, *Robin Hood* (London, 1982), 184–5, and R. B. Dobson and J. Taylor, *Rymes of Robyn Hood: An Introduction to the English Outlaw* (London, 1976), 54–6.

[33] The reference to 'patriotic exertions' derives from radical discourse in the 1790s, and refers to Robin's efforts on behalf of 'the common people' as well as to the 'innovative national concept' suggested by Knight, *Robin Hood*, 156.

years, a circumstance which Butler argues proved difficult for a temperamentally ironic writer such as Peacock.[34] In fact, much of Peacock's wit in *Maid Marian* is at the expense of Robin and his followers, who constitute themselves as 'a high court of foresters' in Sherwood. Their quasi-republican 'congress or court of equity' resolves (like the revolutionary government at Paris in 1792) to 'war against the whole world' to restore 'the . . . natural balance of power, by taking from all who have too much as much of the said too much as we can lay our hands on; and giving to those who have nothing such a portion thereof as may seem to us expedient to part with'.[35] Part of Peacock's joke is directed at the pompous, legalistic jargon adopted by self-appointed committees, then as now. But it also had a topical relevance which depended as much as anything on the mood of England in 1818; in the passage above this is registered most clearly in the way that the 'natural balance of power' is overtaken in the same sentence by the less exalted claims of expedience. The Sherwood congress delightfully parodies the proceedings in radical associations such as the London Corresponding Society, which flourished during the 1790s and gained inspiration from *The Rights of Man* and the republican Convention at Paris. Having passed its equalitarian resolutions, the foresters' congress winds up with wonderful impropriety in a loyal flourish: 'God save King Richard', and the proceedings are signed, again like the minutes of a reformist meeting, by 'LITTLE JOHN, Secretary'.

Peacock published *Maid Marian* in 1822 although, as a prefatory note points out, most of the book was written in autumn 1818. This is worth emphasizing, because Peacock's choice of the Sherwood theme reflects wider interest in Robin Hood that year. When Hunt was preparing *Foliage* for the press in January and February 1818, Keats wrote his two lyrics 'Robin Hood' and 'Lines on the Mermaid Tavern' in what he termed 'the Spirit of Outlawry' (*Letters*, i. 225). Both poems draw on the Sherwood pastorals mentioned already and on the more recent 'radical Robin' of the 1790s, but they do so by way of affirming that Robin, his 'merry men', and the great poets of *As You Like It* and *The Sad Shepherd* are 'gone away'. In these poems and in related

[34] Butler, *Peacock Displayed*, 148–9.   [35] See *Maid Marian*, 160–2.

discussion of them, Keats signalled his dissatisfaction with Hunt and Wordsworth, and gave voice to the growing 'spirit of freedom and independence'—of 'outlawry'—in his imaginative and political life.[36]

Maid Marian, Foliage, and Hazlitt's peroration to his lecture 'On Burns, and the Old English Ballads' all suggest that discussion of Robin Hood was current among Keats's friends early in 1818. Indeed, Hazlitt concluded his lecture by quoting in full a sonnet on Robin Hood by John Hamilton Reynolds—one of the two sonnets on this topic which Keats had received in a letter from Reynolds on 3 February 1818. The manuscript of Reynolds's letter has been lost, but his sonnets were published in John Hunt's journal the *Yellow Dwarf,* 21 February 1818 (a further pointer to radical interest in Robin Hood at this moment), and subsequently in Reynolds's collection *The Garden of Florence and Other Poems* (1821).[37] Reynolds's two sonnets, as published in the *Yellow Dwarf,* follow here:

> To a Friend: On Robin Hood.
> The trees in Sherwood Forest are old and good,—
> The grass beneath them now is dimly green;
> Are they deserted all? Is no young mien,
> With loose slung bugle, met within the wood?
> No arrow found,—foil'd of its antler'd food,—
> Struck in the oak's rude side?—Is there nought seen,
> To mark the revelries which there have been,
> In the sweet days of merry Robin Hood?
> Go there with summer, and with evening,—go
> In the soft shadows, like some wandering man,—

---

[36] For 'Robin Hood' in relation to the disintegration of the Hunt circle of friends, which included Keats, Haydon, and Reynolds, see Thomas R. Mitchell, 'Keats's "Outlawry" in "Robin Hood"', *Studies in English Literature,* 34 (1994), 753–69.

[37] In addition to their social-political interest, the anti-clericalism of the Robin Hood stories would have appealed to Keats; cf. his views on the established Church in his sonnet 'Written in Disgust of Vulgar Superstition'; at the beginning of *Endymion* III; in his letter to Benjamin Bailey, 3 Nov. 1817, *Letters,* i. 178–9; and his letter to his brothers, 14 (?) Feb. 1818 enclosing extracts from Horace Smith's satirical poem 'Nehemiah Muggs, an Exposure of the Methodists' (*Letters,* i. 227–30). Similarly, Reynold's sonnets on Robin Hood coincided with his attack on ecclesiastical corruption in the first of his 'Pulpit Oratory' essays, published in the *Yellow Dwarf: A Weekly Miscellany* (7 Feb. 1818), 46–8: 'Their principles are gorged by their interests, and their religious humility lies fawning at the feet of their worldly pride.' See also *Selected Prose of John Hamilton Reynolds,* ed. Leonidas M. Jones (Cambridge, Mass., 1966), 212.

And thou shalt far amid the Forest know
The archer-men in green, with belt and bow,
Feasting on pheasant, river-fowl, and swan,
With Robin at their head, and Marian.

          To the Same.
With coat of Lincoln green, and mantle too,
And horn of ivory mouth and buckle bright,—
And arrows wing'd with peacock-feathers light,
And trusty bow, well gathered of the yew,—
Stands Robin Hood:—and near, with eyes of blue
Shining through dusk hair, like the stars of night,
And habited in pretty forest plight,
His greenwood beauty sits, young as the dew.
Oh, gentle tressed girl! Maid Marian!
Are thine eyes bent upon the gallant game
That stray in the merry Sherwood? Thy sweet fame
Can never, never die. And thou, high man,
Would we might pledge thee with thy silver Can
Of Rhenish, in the woods of Nottingham![38]

The two sonnets are conventional sentimental exercises, 'a finely-tuned romantic imagination of the past', as Stephen Knight has described them.[39] The first affirms that the 'sweet days of merry Robin Hood' may survive in the life of the imagination, the second that Robin's and Marian's 'fame | Can never, never die'. Reynolds's nostalgia for 'merry Sherwood' is far from the explicitly radical perspective of Joseph Ritson's anthology, but the fact that the sonnets were published in the *Yellow Dwarf* emphasizes how the 'trees in Sherwood Forest' might stand for the origin and continuity of radical opposition (a cause both 'old and good') more overtly expressed elsewhere in that journal.

Keats acknowledged Reynolds's sonnets in an appropriately sylvan image: 'I thank you for your dish of Filberts', his letter begins, '—Would I could get a basket of them by way of desert every day for the sum of two pence—' (*Letters*, i. 223). In return, he enclosed 'a few Catkins' headed 'To J.H.R. In answer to his Robin Hood Sonnets': his poems 'Robin Hood: To a Friend' and 'Lines on the Mermaid Tavern':

[38] *Yellow Dwarf: A Weekly Miscellany* (21 Feb. 1818), 64.
[39] Knight, *Robin Hood*, 161.

Robin Hood: To a Friend

No! those days are gone away,
And their hours are old and gray,
And their minutes buried all
Under the down-trodden pall
Of the leaves of many years:
Many times have winter's shears,
Frozen north, and chilling east,
Sounded tempests to the feast
Of the forest's whispering fleeces,
Since men knew nor rent nor leases.

No, the bugle sounds no more,
And the twanging bow no more;
Silent is the ivory shrill
Past the heath and up the hill;
There is no mid-forest laugh,
Where lone Echo gives the half
To some wight, amaz'd to hear
Jesting, deep in forest drear.

On the fairest time of June
You may go, with sun or moon,
Or the seven stars to light you,
Or the polar ray to right you;
But you never may behold
Little John, or Robin bold;
Never one, of all the clan,
Thrumming on an empty can
Some old hunting ditty, while
He doth his green way beguile
To fair hostess Merriment,
Down beside the pasture Trent;
For he left the merry tale
Messenger for spicy ale.

Gone, the merry morris din;
Gone, the song of Gamelyn;
Gone, the tough-belted outlaw
Idling in the 'grenè shawe';
All are gone away and past!
And if Robin should be cast
Sudden from his turfed grave,
And if Marian should have
Once again her forest days,

She would weep, and he would craze:
He would swear, for all his oaks,
Fall'n beneath the dockyard strokes,
Have rotted on the briny seas;
She would weep that her wild bees
Sang not to her   strange! that honey
Can't be got without hard money!

So it is: yet let us sing,
Honour to the old bow-string!
Honour to the bugle-horn!
Honour to the woods unshorn!
Honour to the Lincoln green!
Honour to the archer keen!
Honour to tight little John,
And the horse he rode upon!
Honour to bold Robin Hood,
Sleeping in the underwood!
Honour to maid Marian,
And to all the Sherwood-clan!
Though their days have hurried by,
Let us two a burden try.

Lines on the Mermaid Tavern

Souls of poets dead and gone,
What elysium have ye known,
Happy field or mossy cavern,
Choicer than the Mermaid Tavern?
Have ye tippled drink more fine
Than mine host's Canary wine?
Or are fruits of Paradise
Sweeter than those dainty pies
Of venison? O generous food!
Drest as though bold Robin Hood
Would, with his maid Marian,
Sup and bowse from horn and can.

I have heard that on a day
Mine host's sign-board flew away,
Nobody knew whither, till
An astrologer's old quill
To a sheepskin gave the story,
Said he saw you in your glory,
Underneath a new old sign

Sipping beverage divine,
And pledging with contented smack
The Mermaid in the zodiac.

  Souls of poets dead and gone,
What elysium have ye known,
Happy field or mossy cavern,
Choicer than the Mermaid Tavern?

The first line of 'Robin Hood'—'No! those days are gone away!'—sets the tone of Keats's response to Reynolds, at once less sentimental than the idyllic vision of his friend's sonnets and markedly unillusioned about the relationship of past and present.[40] In banishing the 'merry' days of Robin Hood to the distant past, 'buried all | Under the down-trodden pall | Of the leaves of many years', Keats may well have been drawing on Hunt's essays 'Christmas and Other Old National Merry-Makings Considered, with Reference to the Nature of the Age, and to the Desireableness of their Revival' published in the *Examiner*—especially the following passage:

Merry Old England died in the country a great while ago; and the sports, the pastimes, the holidays, the Christmas greens and gambols, the archeries, the May-mornings, the May-poles, the country-dances, the masks, the harvest-homes, the new-year's-gifts, the gallantries, the golden means, the poetries, the pleasures, the leisures, the real treasures,—were all buried with her.[41]

Keats mentions that he had read Hunt's 'very proper lamentation on the obsoletion of christmas Gambols & pastimes'—but he adds, 'it was mixed up with so much egotism of that drivelling nature that pleasure is entirely lost' (to George and Tom Keats, 21, 27 (?) Dec. 1817, *Letters*, i. 191). Against this background Keats's austere treatment of the same theme signalled the growing coolness in his relationship with Hunt:

        Many times have winter's shears,
        Frozen north, and chilling east,

[40] For a related discussion of the 'agrarian idyll' as an image of the golden age of England 'against which to try . . . the disjunctions and alienation taking place in the present', see Gary Harrison, *Wordsworth's Vagrant Muse: Poetry, Poverty, and Power* (Detroit, 1994), 49.

[41] See *Examiner* (21 Dec. 1817), 801; further instalments of this essay appeared on 28 Dec. 1817, and 4 Jan. 1818.

> Sounded tempests to the feast
> Of the forest's whispering fleeces,
> Since men knew nor rent nor leases. (6–10)

In Keats's poem the greenwood pastoral has succumbed to the passage of the seasons. And with the encroachments of a capitalist economy traditional English liberties have been mortgaged to vested interests, a change that is pointedly registered in Keats's first draft of the tenth line—'Since men paid no Rent and leases'.[42] So an idyllic past—associated with the 'generous food' at the Mermaid Tavern—has been succeeded by the harsh world of commercial exploitation:

> if Robin should be cast
> Sudden from his turfed grave,
> And if Marian should have
> Once again her forest days,
> She would weep, and he would craze:
> He would swear, for all his oaks,
> Fall'n beneath the dockyard strokes,
> Have rotted on the briny seas;
> She would weep that her wild bees
> Sang not to her—strange! that honey
> Can't be got without hard money! (38–48)

Morris Dickstein rightly notes that this defines a 'state of society that is hostile to romance',[43] although I think one can be more precise in identifying the terms of that hostility. The felled oaks of Sherwood and the rotted timbers of the British fleet attest to the spoliation of the forest, the greenwood community, and the popular freedoms which had existed at a period when 'men knew nor rent nor leases' (10). Keats probably had in mind William Cowper's Whiggish censure of the 'venality' of modern

---

[42] See AP 302 and n., and Knight, *Robin Hood*, 163. Schama, *Landscape and Memory*, 154, establishes the longer historical perspective in which the Robin Hood myth flourished in proportion to exploitation of the forests: 'just at the time when Robin Hood's Sherwood was appearing in children's literature, stage drama, and poetic ballads, the greenwood idyll was disappearing into house beams, dye vats, ship timbers, and iron forges.' It is not a coincidence that in the 1990s widespread concern about the degradation of the English countryside (for example the clearing of ancient woodland to make way for the Newbury bypass) has been accompanied by a resurgence of popular and scholarly interest in Robin Hood.

[43] Morris Dickstein, *Keats and his Poetry: A Study in Development* (Chicago, 1971), 161. See also the discussion of biographical, literary, political, and economic contexts for the poems in Mitchell, 'Keats's "Outlawry"'.

England, part of his meditation on the 'shatter'd' solitary rem-
nant of a forest in 'Yardley Oak':

> In those thriftier days
> Oaks fell not, hewn by thousands, to supply
> The bottomless demands of contest, waged
> For senatorial honours[44]

Like 'Yardley Oak', 'Robin Hood' was also a rebuff to 'Old
father Thames's' panegyric in *Windsor Forest*,

> Thy trees, fair Windsor! now shall leave their woods,
> And half thy forests rush into my floods,
> Bear Britain's thunder, and her Cross display . . . (385–7)[45]

—voicing Keats's opposition to the military, religious, and mercantile powers of imperial Britain in 1818: even the music of the
wild bees has been silenced by the demand for 'hard money!'[46]
Written in 'the Spirit of Outlawry', poetic and political, 'Robin
Hood' also invoked Reynolds's presence as an ally in the outlaw
community. On publication in 1820 it was subtitled 'To a
Friend', recalling the sociable epistles in *Poems, by John Keats*
discussed in Chapter 4. In 'Robin Hood', the 'friend' is invited
to join in celebrating the lost ideals associated with the greenwood life:

> So it is: yet let us sing,
> Honour to the old bow-string!
> Honour to the bugle-horn!
> Honour to the woods unshorn!
> Honour to the Lincoln green!
> Honour to the archer keen!
> Honour to tight little John,
> And the horse he rode upon!
> Honour to bold Robin Hood,
> Sleeping in the underwood!

[44] *The Works of William Cowper*, ed. Robert Southey (8 vols., London, 1853–4), vi.
271. For Keats's response to Cowper's poetry and politics more generally, see
Newey, 'Keats, History, and the Poets', in *K&H* 165–6.

[45] Quoted from *Pope: Poetical Works*.

[46] 'Hard' money is coin 'as opposed to paper currency' (*OED* sense 2). It may be
significant that at the period when Keats wrote 'Robin Hood', the beginning of Feb.
1818, the *Examiner* carried articles on 'the late great increase in the number of
forged Bank Notes'. See for example 'Forged Bank Notes', *Examiner* (8 Feb. 1818),
92–3.

Honour to maid Marian,
And to all the Sherwood-clan!
Though their days have hurried by
Let us two a burden try. (49–62)

In these final lines, Keats and Reynolds are united in their esteem for the 'Sherwood-clan' and reverence for 'poets dead and gone': Shakespeare, Jonson, Milton, and the originator of English poetry, Chaucer. Stephen Knight has found this 'withdrawal from political acuteness' to be 'disappointing', and he explains it in terms of Keats's 'youth and innate tendency towards idealism'—thereby reinstating the nineteenth-century Keats whose 'youthfulness' debarred him from serious engagement with 'political argument'.[47] In fact the 'elision' of politics was not quite so thoroughgoing as Knight believes, for issues touched upon in Keats's poems were resumed in Reynolds's response and in Keats's later correspondence with his friend.[48]

As in the earlier 'Sonnet to Keats—on Reading his Sonnet Written in Chaucer', Reynolds was attuned to the lyrical-political voice of Keats's poems. He took up the 'burden' in a third Robin Hood sonnet which was also published in the *Yellow Dwarf*, 21 February 1818:

To E——, with the Foregoing Sonnets.
Robin the outlaw! Is there not a mass
Of freedom in the name? It tells the story
Of clenched oaks, with branches bow'd and hoary,
Leaning in aged beauty o'er the grass:—
Of dazed smile on cheek of border lass,
List'ning 'gainst some old gate at his strange glory;—
And of the dappled stag, struck down and gory,
Lying with nostril wide in green morass.
It tells a tale of forest days—of times
That would have been most precious unto thee,—
Days of undying pastoral liberty!
Sweeter than music of old abbey chimes,—

---

[47] Knight, *Robin Hood*, 165.
[48] Mitchell, 'Keats's "Outlawry"', 766–7, argues persuasively for the political and personal meanings of Keats's decision to include 'Robin Hood' in the 1820 collection: the poem voiced 'a condemnation of . . . the world of "hard cash" and a defiant determination to create a poetry that would resist that world'. For Mitchell, 'Robin Hood' announces themes which are developed by other poems in the 1820 volume.

Sweet as the virtue of Shakesperian rhymes,—
Days, shadowy with the magic greenwood tree![49]

Reynolds echoes 'forest days' from 'Robin Hood' (line 41) and makes explicit affirmation of the liberal sentiments that had informed Keats's poems: 'a mass | Of freedom in the name', and 'Days of undying pastoral liberty'. These are the values which constitute the 'magic' efficacy of the 'greenwood trees', and the strong social and political force of the 'greenwood' emblem for Keats, Reynolds, Hunt, and others in their circle. Indeed, the currency of Robin Hood and the greenwood in political-literary discussion in Keats's circle is further evident from his subsequent letter to Reynolds, where through recourse to the emblem and idea of the forest he seeks to resolve issues opened in their poetic dialogue.[50]

Ethereal Pigs and Airy Citadels

Those green-rob'd senators of mighty woods,
Tall oaks . . .

(*Hyperion*, I. 73–4)

After thanking Reynolds for the 'filberts' at the opening of his letter, Keats develops a fanciful speculation which the association of poems and nuts had encouraged: 'Would we were a sort of ethereal Pigs, & turn'd loose to feed upon spiritual Mast & Acorns—which would be merely being a squirrel & feed[ing] upon filberts, for what is a squirrel but an airy pig, or a filbert but a sort of archangelical acorn' (*Letters*, i. 223). As John Barnard has said, Keats inverts proverbial wisdom here ('"Pigs might fly" indeed!') opposing wishfulness to reality: 'An "airy pig" is as improbable as an archangelical acorn: if so, where does that leave the "ethereal" status of poetry?'[51] In his letter Keats moves on to compliment Reynolds on 'a throng of delightful Images' in his sonnets, praising 'The trees in Sherwood Forest' as 'the best on account of the first line, and the "arrow—

---

[49] *Yellow Dwarf: A Weekly Miscellany* (21 Feb. 1818), 64.
[50] For further details about the literary-political 'conversation' between Keats and Reynolds, see 'Keats, Reynolds and the "Old Poets"', 183–5.
[51] Ibid. 188.

foil'd of its antler'd food"' (*Letters*, i. 223). He then elaborates at some length his reservations about contemporary poets, citing in particular Wordsworth's egotism and Hunt's affectation; whereas he had formerly championed those moderns against the 'barbarism' of the French School, Keats now admits the selfish limitations of his contemporaries in comparison with the generous amplitude of the 'old Poets' of the sixteenth and seventeenth centuries (*Letters*, i. 223–5).

As we shall see, however, the issue focused in Barnard's question about poetry's 'ethereality' continued to preoccupy Keats. Does the life of the imagination have any relevance to a world 'full of Misery and Heartbreak, Pain, Sickness and oppression'? (*Letters*, i. 281). Keats returns again and again to this problem in his letters and poems, most memorably perhaps in his letter about the 'dark passages' of human life (*Letters*, i. 280–1) and in the dreamer's debate with Moneta in *The Fall of Hyperion*. In February 1818, though, Keats's reference to 'ethereal Pigs . . . turn'd loose to feed upon spiritual Mast & Acorns' transforms the greenwood (where the swine and humans alike fed on the 'mast' of nuts for free) into an ideal commonwealth with no 'rent or leases' imposed on the welfare of the spirit. He was being deliberately fanciful for Reynolds's amusement, but there was I think a serious intention here too which Keats expected his friend to notice. An 'ethereal Pig'—improbable, fantastic, outlandish—was another figure for the outlaw imagination. At the level of verbal allusion, it presented a witty riposte (reminiscent of Richard Porson's satirical *New Catechism*) to Burke's contention in the *Reflections* that in a democracy the nobility and clergy, those 'natural protectors' of 'learning', 'will be cast into the mire, and trodden down under the hoofs of a swinish multitude'.[52] Keats's letter implies the contrary: that, once liberated from an oppressive aristocratic system, the 'swinish multitude' will be transformed into 'a sort of ethereal Pigs', ascending from the 'mire' to draw sustenance from the ideal 'Mast' of the imagination.

That Keats was indeed thinking in such terms is substantiated by his next letter to Reynolds, 19 February 1818, in which he continues to meditate on the 'etherial finger-pointings' of rev-

---

[52] *Reflections*, 173.

FIG. 1. John Collett Ryland (1723–92), Baptist minister and founder of the school which Keats attended at Enfield from 1803 until 1811. Frontispiece to Ryland's *Contemplations on the Beauties of Creation* (1777–82). See Chapters 1 and 2.

FIG. 2. John Keats's school at Enfield, from the *Illustrated London News* (3 Mar. 1849), 133. The picture shows the 'fine old Mansion' which in 1849 was converted into Enfield railway station. For Keats at Enfield School, see Chapters 1 and 2.

FIG. 3. Charles Cowden Clarke (1787–1877) by an unknown artist. Clarke tutored Keats at Enfield, and later encouraged his first efforts at writing poetry. At the time when he was close to Keats, Clarke was a republican for whom Chaucer and Shakespeare (visible as busts in the painting) represented traditional English liberties as well as supreme literary achievement. See Chapter 3 for further discussion. National Portrait Gallery, reproduced with permission.

Fig. 4. James Henry Leigh Hunt (1784–1859) by Thomas Charles Wageman, dated 1815. Poet, journalist, and literary critic, Hunt published some of Keats's earliest poems in the liberal *Examiner* newspaper which he edited. National Portrait Gallery, reproduced with permission.

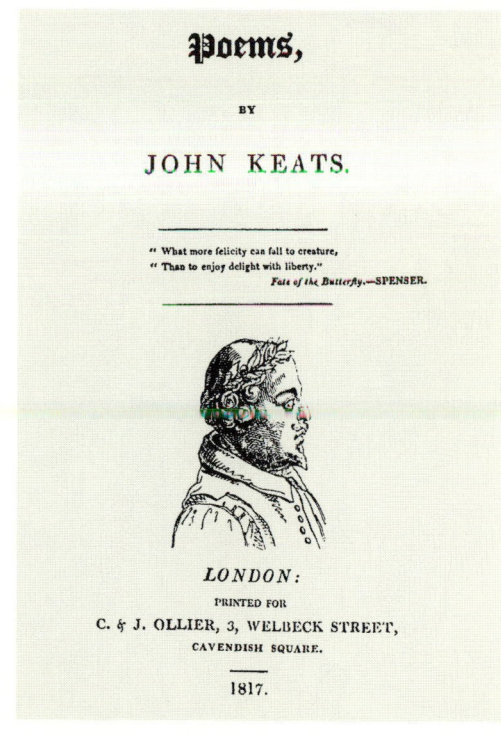

Fig. 5. Frontispiece to *Poems, by John Keats* (1817). The quotation from Spenser and the head of Shakespeare invoked two of Keats's literary heroes, and also formed a calculated announcement of his liberal politics. See Chapter 8 for further discussion.

FIG. 6. *Manchester Heroes*. A satirical cartoon of the Peterloo Massacre, attributed to George Cruikshank. See the epilogue for further discussion of this image in relation to Keats's 'To Autumn'.

erie (*Letters*, i. 231). 'Many have original Minds who do not think it—they are led away by Custom', Keats writes; then, turning to the greenwood as a starting-point for his speculation, he creates for Reynolds an elaborate image of imaginative community in which individuality and fellowship are mutually enhancing:

Now it appears to me that almost any Man may like the Spider spin from his own inwards his own airy Citadel—the points of leaves and twigs on which the Spider begins her work are few and she fills the Air with a beautiful circuiting: man should be content with as few points to tip with the fine Webb of his Soul and weave a tapestry empyrean—full of Symbols for his spiritual eye, of softness for his spiritual touch, of space for his wandering of distinctness for his Luxury—But the Minds of Mortals are so different and bent on such diverse Journeys that it may at first appear impossible for any common taste and fellowship to exist between two or three under these suppositions—It is however quite the contrary—Minds would leave each other in contrary directions, traverse each other in Numberless points, and all at last greet each other at the Journey's end— (*Letters*, i. 231–2)

Keats has moved from an 'airy Pig' to the spider and its web as a more appropriate figure to illustrate how individuals and 'common taste and fellowship' might be reconciled in an harmonious 'greeting' of minds. In seeking to define this ideal community yet more precisely he continues his speculation, echoing Ariel's song in *The Tempest*—'Where the bee sucks, there suck I' (v. i. 88);[53] he also invokes the forest as a representation of a healthy democratic society, in contrast to the solitary oak which for Cowper had been a reminder of the desolate, diminished state of England:

Man should not dispute or assert but whisper results to his neighbour, and thus by every germ of Spirit sucking the Sap from mould ethereal every human might become great, and Humanity instead of being a wide heath of Furse and Briars with here and there a remote oak or Pine, would become a grand democracy of Forest Trees. (*Letters*, i. 232)

Here, 'mould ethereal' recalls the 'spiritual Mast & Acorns' in the letter of 3 February. By a kind of negatively capable

---

[53] For discussion of Keats's sources in Shakespeare, Swift, and Pliny, see D. B. Green, 'Keats, Swift, and Pliny the Elder', *Notes & Queries* (11 Nov. 1950), 499–501.

susceptibility to such 'ethereal' sustenance, quarrelsome and egotistical humanity may be renovated until they resemble 'a grand democracy of Forest Trees'—a truly just commonwealth fittingly represented by the greenwood which had formerly sheltered Robin Hood's outlaw community. The function of passive receptivity in achieving this restoration of humankind is further elaborated in the succeeding sentences of Keats's letter. Drawing upon the traditional association of the beehive with ideal social and political organization, Keats goes on:

> It has been an old Comparison for our urging on—the Bee hive— however it seems to me that we should rather be the flower than the Bee—for it is a false notion that more is gained by receiving than giving—no the receiver and the giver are equal in their benefits—The flower I doubt not receives a fair guerdon from the Bee—its leaves blush deeper in the next spring—and who shall say between Man and Woman which is the most delighted? Now it is more noble to sit like Jove that [sic] to fly like Mercury—let us not therefore go hurrying about and collecting honey-bee like, buzzing here and there impatiently from a knowledge of what is to be arrived at: but let us open our leaves like a flower and be passive and receptive—budding patiently under the eye of Apollo and taking hints from evey noble insect that favors us with a visit—sap will be given us for Meat and dew for drink . . . (*Letters*, i. 232)

This fertile, vernal scene—'budding patiently under the eye of Apollo'—banishes the thrusting, competitive market of a venal world in which 'honey | Can't be got without hard money!' Keats's reverie had, as he said, 'led [him] into thoughts' of how the 'etherial promptings' of imagination might work for good in the social and political life of humankind. Effectively, a society in which human beings emulate the receptivity of flowers suggests what might be involved in forsaking a palpable, Wordsworthian 'knowledge of what is to be arrived at' for a Keatsian politics of negative capability—a consideration to which I shall return in the Epilogue to this book. It is here, I think, we may also find Keats's political imagination prefiguring modern biological thinking in which individuality is no longer to be identified 'with autonomy and separation', as Karl Kroeber summarizes, but with a 'feminized' commonwealth of mutual dependence and support: the spider which created

Keats's image of an ideal 'circuiting' was a 'she'.[54] For the moment, however, it is notable that 'the eye of Apollo' presides over this pastoral reverie as god of the sun, but also of poetry and medicine. My next chapter explores how Keats's medical training may have contributed to his vision of a landscape 'budding patiently'.

[54] See Kroeber, *Ecological Literary Criticism*, 7.

CHAPTER SIX

The Pharmacopolitical Poet

Then with regard to the medical profession, and the claims of its members,—the truth is, that so far from disliking or undervaluing them as individuals, our tendency happens to be quite the contrary,—at least as far as physicians are concerned. We have had the pleasure of knowing one or two most amiable ones; and we believe them in general to be liberal, agreeable, and intelligent men, their very want of acquaintance with petty prices and details tending to make them the one, the necessity of gentle and consoling manners the other, and their studies and intercourse with a variety of people the last.

(Leigh Hunt, 'Apothecaries; and Political Deductions from their Country-Growth')[1]

The Wavering Apprentice

In a letter to William Blackwood, 8 December 1820, William Maginn claimed to know little of Keats's poetry and background:

As for Keats, I know nothing of him or of his writings, except what I see in magazines or reviews, but what I find there strikes me as being supereminently absurd. The very complaint about a jest on him which appeared in your magazine proves him to be a weak, and ridiculous man. You laughed at him, it seems, because he is an apothecary, & this has struck him to the heart. Why Sir the learned professions have at all times been a fair fund of entertainment for the wits, & as I shall certainly not throw my Molière, or Le Sage, or Rabelais, or Swift, or Foote into the fire, because they laugh at the professors of medicine I shall also continue to read your volumes, though in a parody, an article professedly jocose, you have had the audacity to remind Mr Keats of his

[1] *Examiner* (7 Sept. 1817), 561.

Gallipot, glisterbag, cataplasm, bolus.

I do not pretend to be a judge of poetical feelings, but I hope I do not transgress in hinting that a good apothecary is a much more respectable man than a bad poet.[2]

Maginn was a precocious young lawyer at Dublin, who had already published satirical poems about Hunt, Hazlitt, and Keats in *Blackwood's Magazine* over the initials 'R.T.S.' and the pseudonym 'Olinthus Petre'. To disparage Keats while also placing *Blackwood's* in a company of famous satirists was a canny way to ingratiate himself with the proprietor of the journal. In referring to 'magazines or reviews', and to Keats's medical training, Maginn alluded specifically to Z's attack in the fourth 'Cockney School' essay.[3] There, Z had observed that Keats had been 'destined . . . to the career of medicine . . . he was bound apprentice some years ago to a worthy apothecary in town'. The essay concluded:

It is a better and a wiser thing to be a starved apothecary than a starved poet; so back to the shop Mr John, back to 'plasters, pills, and ointment boxes', &c. But, for Heavens sake, young Sangrado, be a little more sparing of extenuatives and soporifics in your practice than you have been in your poetry.[4]

Z knew from Benjamin Bailey that Keats 'had been brought up to the profession of medicine which he had abandoned for the pursuit of Literature', and used this information to lampoon 'the wavering apprentice' who had thrown up a 'useful profession, [which] must have rendered him a respectable, if not an eminent citizen'.[5] This was straightforward abuse, damning Keats's literary pretensions while assigning him to the lowest

[2] NLS, MS 4005, quoted by permission of the Trustees of the National Library of Scotland.

[3] Maginn's reference to the 'complaint about a jest on [Keats]' may have referred to the publisher's advertisement to *Lamia, Isabella, The Eve of St Agnes and Other Poems*, where Keats's 'discouragement' at the reception of *Endymion* was mentioned. Given Maginn's claim to 'know nothing of [Keats] or of his writings', however, it seems more likely that he was thinking of the hostile correspondence received by William Blackwood following publication of each 'Cockney School' essay. A selection from this correspondence is reproduced in the Appendix.

[4] 'Cockney School IV', 519, 524. The quack Doctor Sangrado—'the Hippocrates of Valladolid', a 'learned forerunner of the undertaker'—appears in Le Sage's novel *Gil Blas*.

[5] 'Benjamin Bailey: Notes on his Conversation with Lockhart, 8 May 1821', *KC* i. 246 (see also p. 24 and n. above) and 'Cockney School IV', 519.

category of medical practitioner—the apothecary—as his true station in society. Indeed, 'Z's ' "plasters, pills, and ointment boxes" &c.' was a mocking allusion the Apothecaries' Act of 1815, in which 'the art and mystery of apothecaries' was defined as extending to 'medicines simple or compound, wares, drugs, receipts, distilled waters, chemical oils, syrups, conserves, lohocks, electuaries, pills, powders, lozenges, oils, ointments, plaisters'.[6] In this last respect Z's attack was directed more broadly at the new professionalism of medicine, codified by the Act, and the enhanced social status which was thus acquired by medical practitioners.

Maginn's letter echoes Z's essay almost word for word, while the report that Keats had been 'struck to the heart' by criticism anticipates two well-known responses to his death in 1821: Byron's quip about Keats being 'snuffed out by an Article', and Shelley's more sympathetic claim, in the preface to *Adonais*, that Keats had succumbed to criticism because his heart was 'composed of . . . penetrable stuff'.[7] On hearing of 'poor Keats's death', Maginn commiserated with William Blackwood in a letter of 10 April 1821:

We are unlucky in our butts. It would appear very cruel if any jokes now appeared on the pharmacopolitical poet of Endymion; and indeed when I heard that the poor devil was in a consumption, I was something sorry that I annoyed him at all of late. If I were able I should write a dirge over him as a kind of amende honorable, but my muse I am afraid does not run in the mournful.[8]

His regret was as short-lived as it was disingenuous. Exactly six months later he wrote again to Blackwood:

With respect to Johnny K—it may be said flatly at once that whatever his powers might have been, they were swallowed up by affectation and an aspiring to be Leigh Hunt the second . . . that in fact his poetry as it now stands is bad—bitter bad—And bad poets have always been fair game in all ages—As to his dying of it—that is trash—not worth answering—[9]

  [6] 'The Apothecaries' Act of 1815', *Lancet*, 9 (1825–6), 6.
  [7] See *Don Juan*, XI. 480, *Lord Byron: The Complete Poetical Works*, v. 483, and *Shelley's Poetry and Prose*, ed. D. H. Reiman and S. B. Powers (New York, 1977), 391.
  [8] NLS, MS 4007, quoted by permission of the Trustees of the National Library of Scotland.
  [9] 10 Oct. 1821. NLS, MS 4007, quoted by permission of the Trustees of the National Library of Scotland.

The apothecary-turned-poet and 'aspiring to be Leigh Hunt the second' is a plausible explanation for Maginn's refashioning of Keats as 'the pharmacopolitical poet of *Endymion*'. Furthermore, and although he could not have known this, Maginn's idea of a 'pharmacopolitical poet' struck very close indeed to Keats's sense of the poet's calling as 'physician to all men' (*The Fall of Hyperion*, I. 190), while also evoking some of the distinctive qualities of Keats's verse. This chapter sets out to explain Z's and Maginn's hostile preoccupation with Keats and medicine, through recovering the social-political background to Keats's medical training and tracing the effects this had on his subsequent identity and writings as a 'poet-physician' who was imaginatively responsive to medical wisdom.[10]

Dresser to 'Billy' Lucas: A Cautionary Tale

> There was much candour in that good old Apothecary, who, passing by a country church-yard, shook his head and exclaimed, 'Ah! there lie many of my mistakes'.[11]

Keats's apprenticeship to the Edmonton physician Thomas Hammond dated from summer 1811, when he left Enfield School, until October 1815 when he began his formal training at Guy's Hospital. Cowden Clarke remembered Keats's apprenticeship as an 'arrangement [which] evidently gave him satisfaction . . . it was the most placid period of his painful life; for now, with the exception of the duty he had to perform in the surgery—by no means an onerous one—his whole leisure hours were employed in indulging his passions for reading and translating'.[12] His duties as apprentice would have given him an introduction to basic skills such as vaccination for smallpox, bleeding patients with a lancet or with leeches, dressing wounds, setting bones, pulling teeth, identifying the symptoms of illnesses, making up pills, ointments, poultices, laudanum, and other medicines.[13] Hammond gave his apprentice an excellent training, to judge by Keats's success after his enrolment as

---

[10] See Kroeber, *Ecological Literary Criticism*, 92–3.
[11] 'Apothecaries', *Examiner* (5 Oct. 1817), 635.
[12] 'Recollections of Keats', 125.
[13] See Ward, *Making of a Poet*, 23, and Donald C. Goellnicht, *The Poet-Physician: Keats and Medical Science* (Pittsburgh, 1984), 20.

a student at Guy's Hospital. Sidney Colvin offers a good brief account of his career as a medical student:

His name . . . was entered at Guy's as a six months' student (surgeon's pupil) on October 1, 1815, a month before his twentieth birthday. Four weeks later [29 October] he was appointed dresser to one of the hospital surgeons, Mr Lucas. At the close of his six months' term, March 3, 1816, he entered for a further term of twelve months. On July 25, 1816, he presented himself for examination before the Court of Apothecaries and obtained their licence to practise. He continued to attend lectures and live the regular life of a student; but early in the spring of 1817, being now of age and on the eve of publishing his first volume of verse, he determined to abandon the pursuit of medicine for that of poetry, declared his intention to his guardian, and ceased attending the hospitals without seeking or receiving the usual certificate of proficiency.[14]

This profile is well known but, as with so much else concerning Keats's biography, familiarity has dulled some of the more telling details. The swiftness with which Keats was appointed dresser, just four weeks after enrolling at Guy's, suggests how thoroughly his apprenticeship with Hammond had prepared him for a medical career. As dresser to surgeon 'Billy' Lucas, Keats assumed the considerable responsibilities and duties enumerated in the following description:

He attended to all the accidents and cases of hernia which came in during his week of office, and he dressed hosts of out-patients, drew innumerable teeth, and performed countless venesections, till two or three o'clock, as might be, till the surgery was emptied, for at that time dressers had plenty of practical surgery to learn, and were anxious to avail themselves of the opportunity. When the surgeon arrived the dresser on duty would show him, among the out-patients, any case about which he needed further help or which he thought advisable to be admitted, as likely to issue in an operation.[15]

---

[14] Colvin, *John Keats*, 27–8. Further accounts of Keats's medical training can be found in the biographies by Bate, Ward, and Gittings, and in the following more specialized items: Henry Stephens to G. F. Mathew, Mar. 1847 (*KC* ii. 206–14), the recollections of a fellow medical student; Sir William Hale-White, 'Keats as a Medical Student', *Guy's Hospital Reports*, 75 (1925), 249–62; Robert Gittings, 'John Keats, Physician and Poet', *Journal of the American Medical Association* (2 Apr. 1973), 51–5; Goellnicht, *The Poet-Physician*; Hermione de Almeida, *Romantic Medicine and John Keats* (Oxford, 1991).

[15] Charles Feltoe, *Memorials of John Flint South* (London, 1884), 25.

As one might expect, the long hours of dedicated work required of surgeons' dressers brought them a higher status among their fellow students:

The surgeon, accompanied by his dressers, each carrying their plaister-boxes, which they considered a mark of distinction, as showing their official position, visited both the male and female wards. The pupils accompanied them in shoals, if the surgeon was a favourite, and pushed and jostled, and ran and crowded round the beds, quite regardless of the patients' feelings or condition . . . the working pupils might be seen at other times in the wards, caretaking or watching, and assisting the dressers in carrying out the orders given by their surgeons.[16]

In like circumstances Keats would have attended surgeon 'Billy' Lucas on his visits to the wards. Lucas was popular with the students and (surprisingly!) with patients as well. John Flint South, who studied at Guy's at the same time as Keats, recollected Lucas as a genial man, 'neat-handed, but rash in the extreme' in wielding his knife:

A tall, ungainly, awkward man, with stooping shoulders and a shuffling walk, as deaf as a post, not overburdened with brains of any kind, but very good-natured and easy, and liked by every one. His surgical acquirements were very small, his operations generally very badly performed, and accompanied with much bungling, if not worse. He was a poor anatomist and not a very good diagnoser, which now and then led him into ugly scrapes.

As Billy's dresser Keats surely witnessed many harrowing scenes at the operating table, and when required to tidy up the damage this 'rash' surgeon had inflicted on his patients. South, again, offers us a glimpse of one such dreadful 'scrape', arising not from the crude surgical methods of the day but from Lucas's absent-mindedness:

There was a story current among the pupils, of which I have some grounds to believe the truth. Billy had to amputate the leg, but just as he was about to commence he found himself on the wrong side of the patient, and accordingly shifted his position, but forgetting the (to him) altered position of the limb, he performed his circular

---

[16] Ibid. 26–7. See also 121 for the dressers' 'dignity . . . indicated by each carrying a tin plaister box', and 125–6 for the dressers' kindliness and efficiency in treating patients.

amputation and made the covering for the bone at the wrong end, so that the bone which was to be left in the stump was left projecting and uncovered, whilst that which was removed was furnished with superfluous covering.[17]

South mentions the currency of this story at Guy's while he was a student, and it is difficult to believe that Keats did not know it as well; he would surely also have had first-hand experience of similar mishaps under Lucas's knife.

I have mentioned these disturbing anecdotes about 'Billy' Lucas in order to try to recreate the horrifying actuality of Keats's hospital training; such shocking details tell us much about the kinds of operation Keats would have witnessed and, perhaps, would have been required to undertake himself. Astley Cooper's recollection of his own apprenticeship as dresser, in a lecture Keats may well have attended, offers a glimpse of the dangers involved in a typical 'minor' operation which a dresser would have been expected to perform without anaesthetic:

When I was a dresser at these Hospitals . . . there was a case of sloughing [of gangrenous flesh] opposite to the calf of the leg; Mr Cline, my old master, on going round the wards, said to the dresser, that the projecting ends of the bone had better be removed; there were some granulations [formed during healing] between the bones, which, in sawing, the dresser did not observe, and he cut through them; a slight haemorrhage ensued, and in the same night the patient died.[18]

A fatality such as this could be attributed readily enough to the circumstances and the methods of surgery, as much as to the dresser's oversight. Understandably, though, the possibility of making such a mistake would weigh heavily upon any surgeon, and it particularly oppressed Keats. According to Charles Brown, Keats had told him that his fear of causing a serious haemorrhage by opening an artery (possibly having seen Lucas do just that) had contributed to his 'overwrought apprehension of every possible chance of doing evil in the wrong direction of the instrument'. Such were the 'conscientious motives' which, according to Brown, decided Keats 'to quit the profession, upon

[17] Charles Feltoe, 52–3.
[18] 'Lecture VII: On Granulation', *The Lectures of Sir Astley Cooper on the Principles and Practise of Surgery* (3 vols., London, 1824–7), i. 237–8.

discovering that he was unfit to perform a surgical operation'.[19]
This sanguinary aspect of Keats's medical experience (and
memories of his mother's and brother Tom's deaths) lends a
bitter poignance to Keats's self-diagnosis, again recalled by
Brown, following his first tubercular haemorrhage: 'I know the
colour of that blood;—it is arterial blood;—I cannot be de-
ceived in that colour;—that drop of blood is my death-
warrant;—I must die'. It may be objected that Brown was
embellishing this incident from the perspective of later years, so
that it conformed to the myth that 'poor Keats' had been
doomed to an early death. Yet Brown's response to this emergency was correct according to current medical practice and,
given Keats's 'conscientious motives' in abandoning the lancet,
it was also piercingly ironic: 'I ran for a surgeon; my friend was
bled . . .'[20]

After Keats's promising start to his studies at Guy's his entry
for a further term of twelve months, and his success in the
Society of Apothecaries' examination, demonstrate the high
level of knowledge and practical abilities which he brought to
his medical training. Robert Gittings has said rightly that 'if the
events of late 1816 had not, as a fellow-student remarked,
"sealed his fate" for poetry, he might well have made his mark as
physician or surgeon'.[21] That fellow student was Henry
Stephens, with whom Keats had shared lodgings in 1816. Many
years later Stephens recalled Keats's 'passion . . . for poetry' and
the 'events of late 1816' which had determined him to pursue
a career as poet:

I remember the time of his first introduction to Mr Leigh Hunt
[October 1816], who then Edited the Examiner, & I remember several
pieces of his Poetry being inserted in that Journal, at which he was
exceedingly gratified, I remember his also telling me of an introduction he had to two or three Young Poets of Promise & among them I
remember well the name of Shelley—I also remember his showing me
some time afterwards 'the Examiner' in which was an Article under the
Title of 'the Rising Poets' or 'the Young Poets' or some such Title in
which the names of several were inserted with a brief sketch of them &

---

[19] See Charles Armitage Brown, *Life of John Keats* (London, 1937), 43, and
Gittings, *John Keats*, 132–3.
[20] *Life of John Keats*, 64.   [21] 'John Keats, Physician and Poet', 51.

a Specimen of their Poetry, and the name of John Keats appeared among them, with that of Shelley.

This sealed his fate and he gave himself up more completely than before to Poetry . . . (*KC* ii. 210–22)

Stephens's memoir conveys the tension between Keats's medical studies and his poetry writing, and illustrates very well the decisive effect of his early friendship with Hunt. At the same time, it may indicate too emphatically that medicine and poetry were mutually exclusive alternatives for Keats's future career: the retrospective construction that Keats was 'fated' to become a poet has affinities with William Michael Rossetti's surmise that Keats's early death meant that he had been 'doomed to be the poet of youthfulness'.[22] There was no inevitability in either case: in March 1819, having published two volumes of poetry, Keats had been 'turning it in [his] head whether [he] should go to Edinburgh and study for a physician . . . it is not worse than writing poems, & hanging them up to be flyblown on the Reviewshambles' (*Letters*, ii. 70). In June 1819, the mid-point of his *annus mirabilis* of poetic creativity, he contemplated becoming 'Surgeon [on board] an I[n]diaman' (*Letters*, ii. 114). One year later still, just as *Lamia, Isabella, The Eve of St Agnes, and Other Poems* was about to be published, he remarked to Charles Brown: 'This shall be my last trial; not succeeding, I shall try what I can do in the Apothecary line' (*Letters*, ii. 298). His sense of resignation—'too weary of the world'—was no doubt compounded by his awareness that in adopting such a course he would comply with Z's sneering recommendation: 'back to the shop Mr John, back to "plasters, pills, and ointment boxes", &c.' But there was no sense that he was in any way 'fated' or 'doomed' to do so.[23]

As many later commentators have observed, there was a strong continuity between Keats's medical training and his poetry. Donald C. Goellnicht has traced in detail how Keats's knowledge of anatomy, chemistry, botany, and theories of 'sensation' subsequently affected his poetry, contending that the 'grander, altruistic motives' of the medical profession consti-

---

[22] William Michael Rossetti, *Life of John Keats* (London, 1887), 209.
[23] Cf. D. C. Goellnicht: 'all the circumstantial evidence . . . points to [Keats] having *chosen* medicine as a career,' 'Keats as a Student at Guy's Hospital', *Canadian Bulletin of Medical History*, 3 (1986), 67.

tuted the 'high ideal that appealed most of all to Keats . . . it was the transference of this ideal from medicine to poetry . . . that allowed him to leave the service of the former discipline for that of the latter'.[24] Again, in a more recent study of Keats and Romantic medicine, Hermione de Almeida provided documentary evidence demonstrating that the 'connection between poetry and medicine in Keats's mind . . . was thoroughgoing, obvious, traditional, and ever present in his consciousness'.[25] The thorough interweaving of his medical training and his poetry will be reappraised in Chapter 7. My principal concern in the present chapter is to suggest how the politics of medicine in the revolutionary period after 1789 contributed to Keats's sense of himself as a poet-physician or, more strictly, a 'pharmacopolitical' poet.

Meeting Astley Cooper

> A few minutes before two, Astley Cooper, who was to deliver the first lecture, came briskly though the crowd, his handsome face beaming with delight and animation . . .[26]

When Keats registered at Guy's Hospital at the beginning of October 1815, he enrolled for lecture courses given by some of the most eminent surgeons of the day. His certificate to practise as an apothecary lists his attendance at two courses on 'Anatomy and Physiology', two courses on 'Theory and Practice of Medicine', two Chemistry, and one on 'Materia Medica'.[27] By comparing the certificate with the syllabus of lectures offered at Guy's, it is possible to reconstruct in more detail the lectures Keats actually attended. At St Thomas's Hospital he took two terms' courses 'Anatomy and the Operations of Surgery', taught by Astley Cooper and Henry Cline, and 'Principles and Practice of Surgery' (the latter taught by Cooper only). In Guy's he

---

[24] Goellnicht, *The Poet-Physician*, 163. See also Michael E. Holstein, 'Keats: The Poet Healer and the Problem of Pain', *K–SJ* 36 (1987), 32–49.

[25] *Romantic Medicine and John Keats*, 18.

[26] *Memorials of John Flint South*, 32.

[27] Keats is certified as having taken these courses on the page of the Register of Apothecaries' Hall, which was his licence to practise as an apothecary. The certificate is reproduced in Henry C. Shelley, *Literary By-Paths in Old England* (London, 1909), 249. See also Gittings, *John Keats*, 82; Lowell, *John Keats*, i. 154.

attended a course on 'The Practice of Medicine', taught by William Babington and James Curry; two Chemistry courses, taught by Dr Babington, Dr Alexander Marcet, and William Allen; and 'Theory of Medicine, and Materia Medica' taught by Dr Curry and Dr Henry Cholmeley.[28]

Astley Cooper, the most distinguished surgeon of the day, was held in high esteem by the students for his abilities as a surgeon and anatomist, and also for the practicality of his lectures which were based on 'his own personal work and knowledge'. Henry Cline, 'a tall, sickly, and very plain man, marked with the small-pox, and very shy' seems to have been in Cooper's shadow: he lectured in 'a quiet monotonous tone, and very slowly'. William Babington, like Cooper, was 'a very excellent practical teacher . . . his lectures were full of experience and practical good sense', although his clothes were 'very untidy' and, apparently, he 'rejoiced in dirty hands'. James Curry, the last of Keats's teachers recalled by South, was

rather a buck, in his way; he wore a powdered sandy wavy wig, dressed in black, but always had on a very smart foppish great-coat, and showed a profusion of shirt and an enormous neckcloth; he wore a large gold watch and chain, which, immediately on seating himself at the lecture-table, he placed on one side of his desk, and played with incessantly during the whole lecture, and this at the same time gave him the opportunity of displaying a large seal ring which he wore on his little finger.

Curry was a man of 'very extensive reading and of very observant habits' but also 'fierce and uncompromising in his criticism of . . . other physicians': he 'was not liked as a man'.[29] South's character sketches have been quoted here because they are helpful in establishing the personalities with whom Keats was certainly familiar, although it is notable that his recollections omit any reference to the political environment at Guy's during the revolutionary decades. As we shall see, Jacobin politics and advanced medical science were closely associated with individuals attached to the hospital during the 1790s.

On arriving at Guy's Keats came swiftly to the attention of the

[28] Based on the careful reconstruction of lecture courses Keats is likely to have attended in Goellnicht, *The Poet-Physician*, 23–31.

[29] For Cline, Babington, and Curry see *Memorials of John Flint South*, 32–4, 58, 59–60.

charismatic and distinguished surgeon Astley Cooper, who arranged for his dresser George Cooper and his fellow lodger Frederick Tyrell (both older medical students) to take Keats into their lodgings at 28 St Thomas's Street.[30] As Robert Gittings said, something 'had marked out Keats specially for Astley Cooper',[31] although the reasons cited for this have been varied and in some cases peculiarly far-fetched. W. Jackson Bate thought, reasonably enough, that Cooper had 'sensed the youth's loneliness' in the hurly-burly of students at Guy's, although why he should have picked out Keats in particular is not explained. Esther J. Vincent was perplexed; Cooper's lectures were 'jammed with adoring students', she wrote, yet, '[o]ddly enough, Cooper took notice of little Keats (just over 5 feet) and showed him some attention'.[32] William Hale-White proposed that Cooper, 'a remarkably handsome man, universally regarded as being at the head of his profession, a great teacher, an investigator, a bold and brilliant surgeon, a true and honest friend', had been 'attracted by the poet's dark-brown brilliant eyes and golden red hair'.[33] This may have been true to Cooper's stature and sufficiently flattering about Keats's appearance, but it had nothing to do with the hospital environment in which Cooper and Keats lived and worked in 1815. Robert Gittings conjectured a Keats family link with the famous surgeon Thomas Keate, a friend and colleague of Cooper's, as 'perhaps the most likely cause'.[34] This may well have been the case although I would cite, as an obvious reason for Cooper's interest, Keats's real aptitude for medical studies.

It may have been Hammond, who had trained at Guy's, or possibly Joseph Henry Green who gave Keats an introduction to Cooper. Green (who was related to Hammond by marriage)

---

[30] Ibid. 81: 'George Cooper told me that whilst at Guy's Hospital, where he was dresser to Astley Cooper for eighteen months, he lived in St Thomas's Street . . . where John Keats, the poet, lived with him, having been placed under his charge by Astley Cooper.' See also Gittings, *John Keats*, 81–2.

[31] Gittings, *John Keats*, 81.

[32] Bate, *John Keats*, 47; Esther J. Vincent, 'A Medical Truant', *Surgery, Gynecology & Obstetrics* (Nov. 1955), 648.

[33] Hale-White, 'Keats as a Medical Student', 258. As Wolfson, 'Feminizing Keats', 338, points out, such attention to Keats's appearance 'bespeaks and perpetuates a . . . feminizing attention' which had been common in 19th-cent. accounts of Keats.

[34] Gittings, *John Keats*, 81–2, 639–40.

grew up in London close to the 'Swan and Hoop' at Moorgate, where the Keats family had lived; by 1815 he was lecturer in anatomy at the hospital, and it is likely that at this time Keats and Green had been acquainted for some years. Certainly, there were numerous connections of a personal and professional nature that allowed Keats an introduction at Guy's before he formally entered his training there, and Cooper may have remembered meeting with him. South noted as a 'remarkable gift' Cooper's 'very retentive memory of persons, and their names and circumstances connected with them, so that he immediately recognised those he had not seen for years'.[35] An earlier encounter between Cooper, Hammond, Green, and Keats would offer a plausible background for Keats's enrolment at Guy's and his rapid elevation to become a dresser after only one month at the hospital.[36]

If Cooper was impressed by Keats's medical experience and potential, he may well have noticed other qualities in him too (besides his height, the colour of his eyes and hair). As we have seen, George Felton Mathew remembered Keats at this time as belonging to 'the sceptical and republican school. An advocate for the innovations which were making progress in his time. A faultfinder with every thing established' (*KC* ii. 185–6). If my conjecture about Cooper's early meeting with Keats has any plausibility, it is also possible that Cooper was aware of Keats's religious scepticism and his republicanism. Certainly, in former years Cooper had held similar opinions, and a talented student who resembled his younger self would have drawn his interest.

Family circumstances, the dissenting culture of Enfield School, and Keats's political radicalism all make his choice of a medical career understandable. During the eighteenth century, when the universities and many professions were closed to dissenters, medicine had offered an enlightened and rewarding career unimpeded by the Test Acts:

Denied positions in the church and the law . . . Dissenters turned instead to the cultivation of the natural sciences as the means to personal

---

[35] *Memorials of John Flint South*, 56.
[36] The Hammond family 'might be described as a dynasty of local surgeons', with extensive connections at St Thomas's and Guy's Hospitals; see Phyllis G. Mann, 'John Keats: Further Notes', *K–SMB* 12 (1961), 21–7; F. N. Doubleday, 'John Keats and the Borough Hospitals', *K–SMB* 13 (1962), 12–17; Gerald Hamilton Edwards, 'John Keats and the Hammonds', *K–SMB* 17 (1966), 31–6.

and social improvement and, crucial for them, to political reform. What better pursuit then for a young Dissenter than commerce or the study and practice of medicine?[37]

The legal barriers to religious dissenters demonstrate why the 'practice of medicine' was closely involved with their political aspirations to secure a reform of the parliamentary system and this long association between dissent and medicine may help further to explain Z's ridicule of the profession. Such ambitions had reached a particular intensity during the 1790s, when progressive medical science and revolutionary politics apparently vindicated hopes of the perfectibility of humankind. This regenerative impetus, uniting radical politics with medicine, had considerable impact at Guy's Hospital and on Astley Cooper in particular. Furthermore, the revolutionary associations of medicine in the 1790s subsequently informed Keats's dangerous identity as a 'pharmacopolitical poet', a link which presents an additional reason for Z's animosity towards the physician-turned-poet and the democratic values which he represented.

Radical Medicine: Astley Cooper and John Thelwall

> The Patriot K[osciusko] having had the Sciatic Nerve divided by a pike wound was a long while before his limb recovered its sensibility.[38]

In *Recollections of Writers*, Charles Cowden Clarke wrote that while at Enfield his father had been on close friendly terms with many dissenters who were also prominent in the democratic reform movement. As we have seen in the first chapter of this book, Joseph Priestley, Gilbert Wakefield, George Dyer, and Alexander Geddes were among them. Also of relevance here is John Mason Good, the surgeon whose translation of the Book of Job had, apparently, interested John Clarke.[39] In 1783–4, Mason Good studied medicine in London, and became 'an active member of a society for the promotion of natural philosophy, as well as medical science, then existing among the

---

[37] Christopher Lawrence, *Medicine in the Making of Modern Britain, 1700–1920* (London, 1994), 17.
[38] From Keats's lecture notes, in *John Keats's Anatomical and Physiological Note Book*, ed. M. B. Forman (Oxford, 1934), 55.
[39] *Recollections*, 5.

students at Guy's Hospital'.[40] This was the Physical Society, founded in 1783 and described by a member as 'a society of literary men . . . composed of surgeons, physicians, and men of science in general' who met to hear 'a Dissertation read, on a medical, chirurgical, or philosophical Subject'.[41] The Society became a prestigious forum for debating medical and scientific issues, concerns which in the 1790s also attracted the leading political reformists of the day—Priestley, Coleridge, Thelwall, Beddoes, and others. That this was so is indicated by Mason Good's circle of 'frequent associates' in 1795, some of whom were also acquainted with Keats's schoolmaster John Clarke: 'Drs Disney, Rees, Hunter, Geddes, Messrs. Maurice, Fuzeli, Charles Butler, Gilbert Wakefield.'[42] The appearance of John Disney, Henry Fuseli, and Gilbert Wakefield in this list indicates how medical and dissenting circles overlapped at London in the 1780s and 1790s, as well as a common interest in reformist politics. A crucial figure in this respect was Keats's lecturer and patron Astley Cooper, who had started his career as a surgeon in the late 1780s, just as revolutionary ferment in London was about to reach a new pitch of excitement with the Fall of the Bastille.

Cooper had trained at Guy's Hospital and then at Edinburgh University during the mid-1780s, before returning to London where he procured a 'residence [with] the eminent Mr [Henry] Cline, one of the surgeons of St Thomas's Hospital'.[43] In 1789, aged only 21, Cooper was appointed Demonstrator in Anatomy at St Thomas's—a fact which might bear upon the swift recognition of Keats's abilities, when he became dresser at Guy's just

[40] Olinthus Gregory, *Memoirs of the Life, Writings, and Character of the Late John Mason Good, M.D.* (London, 1828), 22.

[41] See the evidence given by surgeon John Clarke at Thelwall's trial, in *The Life of John Thelwall by his Widow* (London, 1837), 441–2, and *Laws of the Physical Society Held at Guy's Hospital* (London, 1783), 4.

[42] *Memoirs of John Mason Good*, 67. John Disney (1746–1816), Unitarian minister of the Essex Street Chapel; Abraham Rees (1743–1825), independent dissenter and cyclopaedist *or* George Rees (1776–1846), medical writer, student at Guy's Hospital, and member of the Physical Society in the 1780s; John Hunter (1728–93), surgeon; Alexander Geddes (1737–1802), biblical scholar and critic; Thomas Maurice (1754–1824), oriental scholar and historian; Henry Fuseli (1741–1825), painter and writer; Charles Butler (1750–1832), legal writer; Gilbert Wakefield (1756–1801), Unitarian, classical scholar, reformist. See *DNB*.

[43] See Bransby Blake Cooper, *The Life of Sir Astley Cooper* (2 vols., London, 1843), i. 87.

before his twentieth birthday. Cline's politics were democratic, and brought him

the closest intimacy with such men as Horne Tooke, Thelwall, and, indeed, with all the chief of those who, glorying in the rise of the democratic spirit which at that time was spreading itself over Europe, were not only watching with interest the progress of the French Revolution, but were anticipating similar events with unconcealed anxiety of expectation in our own country.[44]

Cline's friendship with the veteran reformist Horne Tooke, and Tooke's protégé John Thelwall, meant that a senior medical figure at Guy's had links with the intellectual leadership of the reform movement in Britain. Tooke had long been connected with the Society for Constitutional Information, and from 1793 Thelwall was a leader of and principal spokesman for the artisan reformers in the London Corresponding Society. When Tooke was imprisoned in the Tower of London during 1794 Cline attended him as his physician, and at Thelwall's trial for treason in December that year Cline gave evidence for the defence.[45] As might be expected, this close friendship between the surgeon and reformist politicians had a marked effect on Astley Cooper, and on the intellectual debate at the Physical Society during the 1790s.

From June to September 1792 Cooper visited Paris to meet the surgeons Pierre Joseph Desault and François Chopart, and to study French methods of surgery. During this summer, he attended the National Assembly where he heard speeches by the revolutionary leaders of the day: Brissot, Vergniaud, Danton, Marat, and Robespierre. Cooper's mother commented ruefully to a friend, 'our young man has imbibed democratic principles at Mr Cline's, and does not feel as he ought for the royal sufferers, and for the aristocratic party'.[46] Cooper was delayed at Paris until mid-September 1792, while trying to obtain passports for his journey home; he may well have witnessed the massacres in the city, although his own safety was ensured 'by a democratic badge and by friendship with leading revolutionists in England to whom Cline adhered'.[47] Intriguingly,

[44] Ibid. 95.   [45] See ibid. 96, and *Life of John Thelwall*, 440–1.
[46] *The Life of Sir Astley Cooper*, i. 217–18.
[47] See S. Wilks and G. T. Bettany, *A Biographical History of Guy's Hospital* (London, 1892), 318.

he nearly coincided with another young English Jacobin, William Wordsworth, who was also at Paris from late September or early October 1792. After his return to Guy's, Cooper regularly attended the Physical Society where, in 1793, 'his old associate Thelwall was one of the most conspicuous of its members'.[48]

Cooper had been a member of the Physical Society since his student days in October 1784. Thelwall was less formally connected to the medical profession; in 1791 he

took a house in the neighbourhood of Guy's and St Thomas's hospitals; not with the intention of attaching himself practically to the medical or chirurgical profession, but . . . to attend the anatomical lectures of Mr Cline, the physiological of Dr Haighton, and the chemical and the materia medica lectures of Dr Babington.[49]

William Babington, who in 1815–16 would lecture to Keats on the Practice of Medicine and on Chemistry, proposed and secured Thelwall's election to the Physical Society on 22 October 1791.[50] Thereafter Thelwall frequently attended meetings in company with his friends Babington, Cline, and Cooper; a little over a year after his election, the Physical Society's minutes record a 'Public Meeting' at the Theatre, Guy's Hospital, 26 January 1793, at which 'Mr Thelwall read his Essay on Vitality which was in part discussed'. The lecture was a great success. Discussion of it was resumed at five subsequent meetings of the Physical Society, and on 2 March 1793 the Society communicated a 'Letter of Thanks' to the lecturer—'the first', as Thelwall's widow recalled, 'that was ever voted to any member on such an occasion'.[51]

Thelwall published his lecture as *An Essay towards a Definition of Animal Vitality . . . in which Several of the Opinions of the Celebrated John Hunter are Examined and Controverted*—a title which is

[48] *The Life of Sir Astley Cooper*, i. 236.

[49] *Life of John Thelwall*, 79. See also Thelwall's 'Prefatory Memoir' in *Poems Chiefly Written in Retirement* (Hereford, 1801), pp. xx–xxi.

[50] All details of Thelwall's membership and activities are from the manuscript records of the Physical Society, now kept at Wills Medical Library, Guy's Hospital, London.

[51] *Life of John Thelwall*, 104, and 'Prefatory Memoir', p. xxii. The long-running discussion of Thelwall's lecture was the more unusual given the rule of the Physical Society which stated 'No Dissertation shall be the Subject of Discussion on more than two Meetings', *Laws of the Physical Society*, 6.

sufficient to indicate the nature of the controversy Thelwall had entered. His purpose was to discriminate between '*a vital principle*, and *the state of vitality*' in order to refute Hunter's 'misleading' theory 'of the Vital Principle being resident in the blood'.[52] Pointing out that 'many of the most imperfect animals have no blood', Thelwall opened the broader question of philosophical materialism that was at issue: 'Whether life itself is to be considered as a distinct and positive essence, or, simply, as the result of a particular harmony and correspondence of the whole, or aggregate combination, preserved and acted upon by a particular stimulus?'[53] Is life to be identified with the separate existence of soul or spirit?—or is it the result of material organization, responding to 'the stimuli necessary for the production and sustainment of Life ... absorbed and properly diffused through the organized frame'?[54] Arguing that '*Spirit*, however refined, must still be material' (though 'our senses have never yet been capable of taking cognizance of it'), Thelwall also speculated on the nature of the 'stimulus' necessary to the production of 'Vital Action':

But what is this something—this vivifying principle?—Is it atmospheric air itself?—Certainly not. The coats of the arteries, and the membranous linings of the cells of the lungs, forbid the access of such an element; besides, it has been proved by experiment, that in the arteries of the living body there is no air. Something, however, it must be, that is contained in the atmosphere, and something of a powerful and exquisitely subtle nature.

Here Thelwall's appeal to empirical 'experiment' underlined the materialist assumptions of his thinking, as did the final paragraph of his *Essay* in which he identified the mysterious 'vivifying principle':

If, then, we look upon the component parts of our atmosphere, what can we discover so competent to the task—so subtle, so powerful, so nearly approaching to that idea of an ethereal medium, which some philosophers have supposed necessary to complete the chain of connection between the divine immortal essence, and the dull inertion of created matter, as the electrical fluid?—that principle, whose presence, under such a variety of forms, is constantly presenting itself to

---

[52] See *An Essay towards a Definition of Animal Vitality* (London, 1793), 7, 13.
[53] Ibid. 19.   [54] Ibid. 20.

the researches of the philosopher!—whose agency, in so many of the phenomena of Nature, we are daily detecting! and which, perhaps, will one time be discovered to be the real principle by which all heat and action are originally generated and maintained![55]

After Thelwall's death, his widow remembered that it had been 'common' in the 1790s 'to charge every active member belonging to political Societies with atheism'.[56] *An Essay towards a Definition of Animal Vitality* shows why, in Thelwall's case, there was some reason for the charge. His lecture sought to define the 'chain of connection' between 'divine immortal essence' and 'created matter' as a 'principle' or 'phenomenon' of Nature. The 'electrical fluid', Thelwall's preferred explanation for such a 'chain', may have 'nearly approached to that idea of an ethereal medium', but it was none the less a material, physical 'presence' which implicitly denied the transcendent influence (and existence) of divinity. At various times Benjamin Franklin, Erasmus Darwin, Joseph Priestley, and other natural philosophers of the later eighteenth century had identified the 'vital principle' of the material universe with 'the all-pervading aethereal electrical fluid . . . seen in the depths and heights of nature'.[57] Furthermore, Thelwall's exploration of 'animal vitality' proved to have implications beyond the immediate medical and scientific concerns of the Physical Society. According to Astley Cooper's biographer, Thelwall's object in attending the Physical Society 'was probably merely to accumulate information to substantiate his peculiar tenets of materialism, to which, by an ill-directed mind, the study of physiology and anatomy might easily be rendered subservient'.[58] The recent discovery of electricity afforded sure evidence that knowledge was progressive: the 'researches of the philosopher' were apparently uncovering the material 'principles' of life itself. On these grounds Thelwall, like his friend William Godwin, could argue that human beings were perfectible, and that the manifold improvements promised by scientific advances and political revolutions

[55] See *An Essay towards a Definition of Animal Vitality* (London, 1793), 39–40.

[56] *Life of John Thelwall*, 147.

[57] See the excellent discussion in Ian Wylie, *Young Coleridge and the Philosophers of Nature* (Oxford, 1989), esp. 66–7, 123–4, 132. See also H. W. Piper, *The Active Universe* (London, 1962).

[58] *The Life of Sir Astley Cooper*, i. 237.

meant that a secular millennium was at hand. *An Essay on Animal Vitality* was, in other words, a coherent philosophical justification of Thelwall's political agenda as a reformist, although the violent course of events in Europe rendered this optimistic conjunction of science and politics increasingly difficult to sustain.

From 1794 Thelwall's political commitments distracted him from anatomical and physiological studies, and from Physical Society meetings. Many years later, he recalled to Cline that the 'excentric fire of youth hurried [him] away to other topics'.[59] Thelwall chose not to remind Cline that he had been obliged to quit the Society because of a particularly controversial paper. On 14 December 1793 he delivered to the Society a lecture 'On the Origin of Sensation', in which he discussed 'the origin of mental action, explain'd on the System of Materialism'—a topic which was likely to have developed the argument (and political implications) of his earlier lecture.[60] His second paper was discussed at three successive meetings thereafter until, on 25 January 1794, a motion was put forward:

That as a paper now before the Society . . . appears to have no application to the Practice of Medicine or Surgery therefore in no degree interesting to a Society which has only for its object the improvement of those arts—moved: that the Discussion of the aforesaid Paper be discontinued & not resumed . . .

A 'tumultuous Debate' followed; the motion was passed, and Thelwall with three other members 'withdrew their Names from the Society'.[61] By this time the British repression was intensifying, and any suggestion that Thelwall's paper and the subsequent discussion had a bearing on politics would have been sufficient to draw the hostile motion. Thelwall was by now the best-known reformist in the country and, on 12 May 1794, five months after giving his paper, he was arrested and imprisoned

[59] John Thelwall, *A Letter to Henry Cline, Esq.* (London, 1810), 2.

[60] See 'Prefatory Memoir', pp. xxii–xxiii. It is significant that in his memoir, Thelwall emphasized that his paper was delivered 'without digression or allusion to other topics'. This may well have been the case, although in seeking to explain 'the phenomena of mind . . . upon principles *purely Physical*', Thelwall inevitably entered political and religious controversy.

[61] Manuscript minutes of the Physical Society, Wills Library, Guy's Hospital, quoted with permission.

in the Tower of London, to await a charge of treason and trial the following December.

Thelwall's various activities as medical student, poet, and political reformer in the 1790s have been emphasized here, for in many respects they prefigure choices that confronted Keats as medical student and aspiring poet from 1815 onwards. Thelwall, like Keats, had been obliged to leave school to earn a living: at 11 years old he began work for the family silk business. He found this irksome, preferring to continue his education through wide reading (again like Keats), while making various attempts to develop a career as a painter and as an actor. He was apprenticed to a master-tailor, but quickly abandoned the trade to make further study as a painter, then took articles as clerk to the lawyer John Impey of Inner Temple Lane. After three and a half years studying for the bar, his articles were cancelled and in 1786 he 'launched into the world as a literary adventurer'. Thelwall had published widely in journals during the early 1780s; in 1787 his *Poems on Various Subjects* appeared, and he became editor of and principal contributor to the *Biographical and Imperial Magazine.* The year 1793 saw the publication of his influential verse and prose miscellany, *The Peripatetic,* and, two years later, *Poems Written in a Close Confinement in Newgate Jail.*

Mrs Thelwall said that in the early 1790s her husband had 'moved in two spheres, the literary and the political', although it would be true to say that he moved in a third—the medical— as well. His literary career developed over the period of his intense activity as a reformist, and while he was pursuing his studies at Guy's and St Thomas's Hospitals. In the first volume of *The Peripatetic,* for example, Thelwall's verse 'Digression for the Anatomists' speculated about the soul's 'pure electric fire' and whether this was 'imbibed from the air . . . [as] certain portions of the electric fluid'.[62] As my previous discussion has shown, Thelwall's different spheres of activity were for a time intellectually compatible, each overlapping with and reinforcing the other. His example suggests that the demarcation of professions was not so strict as it would subsequently become, and that for Thelwall the hybrid physician-politician-poet had been a practical reality. Following the Apothecaries' Act of 1815

---

[62] John Thelwall, *The Peripatetic* (3 vols., London, 1793), 164 and n.

the professional regulation of medical practitioners was more rigorous, and the physician-poet John Keats was obliged to quit his medical studies in order to dedicate himself fully to his calling as poet-physician. Keats's poetry would later draw extensively on his medical training with Hammond and at Guy's, seeking to identify a role for the poet in a world where the revolutionary idealism formerly shared by Thelwall and Cooper seemed banished to a 'faery land forlorn'.

CHAPTER SEVEN

'Apollo's touch':
The Pharmacy of Imagination

> countenance anxious, and spirits very much dejected; skin
> bedewed with moisture; pulse quick, small, and compress-
> ible . . .
>
> (Sir Astley Cooper, 'Of Contused Wounds')[1]

> I see a lily on thy brow,
>   With anguish moist and fever dew;
> And on thy cheek a fading rose
>   Fast withereth too.
> ('La Belle Dame sans Mercy', 9–12)[2]

Where's the Poet?

William Babington's introductory lecture on chemistry, which
Keats attended at Guy's, debated the relative philosophical
merits of the artist and the scientist:

> The Artist is selfish, for he is constantly labouring for his own interest;
> he works from imitation and without principle . . .
>   The Phylosopher or man of Science is in search of truth in order to
> make a general application of it for the benefit of his fellow creatures
> & values his experiments no further than as the[y] tend to the dis-
> covery or establishment of some general Law.[3]

The terms of Babington's comparison—'imitation', 'general
application', 'general Law'—reflected the empirical bases of
eighteenth-century philosophy and science, according to which
the establishment of universal evidence was a higher order of
achievement than the seemingly 'imitative' and 'unprincipled'

---

[1] *The Lectures of Sir Astley Cooper on the Principles and Practise of Surgery*, iii. 176.
[2] *Indicator* (10 May 1820), 248.
[3] Quoted in Goellnicht, *The Poet-Physician*, 51–2.

labours of the artist. The controversy about artistic status and calling, and the question of the poet's selfishness or disinterest, were of pressing concern to Keats and his contemporaries, and would remain an intense preoccupation for poets throughout the nineteenth century. In his lecture 'On Poetry in General', delivered January 1818 at the Surrey Institution, William Hazlitt observed that

poetry is one part of the history of the human mind, though it is neither science nor philosophy. It cannot be concealed, however, that the progress of knowledge and refinement has a tendency to circum-scribe the limits of the imagination, and to clip the wings of poetry. The province of the imagination is principally visionary, the unknown and the undefined: the understanding restores things to their natural boundaries, and strips them of their fanciful pretensions. (Howe, v. 9)

That Keats had recently been thinking in similar terms about conflict between progressive scientific knowledge and the life of the imagination is evident from the conclusion to his review 'Mr Kean' published in the *Champion*, 21 December 1817: 'ro-mance lives but in books', Keats wrote, 'The Goblin is driven from the heath, and the rainbow is robbed of its mystery!'[4] Compare Haydon's recollection of his 'immortal dinner', held 28 December 1817 one week after the appearance of Keats's *Champion* review. On that occasion Keats and Lamb agreed that '[Newton] destroyed all the poetry of the rainbow by reducing it to the prismatic colours'.[5] Keats's anti-Newtonism and Hazlitt's lecture were subsequently united in the following jux-taposition of imagination and 'philosophy', from the second part of *Lamia*:

> Do not all charms fly
> At the mere touch of cold philosophy?
> There was an awful rainbow once in heaven:
> We know her woof, her texture; she is given
> In the dull catalogue of common things.
> Philosophy will clip an Angel's wings,
> Conquer all mysteries by rule and line,

---

[4] See *John Keats: The Complete Poems*, ed. John Barnard (Harmondsworth, 1973), 529.
[5] See *The Life of Benjamin Robert Haydon*, ed. Tom Taylor (2nd edn., 3 vols., London, 1853), i. 385.

> Empty the haunted air, and gnomed mine—
> Unweave a rainbow . . . (II. 229–37)

Keats was writing *Lamia* in July and August 1819, and finished his poem at Winchester 5 September 1819—the same period at which he was also at work on *The Fall of Hyperion*. The overlap is significant, for in the latter poem the dreamer's affirmation that the poet is 'a sage; | A humanist, physician to all men' is more hospitable to diverse modes of knowledge, seeking to accommodate them within the poet's humane ministry. Such a 'power . . . of enormous ken' (I. 303) recalls the 'knowledge enormous' which 'makes a God of [Apollo]' in *Hyperion* (III. 113), and elides the distinction between imagination and science in the 'warm philosophy' of poetry. This would effect a reconciliation of the physician's and the poet's respective callings, while addressing issues that also preoccupied Lamb, Hazlitt, and others in their circle.

In addition to these immediate contexts during 1818–19, however, the dreamer's dialogue with Moneta may also be read as an attempt to resolve Wordsworth's distinction between the poet and the 'Man of science' (physician, philosopher, chemist, botanist) in his 1802 additions to the preface of *Lyrical Ballads*. Wordsworth's preface presents a striking reversal of Babington's priorities in his chemistry lecture:

> The knowledge both of the Poet and the Man of science is pleasure; but the knowledge of the one cleaves to us as a necessary part of our existence, our natural and unalienable inheritance; the other is a personal and individual acquisition, slow to come to us, and by no habitual and direct sympathy connecting us with our fellow-beings. The Man of science seeks truth as a remote and unknown benefactor; he cherishes and loves it in his solitude: the Poet, singing a song in which all human beings join with him, rejoices in the presence of truth as our visible friend and hourly companion.[6]

The poet's knowledge, Wordsworth argues, is a 'necessary', 'natural', 'inalienable' fact of human existence; that of the 'Man of science' is extraneous to humanity. In 'A Poet's Epitaph' Wordsworth had expressed with some robustness this disparity between the humane priorities of the poet and those of the scientist:

---

[6] See *The Prose Works of William Wordsworth*, i. 140–1.

> Physician art thou? One, all eyes,
> Philosopher! a fingering slave,
> One that would peep and botanize
> Upon his mother's grave?
>
> Wrapped closely in thy sensual fleece
> O turn aside, and take, I pray,
> That he below may rest in peace,
> Thy pin-point of a soul away! (17–24)[7]

The Physician/Philosopher that would unfeelingly 'botanize' (search for plants) on the turf of 'his mother's grave' represents the 'Man of science' whose preoccupation with the 'sensual' or material universe blunts his humanity and reduces his soul to a 'pin-point'. The 'Poet's Epitaph' banishes this crude, limited creature from attendance at the grave, invoking eternity as witness to the diminished capabilities of the scientist when compared to those of the poet.

Wordsworth's insistence on the poet's unique humanity arose out of the intellectual crisis which accompanied the faltering of revolutionary progress in the mid-1790s. One manifestation of that crisis, as Wordsworth described it in Book X of *The Prelude*, was his realization of the incompatibility between the abstract rationalism of William Godwin's *Political Justice*, and the emotional and spiritual dimensions of human life. Wordsworth's representation of this conflict was a 'bar', or a court of law, at which he brought his own mind to trial,

> now believing,
> Now disbelieving, endlessly perplexed
> With impulse, motive, right and wrong,
> (*The Prelude* (1805), X. 892–4)

—a figure which in *The Prelude* Book X corresponds to the 'ghastly visions' of 'unjust tribunals' (X. 374, 377) which ruled in Paris during the heyday of Robespierre's Terror. The contrarieties of Wordsworth's inner life are thus made to correspond to a dreadful fracture in contemporary political life, most notably perhaps Robespierre's identification of terror with justice as 'an emanation of virtue', the only means to secure the revolutionary values of liberty, equality, fraternity.[8] Amid

---

[7] Quoted from *William Wordsworth*, ed. Stephen Gill (Oxford, 1984).
[8] See *Wordsworth and Coleridge: The Radical Years*, 209.

the intellectual contradictions and confusions produced by the collapse of the French Revolution Wordsworth refashioned himself as poet of *Lyrical Ballads*, advocating a receptivity to 'the lore which nature brings' against the partial learning of 'sages' and the deadly machinations of the 'meddling intellect'.[9] In the epilogue to this book, I shall argue that a comparable recognition of the limitations of Godwin's philosophy informed Keats's idea of negative capability, and that his most impersonal, negatively capable lyric, 'To Autumn', may be understood as the belated celebration of an ideal commonwealth of humankind and the natural world.

That revolutionary failure was indeed one explanation for Wordsworth's insulation of poetry from other intellectual pursuits is further suggested by his 1802 speculation on a future *rapprochement* between poet and scientist:

If the labours of Men of science should ever create any material revolution, direct or indirect, in our condition, and in the impressions which we habitually receive, the poet will sleep then no more than at present; he will be ready to follow the steps of the Man of science, not only in those general indirect effects, but he will be at his side, carrying sensation into the midst of the objects of the science itself. The remotest discoveries of the Chemist, the Botanist, or Mineralogist, will be as proper objects of the Poet's art as any upon which it can be employed, if the time should ever come when these things shall be familiar to us, and the relations under which they are contemplated by the followers of these respective sciences shall be manifestly and palpably material to us as enjoying and suffering beings. If the time should ever come when what is now called Science, thus familiarised to men, shall be ready to put on, as it were, a form of flesh and blood, the Poet will lend his divine spirit to aid the transfiguration, and will welcome the Being thus produced, as a dear and genuine inmate of the household of man.[10]

Tacitly pointing out that science has hitherto failed to achieve 'any material revolution, direct or indirect, in our condition', Wordsworth marked his distance from the commitments of former years when the universal progress of politics, society, science, religion, and the arts had seemed to give substance to the visionary creations of the poet's 'divine spirit'.

[9] See in particular 'The Tables Turned', 21–8.
[10] *The Prose Works of William Wordsworth*, i. 141.

Just such a 'material revolution' had informed John Thelwall's 1793 paper to the Physical Society at Guy's, and it was intrinsic to Coleridge's creativity in the 1790s: Coleridge's poetry at this period gave voice to the imminent reality of a 'blest future' for which—so he wrote in *Religious Musings*—the works of Milton, Newton, Hartley, and Priestley—'Patriot, and Saint, and Sage'—had been a preparation.[11] *Religious Musings* presented a vision of the 'promis'd years' which the cumulative knowledge of scientists, philosophers, surgeons, botanists, politicians, theologians, and poets would necessarily achieve. It was appropriate, then, that when Coleridge dedicated himself,

> head, heart, and hand,
> Active and firm, to fight the bloodless fight
> Of Science, Freedom, and the Truth in Christ

—he did so in the blank verse of his poem 'Reflections on Entering into Active Life'.[12] At this moment, the poet, the scientist, and the philosopher could believe with confidence that they were united in a cause that would bring about the betterment of humankind—a transformation which Keats, some twenty years later, also hoped to achieve as a poet who might be a sage, humanist, and physician 'to all men'.[13] The cure of suffering that had not proved feasible through political revolution or medical practice might be yet achieved through the pharmacy of imagination.

The Chemistry of Revolution

In his fine study *Keats the Poet*, Stuart Sperry has shown that Lamia's transformation when touched by Hermes' rod

---

[11] See *Religious Musings*, 387–402, in Coleridge, *Poems on Various Subjects*.

[12] 'Reflections on Entering into Active Life', 58–60, in the *Monthly Magazine* (Oct. 1796).

[13] Cf. Robert Gittings's contention that Wordsworth's 1815 *Poems*, and his belief that the poet was 'a healer of the ills of mankind', influenced Keats in a way that was at odds with his medical career: 'from this moment, Wordsworth and Astley Cooper were in competition for the direction that Keats's genius would take'; 'John Keats, Physician and Poet', 54. I argue that Keats's poetry attempts to resolve the Wordsworthian polarization of 'science' and 'poetry', assimilating *both* Wordsworth and Cooper in his idea of the poet's calling.

'resembles nothing so much as the effects of a violent chemical reaction':[14]

> Her mouth foam'd, and the grass, therewith besprent,
> Wither'd at dew so sweet and virulent;
> Her eyes in torture fix'd, and anguish drear,
> Hot, glaz'd, and wide, with lid-lashes all sear,
> Flash'd phosphor and sharp sparks, without one cooling tear.
> The colours all inflam'd throughout her train,
> She writh'd about, convuls'd with scarlet pain:
> A deep volcanian yellow took the place
> Of all her milder-mooned body's grace ... (I. 148–56)

One might add that Lamia's convulsive change also resembles feverish inflammation heightened to the intensity of 'volcanian' combustion:[15] a mocking, ironic use of the medical and scientific knowledge from which, as Sperry goes on to say, 'throughout his career Keats adopts analogies ... to express his own sense of the imagination and its creative processes'.[16] Perhaps the most important instance of this is the long, speculative passage which succeeds Endymion's question 'Wherein lies Happiness?' (*Endymion*, I. 777–815). The passage was described by Keats in his letter to John Taylor, 30 January 1818, as 'a regular stepping of the Imagination towards a Truth ... It set before me at once the gradations of Happiness even like a kind of Pleasure Thermometer' (*Letters*, i. 218). He includes in his letter five lines which he wished Taylor to insert as a 'preface ... necessary to the Subject':

> Wherein lies Happiness? In that which becks
> Our ready Minds to fellowship divine;
> A fellowship with essence, till we shine
> Full alchymized and free of space. Behold
> The clear Religion of heaven— ...
> (*Letters*, i. 218; cf. *Endymion*, I. 777–81)

Sperry observes that these lines have often been read as 'an affirmation of [Keats's] belief in a Platonic or transcendent reality', and that in such metaphysical readings the term 'Thermometer' is noticeably incongruous.[17] In proposing that the

---

[14] Sperry, *Keats the Poet*, 302–3.
[15] 'Volcanian' is Keats's own coinage; see *OED*.
[16] *Keats the Poet*, 307.   [17] See ibid. 46–9.

passage describes the creative process, Sperry emphasizes Keats's use of chemical theory and language. The word 'alchymized' (transmuted, as in alchemy, from a base to a higher substance) indicates how creativity begins with particular sense impressions (the feel of a 'rose leaf round thy finger's taperness', I. 782) which are imaginatively 'concentrated and distilled', leading on to higher and more 'ethereal' forms and, finally, a 'fellowship divine; | A fellowship with essence'.

Chemistry thus enabled Keats to 'set before [himself]' the idealizing processes of imagination, although it is notable that 'fellowship with essence' also signalled the universal principle which John Thelwall had once sought to define as 'the chain of connection between the divine immortal essence, and the dull inertion of created matter'.[18] Thelwall had claimed that future 'researches of the philosopher' would reveal 'the electrical fluid' as the principle by which humanity might achieve 'fellowship with essence'—a materialist argument which I have suggested also reinforced his democratic claims as a reformist. I do not wish to argue that Keats's 'Pleasure Thermometer' constituted a 'regular stepping of the Imagination' towards democracy, although an ultimate realization of community is suggested by 'fellowship',[19] and by the conclusion of Keats's speculations in *Endymion* I:

> at the tip-top,
> There hangs by unseen film, an orbed drop
> Of light, and that is love: its influence,
> Thrown in our eyes, genders a novel sense,
> At which we start and fret; till in the end,
> Melting into its radiance, we blend,
> Mingle, and so become a part of it . . . (I. 805–11)

This genial, renovative idealism cannot be understood to refer to the transformation of any particular social circumstances;

---

[18] Thelwall, *An Essay on Animal Vitality*, 39–40.

[19] For the difficulties in reconciling the themes of 'fellowship' in human and ideal (or 'divine') relationships in *Endymion*, see Jack Stillinger, 'On the Interpretation of *Endymion*: The Comedian as the Letter E', in *Hoodwinking of Madeline*, especially 15–20. Stillinger traces the 'unrelatedness of themes' in *Endymion* to the influence of Shelley's *Alastor*, and argues for a more accommodating response to the thematic diversity of both poems. I go on to argue here that Keats suggests how a reconciliation of ideal and earthly 'fellowship' might be achieved spontaneously and 'unknowingly'.

indeed, Keats seems to have believed that it rendered all activity to that end unnecessary:

> Aye, so delicious is the unsating food,
> That men, who might have tower'd in the van
> Of all the congregated world, to fan
> And winnow from the coming step of time
> All chaff of custom, wipe away all slime
> Left by men-slugs and human serpentry,
> Have been content to let occasion die,
> Whilst they did sleep in love's elysium.
> And, truly, I would rather be struck dumb,
> Than speak against this ardent listlessness:
> For I have ever thought that it might bless
> The world with benefits unknowingly;
> As does the nightingale, upperched high,
> And cloister'd among cool and bunched leaves—
> She sings but to her love . . . (I. 816–30)

The winnowing and purging of 'the congregated world' loses occasion to the 'ardent listlessness' of love, which yet offers a prospect of blessing the world 'with benefits unknowingly'. One presider in this passage is Coleridge's Ancient Mariner, whose salvation begins with the 'spring of love' with which he blessed the water snakes 'unaware' (284–7). Also relevant is Wordsworth's subdued claim in 'Tintern Abbey' for the hidden influence of 'unremembered pleasure' upon 'unremembered acts | Of kindness and of love' (32, 35–6). *Endymion, The Ancient Mariner*, and 'Tintern Abbey' each respond to the revolutionary impetus of the times, while seeking to locate the means of transformation outside the vexed sphere of political action. 'Tintern Abbey', for example, explores how the processes of memory may contribute to personal and social amelioration through 'acts of kindness'.[20] For Keats, one emblem of a comparably imperceptible yet benign influence is the nightingale; as we shall see, the 'Ode to a Nightingale' (which echoes 'Tintern Abbey') develops the nightingale's symbolic role by merging it with the more explicitly political associations of the greenwood lyrics previously discussed in Chapter 5.

For the moment, however, we can understand how Keats

---

[20] See 'Daring to Hope', in *Wordsworth and Coleridge: The Radical Years*, 268–75, and 'The Politics of Kindness', in *The Politics of Nature*, 30–2.

might have cited the 'Pleasure Thermometer' lines from *Endymion* I, to support the dreamer's claims for the poet in his dialogue with Moneta:

> 'sure not all
> Those melodies sung into the world's ear
> Are useless: sure a poet is a sage;
> A humanist, physician to all men.' (I. 187–90)

This certainly elicits a 'direct equation of true poet and true physician', suggesting that 'for Keats, the ideals of the poet are the same as those of the physician'.[21] Yet there is more in play here than this binary relationship: 'sage' and 'humanist' indicate other areas of liberal commitment allied to, but distinct from, medical science and poetry. Indeed, William Maginn's description of Keats as a 'pharmacopolitical poet' gives priority to his medical training but connects this with a second characteristic to create the 'pharmaco*political* poet of Endymion' (my emphasis). Maginn was probably thinking of the invective with which Keats opened *Endymion* III, rather than the 'Pleasure Thermometer' lines discussed above. But to what extent did medicine and politics intersect more widely in Keats's imaginative life in the poetry he wrote from March 1817 onwards?

'Effigies of Pain'

Almost from the first Keats's poetry is alert to the physical manifestations of well-being or distemper; indeed, a few of his most striking lines apparently recall medical lectures he had heard delivered at Guy's Hospital. While listening to Astley Cooper lecture on the nerves, Keats jotted down the observation that 'Injuries may happen so quickly that sensation has no time to be communicated. The pain is proportioned to the degree of quickness or slowness of Wounds being inflicted.'[22] The sense that 'pain [may be] proportioned' to time re-emerged in *Hyperion*, where Keats wrote of the sun-god's prolonged anguish: 'horrors, portion'd to a giant nerve, | Oft made

---

[21] de Almeida, *Romantic Medicine and John Keats*, 37; Goellnicht, *The Poet-Physician*, 235.
[22] See *John Keats's Anatomical and Physiological Note Book*, 56.

Hyperion ache' (I. 175–6). Again, in *The Fall of Hyperion*, the dreamer's terror at Moneta's robes and veils is described as having 'made [his] heart too small to hold its blood' (I. 254). A comparable, physiological symptom had been pointed out in a lecture—'after death the Arteries are found empty, they have power of expelling the Blood in the last Struggles of Life'[23]—and in *The Fall of Hyperion* the dwindling of the dreamer's heart, mysteriously 'seen' by the goddess, encourages her disclosure of 'a wan face . . . bright blanch'd I By an immortal sickness which kills not'. In immediate juxtaposition to the dreamer's near-experience of the 'last Struggles of Life', he beholds a face which is drained of blood as if in death, although 'deathwards progressing I To no death was that visage' (I. 256–8, 260–1).

These close parallels between the poems and Keats's note-book are not evidence that the medical lectures were an immediate 'source' for the poetry, but they are valuable for indicating how noticeably Keats's poetry was inflected by his medical studies and experiences. Keats's distinctive vision, as unique as Wordsworth's romance of childhood and nature in *The Prelude*, represents the world as a gigantic hospital, a global sickroom populated with 'effigies of pain' (*Hyperion*, I. 228). Equally characteristic of Keats's poetry is the diagnostic register of his voice: 'health, and quiet breathing', 'paly lip', 'tender-taken breath', 'anguish moist and fever dew'.[24] Compare the following observations from Astley Cooper's *Lectures*: 'her breathing natural'; 'Chilly pain over his eyes'; 'covered with a cold perspiration, and is unusually pallid'; 'countenance anxious, and spirits very much dejected; skin bedewed with moisture; pulse quick, small, and compressible'; 'face flushed; skin very moist'; 'skin cool'.[25] The 'beadsman' in *The Eve of St Agnes* is an invalid, 'meagre, barefoot, wan' (12); old Angela dies 'palsy-twitch'd, with meagre face deform' (376); the fallen Titans, 'pent in regions of laborious breath', undergo agony like a patient forcibly held down while the surgeon works with his knife:

> Their clenched teeth still clench'd, and all their limbs
> Lock'd up like veins of metal, crampt and screw'd;

---

[23] See *John Keats's Anatomical and Physiological Note Book*, 9–10.

[24] *Endymion*, I. 5, 341; 'Bright Star', 13; 'La Belle Dame', 10.

[25] *The Lectures of Sir Astley Cooper on the Principles and Practise of Surgery*, i. 256, 258; ii. 224; iii. 176, 177.

Without a motion, save of their big hearts
Heaving in pain, and horribly convuls'd
With sanguine feverous boiling gurge of pulse. (II. 22, 24–8)

This scene of titanic anguish represented an intensification of the pain which Keats knew from his years at Guy's was the limit of endurance for humankind.[26] One might claim, in fact, that these fallen gods suffer from the attentions of a sublime counterpart of that rash surgeon 'Billy' Lucas.

By way of contrast, there are many instances where Keats's poetry is attuned to his medical experience in a less strident manner. In 'Ode to a Nightingale', for example, 'hemlock' (2) and the 'dull opiate' laudanum (3) were among the most powerful drugs then available; 'full-throated ease' (10) and 'quiet breath' (54) each imply a comparison with their opposites—a throat choked by haemorrhaging blood, and breath exhaled with the rattle of disease. Elsewhere, the third book of *Endymion* offers a poignant vision of the lovers 'doom'd to die' during Glaucus' 'bondage' until revived by the presence of a '*youth, by heavenly power lov'd and led*' (III. 708, 722–3). The passage recalls Satan's followers in *Paradise Lost* Book I, and the magic of the *Arabian Knights* and Beckford's *Vathek*,[27] but these literary sources embellished more immediate personal experience: the mortuary at Guy's and, perhaps, more distant memories of the deaths of Keats's parents:

So in that crystal place, in silent rows,
Poor lovers lay at rest from joys and woes.—
The stranger from the mountains, breathless, trac'd
Such thousands of shut eyes in order plac'd;
Such ranges of white feet, and patient lips
All ruddy,—for here death no blossom nips.
He mark'd their brows and foreheads; saw their hair
Put sleekly on one side with nicest care;
And each one's gentle wrists, with reverence,
Put cross-wise to its heart. (III. 735–44)

This precise, crystalline vision is distinctively Keats's in its blend of tenderness and detachment. The initial perspective on the

---

[26] See ibid. ii. 246–7, for the three bandages 'required to secure the patient' in cutting for stones, in order to 'prevent the patient from making any movements likely to impede the operation, or occasion danger during its performance'.
[27] See AP 234.

'silent rows' is that of a stranger, although his involvement is suggested by his 'breathless[ness]'; something between clinical observation and sympathetic contact is suggested by the verb 'trac'd'. We are given a sense of the scale of the sight in 'Such thousands of shut eyes . . . | Such ranges of white feet' but this view of massed repose maintains a hold on the particular, just as we were about to lose it in the suggestion that 'here death no blossom nips'. The observation of the way in which hair and wrists have been 'put' is aware not just of the appearance of a resting human form, but also of the care which has been devoted by another person in disposing the body. 'And each one's gentle wrists' intimates the suppleness of limbs not yet stiffened by death, merging the formal posture of crossed arms with a suggestion of the delicacy of touch in so arranging them. 'Gentle wrists' is the choice of a poet who knew how to feel for a patient's pulse and, appropriately, the cure subsequently effected by Endymion is likened to the inspiring moment of 'Apollo's touch'. *The Fall of Hyperion* would reveal Keats far less convinced of imagination's salutary power but, for the moment, and 'in that crystal place', it is the curative power of poetry which has a vital effect in 'reanimating' the lovers with a 'noise of harmony, pulses and throes | Of gladness in the air' (III. 790 2).

A related passage, from *I stood tip toe*, apparently recalls Keats's experience as a dresser, walking the wards at Guy's:

> The breezes were ethereal, and pure,
> And crept through half closed lattices to cure
> The languid sick; it cool'd their fever'd sleep,
> And soothed them into slumbers full and deep.
> Soon they awoke clear eyed: nor burnt with thirsting,
> Nor with hot fingers, nor with temples bursting . . . (221–6)[28]

The attention to symptoms such as 'clear eyed', 'hot fingers', 'temples bursting' suggests that this evocation of how cool fresh air brings relief to the sick was based upon current hospital practice, and Keats's own experiences in attending patients.[29]

[28] For further discussion of this passage, see Ward, *Making of a Poet*, 59–60. Keats's lines may recall Shelley's 'winds that bear sweet music when they breathe | Through some dim latticed chamber' in *Alastor*, 631–2.

[29] Cf. the discussion in Goellnicht, *The Poet-Physician*, 169, which suggests that details in the passage quoted were 'seen often while [Keats was] on duty as a dresser . . . the symptoms of the patients are medically accurate'.

Certainly, John Flint South recalled that the atmosphere in the crowded operating theatre was 'almost stifling', and that in the wards the students used to jostle and crowd around the beds 'quite regardless of the patients' feelings or condition'.[30] This passage from *I stood tip-toe* quoted above comes from the conclusion of the poem, and forms part of Keats's first approach to the story of Endymion and Phoebe; his working title for *I stood tip-toe* was in fact *Endymion*—and the poem is titled *Endymion* in Tom Keats's transcript of it.[31] As in many Romantic poems, the 'ethereal breeze' is a symbolic invocation of imagination; under its genial influence the 'languid sick' recover health, and are 'fill'd with a sweet surprise, | Until their tongues were loos'd in poesy' (234–5). *I stood tip-toe* breaks off after a further seven lines, although the analogy between medicine and the curative power of the imagination is already apparent, and distinctively Keats's own. Written over two years later, 'Ode to a Nightingale' reveals how the vision of the poet-physician intersects with the political concerns that had been explicitly voiced in *Poems, by John Keats, Endymion,* and the 'greenwood' Robin Hood lyrics of early 1818.

A Sylvan Hospice: 'Ode to a Nightingale'

> cloister'd among cool and bunched leaves . . .
> (*Endymion*, I. 829)

Like *I stood tip-toe*, Keats's letters show his sensitivity to the ways in which air affected bodily health. 'Our hea[l]th temperament and dispositions are taken more . . . from the air we breathe than is generally imagined', he wrote to John Taylor, 5 September 1819:

Since I have been at Winchester I have been improving in health—it is not so confined—and there is on one side of the city a dry chalky down where the air is worth six pence a pint. So if you do not get better at Retford do not impute it to your own weakness before you have well considered the nature of the air and soil. (*Letters*, ii. 156)

It has been argued that Keats's letter was indebted to remarks on climate and character in Hazlitt's essay 'On Manner' in *The*

---

[30] *Memorials of John Flint South*, 26–7, 36.
[31] 'I have done little to Endymion lately'; to Charles Cowden Clarke, 17 Dec. 1816, *Letters*, i. 121.

Round Table, and Robertson's comments on the Chinese in his *History of America*.[32] Keats certainly knew these works, but that did not make them necessary contexts for the letter. What he wrote to Taylor about the effects of air and climate on 'health temperament and dispositions' reflected traditional wisdom,[33] on which Milton had drawn for the pastoral simile in *Paradise Lost* Book IX:

> As one who long in populous city pent,
> Where houses thick and sewers annoy the air,
> Forth issuing on a summer's morn to breathe
> Among the pleasant villages and farms
> Adjoined, from each thing met conceives delight,
> The smell of grain, or tedded grass, or kine,
> Or dairy, each rural sight, each rural sound . . . (IX. 445–51)[34]

Lucy Newlyn has shown how, during the eighteenth century, this Miltonic opposition of city and country was repeated in Young's *Night Thoughts*, Thomson's *Seasons*, Cowper's *Task*, and elsewhere.[35] It became a conventional literary figure but, Newlyn demonstrates, it was rescued from cliché in Coleridge's, Wordsworth's, and Lamb's symbolic use of the motif to represent, and discriminate, states of mind. In 'Tintern Abbey', for example, the 'towns and cities' (27–8) are 'symbolic of an alien environment', a 'foil' which Newlyn rightly says serves to highlight the mind's ability to retain 'forms of beauty' and to transcend, through memory, the alienation which the city represents:[36]

> Though absent long,
> These forms of beauty have not been to me,

---

[32] See *Letters*, ii. 156n., and H. E. Briggs, 'Two Notes on Hazlitt and Keats', *PMLA* 59 (1944), 596–8.

[33] For a recent account of Romantic 'proto-ecological' vision, relevant to Keats's concern with air and climate, see Kroeber, *Ecological Literary Criticism*, 56, 61. For Kroeber, 61, however, Keats represented 'the first of the major nineteenth-century poets to move towards segregating poetry into a distinct realm of "the aesthetic"'. In that the present book seeks to qualify the enduring idea of his 'aesthetic' insulation from the world, it may also open the way for a more thoroughgoing reappraisal of Keats's 'green' awareness of the interdependence of all forms of life, the steady consciousness 'of living in a real natural world', which Kroeber associates with modern ecological thought.

[34] In Keats's copy of *Paradise Lost*, IX. 447–51 are underlined.

[35] Lucy Newlyn, ' "In City Pent": Echo and Allusion in Wordsworth, Coleridge, and Lamb, 1797–1801', *Review of English Studies*, 32 (Nov. 1981), 409–10.

[36] Ibid. 413.

> As is a landscape to a blind man's eye:
> But oft, in lonely rooms, and mid the din
> Of towns and cities, I have owed to them,
> In hours of weariness, sensations sweet,
> Felt in the blood, and felt along the heart,
> And passing even into my purer mind
> With tranquil restoration . . . (23–31)

For Wordsworth the experience of 'sensations sweet, | Felt in the blood' leads beyond bodily pleasure; the unusual construction 'felt along the heart' opens an inner space or channel for spiritual renewal, where physical well-being yields an ideal 'purified' expression as 'tranquil restoration'. So understood, 'sensation sweet' may be the precursor of 'another gift, | Of aspect more sublime', the visionary moment when 'We see into the life of things' (37–8, 50). Newlyn shows how this fulfilling moment, followed by the turn 'If this | Be but a vain belief' (50–1), contributes to Wordsworth's recognition of the city as a life-consuming environment now fully associated with a particular psychological state:

> how oft,
> In darkness, and amid the many shapes
> Of joyless day-light; when the fretful stir
> Unprofitable, and the fever of the world,
> Have hung upon the beatings of my heart,
> How oft, in spirit, have I turned to thee,
> O sylvan Wye! (51–7)

The city's random and turbulent activity is a debilitating burden, eased only when displaced by the heart's recourse to the memory of scenes formerly known and loved. As is well known, Keats echoed these lines from 'Tintern Abbey' in 'Ode to a Nightingale', evoking a comparable state of oppression in which he turns to the consolation of the nightingale's song:

> That I might drink, and leave the world unseen,
>   And with thee fade away into the forest dim:
>
> Fade far away, dissolve, and quite forget
>   What thou among the leaves has never known,
> The weariness, the fever, and the fret
>   Here, where men sit and hear each other groan;
> Where palsy shakes a few, sad, last gray hairs,

> Where youth grows pale, and spectre-thin, and dies;
> Where but to think is to be full of sorrow
> And leaden-eyed despairs . . . (19–28)

Often cited as Keats's memory of his brother Tom's death from tuberculosis, these lines undoubtedly also respond to the powerful sense of physical distemper conveyed in 'Tintern Abbey', where the city's 'fretful stir' and 'the fever of the world' had combined to 'h[a]ng upon the beatings of [the] heart'. And in this respect 'Ode to a Nightingale' shows Keats's distinctive transformation of the Wordsworthian and Miltonic figures of city and country.

Milton's simile had been invoked by Keats in an early sonnet, which begins like this:

> To one who has been long in city pent,
> 'Tis very sweet to look into the fair
> And open face of heaven,—to breathe a prayer
> Full in the smile of the blue firmament. (1–4)

Miriam Allott suggested that here Keats was recalling the Coleridgean echoes of Milton in 'The Nightingale' or 'This Lime-Tree Bower', rather than the original passage in *Paradise Lost* Book IX, quoted above. Yet, although Keats's close study of *Paradise Lost* dated from his visit to Oxford in autumn 1817, over a year after this sonnet was written, the progression of the quatrain recalls Milton's poem very precisely. Keats's opening line is a direct quotation of Milton's simile, 'As one who long in populous city pent' (IX. 445); Keats's rhyme-word 'fair' in the second line chimes with (and contains) Milton's 'air' (IX. 446), and Keats's 'breathe a prayer | Full in the smile of the blue firmament' is a sentimental abstraction of Milton's line 'Forth issuing on a summer's morn to breathe' (IX. 447). I have elaborated these echoes to demonstrate that Keats was indeed aware of Milton's simile at an early date, and because in his sonnet the release of one who has been 'long in city pent' is associated with the recovery of 'heart's content' and 'an ear | Catching the notes of Philomel': a decorative and in this case probably Coleridgean allusion to the nightingale. A comparable pattern in which the desire to escape from suffering is

---

[37] AP 45 n.

associated with the greenwood and the nightingale's greeting appears in 'Ode to a Nightingale'.

Whereas Wordsworth and Coleridge had developed the 'populous city' into the symbolic environment of alienated mental and spiritual life, 'Ode to a Nightingale' dwells upon the realities of bodily contamination arising from the cramped and unhealthy conditions of city life, as a burden afflicting all humankind:

> The weariness, the fever, and the fret
>   Here, where men sit and hear each other groan;
> Where palsy shakes a few, sad, last gray hairs,
>   Where youth grows pale, and spectre-thin, and dies . . . (23–6)

Here Keats modifies the symbolic associations of the city by drawing language and imagery from his medical training, presenting 'the fever, and the fret' as typical of the wasting of all humankind. At the same time, the poem moves beyond the personal circumstances of illness and bereavement: 'men' are both old and young, some 'shaken' by palsy, others 'growing' pale. The eye of the physician discriminates one affliction coming to its 'last' acute stage, and another of lingering 'chronic' decline. In response to these effigies of pain, the imagination of the poet creates a sylvan retreat or hospice, 'some melodious plot | Of beechen green . . . far away . . . among the leaves' (8–9, 21–2), where dying seems to hold no mortal agony. In marked juxtaposition to the torment of 'weariness, fever, fret', this darkling bower is also an intense re-visioning of the passage in *I stood tip-toe*,

> The breezes were ethereal, and pure,
> And crept through half closed lattices to cure
> The languid sick; it cool'd their fever'd sleep
> And soothed them into slumbers full and deep.

In the 'forest dim' of 'Ode to a Nightingale' the 'full-throated' melody of the bird has an identically ethereal, purifying effect although this does not produce the forgetful escape from actuality anticipated in the second and third stanzas of the poem. The 'magic greenwood', which (as we saw in Chapter 5) had represented pastoral and political liberties in Keats's and Reynolds's Robin Hood poems, is transformed in 'Ode to a Nightingale' into the verdurous dwelling of reverie, the 'embalmed darkness' of vision. So internalized, the woodland home of freedom and justice is recognized as the resort of self-forgetfulness or 'negative capability'—where the poet may become outlaw to his own identity and 'half in love with easeful Death' (52). The desire to pass beyond earthly existence,

> To cease upon the midnight with no pain,
> While thou art pouring forth thy soul abroad
> In such an ecstasy! (56–8)

—would of course transgress the melancholy laws of mortality, and it is this realization which revives that aspect of the poet's consciousness still 'half in love' with selfhood:

> Still wouldst thou sing, and I have ears in vain—
> To thy high requiem become a sod. (59–60)

The recognition leads in stanza vii of the ode to a curious echo or half-memory of the earlier lament for Robin Hood:

> No! those days are gone away,
> And their hours are old and gray,
> And their minutes buried all,
> Under the down-trodden pall
> Of the leaves of many years . . . ('Robin Hood', 1–5)

Much as the outlaw life of Sherwood had served to highlight the harsh realities of the present, the 'Immortal Bird'—which sings beyond the boundaries of human life—brings an intimation of the unescapable facts of existence: 'hungry generations' downtrodden by the passage of many years; the divisions of life between 'emperor' and 'clown', ruler and subject; and the misery of another, unwilling outlaw, the exiled Ruth 'in tears amid the alien corn'. At the close of 'Ode to a Nightingale', vision unravels to reveal a world forlorn as that in 'Robin Hood'; like that earlier lyric, Keats's ode bids farewell to romance as a 'deceiving elf':

> Adieu! adieu! thy plaintive anthem fades
> Past the near meadows, over the still stream,
> Up the hill-side; and now 'tis buried deep
> In the next valley-glades . . . (75–8)

Both Sherwood Forest, where Robin Hood lies in 'his turfed grave', and the 'valley-glades' of the 'Ode' are sites of romantic interment; they remind of 'music fled' and the confused possibility (vision or dream?) of an ideal existence that has already passed 'over the still stream', or bourne, into the otherwhere beyond.

'Ode to a Nightingale' is, in effect, a subtle elaboration of the greenwood poems written by Keats and Reynolds early in 1818. Imaginatively assimilating Keats's medical training with the political interests of his outlaw lyrics, the 'Ode' is definitively the creation of a 'pharmacopolitical poet'—but it is also, of course, much more than William Maginn's label comprehends. The 'Ode' intensifies those circumstantial concerns to reveal how tragedy dwells inside romance: to aspire to a perfected existence—through the use of medicine, by means of political revolution, or in achieving unity with 'divine immortal essence'—is to know oneself already forlorn. As fevered creatures existing amid 'uncertainties, Mysteries, doubts' (*Letters*, i. 193), the only course open for humankind may be to live in and through negative capability, aware that our welfare depends upon the interdependence—or 'interassimulation' (*Letters*, ii. 208)—of self, humankind, and the natural world.

CHAPTER EIGHT

Lisping Sedition: *Poems*, *Endymion*, and the Poetics of Dissent

> I don't defend that rhyme; I know 'tis bad,
> Though used by Hunt & Keats, & all that squad.
> (William Maginn to William Blackwood,
> 8 Dec. 1820)[1]

> Hear how their bantling has already learned to lisp
> sedition.
>
> (Z, 'On the Cockney School of Poetry: No IV')

A Cockney Bantling

Richard Woodhouse wrote in his copy of *Endymion*, 'K. said, with much simplicity, "It will easily be seen what I think of the present Ministers by the beginning of the 3d Book"'.[2] If not quite 'easily', one can see readily enough from the opening of *Endymion* III that Keats was unimpressed by the establishment:

> There are who lord it o'er their fellow-men
> With most prevailing tinsel: who unpen
> Their baaing vanities, to browse away
> The comfortable green and juicy hay
> From human pastures; or, O torturing fact!
> Who, through an idiot blink, will see unpack'd
> Fire-branded foxes to sear up and singe
> Our gold and ripe-ear'd hopes. With not one tinge
> Of sanctuary splendour, not a sight
> Able to face an owl's, they still are dight
> By the blear-eyed nations in empurpled vests,
> And crowns, and turbans. With unladen breasts,

---

[1] NLS, MS 4005, quoted by permission of the Trustees of the National Library of Scotland.

[2] See AP 206n.

> Save of blown self-applause, they proudly mount
> To their spirit's perch, their being's high account,
> Their tiptop nothings, their dull skies, their thrones—
> Amid the fierce intoxicating tones
> Of trumpets, shoutings, and belabour'd drums,
> And sudden cannon. (III. 1–18)

Keats wrote the third book of *Endymion* in September 1817 at Magdalen Hall, Oxford, where he was staying with Benjamin Bailey, and he completed it by 28 September (*Letters*, i. 168). Many years afterwards Bailey, now Archdeacon at Colombo, Ceylon, wrote a series of letters to Richard Monckton Milnes in which he made much of his short acquaintance with Keats: 'I knew his *inner* man so thoroughly that I may be able to throw light upon his genius and character' (15 October 1848, *KC* ii. 263–4). When he recalled the composition of *Endymion* III, however, Bailey grew thoroughly stern and censorious, claiming that Keats had written 'the first few introductory lines which he read to me, before he became my guest':

I did not then, & I cannot now very much approve that introduction. The 'baaing vanities' have something of the character of what was called 'the cockney school'. Nor do I like many of the forced rhymes, & the apparent effort, by breaking up the lines, to get as far as possible in the opposite direction of the Pope school. (7 May 1849; *KC* ii. 269)[3]

He labours the point, emphasizing that this was his impression 'at the time of the composition of this Book, & remains so now' (*KC* ii. 269–70). Bailey may indeed have consistently disliked the passage, although in September 1817 he could not have associated 'baaing vanities' with 'Cockney School' poetics since Z's first essay, inventing and then denouncing the sect, had not yet appeared in *Blackwood's Magazine*.

It is more probable that Bailey would have been reluctant to approve the introduction to Book III because of its anti-clerical sentiments:

> With not one tinge
> Of sanctuary splendour, not a sight

---

[3] The likelihood is that Keats composed all of Book III at Oxford; Woodhouse noted in his copy of *Endymion* 'At the End of this line [in the draft] is written "Oxford Septr 5".' See also *The Poetical Works of John Keats*, ed. H. W. Garrod (2nd edn., Oxford, 1958), p. xci.

> Able to face an owl's, they still are dight
> By the blear-eyed nations in empurpled vests . . .

These lines are too awkward and convoluted to be effective as
anti-clerical polemic, although for Bailey they came to represent one of the 'errors of Keats's character' (*KC* ii. 260). 'On
religion, for instance, he had . . . the most lax notions', Bailey
informed Milnes, adding that at the time of their friendship
'[his] own mind was fully & gravely determined to [his] sacred
profession' (*KC* ii. 291). Oddly enough, it was Bailey's disappointment at not gaining a curacy in the diocese of Lincoln
which had prompted an angry outburst in Keats's letter to him
of 3 November 1817:

it must be shocking to find in a sacred Profession such barefaced
oppression and impertinence—The Stations and the Grandeurs of the
World have taken it into their heads that they cannot commit themselves towards an inferior in rank—but is not the impertinence from
one above to one below more wretchedly mean than from the low to
the high? There is something so nauseous in self-willed yawning impu-
dence in the shape of conscience—it sinks the Bishop of Lincoln into
a smashed frog putrifying: that a rebel against common decency
should escape the Pillory! That a mitre should cover a Man guilty of
the most coxcombical, tyranical and indolent impertinence! I repeat
this word for the offence appears to me to be most especially *imperti-
nent*—and a very serious return would be the Rod   yet doth he sit in
his Palace. Such is this World . . . (*Letters*, i. 178–9)

Endymion III demonstrates that Keats was most unlikely to have
been astonished at the 'tyranical impertinence' of any bishop
and, as Robert Ryan has shrewdly pointed out, this letter probably expressed what Keats assumed his friend Bailey must be
feeling (something akin to 'negative curacy'). Ironically, too,
Bailey's disappointment may well have resulted from the conscientious efforts by George Tomline, Bishop of Lincoln, to eradi-
cate corruption in ecclesiastical appointments by raising the
educational requirements for ordination.[4] A little later in his
letter to Bailey, Keats followed his invective about bishops and
mitres by mentioning the first of Z's essays, 'a flaming attack
upon Hunt in the Endinburgh Magazine—I never read any

---

[4] See the very informative discussion in Robert M. Ryan, *Keats: The Religious Sense*
(Princeton, 1976), 121–4.

thing so virulent... These Philipics are to come out in Numbers—calld "the Cockney School of Poetry"' (*Letters*, i. 179–80). In bringing together strenuous anti-clericalism and the Cockney School essays, I suspect that Keats's letter (which remained in Bailey's possession) provided materials for the censorious remarks passed many years later to Milnes.[5]

When *Endymion* was published in April 1818, the anti-clerical sentiment which so preoccupied Bailey passed almost without notice in reviews. The *British Critic* observed: 'The third book begins in character, with a jacobinical apostrophe to "crowns, turbans, and tiptop nothings"; we wonder how mitres escaped from their usual place.'[6] In *Blackwood's*, Z prefaced his quotation from the opening of Book III with these remarks:

> We had almost forgot to mention, that Keats belongs to the Cockney School of Politics, as well as the Cockney School of Poetry.
>
> It is fit that he who holds Rimini to be the first poem, should believe the Examiner to be the first politician of the day. We admire consistency, even in folly. Hear how their bantling has already learned to lisp sedition.[7]

The terms of Z's criticism in this passage have received less attention than they deserve. Keats is a 'bantling'—a bastard child—taught by the 'Cockney School' to versify in a 'lisp', associated at this period with childish or 'effeminate' sensibility. The beginning of *Endymion* III is indeed characterized by a sort of unstable, childish exuberance. But the verse is clogged with awkward parentheses: 'or, O torturing fact! | Who'; forced 'Cockney' rhymes 'fact! | Unpack'd', 'past and gone— | Babylon'; archaic words such as 'dight'; and elliptical phrases like 'There are who lord it', 'most prevailing tinsel', 'a sight | Able to face an owl's', 'unladen breasts, | Save of blown self-applause'. As political invective, the lines are almost wholly obscure. In the *Quarterly Review*, September 1818, John Wilson Croker contended that Keats had written *Endymion* 'at random', so that the poem wandered from one subject to another as the

---

[5] The letter was in Bailey's 'Ceylon Scrapbook'; see Hyder E. Rollins, 'Benjamin Bailey's Scrapbook', *K–SJ* 6 (Winter 1957), 15–35, esp. 18. Bailey's recollection of his determination to enter the 'sacred Profession' echoes Keats's observation, 'it must be shocking to find in a sacred Profession such barefaced oppression and impertinence'.

[6] *British Critic* (June, 1818), rpt. in *KCH* 94.   [7] 'Cockney School IV', 524.

rhymes suggested fresh thoughts and images.[8] But to Z the poem's marred and imperfect verse, its 'lisping' voice, was a further expression of the political agenda which he associated with Hunt and the Cockney School. Was this simply one more gibe to ridicule the 'young Cockney rhymester'?—or should we take Z's observation seriously as an insight that reveals the ideological grounds on which Keats's poems were identified with 'the Cockney school of versification, morality, and politics'?

The ways in which *Poems, by John Keats* deliberately announced the author's relationship to Leigh Hunt have been discussed already, but the complex design of this volume deserves further consideration here. Keats had divided his book into five parts: following the dedicatory sonnet to Hunt were three sections— 'Poems', 'Epistles', 'Sonnets'—and the book concluded with *Sleep and Poetry*. The contents comprised occasional verses, 'To Some Ladies', 'On Receiving a Curious Shell', 'On Leaving Some Friends'; two imitations of Spenser, the 'Specimen of an Induction' and 'Calidore'; and familiar and fraternal verse epistles to friends and his brother George. As we have seen, many of these poems were explicit in announcing Keats's politics, most obviously so in the sonnets to Hunt and Kosciusko, and in the epistles to Mathew and George Keats. The ode 'To Hope', probably written shortly after Hunt's release from gaol on 2 February 1815, declared:

> Let me not see the patriot's high bequest,
>   Great Liberty! how great in plain attire!
> With the base purple of a court oppress'd,
>   Bowing her head, and ready to expire . . . (37–40)

'To Hope' is written in a conventional eighteenth-century libertarian idiom and, along with the other poems already mentioned, it reinforces the political interests directly voiced by Keats's first book.[9] In some of these early poems Keats interweaves comparably explicit liberal sentiments with passages of luxurious description in which a decorative Spenserian bower is identified as a place of imaginative retirement and recreation:

---

[8] See *Quarterly Review*, 19 (1818), 206, and *KCH* 112.
[9] See also the discussion in Newey, ' "Alternate uproar and sad peace" ', 267–8, and, for the 'hard-driving Whig perspective' of the early verse, Newey, 'Keats, History, and the Poets', *K&H* 165–93.

> a bowery nook
> Will be elysium—an eternal book
> Whence I may copy many a lovely saying
> About the leaves, and flowers—about the playing
> Of nymphs in woods, and fountains; and the shade
> Keeping a silence round a sleeping maid;
> And many a verse from so strange influence
> That we must ever wonder how, and whence
> It came. (*Sleep and Poetry*, 63–71)

This arbour of fancied sequestration may be read as 'an eternal book' which expresses Keats's wish to lose the responsibilities of life to erotic enchantment and the 'strange influence' of poetry. But, as we saw in Chapter 4, the luxurious bower also defined a space of imagined 'elysium' comparable to Hunt's 'Places of nestling green for Poets made', and intelligible as an expression of the liberal ideals announced more directly elsewhere in the book. When critics noticed Keats's 'natural freedom of versification', or observed that 'in his enmity to the French school, and to the Augustan age of England, he seems to have a principle, that plan and arrangement are prejudicial to natural poetry', they were responding to the stylistic signature of the 'natural freedom' that also defined his opposition to 'the present Ministers'.[10]

Keats's 'bowery nooks'—'Some flowery spot, sequester'd, wild, romantic' ('To George Felton Mathew', 37), the 'fresh woodland alley . . . the bowery cleft' (*I stood tip-toe*, 20–1)—are resorts of imaginative life which at the levels of poetic style, vocabulary, and imagery link with the ideological contexts of his creativity. In some instances this association is more fully drawn out, as in the 'outlaw' or greenwood lyrics of January 1818. In an earlier lyric, 'Oh! how I love', the fanciful retreat to 'A fragrant wild, with Nature's beauty drest' awakens thoughts of

> patriotic lore,
> Musing on Milton's fate—on Sydney's bier—
> Till their stern forms before my mind arise . . . (7, 9–11)

A comparably patriotic inflection of retreat appears in *Sleep and Poetry*, where withdrawal into 'the bosom of a leafy world' (119)

---

[10] See the following two reviews of *Poems, by John Keats*: J. H. Reynolds in *Champion* (9 Mar. 1817), rpt. *KCH* 49, and George Felton Mathew in the *European Magazine* (May 1817), rpt. *KCH* 52.

gives rise to thoughts of the fully humanized poetry which Keats
hoped to write in the future:

> And can I ever bid these joys farewell?
> Yes, I must pass them for a nobler life,
> Where I may find the agonies, the strife
> Of human hearts . . . (122–5)

Here, and elsewhere in Keats's early poems, the bower serves as
a temporary refuge in the poet's quest towards a humane,
historicized imagination—indeed, Jack Stillinger has seen the
whole of the 1817 collection as a narrative addressing issues
related to Keats's career as a poet.[11] A similar progression appears in 'Ode to a Nightingale', where 'verdurous glooms and
winding mossy ways' (40) lead into the 'embalmed darkness' of
reverie figured as a woodland bower in which the poet may

> guess each sweet
> Wherewith the seasonable month endows
> The grass, the thicket, and the fruit-tree wild;
> White hawthorn, and the pastoral eglantine;
> Fast fading violets cover'd up in leaves;
> And mid-May's eldest child,
> The coming musk-rose, full of dewy wine,
> The murmurous haunt of flies on summer eves (43–50)

—much as he had delighted to catalogue 'luxuries' in his earlier poems. But in 'Ode to a Nightingale' this child-like poring
over 'sweets' of the imagination (which Yeats thought was characteristic of Keats) gives way to an awareness of mortality, the
passage of time, and the tread of 'hungry generations' of
humankind. This movement from 'sweets' or 'luxuries' to a
chastened awareness of history is a recurrent pattern in
Keatsian romance, and in his early verse it is accompanied by a
more evident preoccupation with the political life of England.

A Time when Pan is not Sought

> these are times to make the most delicate-minded look
> warily about them . . . we must confess, that the idea of ten

[11] See 'The Order of Poems in Keats's First Volume', in *The Hoodwinking of
Madeline*, 1–13.

poor wretches huddling together in ragged starvation on a
bridge at night is at least as much calculated to make us
grave and shuddering, as that of a single high-living PRINCE
who has his coach-window cracked.[12]

The title-page of *Poems, by John Keats* was carefully arranged to
announce the relationship between liberal politics and the
poet's imaginative life (see Fig. 5). On opening the book,
Keats's first readers saw an epigraph from Spenser's complaint
Muiopotmos; or, The Fate of the Butterfly:

> 'What more felicity can fall to creature,
> Than to enjoy delight with liberty'

Just beneath this verse is a laurelled head of William Shakespeare,[13] a juxtaposition that is worth exploring a little further.
In bringing together Spenser and Shakespeare, Keats paid tribute to his poetic heroes (two months after *Poems* appeared he
'dared' to acknowledge Shakespeare as his 'good Genius' *Letters*, i. 142) and also made a public declaration of his political
allegiances. By coupling 'delight' and 'liberty' with Shakespeare, Keats neatly focused a theme in Hunt's leaders for the
Examiner where Shakespeare was invoked as presiding over 'our
liberties' in a liberal pantheon that included King Alfred,
Chaucer, Milton, Sydney, and Marvell.[14] Keats may well have
expected his readers to know that in Spenser's poem libertarian
'felicity' is immediately succeeded by 'mishap', and an elegiac
meditation on the vulnerability of joy:

> But what on earth can long abide in state?
> Or who can him assure of happie day;
> Sith morning faire may bringe fowle evening late,
> And least mishap the most blisse alter may? (217–20)[15]

[12] 'Attack on the Prince Regent, and a Word or Two of Plain Comment upon it',
Examiner (2 Feb. 1817), 65.

[13] For the identification of Shakespeare, and Keats's 'deliberate design' of the
title-page in *Poems*, see Stuart M. Sperry, 'Richard Woodhouse's Interleaved and
Annotated Copy of Keats's *Poems* (1817)', in E. Rothstein and T. K. Dunseath (eds.),
Literary Monographs (Madison, 1967), 120–1.

[14] See for example *Examiner* (2 Mar. 1817), 129, 138, and (9 Mar. 1817), 145.
For Hunt, Chaucer was 'a Reformer in his day' *Examiner* (9 Mar. 1817), 145; 'a
politician and a reformer, zealous enough even in his old age to get imprisoned for
the space of four years, [who] took a special delight in rural pleasures'; *Examiner* (10
May 1818), 289. See also the discussion of Chaucer's significance for Reynolds and
Keats in Ch. 5, pp. 134–40.

[15] *Spenser: Poetical Works*, ed. J. C. Smith and E. de Selincourt (Oxford, 1912).

Earthly mutability also characterized the first poem in Keats's volume, the dedicatory sonnet to Leigh Hunt. The sonnet echoes in its first line the 'May-morning' festival of Wordsworth's 'Immortality' ode, recalling Wordsworth's loss of visionary power ('there hath passed away a glory from the earth') as a comment on the historical moment of Keats's compliment to Hunt:

> *To Leigh Hunt, Esq.*
> Glory and loveliness have passed away;
>   For if we wander out in early morn,
>   No wreathed incense do we see upborne
> Into the east, to meet the smiling day:
> No crowd of nymphs soft voic'd and young, and gay,
>   In woven baskets bringing ears of corn,
>   Roses, and pinks, and violets, to adorn
> The shrine of Flora in her early May.
> But there are left delights as high as these,
>   And I shall ever bless my destiny,
> That in a time, when under pleasant trees
>   Pan is no longer sought, I feel a free,
> A leafy luxury, seeing I could please
> With these poor offerings, a man like thee.

The impact that this impressive dedicatory poem would have made on Keats's readers and reviewers should not be underestimated. By placing it on the first page of his first collection Keats deliberately identified himself with an outspoken figure of public opposition to the government, but, more than this, he did so in the unsettled period following the Spa Fields riot—'a crisis of . . . general and unexampled pressure and calamity'.[16] On 2 March 1817, the day before *Poems* was published in London, the front page of the *Examiner* carried an article 'On the Proposed Suspension of the Habeas Corpus Act', denouncing the Foreign Secretary Lord Castlereagh—'a man, who is proved guilty in the House of Commons of violating the Constitution and setting at nought the representative rights of the people, coming forward and asking for a suspension of our most sacred privilege'—and warning that 'The Suspension Bill, if it pass, will be an unconstitutional assumption of power by the

---

[16] From the first resolution taken at the 'Meeting for a Reform' reported in *Examiner* (26 Jan. 1817), 58.

House of Commons illegally constituted.'[17] By appearing the day following Hunt's attack in the *Examiner*, Keats's lyrical compliment to Castlereagh's opponent would have seemed markedly controversial—and not only because of the political stakes it so clearly announced. In the economy of Keats's sonnet national crisis is associated with dislocation from the classical world, with the loss of pastoral innocence and 'a time, when under pleasant trees I Pan is no longer sought'.[18] The contemporary association of paganism and the cult of Pan with liberty of conscience has been discussed already in Chapter 2. More relevant here, I think, is what Keats may have intended by that slightly elliptical reference to the present as 'a time, when . . . I Pan is no longer sought'. One could cite the mass meeting of reformists in Spa Fields, London, 2 December 1816, which was followed by rioting; the frequent petitions to the Commons for reform; the attack on the Prince Regent's coach, 28 January 1817; the numerous bankruptcies caused by the post-war depression; capital trials of the rioters, and the suspension of the Habeas Corpus Act on 4 March.[19] All of these developments afforded evidence of mounting national emergency; circumstances in which 'Pan is [not] sought'; a time when, as Hunt wrote,

sophisticated men set up and deify their own selfish and petty feelings of all sorts, and then make virtue consist in maintaining them. The business of society is thus turned into shewing an outward reverence for a hundred stupidities, and resenting them with involuntary spleen all the while; and nations become formal, morose, and evil-thinking.

---

[17] *Examiner* (2 Mar. 1817), 129–30. Castlereagh had introduced the Suspension Bill in the Commons on 24 Feb.

[18] Martin Aske has emphasized how this default may register an anxiety of belatedness in Keats, an imagination seeking consolation for the impossibility of recovering a pure classical inspiration. Aske foregrounds the role of the classics in Keats's quest for poetic identity, and differentiates his '*privatisation*' of response from the ideologically driven poetry of Shelley and Peacock. See *Keats and Hellenism*, 3, 47–52. I differ from Aske in seeing Keats's troubled invocation of classical literature and myth, and the dedicatory sonnet in particular, as inseparable from the poet's engagement with contemporary social and political issues.

[19] *Examiner* (2 Mar. 1817), 133, reports that in the previous week the Commons received petitions for reform from Ludlow, Blackburne, Duffield, Stuarton, Perth, Hull, 'and other places', and one from an individual, Henry Hunt. In the same issue, 138, forty-eight bankruptcies are listed, most of them small businesses; a comparable number of bankruptcies appeared in the paper each week at this period. For more, see E. P. Thompson, *The Making of the English Working Class* (Harmondsworth, 1968), 691–700.

The best piety is that which is most alive to the beauty of the creation, and would see all enjoy it alike; but the weak, the hypocritical, and the greedy, turn aside from it to jostle for absurdities, to keep up despicable possessions and superfluities in its stead, and to sing damnatory hymns at each other in ill-built sepulchres, where they thank GOD for giving them certain commandments, and saving from their own madness those who do not keep them.—For GOD's sake, let us get out of this subject, and breathe again the fresh air of reason and nature.[20]

Hunt's final remark finds an echo in Keats's sonnet where ('in a time' that is 'formal, morose, and evil-thinking') he too associates release from present oppressions with nature and 'a free, | A leafy luxury'. The greenwood flourish, emulating Hunt's poetic style,[21] was a compliment and also a libertarian signal bringing Keatsian 'luxury' within the compass of history. Against Castlereagh's suppression of 'the representative rights of the people', and in spite of 'despicable possessions and superfluities', Keats brings his 'poor offerings' in *Poems* as a witness to the renewal of what Hunt called 'our green and glorious country'.[22]

The Suburban School

> How Cockneyish it was of me to be delighted with this
> scene, which I was, unfeignedly!
> > (Cornelius Webb, 'A Walk Near Town')

> But mostly it was footsteps, rustling leaves,
> And blackbirds fluting over miles of Heath.
> > Then Millfield Lane looked like a Constable
> And all the grassy hillocks spoke of Keats.
> > (John Betjeman, 'Before MCMXIV')[23]

After the politically motivated attacks on Keats in the *Quarterly* and *Blackwood's*, Keats's friends rallied to his defence. One of their tactics was to insist upon the separation of poetry and

[20] 'Attack on the Prince Regent, and Thanksgiving in the Churches', *Examiner* (16 Feb. 1817), 98.
[21] Compare Hunt's Hampstead sonnet quoted in full on p. 126.
[22] *Examiner* (2 Mar. 1817), 139.
[23] See Cornelius Webb, *The Man about Town* (2 vols., London, 1838), ii. 108; Betjeman, *Summoned by Bells*, 3.

history, the aesthetic and the political. John Hamilton Reynolds, for example, asserted Keats's rural 'independence':

We have the highest hopes of this young poet. We are obscure men, it is true . . . We live far from the world of letters,—out of the pale of fashionable criticism,—aloof from the atmosphere of a Court; but we are surrounded by a beautiful country, and love Poetry, which we read out of doors, as well as in. We think we see glimpses of a high mind in this young man . . .[24]

The poet's 'high mind', by implication, was disengaged from the traffic of letters, criticism, and politics. Yet each of Reynolds's claims for Keats's 'obscurity' was socially definitive: 'fashionable criticism', for instance, denoted criticism which was currently 'stylish', but also a manner 'current in upper-class society' or 'in vogue among persons of the upper class' (*OED*)— that is, the coterie of 'fashionables' who contributed to 'the atmosphere of a Court'.[25] Reynolds's purpose was to defend Keats by insulating him in 'beautiful country', although the poet's distance from 'fashionable criticism' and 'the atmosphere of a court' might readily be interpreted as reprobate—a characteristic of the literary revolution announced in *Sleep and*

[24] John Hamilton Reynolds, *Alfred, West of England Journal and General Advertiser* (6 Oct. 1818), rpt. *KCH* 120.

[25] For 'the atmosphere of a Court' see for example 'Court and Fashionables', *Examiner* (3 May 1818), 284. The report describes the Queen's visit to the Mansion-house, for the examination of children educated in the London National Schools: 'About 300 girls and 700 boys were paraded before the Company, and underwent some examination, after singing a hymn and repeating part of the Church Service. This being over, they sang another hymn, and said some prayers; they then sang "God save the King", with an additional verse about the QUEEN's letting her "gentle and serene brow grace the fair wreath".—The LORD Mayor then addressed the little children, reminding them of the high honour which had been done them by her MAJESTY, and ordering them a small sum of money each (sixpence we believe) by order of the QUEEN.—The children conducted themselves with military precision.— The Royal Party, having first partaken of a choice collation, left the Mansion-house amidst the shouts of the populace. After this exhibition the Royal Dukes, the Bishops, the Lord Mayor, &c. went to dine at the City of London Tavern, upon "all the delicacies of the season". "Church and State" was drank by the Princes and Bishops in great style; and their happy union was commented upon with much gravity by the Archbishop of CANTERBURY.' For 'fashionable criticism', see the article on 'the *Government Critic* . . . an invisible link, that connects literature with the police'; 'Literary Notices', *Examiner* (14 June 1818), 378: 'He is under the protection of *the Court*; and his zeal for his King and country gives him a right to say what he pleases of every writer who does not do all in his power to pamper the one into a tyrant, and to trample the other into a herd of slaves.'

Poetry and championed by Hunt in his 'Young Poets' essay and in the preface to *Foliage*.[26] Certainly, Z took this view and contrived to frustrate Keats and the other Cockneys by banishing them to a cultural limbo on the fringe of metropolitan civilization, yet not quite removed to the country. In retrospect the strategy of enforcing Keats's isolation from 'the world', adopted by friends and hostile critics alike, can be seen to have initiated the long-standing critical consensus which agreed that historical analysis was 'irrelevant' to the understanding of Keats's poetry.[27]

The London 'mob' had always been seen as a vulgar, dangerously turbulent mass, and it was probably this historical association with social upheaval that Z wished to invoke with the 'Cockney' label. But his criticism displaced the Cockney territory from the inner city to the northerly village of Hampstead, and confined it there by coining the disagreeable adjective 'suburban'. The *Oxford English Dictionary* dates the pejorative sense of 'suburban' to 1817, its first recorded use being Laura's 'pitying survey' of her 'dearest friends' in Byron's *Beppo*—completed October 1817, published February the following year:

> One has false curls, another too much paint,
>   A third—where did she buy that frightful turban?
> A fourth's so pale she fears she's going to faint,
>   A fifth's look's vulgar, dowdyish, and suburban . . . (521–4)

One might argue further that it was Z's essays on the Cockney School, which also dated from October 1817, that served to fix the modern, pejorative senses of 'suburban' as part of his caricatures of Hunt, Hazlitt, Keats, Reynolds, and Webb.

In his first essay, Z writes about Hunt's poetry of nature and place:

He is the ideal of a Cockney Poet. He raves perpetually about 'green fields', 'jaunty streams', and 'o'er-arching leafiness', exactly as a Cheapside shop-keeper does about the beauties of his box on the Camberwell road. Mr Hunt is altogether unacquainted with the face of nature in her magnificent scenes; he has never seen any mountain

---

[26] See Jones, 'The Suburban School', 14, for the suburbs as a representation of the 'bourgeois ideal' of a landscape in which nature and culture coexist 'within a carefully constructed domestic environment'.

[27] See KHM 26.

higher than Highgate-hill, nor reclined by any stream more pastoral
than the Serpentine River. But he is determined to be a poet eminently rural, and he rings the changes—till one is sick of him, on the
beauties of the different 'high views' which he has taken of God and
nature, in the course of some Sunday dinner parties, at which he has
assisted in the neighbourhood of London.[28]

Cockney nature poetry, for Z, was a Cheapside sublime expressed in catch-phrases and jingles. In Hunt's poems, nature's
'magnificent scenes' had been reduced to a familiar local territory—'Hampstead's whole merits,—heath, wood, hill, and vale'
('To Thomas Moore'); Romantic ecstasy had dwindled to table
talk, 'Too witty, for tattling,—too wise, for dogmatic' ('To
W.H.'). A comparable citation of Cockney faults had appeared
in Byron's 'Second Letter on Bowles's Strictures', which dis-
criminated 'two sorts of Naturals;—the Lakers, who whine
about Nature because they live in Cumberland; and their *under-
sect* (which some one has maliciously called the "Cockney
School"), who are enthusiastical for the country because they
live in London'. Byron agreed with Z in that he too associated
Cockney imagination with the bogus sublimities of Hunt's
poetic landscape: 'the far distant boundaries of the wilds of
Middlesex', 'the Alps of Highgate', and 'the Nile of the New
River'.[29] Although Byron was principally concerned in his
'Second Letter' to vindicate Pope as a nature poet, his essay
also shows that the Cockney controversy generated a public
revaluation of Wordsworth as an ornament of the literary and
political establishment.[30] The consequences of this alteration
for later criticism of Wordsworth and Keats are notable. Generally

[28] 'Cockney School I', 39.
[29] 'Observations upon "Observations"', vi, 410, 412.
[30] William Blackwood's correspondence discloses Coleridge's significant role in
encouraging *Blackwood's* popularizing of Wordsworth. In spring 1819 *Blackwood's
Magazine* was trying to woo Coleridge as a contributor, using William Davies (of the
London publishing house Cadell and Davies) as an intermediary. Davies reported
Coleridge's opinion that *Blackwood's* should avoid 'any perceptible bias to either
political party, and . . . every disposition to indulge in personalities'. He added, 'as
I discover that Mr W. is a very great favorite with Mr C. I am rather inclined to
recommend that you occasionally say something kind and conciliatory, about Mr
W., in your future Nos, though merely to shew a kindly feeling towards Mr C.' NLS,
MS 4004, quoted by permission of the Trustees of the National Library of Scotland.
For *Blackwood's* championing of Wordsworth, see Alexander, '*Blackwood's*: Magazine
as Romantic Form', 57–68, esp. 61, and for Z's approbation of Wordsworth, see
p. 227 below.

speaking, modern critics and editors lose interest in Wordsworth from this period of the poet's career. On the other hand, adverse criticism of Keats at this time has obscured the ideological force of his early poems, which Z and other contemporary readers understood as a revival of the English Jacobin movement of the 1790s.

Z's attacks on the Cockney School included a mock-obituary of Hunt which also identified his distinction in establishing the terms of suburban vision for the nineteenth and twentieth centuries:

It is much to be regretted, that the deceased bard's rural life was so limited and local. He had no other notion of that sublime expression, 'sub Dio', than merely 'out of doors'. One always thinks of Leigh Hunt, on his rural excursions to and from Hampstead, in a great-coat or spencer, clogs over his shoes, and with an umbrella in his hand. He is always talking of lanes, and styles, and hedgerows, and clumps of trees, and cows with large udders. He is the most suburban of poets. He died, as might have been prophesied, within a few hours saunter of the spot where he was born, and without having been once beyond the well-fenced meadows of his microcosm. Suppose for a moment, Leigh Hunt at sea—or on the summit of Mont Blanc! It is impossible. No. Hampstead was the only place for him.

> 'With farmy fields in front and sloping green.'

Only hear how he revels in the morning before breakfast, when out on an adventurous constitutional stroll.

> Then northward what a range,—with heath and pond,
> Nature's own ground; woods that let mansions through,
> And cottaged vales with pillowy fields beyond,
> And clump of darkening pines, and prospects blue,
> And that clear path through all, where daily meet
> Cool cheeks, and brilliant eyes, and morn-elastic feet.

Mr Hunt is the only poet who has considered the external world simply as the 'country', in contradiction to the town—fields in place of squares, lanes *vice* streets, and trees as lieutenants of houses. That fine line of Campbell's,

> 'And look on nature with a poet's eye,'

must, to be applicable to him, be changed into,

> 'Look on the country with a cockney's eye.'[31]

[31] 'Cockney School VI', 74.

Z's remarks were calculated to present a kind of suburban grotesque, 'in a great-coat or spencer, clogs over his shoes, and with an umbrella', but they actually locate Hunt in the midst of a scene which is dismayingly akin to the densely populated modern landscape of southern England. And more than this, Hunt's Cockney, suburban microcosm has expanded to form the reality of modern life in the western world—and increasingly so elsewhere; the globe itself is becoming local, limited, socialized, well fenced: Hampstead is the only place left for us—a suburban patch known and frequented by all. We need also to recognize that Z's criticism succeeded in making suburban life and literature synonymous with cultural vulgarity, for later generations followed him in regarding the '*Suburban School*' of English writing (so Byron termed it) as beyond the pale of serious critical attention.[32] As part of this systematic cultural depreciation, the 'Cockney School' essays worked further to prejudice understanding of Keats's politics from an early date, by establishing a powerful idea of Keats as an immature poet and thinker.

John Hamilton Reynolds had recommended Keats's poetry by drawing attention to his youth, and other critics made similar points, so that William Rossetti, writing in 1887, could claim that Keats had been 'doomed' to 'youthfulness'.[33] Hunt had introduced Keats in the *Examiner*, 1 December 1816, under the heading 'Young Poets': 'The last of these young aspirants . . . is, we believe, the youngest of them all, and just of age. His name is JOHN KEATS.'[34] Reviews of *Poems* and *Endymion* refer to Keats as 'a very young man'; 'our young poet'; 'the young writer'; 'a young poet giving himself up to his own impressions'; 'an immature promise of possible excellence'; 'sentiments sometimes bordering upon childishness'; 'a very young man'; 'our young friend'; 'the young aspirant'; 'a young man of genius'.[35] For Wordsworth, too, 'young Keats' was 'a youth of [great] promise'.[36]

---

[32] Byron to John Murray, 4 Aug. 1821, *BLJ* viii. 166.

[33] See Rossetti, *Life of John Keats*, 209.

[34] *Examiner* (1 Dec. 1816), 761.

[35] *Champion* (9 Mar. 1817), *KCH* 45; *European Magazine* (May 1817), *KCH* 52; *Examiner* (1 June 1817), *KCH* 55; *Eclectic Review* (Sept. 1817), *KCH* 67; *Edinburgh Magazine, and Literary Miscellany* (Oct. 1817), *KCH* 71; *Examiner* (27 Sept. 1818), 609; *Chester Guardian*, rpt. in *Examiner* (1 Nov. 1818), 696; *Alfred, West of England Journal and General Advertiser* (6 Oct. 1817), *KCH* 117.

Nevertheless, in April 1818, when *Endymion* was published, Keats was 22½ years old: hardly young any longer, and certainly not 'bordering on childhood'. Wordsworth had been not quite 23 when he published *An Evening Walk* and *Descriptive Sketches* in 1793; Byron was just 24 when *Childe Harold* was published in 1812, and the reviews certainly did not dwell at length upon his young manhood. So while many of Keats's first reviewers welcomed his poetry, their preoccupation with youth pointed to qualities that other less sympathetic critics found suspect: the callow sentiments of a poet 'just of age', the unformed imagination of a man still 'bordering on childishness, the 'lisped' verses of a 'bantling'.

Keats himself tried to deflect hostile criticism of *Endymion* by alerting readers to his own 'great inexperience [and] immaturity'. 'The imagination of a boy is healthy', Keats wrote in his preface to the poem, 'and the mature imagination of a man is healthy; but there is a space of life between, in which the soul is in a ferment, the character undecided, the way of life uncertain, the ambition thick-sighted: thence proceeds mawkishness.' 'Mawkishness' (denoting sickly sentimentality) is derived from 'mawk', a maggot, and in this context may also be related to the auxiliary sense of 'maggot', meaning 'a whimsical fancy'. The pathology of 'mawkishness', outlined by Keats, appeared more fully in an 1806 review of Charlotte Dacre's novel *Zofloya* in which her 'maggotty' prose style was diagnosed as the symptom of an infectious 'disease . . . in the brain . . . overwhelming all meaning in a multitude of words':

The ravings of persons under its influence, whenever they are heard or read, have a sensible effect upon brains of a weak constitution, which themselves either putrify and breed maggots, or suffer a derangement of some kind. It might be a charitable thing to have an hospital for the reception of these unfortunate people while under the influence of the disease, where they might be confined in such a manner as not to infect others; the incurables being of course kept separate from the rest.[37]

[36] See *The Letters of William and Dorothy Wordsworth*, ed. E. de Selincourt, 2nd edn., *The Middle Years Part II, 1812–1820*, rev. M. Moorman and A. G. Hill (Oxford, 1970), 360, 578.
[37] *Literary Journal: A Review of Domestic and Foreign Literature* (1806), 633, 635. I am grateful to Dr Nicola Trott for this reference.

Z. recognized the symptoms of this 'maggotty' disease in the 'drivelling idiocy' of *Endymion*, responding to the poem's style but also to the preface where Keats associated mawkishness with a 'space of life between' at which the imagination is 'sickly' (and fantastical) in that it lacks character and steadiness of purpose. *Endymion*, according to the preface, is a 'feverish attempt', a 'youngster' which 'should die away'. In December 1817 Keats had identified a comparable uncertainty of self as one characteristic of imaginative genius, a quality he defined as 'negative capability' (*Letters*, i. 193). Reviews of *Poems* and *Endymion* described the poetry as 'remarkably abstracted', 'indiscriminate', 'the shadowings of unsophisticated emotions', and 'indistinct and confused'[38]—and some of the reviewers found these effects attractive. For example, the *Edinburgh Magazine*[39] drew attention to Keats's 'licentious brilliancy of epithet', describing the following passage from the epistle 'To Charles Cowden Clarke' as 'the very pink of the smart and flowing conversational style . . . such elegant *badinage*':

> But many days have past since last my heart
> Was warm'd luxuriously by divine Mozart;
> By Arne delighted, or by Handel madden'd;
> Or by the song of Erin pierc'd and sadden'd:
> What time you were before the music sitting,
> And the rich notes to each sensation fitting;
> Since I have walk'd with you through shady lanes
> That freshly terminate in open plains,
> And revel'd in a chat that ceased not
> When at night-fall among your books we got:
> No, nor when supper came, nor after that,—
> Nor when reluctantly I took my hat;
> No, nor till cordially you shook my hand
> Mid-way between our homes:—your accents bland
> Still sounded in my ears, when I no more
> Could hear your footsteps touch the grav'ly floor.
> Sometimes I lost them, and then found again;
> You chang'd the footpath for the grassy plain.
> In those still moments I have wish'd you joys

[38] See J. H. Reynolds in *Champion* (9 Mar. 1817), rpt. *KCH* 46; Hunt in *Examiner* (6 July 1817), 429, rpt. *KCH* 57; *Edinburgh Magazine, and Literary Miscellany* (Oct. 1817), rpt. *KCH* 73; Baldwin's *London Magazine* (Apr. 1820), *KCH* 137.
[39] See *KCH* 72.

That well you know to honour:—'Life's very toys
With him', said I, 'will take a pleasant charm;
It cannot be that ought will work him harm'.
These thoughts now come o'er me with all their might:—
Again I shake your hand, friend Charles, good night. (109–32)

After quoting this 'banter' in full, the *Edinburgh Magazine*'s reviewer described it as 'ground very dangerous for a young poet'—although why the epistle should have drawn this judgement may not be immediately apparent to a modern reader. A principal danger was that its easy, colloquial manner ('before the music sitting'; 'chat that ceased not'; 'among your books we got'; 'nor when supper came, nor after that') was insufficiently considered to achieve a 'permanent effect':

That style is vivacious, smart, witty, changeful, sparkling, and learned—full of bright points and flashy expressions that strike and even seem to please by a sudden boldness of novelty,—rather abounding in familiarities of conception and oddnesses of manner which shew ingenuity, even though they be perverse, or common, or contemptuous.

At a first glance, 'vivacious', 'smart', 'witty', 'sparkling', 'learned' would seem to be a full approbation for the brisk and lively manner of Keats's poetry. But the critic's unease is registered through a second strand of vocabulary in the review: the poetry is 'licentious', 'changeful', 'flashy', mingling a 'boldness of novelty' with familiarities and commonplaces. Evidently, this novel (and 'maggotty') style was perceived as a challenge to received literary values, and specifically to the neoclassical ideal of stylistic and intellectual 'decorum'. But, as Olivia Smith has demonstrated, such criticism had an agenda that extended far beyond linguistic and literary matters. Its core vocabulary had a social register which derived from the preface to Johnson's *Dictionary of the English Language* (1755), in which 'such terms as "elegant", "refined", "pure", "proper", and "vulgar" . . . conveyed the assumptions that correct usage belonged to the upper classes and that a developed sensibility and an understanding of moral virtue accompanied it'.[40] In direct contrast to this authorized language was what Johnson termed the 'fugitive cant' of current usages among 'the laborious and mercantile part of the people': 'illiterate writers will at one time or other,

---

[40] Olivia Smith, *The Politics of Language 1791–1819* (Oxford, 1984), 9.

by publick infatuation, rise into renown, who, not knowing the original import of words, will use them with colloquial licentiousness, confound distinction, and forget propriety.'[41] The *Edinburgh*'s reviewer makes Keats's poetry conform exactly to Johnson's paradigm of the 'illiterate'. It is 'licentious', which was glossed by Johnson as 'unrestrained by law or morality'; and when carried over into literary criticism, the word retained its unsettling legal and moral associations. Those senses of 'licentious' are echoed by 'changeful', defined by Johnson as 'Full of change; inconstant; uncertain; mutable; subject to variation; fickle', and also by 'flashy', that is, 'Empty; not solid; showy without substance'. The 'boldness of novelty' in Keats's poems, which one might expect to be a praiseworthy quality, was in fact a persistent fault: rather than expressing a courageous break with literary precedent, for the *Edinburgh*'s critic (as for Johnson) Keats's 'boldness of novelty' signalled a lack of caution; an aspiration to liberty without responsibility (after the pattern of revolutionary France) through which proper 'distinctions' were overturned and 'confounded'.

All of these critical terms show how Keats's vocabulary, poetic idiom, and style were intensely freighted with moral, social, and political meanings. His 'mawkishness' was not just the impotence of an adolescent poet; it represented a more radical unsettlement, the poetics of dissent which defined Keats's opposition to establishment ideology. Like Hunt's and Hazlitt's writings, Keats's innovative poetry is 'full of conceits and sparkling points' which were understood as the voice of a reformist political agenda: their writing is 'alive to the socialities . . . of life', and is 'too fond, even in their favourite descriptions of nature, of a reference to the factitious resemblances of society'. John Wilson Croker, reviewing *Endymion* in the *Quarterly*, elucidated the politics of Keats's style by characterizing his poetry as an anarchy of neologisms and run-on couplets, to be understood only in so far as Keats was 'a copyist of Mr Hunt, but . . . more unintelligible'.[42] Byron, like Croker, felt threatened by Keats's mawkish novelty. But for him Keats's

[41] From the 'Preface' to Samuel Johnson, *A Dictionary of the English Language* (London, 1755), unpaginated.

[42] See *KCH* 111. For Keats as a 'copyist' of Hunt, compare Keats's 'among your books we got' with 'get among trees' from Hunt's epistle 'To William Hazlitt'. See Ch. 4, p. 127.

imagination was less involved with 'soul . . . character . . . [and] way of life' and rather more absorbed by the sexual awakening of an adolescent 'Mankin': his imaginative impotence was integral to his '*Vulgarity . . .* a sad abortive attempt at all things, "signifying nothing"'.[43] The Tory journals demonstrated a comparable preoccupation with Keats's 'mankin' sexuality, but more distinctly in the context of childish and 'effeminate' sensibility and seditious politics. And, as with the review from the *Edinburgh Magazine* discussed above, this politically oriented criticism reflected eighteenth-century preoccupations with language.

The politics of childish poetry link reviews of Keats and Hunt with the critical reception of the earlier generation—Coleridge, Wordsworth, and Southey—in the 1790s. Criticism of Keats's poetry from 1817 was, as Jerome McGann has observed, 'in many respects a repetition of the attack upon Wordsworth's programme in the Lyrical Ballads'.[44] Favourable reviews of *Poems* were attracted by Keats's devotion to simplicity. Leigh Hunt found in the poems a 'most natural and least expressible simplicity'; the *European Magazine* and the *Eclectic Review* pointed respectively to poetry 'as pretty and as innocent as childishness can make it', and to 'sentiment sometimes bordering upon childishness'.[45] John Hamilton Reynolds recommended Keats's simplicity in more complex terms: 'He relies directly and wholly on nature. He marries poesy to genuine simplicity. He makes her artless,—yet abstains carefully from giving her an uncomely homeliness:—that is, he shows he can be familiar with nature, yet perfectly strange to the habits of common life.'[46] Here the function of poetic 'simplicity' is a 'marriage' which will domesticate and subdue a consciously feminized nature, 'mak[ing] her artless'. The crucial word is *artless*. It denotes stylistic transparency and directness (as opposed to metaphysical 'mystery'), but also gathers a cluster of social, moral, and gendered resonances. Feminine nature is 'artless' in that it is sexually and

[43] Byron's 'Addenda' to his *Letter to John Murray Esqre*. See *Lord Byron: The Complete Miscellaneous Prose*, ed. Andrew Nicholson (Oxford, 1991), 160, and Byron to John Murray, 12 Mar. 1821, *BLJ* viii. 92.

[44] See KHM 30.

[45] *Examiner* (6 July 1817), 429, rpt. *KCH* 59; *European Magazine* (May 1817), rpt. *KCH* 53; *Eclectic Review* (Sept. 1817), rpt. *KCH* 67.

[46] *Champion* (9 Mar. 1817), rpt. *KCH* 46.

socially conformative: 'sincere, guileless, ingenuous' (*OED* 4), ideally passive, tractable, and (as for Samuel Johnson) 'comely' because averse to 'habits of common life'. Reynolds laboured this point to refute those critics who claim that 'artlessness is a vice'; Keats's 'natural freedom of versification' does not descend into licentiousness—indeed, the 'best poets of the day might not blush to own it'.[47]

Early reviews of *Lyrical Ballads* (1798) had been remarkably similar. Joseph Johnson's *Analytical Review* praised 'the studied simplicity, which pervades many of the poems', noting 'poems which particularly pleased us from their character either of simplicity or tenderness, or both'. For the *British Critic* the poems aimed at 'simplicity and nature', and 'succeeded in attaining [a] judicious degree of simplicity'. The *Monthly Review* found Wordsworth's 'natural delineations of human passions, human characters, and human incidents' to be 'pleasing and interesting in no common way', and described one poem, 'We are Seven', as 'innocent and pretty infantine prattle'.[48] Each of these reviews responded to Wordsworth's advertised desire to offer 'a natural delineation of human passions, human characters, and human incidents' in an appropriately democratic idiom. But to an anti-Jacobinical reader poetry (and poetic theory) of this character might appear dangerously 'levelling' in that it sought 'to ascertain how far the language of conversation in the middle and lower classes of society is adapted for the purposes of poetic pleasure'.[49]

The *Anti-Jacobin* magazine (20 November 1797) substantiated this political context by elaborating 'the elements of a *Jacobin* Art of Poetry' to illustrate 'the poetical, as well as the political, doctrine of the NEW SCHOOL'. The 'Ode to Jacobinism' (26 March 1798) represented the French Revolution as a 'darling child' whose 'infant mind' had been infected with Voltaire's writings—a scene which was depicted with deathly, nightmarish intensity in James Gillray's oil sketch of *Voltaire Instructing the Infant Jacobinism*. A little later in 1798, the satirical

[47] See *KCH* 46, 49.

[48] See *Analytical Review* (Dec. 1798); *British Critic* (Oct. 1799); *Monthly Review* (June 1799). All are rpt. in 'Appendix C' of *Wordsworth and Coleridge: Lyrical Ballads*, ed. R. L. Brett and A. R. Jones (2nd edn., London, 1991), 322–40.

[49] See the 'Advertisement' to *Lyrical Ballads* (1798) in *The Prose Works of William Wordsworth*, i. 116–17.

poem *New Morality* (9 July) identified a proto-Keatsian 'mawkish strain' as the unstable residue of '*French* Philanthropy . . . filtered through the dregs of Paine'. And the same poem offered another genealogy, this time of Rousseau's foster-child, 'Sweet Sensibility':

> Sweet child of sickly Fancy! her of yore
> From her loved France Rousseau to exile bore;
> And, while midst lakes and mountains wild he ran,
> Full of himself, and shunn'd the haunts of man,
> Taught her o'er each lone vale and Alpine steep
> To lisp the story of his wrongs, and weep;
> Taught her to cherish still in either eye,
> Of tender tears a plentiful supply,
> And pour them in the brooks that babbled by;—
> —Taught by nice scales to mete her feelings strong,
> False by degrees, and exquisitely wrong;—
> —For the crushed beetle *first*,—the widow'd dove,
> And all the warbled sorrows of the grove;—
> *Next* for poor suff'ring *guilt*;—and *last* of all,
> For Parents, Friends, a King and Country's fall.[50]

The *Anti-Jacobin* argued repeatedly that the cult of sensibility had been exploited by Rousseau and Paine to enlist sympathetic and tender feeling as motives for a democratic revolution: a revolutionary mawkishness in which emotional susceptibility and changeful politics were combined. Indeed, another famous cartoon by Gillray, *New Morality* (which illustrated the poem), showed the English Jacobins (including Coleridge, Southey, Thelwall, and—as 'toad and frog'—the Charleses Lamb and Lloyd) paying homage to an icon of 'SENSIBILITY': a bedraggled *citoyenne* wearing a cap of liberty, cradling a dead dove in one hand and, in the other, a book inscribed 'Rousseau'.

Sensibility was identified with democratic revolution by the *Anti-Jacobin* because its franchise extended beyond the social and political distinctions of class or status, to hitherto marginal, vulnerable, and inarticulate sections of the community—especially women and children. Such 'prodigals of grief' possessed the dangerous capacity to feel ('falsely', 'wrongly', according to

---

[50] *The Poetry of the Anti-Jacobin* (6th edn., London, 1828), 225. For more on the politics of childish poetry in the 1790s, see Fairer, 'Baby Language and Revolution', 33–52.

the *Anti-Jacobin*) for all humankind, generating 'a universal benevolence' through which 'the widest communal good' superseded established social structures and categories.[51]

Besides lending a sense of revolutionary possibility to Keats's
mawkishness, the democratic sensibility of the 1790s foreshadowed the unselfish principle of Keats's negative capability,
which identified a universal hospitality as the prerogative of
poetic genius. I shall explore the implications of this relationship in greater detail in the Epilogue, but for now it is sufficient
to notice that when Keats pondered negative capability in his
letter of late December 1817, he concluded: 'This pursued
through Volumes would perhaps take us no further than this,
that with a great poet the sense of Beauty overcomes every other
consideration, or rather obliterates all consideration' (*Letters*,
i. 194). Here, Keats's idea of beauty authenticated creative
genius—especially Shakespeare's—but its power to 'overcome'
and 'obliterate' presented a combative aesthetic appropriate to
an age of revolutionary struggle. Writing sixty years previously,
Edmund Burke had said that beauty invokes ideas of 'weakness
and imperfection', arguing further that '[w]omen are very sensible of this; for which reason, they learn to lisp, to totter in their
walk, to counterfeit weakness, and even sickness'.[52] For Keats
'feminine' sickliness and imperfection were overcome and assimilated by the imagination as a paradoxical source of human
strength which, unlike the French Revolution, might offer a
lasting renewal for the world: 'a joy for ever'. And the diction
of Keats's poetry, glossed by reviewers as an 'effeminate' and
childish lisp, articulated the challenge of beauty to the authorized 'masculine' discourses of the political and cultural
establishment.

So, twenty years after the publication of 'New Morality', critics
of Keats identified him as the latest offspring of 'sickly Fancy':
Leigh Hunt's foster-child, or 'bantling' illegitimate son, taught
to 'lisp' sedition not 'midst lakes and mountains wild' but in the
studio of a suburban villa at Hampstead—'a poet's house' (*Sleep
and Poetry*, 354). By insisting on Keats's 'youth' and 'effeminacy', these critics sought to disperse the Jacobin potential in

[51] For the 'potentially radical strain of sensibility' see in particular Chris Jones,
Radical Sensibility: Literature and Ideas in the 1790s (London, 1993), esp. 1–19.
[52] See Burke, *A Philosophical Enquiry*, 100.

his poems. The extent to which later generations have been unwilling to treat Keats's political interests seriously is one measure of the reviewers' success in enforcing earlier, Burkean standards according to which Keats's distinctive poetic voice could be identified with stereotypes of passivity and weakness, and thus accommodated to the prevailing masculine structures of social and cultural authority.

As we have already seen, for Z childishness was a definitive characteristic of the 'Cockney School' of 'politics, versification, and morality', and of Keats in particular as 'a young Cockney rhymester'. In Z's essays the following profile of Cockney culture is firmly outlined: 'exquisitely bad taste', 'vulgar modes of thinking', 'low birth and low habits', 'ignorant', 'under-bred', 'suburban', 'paltry', 'morally depraved', 'indecent and immoral', 'licentious', 'obscene and traitorous'. The occasion for this sexual slander was Hunt's poem *The Story of Rimini*, that 'lewd tale of incest, adultery, and murder',[53] and Byron used much the same language in his abusive remarks about Keats. Yet in Z's essay on Keats, the social-sexual hostility aimed at Hunt gives place to the different, more radical sense of 'Cockneyism' associated with childishness. In the fourth Cockney School essay the political charge of 'Cockneyism' had less to do with Keats's social circumstances and origins than with Z's recognition of the disruptive possibilities of Keatsian 'childishness'. But what precisely did Z intend by disparaging Keats as a young *Cockney* rhymester?

In Samuel Johnson's *Dictionary of the English Language* (1755) the leading sense of 'Cockney' is 'A native of London' (which fits Keats surely enough). But Johnson also lists a second sense of Cockney, which has obvious gendered and social inflections: 'Any effeminate, low citizen'. So there we have it: Cockney Keats: effeminate, common, and a Londoner. This tells us a lot about how the 'Cockney' tag might be employed in sexual-social conflict, but perhaps not very much, yet, about how the word was intended to apply to Keats's poetry. In the *Oxford English Dictionary*, the four primary senses of 'Cockney' are glossed as follows:

Cockney: egg; lit. 'cocks' egg'
1. An egg . . . hen's egg . . . one of the small or misshapen eggs occa-

[53] 'Cockney School III', 453.

sionally laid by fowls . . . 2. 'A child that sucketh long', 'a nestle-cock', 'a mother's darling' . . . 'a child tenderly brought up'; hence, a squeamish or effeminate fellow, 'a milksop'. 3. A derisive appellation for a townsman, as the type of effeminacy in contrast to the hardier inhabitants of the country. 4. One born in the city of London . . .

For Z Keats was a Cockney not merely because he was supposedly a 'young man', and an admirer of Leigh Hunt and Hazlitt. The charge was more specific: Cockney Keats was an unweaned boy-child, unwilling to 'bid farewell' to the exuberant joys of early, sensual experience at his mother's breast. His 'simplicity' was a token of his opposition to the 'artful' duplicity of government (compare William Hone's *Political House that Jack Built*, dedicated to 'The Nursery of Children Six Feet High, His Readers', in which the nursery rhyme was adapted in a satirical exposure of state oppression after the Peterloo Massacre of August 1819).[54] Keats's vulnerable 'tenderness' enervated the discourse of masculine authority, which Z now associated with those ('classical') writers who had formerly appeared amid the Jacobin rabble of *New Morality*. In his first essay on the Cockney School, Z admired the one-time republican William Wordsworth as a figure of austere 'patriarchal simplicity'. Charles Lamb, Gillray's toad or frog, was happily re-embodied by Z as 'that simple-minded man of genius'.[55] Keats, meanwhile, had become potentially more dangerous than his natural father Leigh Hunt, as the 'new brood' of treacherous sensibility that had formerly been associated with Rousseau and the French Revolution.

As the political unrest of the post-Waterloo years grew more distant, or moved through different channels, the unsettling aspects of Keats and Hunt (which had seemed so alarming in an age of revolutions) gradually vanished. During the nineteenth century both writers were accommodated by sustaining the stereotypes of childish and effeminate passivity established by Z and others after 1817. In this manner, Hunt and Keats were publicly depoliticized, and disengaged from the ideological context which had so powerfully informed their creativity and their thinking about literature. Z's caricature in *Blackwood's* had

---

[54] *The Political House that Jack Built* (47th edn., London, 1820).
[55] See *Blackwood's Magazine* (Oct. 1817), 40, and *Blackwood's Magazine* (Oct. 1819), 72.

transformed Hunt into a figure of fun. Thirty-five years later Hunt was no longer a force in political affairs, although still very much alive. In 1853 he reappeared as the amiably childish Harold Skimpole in *Bleak House*:

'I don't mean literally a child,' pursued Mr Jarndyce; 'not a child in years. He is grown up—he is at least as old as I am—but in simplicity, and freshness, and enthusiasm, and a fine guileless inaptitude for worldly affairs, he is a perfect child.' (chapter 6)

Hunt, once the most articulate radical journalist in England, was doomed by Dickens to eternal childishness, and Keats's reputation developed in a similar manner during the nineteenth century. Once his 'mawkish' sensibility no longer appeared as a token of Jacobin sympathies, Keats survived as the poet of 'delicate and fragile' genius lamented by Shelley in *Adonais*. According to William Howitt in 1847: 'On this world and its concerns he could take no hold, and they could take none on him'; for David Macbeth Moir, in 1851: 'all . . . was the result of imaginative wealth and youthful inexperience'; the *Encyclopaedia Britannica* of 1857 (Alexander Smith) thought that 'he still wrote in a style of babyish effeminacy . . . [and] of a . . . nauseous sweetness'.[56] These judgements were echoed by much weightier critics: David Masson wrote of 'an intellectual invalid, . . . a poor youth too conscious of 'the endeavour of the present breath', watching incessantly his own morbid symptoms' (1860); Algernon Swinburne of 'some of the most vulgar and fulsome doggrel ever whimpered by a vapid and effeminate rhymester in the sickly stage of whelphood . . . [who] lived long enough only to give promise of being a man' (1886). Gerard Manley Hopkins thought Keats 'one of the beginners of the Romantic movement, with all the extravagance and ignorance of his youth . . . His contemporaries, as Wordsworth, Byron, Shelley, and even Leigh Hunt, right or wrong, still concerned themselves with great causes, as liberty and religion; but he lived in mythology and fairyland the life of a dreamer' (1887–8). Matthew Arnold commented that Keats was 'let and hindered with a short term and imperfect experience,—"young" as he

---

[56] William Howitt, *Homes and Haunts of the Most Eminent British Poets* (1847), *KCH* 311; D. M. Moir, *Sketches of the Poetical Literature of the Past Half-Century* (1851), *KCH* 351; 'Keats in the *Encyclopedia Britannica*', *KCH* 365.

says of himself' (1880, 1886).[57] The feminizing of Keats during the nineteenth century, apparent in some of these criticisms, has been analysed in detail by Susan Wolfson,[58] who shows how during this period Keats was 'deemed to have particular appeal to women'; his poetry was marketed in particular 'to female audiences'. This was one way of assimilating Keats's threat to prevailing codes of masculinity, and was effectively a continuation of Z's polemical criticism in *Blackwood's Magazine*. The prolonged feminizing of Keats helps one to make sense of the otherwise laughable masculine over-compensation in David Masson's Sweeney-Keats: 'a slack, slouching youth, with a thick torso, a deep grave voice, and no fixed principles ... [who] kept aloof from opinion, doctrine, controversy, as by a natural instinct.'[59]

In all of these nineteenth-century responses to Keats, the revolutionary potential of his 'style of babyish effeminacy' has been forgotten: Keats entered the canon as the Romantic poet widely believed to have had no interest in politics and the events of contemporary history. My previous chapters have shown how a recovery of the historical, cultural, and ideological contexts in which Z could detect Keats's poems 'lisping sedition' reveals that his poetry was more thoroughly (and, to some eyes, dangerously) politicized than has frequently been allowed. Furthermore, Keats's thinking about creative genius and ideal beauty (so often regarded as aesthetic 'escapism') can be seen as developments of the democratic sensibility formerly identified with Jacobin revolution in France. My 'Epilogue' explores the radical inflections of Keats's concept of 'negative capability', relating that theory to a poem which has often been viewed as serenely detached from history: 'To Autumn'.

[57] David Masson, 'The Life and Poetry of Keats', *Macmillan's Magazine* (Nov. 1860), *KCH* 371; Algernon Swinburne, *Miscellanies* (London, 1886), 211, 213; G. M. Hopkins to Coventry Patmore, 20, 24 Oct. 1887 and 6 May 1888 in *G. M. Hopkins, Selected Prose*, ed. G. Roberts (Oxford, 1980), 154, 159; Matthew Arnold, 'John Keats', first published 1880, rpt. in *Essays in Criticism: Second Series* (1888) quoted from *The Complete Prose Works of Matthew Arnold*, ed. R. H. Super (11 vols., Ann Arbor, 1960–77), ix. 214.

[58] See Wolfson, 'Feminizing Keats', 317–56.

[59] Masson, 'The Life and Poetry of Keats', *KCH* 373–4.

Epilogue:
John Keats's Commonwealth:
The 1820 Collection and 'To Autumn'

Autumne is ycomen in
Ceres fill thy horn;—
Reaper swinketh, Farmer drinketh,
And creaketh wain with newe corne.[1]

*Negative Capability and its Backgrounds: Shakespeare,
Politics, Theatre*

I have had two very pleasant evenings with Dilke yesterday & today; & am at this moment just come from him & feel in the humour to go on with this, began in the morning, & from which he came to fetch me. I spent Friday evening with Wells & went the next morning to see *Death on the Pale horse.* It is a wonderful picture, when West's age is considered; But there is nothing to be intense upon, no women one feels mad to kiss; no face swelling into reality. the excellence of every Art is its intensity, capable of making all disagreeables evaporate, from their being in close relationship with Beauty & Truth—Examine King Lear & you will find this examplified throughout; but in this picture we have unpleasantness without any momentous depth of speculation excited, in which to bury its repulsiveness—The picture is larger than Christ rejected—I dined with Haydon the sunday after you left, & had a very pleasant day, I dined too (for I have been out too much lately) with Horace Smith & met his two Brothers with Hill & Kingston & one Du Bois, they only served to convince me, how superior humour is to wit in respect to enjoyment—These men say things which make one start, without making one feel, they are all alike; their manners are alike; they all know fashionables; they have a mannerism in their very eating & drinking, in their mere handling of a Decanter—They talked of Kean & his low company—Would I were in that company instead of yours said I to myself! I know such like acquaintance will never do for

[1] From 'Four Seasons', in a Notebook kept by Charles Cowden Clarke dated 'Enfield. 1814', fo. 19ʳ. The Brotherton Collection, Leeds University Library.

me & yet I am going to Reynolds, on wednesday—Brown & Dilke walked with me & back from the Christmas pantomime. I had not a dispute but a disquisition with Dilke, on various subjects; several things dovetailed in my mind, & at once it struck me, what quality went to form a man of Achievement especially in Literature & which Shakespeare posessed so enormously—I mean *Negative Capability*, that is when man is capable of being in uncertainties, Mysteries, doubts, without any irritable reaching after fact & reason—Coleridge, for instance, would let go by a fine isolated verisimilitude caught from the Penetralium of mystery, from being incapable of remaining content with half knowledge. This pursued through Volumes would perhaps take us no further than this, that with a great poet the sense of Beauty overcomes every other consideration, or rather obliterates all consideration. (*Letters*, i. 191–4)

This famous passage from Keats's letter to his brothers of late December 1817 has been the subject of numerous critical discussions, in which the intellectual origins of 'Negative Capability' were traced in eighteenth-century aesthetic, literary, and philosophical backgrounds. Best known is Walter Jackson Bate's analysis of the 'interplay and coalescence of impressions' in the letter, showing how Edmund Kean's acting, Benjamin West's *Death on the Pale Horse*, and the 'intensity' of *King Lear* formed an aesthetic constellation which was shaped by Keats's assimilation of Hazlitt's thought, especially his essay 'On Gusto' from *The Round Table*.[2] On 21 December 1817 Keats's review 'Mr Kean' used Hazlitt's admirable term 'gusto' ('power or passion defining any object', 'expression [in its] highest degree'[3])—to express the 'instant feeling' focused by Kean's acting, 'an indescribable gusto in his voice, by which we feel that the utterer is thinking of the past and the future, while speaking of the instant'.[4] As Bate shows, 'gusto' as an aesthetic ideal prefigured aspects of Keats's later poetic style, 'an imaginative "intensity" of conception' which Keats also associated with Milton 'pursu[ing] his imagination to the utmost' in *Paradise Lost*,[5] and

[2] See Bate, *John Keats*, 242–63, and 'Negative Capability and the Question of Identity', in James Engell, *The Creative Imagination: Enlightenment to Romanticism* (Cambridge, Mass., 1981), 288–92.

[3] 'On Gusto', *The Round Table*, ii. 20–1; see also Engell, *Creative Imagination*, 204–5.

[4] See *John Keats: The Complete Poems*, 528.

[5] See Bate, *John Keats*, 246, quoting Keats's marginal comment to *Paradise Lost*, vi. 420–3.

Shakespeare's 'intensity of working out conceits' (*Letters*, i. 188). That last observation about Shakespeare appears in a letter to John Hamilton Reynolds dating from 22 November 1817, about one month before the Kean review and the 'negative capability' letter. This is notable, in that his remark to Reynolds is qualified in a way which suggests that he was already responding to the sympathetic, intuitive qualities of Shakespeare's imagination. 'I neer found so many beauties in the sonnets—they seem to be full of fine things said unintentionally—in the intensity of working out conceits' (*Letters*, i. 188). Here the 'intensity' of imagining releases 'fine things said unintentionally'— seemingly without consciously directed attention. This Shakespearian paradox is focused neatly in that 'intensity' and 'unintentionally' are both adapted from a common Latin root, *intendere*, meaning 'to stretch out or forth, to strain, direct' but also to 'turn one's attention, purpose, [and] endeavour' (*OED*). Keats suggests that, at its highest pitch, Shakespeare's creativity coexists with a unique passivity—or, as Keats refines this in his letter to his brothers, '*Negative Capability*, that is when man is capable of being in uncertainties, Mysteries, doubts, without any irritable reaching after fact & reason'.

Once again, Bate gives a thorough analysis of Keats's statement in the immediate context of his dinners with Horace Smith and Haydon, the pantomime he attended with Brown and Dilke, and more broadly in relation to his early life, personality, and reading. Bate shows how Keats had an innate 'capacity for sympathetic identification', a potential which had been apparent to Charles Cowden Clarke in Keats's 'intensely tender affection for his brothers' while at Enfield School.[6] Additionally, perhaps there was what Jack Stillinger has termed 'some non-egotistic element in Keats's own personality', a genuine and personal appeal in 'something close to mere passivity . . . something not far from Wordsworth's "wise passiveness"', which fostered 'his growing interest in the impersonality of genius'.[7]

We see this concern with impersonality in process of evolution in the letter to Reynolds, 22 November 1817. Keats asks 'a very silly Question . . . Why dont you, as I do, look unconcerned at what may be called more particularly Heart-vexations? They

[6] See Bate, *John Keats*, 253, and 'Recollections of Keats', 123.
[7] See Stillinger, 'Wordsworth and Keats', 188, and Bate, *John Keats*, 250, 252.

never surprize me—lord! a man should have the fine point of his soul taken off to become fit for this world' (*Letters*, i. 188). From this recommendation of worldly equanimity, Keats passes to Shakespeare's 'unintentional intensity' and his power of universal sympathy:

> He has left nothing to say about nothing or any thing: for look at Snails, you know what he says about Snails, you know where he talks about 'cockled snails'—well, in one of these sonnets, he says—the chap slips into—no! I lie! this is in the Venus and Adonis: the Simile brought it to my Mind.

> > Audi—As the snail, whose tender horns being hit,
> > Shrinks back into his shelly cave with pain,
> > And there all smothered up in shade doth sit,
> > Long after fearing to put forth again . . . (*Letters*, i. 189)

Keats was attracted to this passage as an instance of Shakespeare's 'intensity of working out conceits', a concentrated realization of the snail's tender existence, although it also shows us the quicksilver alacrity of Keats's own mind—darting from *King Lear* to the 'cockled snails' of *Love's Labour's Lost* (iv. iii. 334) to the sonnets to the quotation from *Venus and Adonis*. The brief, colloquial surmise '—the chap slips into . . .' is brilliantly attuned to the limitless possibility of Shakespearian imagination, while intimating a comparable sympathetic power in Keats himself.

As has frequently been observed, an immediate source for Keats's developing sense of Shakespeare's dramatic power was Hazlitt's *Round Table* essay 'On Posthumous Fame,—Whether Shakspeare was influenced by a love of it?': 'He seemed scarcely to have an individual existence of his own, but to borrow that of others at will, and to pass successively through "every variety of untried being,"—to be now *Hamlet*, now *Othello*, now *Lear*, now *Falstaff*, now *Ariel*.'[8] Keats had been reading *The Round Table* from September 1817 onwards, and responding to Hazlitt's criticism and thought with admiration. While his personal impact on Keats was immediate, Hazlitt also transmitted to him the eighteenth-century tradition of sympathy which had been evolved by critics, aestheticians, and philosophers as the touchstone of moral and critical worth supremely embodied by

[8] *The Round Table*, i. 76.

Shakespeare.[9] Coleridge's, Schlegel's, and Hazlitt's ideas of Shakespeare as a protean dramatist, able to assume others' identities, had long been present in British and European criticism.[10] To take just a few examples from the many that could be cited: Elizabeth Montagu had noticed how Shakespeare's plays find

the direct and immediate way to the heart . . . Shakespeare seems to have had the art of the Dervise, in the Arabian tales, who could throw his soul into the body of another man, and be at once possessed of his sentiments, adopt his passions, and rise to all the functions and feelings of his situation.[11]

A few years afterwards, William Richardson, in his *Philosophical Analysis and Illustration of Some of Shakespeare's Remarkable Characters*, declared: 'the genius of Shakespeare is unlimited. Possessing extreme sensibility, and uncommonly susceptible, he is the Proteus of the Drama: he changes himself into every character, and enters easily into every condition of human nature.'[12] Susceptibility is often associated, now, with a sensitivity to feeling which might be closely aligned with 'extreme sensibility'; indeed, this is the principal sense in which susceptibility is understood in James Engell's encyclopaedic study of the creative imagination, where 'sensibility' is presented as an Enlightenment (and Romantic) replacement for classical clichés such as ' "poetic transport" or "divine inspiration" '.[13] But it may be that Richardson meant 'uncommonly susceptible' to discriminate a peculiarly Shakespearian responsiveness: an acute attention to feeling, certainly, but also, and above all, an imaginative hospitality of global generosity. This sense of unfathomable capa-

---

[9] See especially Engell, *Creative Imagination*, 146–7, 153–5, and also Jonathan Bate, *Shakespeare and the English Romantic Imagination* (Oxford, 1986), 157–74. For an important essay which distinguishes Hazlitt's response to Shakespeare's genius from his view of the 'biased' working of genius more generally, see Uttara Natarajan, 'Power and Capability: Hazlitt, Keats and the Discrimination of Poetic Self', *Romanticism*, 2/1 (1996), 54–67.

[10] See Engell, *Creative Imagination*, 8, 154.

[11] Elizabeth Montagu, *An Essay on the Writings and Genius of Shakespeare* (3rd edn., London, 1772), 34, 37.

[12] William Richardson, *A Philosophical Analysis* (London, 1780), 42.

[13] ' "[S]ensibility" really stood for the susceptibility or ability of the poet to identify with his creations in a feeling way and to express that feeling in passionate and natural language'; see Engell, *Creative Imagination*, 155–6.

ciousness is I think underlined in Samuel Johnson's *Dictionary* where 'susceptible' is glossed as an ultimate, limitless receptivity: 'capable of admitting'. Shakespeare's uncommon susceptibility accommodates itself to all manifestations of life, displaying an active ability to 'change himself' and 'enter' those other dimensions of being. In these terms, Richardson prefigured August Schlegel's sense of Shakespeare's distinguishing properties: 'the capability of transporting himself so completely into every situation . . . the power of endowing the creatures of his imagination with such self-existent energy . . . the gift of looking into the inmost recesses of [the characters'] minds'.[14] Still closer in time to Keats's negative capability letter, Coleridge remarked in *Biographia Literaria* (1817) on 'the greatest genius, that perhaps human nature has yet produced, our *myriad-minded* Shakspear . . . SHAKSPEARE becomes all things, yet for ever remaining himself'.[15]

Keats's preface to *Endymion* (dated 10 April 1818) noticed the unhealthy 'space of life between' boyhood and adult life, at which 'the character [is] undecided': a mawkish incapacity which—as Keats was surely aware—contrasted tellingly with Coleridge's and Hazlitt's profiles of Shakespeare. Both critics recognized Shakespeare's protean genius, while being careful to discriminate the residual presence of a Shakespearian ego which imagines 'at will' (Hazlitt), 'yet forever remaining himself' (Coleridge). Keats took his cue from Hazlitt and Coleridge when he said that Shakespeare 'posessed' negative capability 'so enormously', affirming a ballast of self-identity lacking in the 'dwindling', 'undecided', orphaned imagination Keats at times feared in himself. 'Negative capability' as Keats explains it in his letter might indeed be thought of as a state of mind or mood akin to the contemplative, 'wise passiveness' of Wordsworth's 'Expostulation and Reply', but it is not limited to this quiescent paradigm. It evokes too a more dynamic, assertive consciousness which is *simultaneously* assimilative and projective—'capable of being', as Keats expresses it in his letter. In Johnson's *Dictionary* the various aspects of 'capability' comprise receptive and out-going capacities:

---

[14] A. W. von Schlegel, *A Course of Lectures on Dramatic Art and Literature*, trans. John Black (2 vols., London, 1815), ii. 128–9.
[15] Ch. 15 of *Biographia Literaria*, ii. 19, 28.

1. Endued with powers equal to any particular thing.
2. Intelligent; able to understand.
3. Capacious; able to receive or understand.
4. Susceptible.

The prefix 'negative' does not work to cancel any one or all of these capabilities; rather, it seems to unsettle them so as to suggest the flux of a truly protean intellect—wisely passive, watchful, receptive, but also powerfully equal to all things.

In what follows here I explore some of the other dimensions of Keats's ideal 'dovetail', in the philosophical and political backgrounds of 'sympathy' which Keats assimilated along with his reading of Shakespeare and his critics. My concern is to draw attention to the social inflection of negative capability which aligns Keats's idea of Shakespeare's genius with the revolutionary potential discovered in his plays by an earlier generation. While negative capability agreed in some respects with Wordsworth's 'wise passiveness', other poems in *Lyrical Ballads* —'Simon Lee', 'The Last of the Flock', 'Goody Blake and Harry Gill'—had evoked a Shakespearian susceptibility to unaccommodated human beings which spoke powerfully for Jacobin aspirations during the 1790s and the Napoleonic period. It is surely significant, too, that this aspect of Shakespearian sympathy also appealed to the tragic circumstances of Keats's family life: 'Do poor Tom some charity' (III. iv. 59).

For nearly half of Keats's lifetime, 1811–20, *King Lear* was not staged because its portrayal of a mad old king might readily be identified with the recurring insanity of George III.[16] Audiences might well have done this, although the 'seditious' force of the analogy was perhaps secondary to Lear's impassioned identification with 'houseless poverty' against injustice and arbitrary power:

> Poor naked wretches, whereso'er you are,
> That bide the pelting of this pitiless storm,
> How shall your houseless heads and unfed sides,
> Your loop'd and window'd raggedness, defend you
> From seasons such as these? (III. iv. 28–32)

It is the thought of a pitiless, famishing season such as this that the milder, fruited music of 'To Autumn' seeks for the moment

---

[16] See Bate, *Shakespearean Constitutions*, 85.

to hold at bay. Whereas Wordsworth's ballads had responded to Lear's recognition of the claims of humankindness and common humanity, Keats's 'negative capability' might seem akin to a limitless capacity for patience in confronting acute distress— 'give me that patience, patience I need' (*King Lear*, II. iv. 269). These two responses to Shakespeare (sympathetically engaged; divinely hospitable) prefigure Seamus Heaney's account of the poet's role in responding to the violence of civil war: 'stretched between politics and transcendence . . . displaced from a single position by his disposition to be affected by all positions, negatively rather than positively capable'.[17] In Heaney's account the negatively capable, protean imagination transcends the contingencies of war between Catholic and Protestant, Irish nationalist and unionist:

> Escaped from the massacre,
> Taking protective colouring
> From bole and bark, feeling
> Every wind that blows.[18]

Yet in the ideological frames of the French revolutionary period Shakespearian sympathy was not so readily extricable from a political and social conflict in which one party claimed a comparably universal franchise for the 'natural rights' of men and women. Helen Williams, writing at Paris in 1790, described the *Fête* on 14 July marking the first anniversary of the Revolution as 'the triumph of humankind'; 'it required but the common feelings of humanity to become in that moment a citizen of the world', she wrote, 'my heart caught with enthusiasm the general sympathy'.[19] For Williams, the Shakespearian virtues of 'common feeling' and 'general sympathy' were aligned with the democratic zeal of the revolutionaries.

In that respect it may be significant that on 14 December 1817 (the week before Keats began his 'negative capability' letter) the *Examiner* carried a leader on 'Liberty of the Press' in which Hunt wittily demolished the *Courier*'s claim that government ministers 'have . . . never been actuated by *selfish* or *narrow*

[17] Seamus Heaney, *Place and Displacement: Recent Poetry of Northern Ireland* (Grasmere, 1985), 8.

[18] Seamus Heaney, 'Exposure', in *North* (London, 1975).

[19] Helen Maria Williams, *Letters Written in France, in the Summer of 1790* (London, 1790), 14.

principles'. Hunt invoked repeated instances of the ministerial '*selfishness*' which had been palliated and denied in the columns of the *Courier* and the *Quarterly Review.*

And you, foolish people all, who think that there ever was anything like personal irritability against my Lord FOLKSTONE, Mr. BROUGHAM, and others;—and who have held it 'selfish or narrow' in Mr. CANNING to put thousands in his pocket for bowing to the King of the Brazils across the Atlantic,—who have held it 'selfish or narrow' in Mr. CROKER, in times like these, to struggle hard for his war salary when the peace had come,—who have held it 'selfish or narrow', or like 'personal provocation' in the *Quarterly Review* and its poor-souled—we beg pardon,—worthy brethren, to pretend they wrote disinterestedly, to heap BONAPARTE in his prison with all sorts of petty abuse . . . turn round, all ye, whoever ye are, that think these things irritable, and selfish, and narrow, and at the very moment that further measures are in contemplation against your liberty, take the *Courier*'s word for it, that you are all in the wrong.[20]

The article shows the currency of terms such as 'selfishness' and 'disinterest' and 'irritability' in contemporary political debate, presenting some suggestive similarities to the vocabulary of Keats's letter of 21–7 December 1817. At the very least, Hunt's journalism shows how the qualities which for Keats 'went to form a Man of Achievement in Literature' (*Letters*, i. 193) would in Hunt's view also have made for distinction in opposing the 'selfishness' and 'narrowness' of contemporary ministerial policies. In the same issue of the *Examiner* the 'Theatrical Examiner' censured the attempt at '*managing* public opinion' in favour of the actor David Fisher as

substitute for Mr. KEAN during his indisposition, in the characters of *Richard, Macbeth,* and *Hamlet.* . . . They will hardly *continue* to pay out of their own pockets for empty benches and empty boxes. The perverse public spirit and petty spite of such persons must be strong indeed to do this. Their self-love must be most disinterested, as well as irritable.[21]

Once again, there are significant verbal parallels here between the 'Theatrical Examiner' and Keats's letter of 21–7 December, and it is notable too that Keats mentions a dinner at which Edmund Kean was discussed immediately before he tells his

[20] *Examiner* (14 Dec. 1817), 786.
[21] 'Theatrical Examiner: No. 306', *Examiner* (14 Dec. 1817), 793.

brothers how the idea of negative capability had 'struck' him. All of this is, I think, indicative of the immediate backgrounds to Keats's intellectual and imaginative life in December 1817; the *Examiner*'s articles about self-love, disinterest, and irritability in politics and the theatre surely featured in numerous irrecoverable conversations, arguments, and jokes in which Keats participated at a time when, as he said, he had 'been out too much lately' (*Letters*, i. 192).[22] Most telling of all, perhaps, was an article which contrasted sharply with the self-seeking spite of politicians and theatre managers. On the page following the 'Theatrical Examiner' was an item which would certainly have drawn Keats's attention, since it concerned the impoverished fortunes of 'The Family of Shakespeare'. The article traces the family line, and notes that having 'as yet profited nothing by their family renown, they expected nothing': here was further evidence of an enduring, Shakespearian equanimity in the midst of '*every kind of privation*', a circumstance by which the editor of the *Examiner* claimed to have been 'forcibly struck'.[23]

Sympathetic Imagination

> Oh Charles! will the time ever arrive when men will sink their individual feelings in the general mass of existence? Is human nature capable of divesting itself of that sensation of private emolument which now coalesces with all the active motives of man? We are all unhappy; all complaining; all friendless; all lamenting the want of an object in life! When, if we would but annihilate selfishness; regard the interests of others as our own; narrow our physical sphere, and widen our intellectual one; sink our own

---

[22] A further background for Keats's letter can be found in Benjamin Haydon's *Diary*. Jack Stillinger points out how, just five or six days before Keats's 'negative capability' letter, Haydon had been reflecting on Wordsworth and Shakespeare: 'Wordsworth's great power is an intense perception of human feelings regarding the mystery of things by analyzing his own, Shakespeare's an intense power of laying open the heart & mind of man by analyzing the feelings of others acting on themselves.' Entry for 22 Dec. 1817, *The Diary of Benjamin Robert Haydon*, ed. W. B. Pope (5 vols., Cambridge, Mass., 1960), ii. 171, and Stillinger's review in *Journal of English and Germanic Philology*, 60 (Apr. 1961), 334–6. Six days later Keats joined Haydon, Wordsworth, and Lamb for the 'immortal dinner' at which they had 'a glorious set to on Homer, Shakespeare, Milton, & Virgil'; *Diary*, ii. 173.

[23] 'The Family of Shakespeare', *Examiner* (14 Dec. 1817), 795.

> wants, and live in the happiness of others: throw aside the
> panoply of artificial and personal distinction, and feel a
> common identity with mankind at large, we might be
> happy at all times . . .
> (Charles Lloyd, *Edmund Oliver* (2 vols., Bristol,
> 1798), i. 103)

As Walter Jackson Bate and, more lately, David Bromwich and
James Engell have shown, the political and philosophical backgrounds of negative capability may be traced in the cultivation
of sympathetic imagination as a reaction to Thomas Hobbes's
argument for the innate selfishness of human beings. Both Bate
and Engell demonstrate that this aspect of eighteenth-century
thought developed from Shaftesbury, and that it included
(among many) James Arbuckle's *Collection of Letters and Essays on
Several Subjects* (1729), Adam Smith's influential *Theory of Moral
Sentiments* (1759), and John Ogilvie's *Philosophical and Critical
Observations* (1774).[24] A late addition to this argument was
William Hazlitt's *Essay on the Principles of Human Action* (1805),
which Keats had probably bought and read at Benjamin Bailey's
urging.[25] Certainly, a copy was listed among his books at the
time of his death (*KC* i. 254). Against those who, like Hobbes,
'have maintained the doctrine of the natural selfishness of the
human mind', Hazlitt asserted that the human mind was 'naturally disinterested' by virtue of the same faculty which encouraged the pursuit of self-fulfilment:

The imagination, by means of which alone I can anticipate future
objects, or be interested in them, must carry me out of myself into the
feelings of others by one and the same process by which I am thrown
forward as it were into my future being, and interested in it. I could not
love myself, if I were not capable of loving others. Self-love, used in this
sense, is in it's fundamental principle the same with disinterested
benevolence (Howe, i. 1–2)

Hazlitt's emphasis on the sympathetic power of imagination,
carrying him 'out of [the self and] into the feelings of others',
serves 'as a general premise to much of [Hazlitt's] literary criti-

---

[24] See Bate, *John Keats*, 256–7; the same author's *From Classic to Romantic: Premises
of Taste in Eighteenth-Century England* (Cambridge, Mass., 1946; rpt. New York, 1961),
129–59; and Engell, *Creative Imagination*, 143–60.
[25] Bate, *John Keats*, 255–6.

cism, especially his writing on Shakespeare',[26] and also has strong affinities with Keats's developing idea of Shakespeare's ability to 'slip into' other identities. Compare Hazlitt's third lecture at the Surrey Institution, 'On Shakespeare and Milton', delivered 27 January 1818 and very likely attended by Keats:

The striking peculiarity of Shakespeare's mind was its generic quality, its power of communication with all other minds—so that it contained a universe of thought and feeling within itself, and had no one peculiar bias, or exclusive excellence more than another. He was just like any other man, but that he was like all other men. He was the least of an egotist that it was possible to be. He was nothing in himself; but he was all that others were, or that they could become. He not only had in himself the germs of every faculty and feeling, but he could follow them by anticipation, intuitively, into all their conceivable ramifications, through every change of fortune or conflict of passion, or turn of thought. . . . He had only to think of any thing in order to become that thing, with all the circumstances belonging to it. (Howe, v. 47–8)

This lecture was delivered about one month after Keats's negative capability letter, and although Keats's response to it is not known it would certainly have impressed him favourably. Along with Hazlitt's other writings discussed above the lecture indicates the extent to which, at the turn of the year 1817–18, Hazlitt's criticism permeated Keats's thinking about Shakespeare, the sympathetic imagination, and the disparity between egotistical writers of the present day (especially Hunt and Wordsworth) and the more objective amplitude of English renaissance literature as represented by Spenser, Shakespeare, and Jonson (*Letters*, i. 223–5). As David Bromwich has well said, 'there was no contemporary who was more often in Keats's mind': 'Hazlitt's argument against egotism, which reached back to Shakespeare as a deeper source of poetic truth, seems to have calmed Keats's irritability and fortified his resolve.'[27]

It was in early February 1818 that Keats sent Reynolds his 'outlaw lyrics', affirming his growing confidence and independence as a writer: 'Let us have the old Poets, & robin Hood Your letter and its sonnets gave me more pleasure than will the 4th

[26] Bate, *John Keats*, 259. See also the excellent discussion of Hazlitt's *Essay* in David Bromwich, *Hazlitt: The Mind of a Critic* (Oxford, 1983), 46–57.

[27] Bromwich, *Mind of a Critic*, 363.

Book of Childe Harold & the whole of any body's life & opinions' (*Letters*, i. 225).[28] The near-coincidence of negative capability and Keats's poems of the greenwood is significant. When Keats projected an image of society in the ideal form of Sherwood—'a grand democracy of forest trees'—he prefaced his remark with the suggestion that human beings should not 'dispute or assert but whisper results' in a manner quietly receptive to the 'ethereal' promptings of imagination. In other words, social renovation might be achieved through the imaginative susceptibility which at this time Keats also associated with negative capability. The social force of this statement becomes fully apparent when one realizes that Keats associated 'dispute' and 'assertion' with the rational theories for disinterested benevolence and human perfectibility put forward in one of the most celebrated radical texts of the 1790s, a book which Keats had most likely looked into: William Godwin's *Political Justice* (1793).[29] While Keats's idea of negative capability was related to eighteenth-century theories of sympathetic imagination, it was also (like Book X of *The Prelude*, and Hazlitt's *Principles of Human Action*) an imaginative response to Godwin's severely rational arguments for disinterested benevolence.[30] *Political Justice* dated from February 1793, more than two years before Keats's birth, but we can trace the immediate impact of Godwin's thought on Keats in the 'disquisition with Dilke' which sparked his insight into Shakespeare's genius.

The Godwinian Inheritance

> What delight!—
> How glorious!—in self-knowledge and self-rule
> To look through all the frailties of the world . . .
>   (*The Prelude* (1805), X. 818–20)

In the two massive volumes of *Political Justice* Godwin set out a detailed argument that refuted 'the theory of self-love', and all

---

[28] Keats's reference to 'any body's life & opinions' was a reminder of Coleridge's *Biographia Literaria; or, Biographical Sketches of my Literary Life and Opinions. Biographia* was published in July 1817.

[29] For Keats's reading of *Political Justice*, see *Letters*, i. 397 n.

[30] For Hazlitt and 'disinterestedness' in *Political Justice*, see Bromwich, *Mind of a Critic*, 79–91.

sentimental preferences, proving instead that humankind was 'capable of justice, virtue and benevolence' and necessarily motivated to act by a disinterested preference for good.[31] One background to *Political Justice* was David Hartley's analysis in *Observations on Man* of the emotional transformation which leads to 'disinterest', although in *Political Justice* Godwin elaborated a wholly rational foundation for the 'system of disinterestedness'.

Like Hartley, Godwin brings forward the case of a child:

Before he can feel sympathy, he must have been led by a series of observations to perceive that his nurse for example, is a being possessed of consciousness and susceptible like himself to the impressions of pleasure and pain. Having supplied him with this previous knowledge, let us suppose his nurse to fall from a flight of stairs and break her leg. He will probably feel some concern for the accident; he will understand the meaning of her cries, similar to those which he has been accustomed to utter in distress; and he will discover some wish to relieve her.[32]

After this follows Godwin's psychological explanation of the child's 'discovery' of that wish to help the nurse:

Pity is perhaps first introduced by a mechanical impression upon the organs, in consequence of which the cries uttered by another prompt the child without direct design to utter cries of his own. These are at first unaccompanied with compassion, but they naturally induce the mind of the infant to yield attention to the appearance which thus impressed him.[33]

That 'natural inducement' to the mind prompts attention, understanding, and consequent action to relieve another person's distress. But the mind's 'natural' bias towards sympathy, explained here as arising from formative childish experience, is based upon the mechanist theory in which mind is stimulated by 'mechanical impressions' to form and associate ideas. Cumulative experiences of pain, or 'uneasiness', gradually produce an ideal disposition to good arising as a phenomenon of rational understanding. 'Why do I feel pain in the neglect of an act of benevolence, but because benevolence is judged by me to be a

[31] William Godwin, *An Enquiry Concerning Political Justice* (2 vols., London, 1793), i. 359.
[32] Ibid. 348–9.   [33] Ibid. 349.

conduct which it becomes me to adopt? . . . [No] objects would ever have been pursued, if the decisions of the intellect had not gone first, and informed us that they were worthy to be pursued.'[34]

The 'last perfection' of the disinterested intellect, Godwin claims, 'consists in that state of mind which bids us rejoice as fully in the good that is done by others, as if it were done by ourselves'. The truly wise man will be actuated neither by interest nor ambition, the love of honour nor the love of fame. He has no emulation . . . All men are his fellow labourers, but he is the rival of no man.'[35] Godwin's perfect, disinterested mind is thoroughly disconnected from the emotional frailties of interest, ambition, love, and desire; it was of course this extreme commitment to rationalism, on which Godwin had hoped to base the renovation of society, that Wordsworth, Coleridge, and others in the 1790s had found humanly and morally disabling to the philosophy of *Political Justice*. Wordsworth's quarrel with bookish 'sages' in 'Expostulation and Reply' and 'The Tables Turned' was, in part at least, directed against Godwin's desiccated rationality, asserting natural spontaneity and cheerfulness as the sources of wisdom and truth—not the labouring mind worrying away at 'decisions of the intellect'.

Wordsworth's reaction to Godwin in *Lyrical Ballads* is significant here, for in many ways it prefigures (and almost certainly influenced) Keats's statement in his letter to Bailey, 22 November 1817: 'Can it be that even the greatest Philosopher ever arrived at his goal without putting aside numerous objections— However it may be, O for a Life of Sensations rather than of Thoughts!' (*Letters*, i. 185). Many years ago H. W. Garrod, arguing that Keats 'was more the child of the Revolutionary Idea than we commonly suppose', had quoted the 'famous and much misapplied' passage from the letter to Bailey and commented: 'It is no more than if he had said, "O for the pure gospel of the *Lyrical Ballads!*"'.[36] If in one respect Keats's preference for 'sensation' over 'thought' reflected a Wordsworthian valuation of human feeling above abstract reason, it was also and more immediately a response to his own experience of Godwin's philosophy as this was presented to him by his friend

---

[34] William Godwin, 352–3.   [35] Ibid. 360–1.
[36] See Garrod, *Keats*, 28, 33.

Charles Wentworth Dilke. Furthermore, Keats's response to the influence of the rational sage Godwin was an important component in the imaginative 'dovetailing' (both intersection and unfolding) which formed 'negative capability'.

A Godwin Perfectibility Man

Keats's close friendship with Dilke dated from 1816[37] and during the following winter 1817–18 the two men saw each other frequently—especially so during the latter half of December. At this time Dilke was a civil servant in the Naval Pay Office, Somerset House, but he was also an antiquary, a radical,[38] and a convinced admirer of *Political Justice*,—in short, a 'Godwin perfectibil[it]y Man' as Keats described him in October 1818 (*Letters*, i. 397). A year later, Keats elaborated further on Dilke's Godwinian cast of mind in a passage which has a direct bearing on his idea of negative capability:

He thinks of nothing but 'Political Justice' . . . I wrote Brown a comment on the subject, wherein I explained what I thought of Dilke's Character. Which resolved itself into this conclusion. That Dilke was a Man who cannot feel he has a personal identity unless he has made up his Mind about everything. The only means of strengthening one's intellect is to make up ones mind about nothing—to let the mind be a thoroughfare for all thoughts. Not a select party. The genus is not scarce in population. All the stubborn arguers you meet with are of the same brood—They never begin upon a subject they have not preresolved on. They want to hammer their nail into you and if you turn the point, still they think you wrong. Dilke will never come at a truth as long as he lives; because he is always trying at it. He is a Godwin-methodist. (*Letters*, ii. 213)

Dilke's commitment to *Political Justice* (which Keats compares to the zealous evangelism of the Methodists[39]) shows a dogmatic single-mindedness exactly contrary to negative capability,

[37] See *Letters*, i. 73, and *The Papers of a Critic Selected from the Writings of the Late Charles Wentworth Dilke* (2 vols., London, 1875), i. 2.

[38] *Papers of a Critic*, i. 1–2.

[39] See his disparaging remarks on Methodism in *Letters*, ii. 169, 'he's favour'd—he's had a Call—a Hercules Methodist', and his transcription of Horace Smith's satirical poem 'Nehemiah Muggs, an Exposure of the Methodists' in his letter to his brothers, 14 (?) Feb. 1818, *Letters*, i. 227, 229–30.

'mak[ing] up ones mind about nothing', or, as Keats had phrased this in his earlier letter, 'capable of being in uncertainties, Mysteries, doubts, without any irritable reaching after fact & reason'. The similarities between the two letters can be traced further: Keats's broad contrast between negatively capable equanimity and an *irritable* quest for 'fact & reason' is resumed in the reference to 'stubborn arguers' and the example of Dilke in particular 'always trying' to attain a preresolved 'truth'. Interestingly, Keats's attitude to his Godwinian friend bears remarkable similarities to Hazlitt's response to Godwin's associate Thomas Holcroft: 'I complained that he would not let me get on at all, for he required a definition of every the commonest word, exclaiming, "What do you mean by a *sensation*, Sir? What do you mean by an *idea*?"'. Coleridge too remarked on Holcroft's 'fierceness and *dogmatism* of conversation', while Lamb had noticed how 'Professor Godwin' always required 'explanations, translations, limitations . . . when you make an assertion'.[40] In all three cases Godwin was associated with an intellectual fussiness and impatience comparable to Dilke's, and which very likely characterized the 'disquisition with Dilke, on various subjects' which precipitated Keats's realization: 'at once it struck me, what quality went to form a man of Achievement especially in Literature & which Shakespeare possessed so enormously—I mean *Negative Capability*'. In response to the mechanism of Godwinian reason, and its stubborn assertion of disinterest and benevolence, Keats intuited a Shakespearian— or 'poetical'—susceptibility to other human beings, to nature, to the universe. He described this quality in his letter to Richard Woodhouse, 27 October 1818, implicitly associating Godwinian 'preresolution' with Wordsworth's egotism:

As to the poetical Character itself, (I mean that sort of which, if I am any thing, I am a Member; that sort distinguished from the wordsworthian or egotistical sublime; which is a thing per se and stands alone) it is not itself—it has no self—it is every thing and nothing—It has no character—it enjoys light and shade; it lives in gusto, be it foul or fair, high or low, rich or poor, mean or elevated— It has as much delight in conceiving an Iago as an Imogen. What

---

[40] See 'My First Acquaintance with Poets', Howe, xvii. 112, and *Collected Letters of Samuel Taylor Coleridge*, i. 138, and *The Letters of Charles and Mary Anne Lamb*, ed. E. W. Marrs, Jr. (3 vols., Ithaca, NY, 1975–8), i. 244.

shocks the virtuous philosop[h]er, delights the camelion Poet. (*Letters,* I. 386–7)

This famous passage, distinguishing Keats's 'poetical character' from the egotism of 'wordsworthian' imagination, reflects the powerful yet subtle influence of Hazlitt, and through him Zachary Mayne's *Two Dissertations Concerning Sense and the Imagination* (1728), in which the imagination is alikened to 'the Cameleon'.[41] A more immediate, and I think more likely influence on Keats's striking juxtaposition of 'virtuous philosopher' and 'camelion Poet' was the virtuous philosopher Godwin himself. In his essay 'Of an Early Taste for Reading' in the *Enquirer* (1797) Godwin had admitted to an imaginative susceptibility which closely prefigures Keats's: 'When I read Thomson', Godwin claimed, 'I become Thomson; when I read Milton, I become Milton. I find myself a sort of intellectual camelion, assuming the colour of the substances on which I rest.'[42] Here, in brief outline, was an account of the 'poetical character', formulated by the author of *Political Justice* himself yet directly at odds with the rational argument of that earlier work. As further developed by Keats, the idea of a poetical character which 'lives in gusto, be it foul or fair, high or low, rich or poor, mean or elevated' constituted an imaginative capacity for the commonwealth which Godwin and his followers had mistakenly hoped to bring about through the exercise of rational thought. In its immediate contexts, both intellectual and personal, negative capability was (among other things) a response to the rationalistic version of eighteenth-century mechanistic psychology which informed *Political Justice.* Godwin had been proved wrong, but Shakespearian sympathy might offer a boundless yet humane means for social renovation—the negatively capable aspect, as it were, of the over-confident and at times irritable belief in revolutionary change which dated from the early 1790s.[43]

---

[41] See Bromwich, *Mind of a Critic,* 362, 374–5, and Engell, *Creative Imagination,* 146–7.

[42] See *Political and Philosophical Writings,* v. 97.

[43] It follows that I understand the chameleon poet as being more 'tendentious' than Paul Fry is prepared to allow, although I agree with Fry that Keats remains the antithesis of the 'man of power'. See Fry, 'History, Existence, and "To Autumn"', *KP* 213.

John Keats's Commonwealth

> Evil communications corrupt good manners. This is a cer-
> tain maxim we all know, therefore let every Man act for
> himself, and avoid the insinuations of such Agents that
> subtly delight to ensnare the Innocent, to promote their
> own evil designs; such Persons we shall find will be suffi-
> ciently active this Month, but few of them will be so happy
> as to accomplish their crafty ends.
>> ('August 1819: Monthly Observations', *Vox Stellarum;*
>> *or, A Loyal Almanack . . . by Francis Moore, Physician*
>> (London, 1819), 19)

> Sad sixteenth of August! accursed be the day;
>> When thy field, oh, St Peter! was crimson'd with gore . . .
>> ('Manchester Y——Y Valour', *Manchester Observer*,
>> 18 Sept. 1819)

When Keats's first readers opened *Lamia, Isabella, The Eve of St
Agnes, and Other Poems* they discovered that the book began with
an apology. The publisher's Advertisement (which angered
Keats) drew attention to 'the unfinished poem of HYPERION',
explaining that the unfavourable reception of *Endymion* had
'discouraged the author from proceeding'. By noticing Keats's
discouragement, Taylor and Hessey may have hoped to forestall
hostile criticism of his third collection of poetry, although their
identification of the author—'By John Keats, Author of
Endymion'—suggests just the opposite, as if Keats and/or
Taylor were taunting the reviewers.[44] Certainly, it has been suggested that a quality of passive reconciliation is characteristic of
the volume as a whole. 'Keats's 1820 poems . . . were issued not
to provoke, but to allay conflict', Jerome McGann has said,
representing the book as Keats's attempt to subdue the hostility
stirred up by his earlier publications:

The *Lamia* volume represented Keats's effort to show his readers how
they might, by entering his poetic space, step aside from the conflicts
and tensions which were so marked an aspect of that period. The
whole point of Keats's great and (politically) reactionary book was not
to enlist poetry in the service of social and political causes—which is

---

[44] I am grateful to Jack Stillinger for this point about the identification of the
author of the 1820 collection.

what Byron and Shelley were doing—but to dissolve social and political conflicts in the mediations of art and beauty.[45]

In McGann's account the poems in Keats's 1820 volume define
a 'reflexive world' that the same critic has elsewhere identified
with Romantic Ideology, an ideal space far, far removed from
contemporary history. My readings in the previous pages of
Keats's sonnets, *Hyperion*, the 'Robin Hood' lyrics, the 'Ode on
a Grecian Urn', and 'Ode to a Nightingale' may have served, I
hope, to qualify that claim for the 'reactionary' meaning of the
1820 collection.[46] Ironically, in seeking to historicize Keats's
poems, McGann has emphasized their distance from the turbulent world in which they were written, first published, and
reached their earliest readers. But that distance, or 'displacement', becomes in turn a measure of historical pressures at
work on and in the poetry. So McGann argued in *The Romantic
Ideology* that 'Shelley's idealism, Byron's sensationalism, and
Keats's aesthetic poetry are all displaced yet fundamental vehi-
cles of cultural analysis and critique: a poetry of extremity and
escapism which is the reflex of the circumstances in which their
work, their lives, and their culture were all forced to develop.'
And, yet more emphatically: 'Byron and Shelley are most deeply

---

[45] See *The Romantic Ideology*, 117, 124, and KHM 61–2, where McGann defines
the 'reflexive world of Romantic art' as 'the very negation of negation itself, wherein
all events are far removed from the Terror, King Ludd, Peterloo, the Six Acts, and
the recurrent financial crises of the Regency, and where humanity escapes the
inconsequence of George III, the absurd Prince Regent, the contemptible Wellington'. For a questioning response to this assertion, see the conclusion of Newey,
' "Alternate uproar and sad peace" ', 265–89.

[46] For essays which develop McGann's readings of Keats, and 'To Autumn' in
particular, see William Keach, 'Cockney Couplets: Keats and the Politics of Style'
and David Bromwich, 'Keats's Radicalism'. For a more sceptical response, see Paul
H. Fry, 'History, Existence, and "To Autumn" '. All three essays appear in RP. More
recently Andrew Bennett's *Keats, Narrative, and Audience* (Cambridge, 1994), 159–
71, offers a fine intertextual reading of 'To Autumn' arguing that politics in the
poem are 'most explicitly articulated within the terms of the contemporary politics
of agriculture', notably in the contemporary discourse of , and controversy about,
gleaning: 'By attending to the disruptive intertextual noises of history, politics,
economics we find that the attempt to silence the noise of history in "To Autumn",
rather than an escape from the historical, is itself a strategic silencing, a silencing
that echoes most profoundly the political effacement, which we might call the
"noise" of the oppressed' (170–1). Bennett's sense of the closeness with which the
poem is attuned to contemporary political discourses parallels my own reading of
the poem, although our emphases—his on 'silencing', mine on articulate redress—
differ somewhat.

engaged (in a socialist-activist sense) when they have moved furthest along their paths of displacement and escape.'[47]

In differentiating Keats's 'reactionary' poems from the socially and politically 'enlisted' writings of Byron and Shelley, McGann apparently concedes the inadequacy of Romantic ideology to account for the full spectrum of the poets' various relations to historical conflicts and tensions. Furthermore, printing '*engaged*' in italics does not effectively demonstrate how social-political enlistment, in Byron's and Shelley's poems, coincides with ideal displacement. An obvious difficulty appears in the strong polarization of this view of Romantic poetry and history, which obscures the wide range of possible attitudes and responses that intervene between 'engagement' and 'paths of escape': the subtle contextual negotiations which inform all aspects of a poem's vocabulary, shape, style, and generic identity.[48] The present book will have shown, I hope, how a more accommodating view of the 'mediations of art and beauty' at the levels of word, image, emblem, may disclose the ways in which Keats's poetics of dissent comprehended history and the ideal world at a period when 'Pan [was] no longer sought'.

Critical responses to the 1820 volume were generally welcoming, with *Lamia* and *Isabella* attracting favourable comment, although the volume did not allay conflict altogether. A number of reviewers continued to distrust Keats's political sympathies, indicating that some contemporaries did not perceive the reactionary, escapist tendencies of the poems dwelt upon by some later critics. John Scott, writing in Baldwin's *London Magazine* (September 1820), protested against Keats's treatment by *Blackwood's* and the *Quarterly*, observing that 'the miserable selfishness of political party has erected itself into a literary authority'. Yet his review actually conceded the political ground on which Tory critics such as Z had attacked Keats: 'his spirit is

[47] Compare Anne Barton's observation about the affinity between Byron and Keats as poets who both aspired to benefit the world, and in so doing confronted 'one of the central dilemmas of the romantic movement, the dark side of its exalted view of art'. 'Keats perhaps came closest of all, in the "Ode to Autumn", although one may feel that what is recorded there is a kind of inspired surrender, the letting-go of a problem, in which defeat has been transformed, strangely, into a celebration.' See 'Byron and the Mythology of Fact', *The Nottingham Byron Lecture 1968* (Nottingham, 1968), 5–6.

[48] See in particular Bennett, *Keats, Narrative*, 161, for the 'density of intertextuality' in 'To Autumn'.

impregnated with a flippant impatience, (irritated and justified with a false philosophy) of the great phenomena of society, and the great varieties of human nature.' According to Scott, the caricature of Isabella's brothers ('these same ledger-men . . . these money-bags', 137, 142) betrayed 'all sorts of dissenting, and altercating principles and opinions', and he concluded 'it will very easily be seen that [Keats] has very much, and very incautiously exposed himself to attack'. Josiah Conder, in the *Eclectic Review* (September 1820), agreed with Scott in asserting that 'there does not occur, if our recollection serves us, throughout [Keats's] present volume, a single reference to any one object of *real* interest, a single burst of virtuous affection or enlightened sentiment, a single reference, even of the most general kind, to the Supreme Being, or the slenderest indication that the Author is allied by any one tie to his family, his country, or his kind'. It comes as a surprise to find that both of these critics were in fact well disposed to Keats's ambitions as a poet; nevertheless, each recognized him as a 'malcontent'. An alternative view of Keats's politics appeared in the *Indicator* (2 August 1820), where Leigh Hunt argued that the 1820 poems were 'coloured by the modern philosophy of sympathy and natural justice' and 'a high feeling of humanity'; the voice of 'an age of poetry [that] has grown up with the progress of experiment'.[49]

As with *Poems, by John Keats* and *Endymion*, therefore, the response to his 1820 collection was divided according to political party. The liberal disposition welcomed by Hunt was condemned by reviewers such as Conder, for whom Keats's poems expressed a treacherous sensibility recalling the Jacobins of the 1790s: 'At present, there is a sickliness about his productions, which shews there is a mischief at the core'.[50] As for Z, 'sickliness' was a symptom of the deeper, ideological canker of dissent. Furthermore, by echoing 'To Autumn', Conder associates that 'mischief' with a poem that has been widely understood as an expression of Keats's quietism. In Geoffrey Hartman's celebrated essay 'Poem and Ideology', for instance, 'To Autumn' was presented as 'a poem without explicit social context', the

---

[49] For Scott, Conder, and Hunt, see *KCH* 219–27; 232–9; 165–77.
[50] *KCH* 238.

voice of a 'true impersonality'.[51] Taken together, all of these contrasting responses to the poetry suggest that the liberalism of the 1820 volume may have been covertly expressed in 'To Autumn', the more potent for working under the sign of disinterested imagination, or negative capability.

'To Autumn' offers an ideal, 'impersonal' image of the season, an 'impersonality' which has been invoked repeatedly as definitive of the poem's 'perfection'.[52] History, in this lyric, has been assimilated to the natural revolutions of seasonal change, processes that are arrested, almost, and redeemed by autumnal beauty and plenitude. For Hartman 'To Autumn' was best understood as a *Convito*, a banquet of English sounds and foods that nourished Keats's imagination after he had abandoned the sublime, Miltonic voice of the *Hyperion* poems.[53] A collateral interpretation has been offered by Jerome McGann, who reads 'To Autumn' as 'the finished expression' of Keats's tranquil mood at Winchester during September 1819; 'Winchester, and his time there, are repeatedly seen [in Keats's letters] as a respite from the tensions not only of his own personal affairs, but of the contemporary social scene at large.' As McGann puts it, Keats 'found Winchester a wonderful refuge'; 'The city and its environs [were] magical in their ability to carry him away to a charmed world far removed from the quotidian press of his money affairs and the dangerous political tensions of his society.'[54] In this contextual reading of 'To Autumn' McGann coincides with Hartman's manifestly anti-historical understanding of the poem as 'enchanted ground', a spellbound refuge from history. But maybe a less mysterious interpretation of history in 'To Autumn' is possible. In the closing pages of this book I seek to locate the impersonal voice of the poem in relation to contemporary discourses of political and social conflict, so angling the poem that it may be understood as a negatively capable

[51] 'Poem and Ideology: A Study of Keats's "To Autumn"', in *The Fate of Reading and Other Essays* (Chicago, 1975), 126, 146.

[52] For a current reiteration of this view, see Morse Peckham, *The Romantic Virtuoso* (Hanover, 1995), 113: 'the exquisite "To Autumn", the most perfect of [Keats's] poems and perhaps the most perfect in the English language.'

[53] 'Spectral Symbolism and the Authorial Self in Keats's *Hyperion*', in *The Fate of Reading*, 57–73.

[54] *KHM* 58.

intervention rather than as 'an attempt to "escape" the period which provides the poem with its context'.[55]

To be sure, Keats was impressed by the 'ancient aristocratical' city of Winchester, although his letters at this time dwelt at greater length on his vexing financial problems, his fragile health, and his need to 'wean' himself from Fanny Brawne: 'I am all in a mist; I scarcely know what's what'; 'I am all in a Mess here—embowell'd in Winchester'; 'I should *do* something for my immediate welfare'; 'were it not for the assistance of Brown & Taylor, I must be as badly off as a Man can be . . . I have pass'd my time in reading, writing, and fretting.'[56] For a while he believed his letters were being opened in the post, a paranoia driven by his personal distress and by the extremity of the times. Indeed, between 10 and 15 September Keats's private affairs overlapped with public events, when he returned to London to try to secure funds for his brother George. It is this brief visit which provides a focus for the composition of 'To Autumn' during a period of acute unsettlement—personal, public, political, and social.

A Serious Conspiracy in Manchester

> Just published. THE GAME BOOK FOR 1819 . . . by means of which an account may be kept with ease and accuracy of the different kinds of Game, when, where, and by whom killed, how disposed of, and other particulars.
>
> (Advertisement in the *Champion*, 29 Aug. 1819)

On the afternoon of Monday 13 September 1819 Keats joined the large crowd gathered in The Strand to welcome 'Orator' Henry Hunt in the procession organized to mark his arrival in London. 'I[t] would take me a whole day and a quire of paper to give you any thing like detail,' Keats wrote to his brother and sister-in-law: 'I will merely mention that it is calculated that

---

[55] *KHM* 61. See also Paul Fry's account of McGann's troubled response to Hartman in 'History, Existence, and "To Autumn"', KP 216–18.

[56] Keats to Fanny Brawne, 13 Sept. 1819; to J. H. Reynolds, 21 Sept. 1819; to Richard Woodhouse, 21–2 Sept. 1819; to C. W. Dilke, 22 Sept. 1819; to George and Georgiana Keats, 17–27 Sept. 1819; in *Letters*, ii. 160, 167, 169–75, 178, 185.

30.000 people were in the streets waiting for him—The whole distance from the Angel Islington to the Crown and anchor was lined with Multitudes' (*Letters*, ii. 194). Henry Hunt had been the principal speaker at the mass meeting of reformists in St Peter's Fields, Manchester, a little under a month before on 16 August 1819. When the Manchester and Salford Yeomanry, on horseback, moved into the crowd to apprehend Hunt and the others, the peaceful meeting was swiftly transformed to violent confusion in which (perhaps) eleven were killed and as many as 500 people wounded: the Peterloo Massacre. 'Confusion' and 'perhaps', because what exactly happened in Manchester that day remains controversial. Certainly, the emotive and often contradictory accounts of the tragedy in the newspapers encouraged rumour and dismay throughout the country. 'Within two days of Peterloo, all England knew of the event', according to E. P. Thompson: 'Within a week every detail of the massacre was being canvassed in ale-houses, chapels, workshops, private houses.'[57] Hunt and the other speakers on the tribune were arrested and imprisoned, although the immediate charge of 'conspiracy and sedition' was soon dropped. As we have already seen, his triumphal reception in London on 13 September reflected widespread jubilation among the reformists, but this was mingled with hardening resentment at the behaviour of the militia, the judiciary, and especially the government which had endorsed without delay the actions of the soldiers and the magistrates at Manchester.

In this very highly charged political environment, conspiracy theories flourished. When one reads 'To Autumn' with this context in mind, the opening lines start to resonate in unusual and, I think, intriguing ways:

> Season of mists and mellow fruitfulness,
>   Close bosom-friend of the maturing sun;
> Conspiring with him how to load and bless
>   With fruit the vines that round the thatch-eves run . . .

The verb 'to conspire', from the Latin *conspirare*, literally means 'to breath together' and thus 'to accord, harmonize, agree, combine or unite in a purpose' (*OED*). So in 'conspiring' to-

---

[57] *The Making of the English Working Class*, 753–6. For a full-length reassessment of Peterloo, see Robert Walmsley, *Peterloo: The Case Reopened* (Manchester, 1969).

gether the powers of the season and sun combine to make earth fruitful. Yet this genial conspiracy is shadowed by the contrasting sense of the word, glossed by the *Oxford English Dictionary* as to 'plot mischief together secretly', and this mischievous sense of conspiracy was a primary definition of the word in Samuel Johnson's *Dictionary*. In one reading, 'conspiracy' in 'To Autumn' is a plot of nature to 'fill all fruit with ripeness to the core' (6)—an impersonal process of natural abundance. But that expression of nature's fruitfulness is modified by the alternative, treasonable discourses of conspiracy that were circulating widely in September 1819.

On behalf of the government, the Home Secretary Lord Sidmouth advised that the ringleaders were to be charged 'for a treasonable conspiracy to alter by force the constitution of the realm as by law established'. To Lord Eldon, the Chancellor, the meeting had been 'an overt act of conspirators, to instigate . . . specific acts of treason'.[58] *The Times* pronounced on the 'dreadful fact' of the violence at Manchester *before* the detailed account from the paper's reporter, John Tyas, had arrived in London. This leading article established the popular belief 'that nearly a hundred of the King's unarmed subjects have been sabred by a body of cavalry in the streets of a town of which most of them were inhabitants'—although Tyas's eyewitness version, published in the same edition of *The Times*, 19 August 1819, contradicted the leading article in some details. Both the leader and Tyas's report were widely reprinted and appeared in two opposition newspapers that published Keats's writings and which he is known to have read. These were the *Examiner*, and the *Champion*, which in 1819 was edited by John Thelwall—a prominent reformist since the 1790s. Both journals followed the *Times* in agreeing on the 'dreadful fact' of what had happened at Manchester, but of course interpretations of the event differed (and still do so today). The *Examiner* reported the 'disturbance' and 'atrocities' at Manchester; the *Champion* warned about 'ANARCHISTS in MILITARY UNIFORM', the breakdown of justice, and the possibility that military action against the people might provoke a violent revolution. When Henry Hunt and other reformists were arrested and imprisoned,

58 Walmsley, *Peterloo*, 247, 339–40.

the *Champion* noted that the magistrates 'brought against them a charge of *conspiracy* to alter the laws by force and threats'.[59] During the weeks after Peterloo, the *Champion* elaborated an alternative theory of conspiracy in which the powers of the State were aligned against the liberties and democratic aspirations of the people.

For Thelwall the reformists at St Peter's Fields—like those who had met at Copenhagen Fields back in October 1795—were to be identified with 'the cause of the people at large—of the Laws and the Constitution'. They called for annual parliaments and universal suffrage, and in one section of the crowd a banner was held aloft on which 'Justice' was represented 'holding the scales in one hand, and a sword in the other'. From Thelwall's point of view, the military intervention was an act of 'lawless, and ruthless murder', an 'abhorrent massacre'.[60] Then, on Sunday 19 September 1819—the day on which Keats first drafted 'To Autumn'—the *Champion* published the following analysis of contemporary events:

There is indeed, we believe, A SERIOUS CONSPIRACY IN MANCHESTER— a Conspiracy of those whom fortune has favoured, to depress and keep down the less fortunate multitude whose labour has been the instrument of that favour:—a Conspiracy of the Rich against the Poor—a species of conspiracy certainly not less frequent (as it is certainly much more practicable) than a conspiracy of the poor against the rich: nay a conspiracy which we might almost venture to say, always precedes, and not unfrequently produces, that of the latter description. These Opulent Conspirators wish to prevent the labouring classes from aspiring to any political rights—because political rights have a tendency to secure personal liberty and personal consideration. The confederacies and combinations they practice among themselves, they would interdict entirely their poorer brethren, that they may keep them in abject and entire dependence: and what the law cannot, or will not insure for them, in this respect, they would accomplish by the terrors of the sword. If nothing else will keep down the half-famishing labouring poor and stifle the cry of their complaints, it has been thought that massacre would. But let them beware of a reaction;—in case of which, victory might be to them as fatal as defeat.[61]

[59] See *The Times* (19 Aug. 1819); *Examiner* (23 Aug. 1819); *Champion and Sunday Review* (22 Aug. 1819), 525; (19 Sept. 1819), 595.
[60] *Champion and Sunday Review* (22 Aug. 1819), 526, 532; (12 Sept. 1819), 574.
[61] *Champion and Sunday Review* (19 Sept. 1819), 591.

Keats could not have read this column on 19 September: it would have taken a day for copies to reach Winchester from London. On the other hand, political debate in August and September 1819 focused on the word 'conspire'. Thelwall was evidently responding to—and amplifying—rumours of state conspiracy canvassed in the broad range of reformist discourse which was also available to Keats in the national journals, and in material from those papers reprinted locally in the *Salisbury and Winchester Journal*.[62] But, as Jerome McGann and others have pointed out, Keats's poem is not radical polemic like Thelwall's articles in the *Champion* or, for that matter, Shelley's incandescent response to Peterloo in *The Masque of Anarchy*.[63] Throughout this book I have suggested ways in which Keats's verse responded to contemporary journalism in the post-war period. My purpose has been to show how, once we are alerted to contemporary resonances of his poems apparent to his first readers, we can recover a fuller sense of Keats's witty, sparkling, changeful, and controversial arrival on the literary scene. But how can we make a credible link between the ongoing discussion of national crisis in the newspapers and conspiracy in 'To Autumn', so as to elucidate the politics of autumnal beauty in Keats's poem?

The Calendar of Nature

> And Libra weighs in equal scales the year . . .
> (James Thomson, *The Seasons*, 'Autumn')

The *Examiner* for 5 September 1819 (just before Keats's visit to London) contained much on Peterloo, and also Hunt's regular monthly column entitled 'The Calendar of Nature'. The 'Calendar' has been noticed before in criticism of 'To Autumn', most recently by William Keach;[64] it has not yet been reproduced fully

---

[62] I am grateful to John Barnard for information about the political columns of the *Salisbury and Winchester Journal* in 1819.

[63] But see Charles Cowden Clarke's letter to Leigh Hunt, 14 Nov. 1832, in which he welcomes *The Masque of Anarchy* as a belated harvest from 'the insolent age of the villain Castlereagh': 'it is the product of a young, fruitful, *teeming* soil, unploughed, unforced, unharrowed . . . It appears to me worthy of any country & any age— Greek, Roman, or British.' Novello-Clarke Collection, Brotherton Library, Leeds University.

[64] See 'Cockney Couplets', *KP* 194–5.

in this context, however, so that its relation to Keats's poem may reward some further consideration. The 'Calendar' begins with the 'September' stanza from Spenser's *Mutabilitie Cantos,* long recognized as the source for some images in 'To Autumn':

> September.
> Next him September marched eke on foot;
> Yet was he heavy laden with the spoyle
> Of harvest's riches, which he made his boot,
> And him enriched with bounty of the soyle:
> In his one hand, as fit for harvest's toyle,
> He held a knife-hook; and in th'other hand
> A paire of weights, with which he did assoyle
> Both more and lesse, where it in doubt did stand,
> And equal gave to each as justice duly scanned.
>
> Spenser.

The poet still takes advantage of the exuberance of harvest and the sign of the Zodiac in this month, to read us a lesson on justice.

Autumn has now arrived. This is the month of the migration of birds, of the finished harvest, of nut-gathering, of cyder and perry-making, and, towards the conclusion, of the change of colour in trees. The swallows, and many other soft-billed birds that feed on insects, disappear for the warmer climates, leaving only a few stragglers behind, probably from weakness or sickness, who hide themselves in caverns and other sheltered places, and occasionally appear on warm days. The remainder of harvest is got in; and no sooner is this done, than the husbandman ploughs up his land again, and prepares it for the winter grain. The oaks and beeches shed their nuts, which in the forests that still remain, particularly the New Forest in Hampshire, furnish a luxurious repast for the swine, who feast of an evening in as pompous a manner as any alderman, to the sound of the herdsman's horn.

But the acorn must not be undervalued, because it is food for swine, nor thought only robustly of, because it furnishes our ships with timber. It is also one of the most beautiful objects of its species, protruding its glossy green nut from its rough and sober-coloured cup, and dropping it in a most elegant manner beside the sunny and jagged leaf. We have seen a few of them, with their stems in water, make a handsome ornament to a mantle-piece, in this season of departing flowers.

The few additional flowers this month are corn-flower, Guernsey-lilies, starwort, and saffron, a species of crocus, which is cultivated in separate grounds. The stamens of this flower are pulled, and dried into flat square cakes for medicinal purposes. It was formerly much esteemed in cookery. The clown in the Winter's Tale, reckoning up what he is to buy for the sheepshearing feast, mentions 'saffron to colour the warden-pies'. The fresh trees and shrubs in flower are bramble, chaste-tree, laurustinus, ivy, wild honeysuckle, spires, and arbutus or strawberry-tree, a favourite of Virgil, which, like the garden of Alcinous, in Homer, produces flower and fruit at once.—Hardy annuals, intended to flower in the spring, should now be sown; annuals of curious sorts, from which seed is to be raised, should be sheltered till ripened; and auriculas in pots, which were shifted last month, moderately watered.

The stone-curlew clamours at the beginning of this month, woodowls hoot, the ring-ouzel reappears, the saffron butterfly is seen, hares congregate; and, at the end of it, the woodlark, thrush and blackbird, are heard.

September, though its mornings and evenings are apt to be chill and foggy, and therefore not wholesome to those who either do not or cannot guard against them, is generally a serene and pleasant month, partaking of the warmth of summer and the vigour of autumn. But its noblest feature is a certain festive abundance for the supply of all creation. There is grain for men, birds, and horses, hay for the cattle, loads of fruit on the trees, and swarms of fish in the ocean. If the soft-billed birds which feed on insects miss their usual supply, they find it in the southern countries, and leave one's sympathy to be pleased with an idea, that repasts apparently more harmless are alone offered to the creation upon our temperate soil. The feast, as the philosophic poet says on a higher occasion,

> The feast is such as earth, the general mother,
>   Pours from her fairest bosom, when she smiles
> In the embrace of Autumn. To each other
>   As some fond parent fondly reconciles
> Her warring children, she their wrath beguiles
>   With their own sustenance; they, relenting, weep,
> Such is this festival, which from their isles,
>   And continents, and winds, and oceans deep,
> All shapes may throng to share, that fly, or walk, or creep.
>   Shelley.

Just below the stanza from the 'philosophic poet' Shelley's *Revolt of Islam* is the heading 'LAW. Surrey Sessions. *Tuesday, Aug. 31*. Seditious Placards', returning the reader to an article which reports directly on the controversial politics of the day.

The similarities between Hunt's 'Calendar of Nature' and 'To

Autumn' extend beyond 'harvest's riches' and the harvester's 'knife-hook' in Spenser. Details such as the migrating birds, cider-making, swallows and insects, warm days, and even the chill and fog all reappear in Keats's poem.[65] Most interesting in the present context, however, is the schooling that Hunt draws from Spenser and elaborates in his commentary and with the quotation from Shelley: 'The poet still takes advantage of the exuberance of harvest and the sign of the Zodiac in this month, to read us a lesson on justice.'

Spenser's harvester uses a 'paire of weights' to divide the produce of autumn justly and equably. The image of the balance is especially appropriate to September (as Hunt notices) because the latter part of this temperate month lies under the constellation Libra, which depicts a pair of scales. Keats had been familiar with the image and seasonal significance of Libra since his schoolboy reading at Enfield in Bonnycastle's *Introduction to Astronomy*: 'LIBRA, the Balance, one of the twelve signs of the zodiac, into which the sun comes about the 20th of September, or the beginning of autumn.'[66] In addition to these seasonal and astronomical associations, during autumn 1819 the scales had an immediate emblematic force in political debate. The reformists' banners at St Peter's Fields had been emblazoned with the figure of Justice holding her scales, as an expression of their call for democratic rights and universal suffrage. And contemporary satirical prints such as *Manchester Heroes* represented the *injustice* of Peterloo and its aftermath in a cartoon image of the Prince Regent as the fulcrum of a set of unbalanced scales (see Fig. 6). In this wider emblematic context, the point of Leigh Hunt's 'lesson on justice' in his September 'Calendar of Nature' becomes apparent in mediating between political oppression and seasonal fruitfulness. The 'exuberance of harvest' (literally *ex-uber*, from the breast of nature) is appropriately the season of justice; it is depicted by Hunt as a commonwealth, 'a certain festive abundance for the supply of all creation', which might assuage even the dearth

---

[65] Other sources for the autumnal imagery of Keats's poem included illustrated editions of James Thomson's *Seasons*; John Aikin's *Natural History of the Year: Being an Enlargement of Dr. Aikin's Calendar of Nature: By Arthur Aikin* (4th edn., London, 1815). See *KC* i. 254 for Keats's copy of this book, AP 655 n., and Ian Jack, *Keats and the Mirror of Art* (Oxford, 1967), 238–40, 292 n.

[66] *An Introduction to Astronomy*, 420.

endured by those New Forest swine in Richard Porson's satire: 'What is the property of a hog?—A wooden trough, food and drink just enough to keep in life; and a truss of musty straw, on which ten or a dozen of us *pig together*.'[67] Shelley's autumnal *Convito*, the 'banquet of the free' in Canto V of *The Revolt of Islam*, points the revolutionary meaning of Hunt's observations. The exuberance of 'earth, the general mother' feeds and reconciles the 'warring children', who share with all creation in the plenty of the season.

When we turn from Spenser, Shelley, and 'The Calendar of Nature' to Keats's 'To Autumn', the conspiracy of sun and season may now appear less of an escape from historical tensions, than as a harvest-home fulfilling the call for justice from 'the less fortunate multitude'—the 'swine' of Burke's *Reflections*. There are of course no scales of justice overtly represented in 'To Autumn' (as they had been in Spenser's verse, and as depicted on the protesters' banners at St Peter's Fields). Nevertheless in formal terms and in some verbal details the three stanzas of Keats's poem exhibit a fine equity, resuming the current discourse of (in)justice as a politics of style; as Geoffrey Hartman has already pointed out, 'Each stanza . . . is so equal in its poetical weight, so loaded with its own harvest.'[68] Hartman's perception of the poem's global equipoise can be substantiated further in specific images and emblems of balance, disclosed in the central stanza amid the store of autumn's plenty. The tress of hair, for example, is 'soft-lifted', floating upon the breath of the 'winnowing wind'; indeed, the version of the poem transcribed in Keats's letter to Richard Woodhouse, 21 September 1819 (*Letters*, ii. 170–1), has 'winmowing wind', a misspelling that seems to concentrate in a single word the whole process of harvest in mowing, winnowing, and—perhaps—wind milling. The furrow of corn is 'half-reap'd', the next swath 'and all its twined flowers' yet to be harvested. And then there is the marvellously composed movement of

> . . . sometimes like a gleaner thou dost keep
> Steady thy laden head across a brook . . .

—'Stready', as Keats wrote in his copy of the poem for Woodhouse (*Letters*, ii. 170), intimating, as Christopher Ricks

---

[67] *Examiner* (30 Aug. 1818), 550; see also the discussion in Ch. 3.
[68] 'Poem and Ideology', 129.

notes, both 'straight and steady': a justified progress.[69] In all of these verbal and emblematic details the poem identifies balance and equity as particularly appropriate to autumn, 'a medium between summer and winter', articulating the beauty of the season in language and imagery that were also circulating in discourses of political and social justice after the outrage of Peterloo.

The third stanza of 'To Autumn' returns to the westering world of change, loss, mortality—already sensed, perhaps, in the 'clammy cells' of the bees—but with an acceptance of those processes of time which is a characteristic of the negatively capable imagination. Crucially, however, that acceptance has been achieved through contemplation of natural abundance that was laden with intense social and ideological consequence at the season of the poem's composition. There is, moreover, a biblical resonance to the language and imagery of 'To Autumn' which deserves to be mentioned, for it enables us to hear the distant commotion of Peterloo even in the final *sotto voce* cadences of Keats's poem. Behind Keats's benign harvest was the terrifying, apocalyptic reaping of the earth in Revelation 14:

19. And the angel thrust in his sickle into the earth, and gathered the vine of the earth, and cast it into the great winepress of the wrath of God.

20. And the winepress was trodden without the city, and blood came out of the winepress, even unto the horse bridles, by the space of a thousand and six hundred furlongs.

Some contemporary responses to Peterloo echoed these dreadful, sanguinary 'last oozings' from the winepress,

> —may the ghosts of the murdered your slumbers infest,
> And drops of their blood be found in your wine . . .[70]

—and Shelley in his *Masque of Anarchy* draws from the same source to orchestrate the 'ghastly masquerade' of the murderers,

> Drunk as with intoxication
> Of the wine of desolation. (48–9)[71]

---

[69] See *Keats and Embarrassment*, 72–3.
[70] 'Manchester Y——y Valour', in Walmsley, *Peterloo*, 263–4.
[71] *The Masque of Anarchy: A Poem* (London, 1832).

Elsewhere, 'the conspirators against the privileges of the People' were denounced in the prophetic voice of Revelation:

> They shall not smell sweet and blossom in the dust; the wrongs which they have heaped upon society will adhere to them like the leprosy . . . time will disclose the secret; and then they may call on the heavens to hide, and the hills to cover them, but the outstretched arm of Offended Justice will seize these children of blood, even at the uttermost bounds of the earth.[72]

In the temperate lyrical clime of 'To Autumn', these sanguinary tones are chastened, residual, but discerned none the less, I think, in the reaping 'hook', the 'last oozings' of the 'cyder-press', the 'soft-dying day', and the 'rosy hue' of the 'stubble-plains'. Through such verbal details the apocalyptic harvest of the fields of St Peter is acknowledged, even as it is subdued in the slow gathering of the season and the poem itself towards a close. The figure of 'Offended Justice' remains, and it is to this focus of restitution in Keats's poem that I now turn.

'Who hath not seen thee?'

> pray tell me what that tall majestic lady is, that stands there, beautified with yellow hair, and crowned with a turbant composed of ears of corn; her bosom swells with breasts as white as snow. Her right-hand is filled with poppies and ears of corn, and in her left is a lighted torch.
>
> (Andrew Tooke, The Pantheon)[73]

> Scarcity and want shall shun you;
> Ceres' blessing so is on you.
> (The Tempest, IV. i. 116–17)

'Who hath not seen thee oft amid thy store?' As has frequently been pointed out (by Ian Jack, Helen Vendler, John Creaser, and most recently Andrew Bennett), Keats's personification of autumn has numerous mythical referents, the most notable of these being the goddess Ceres.[74] Keats had known about Ceres

---

[72] 'Manchester Politics', *Manchester Observer* (11 Sept. 1819), in Walmsley, *Peterloo*, 273.

[73] *The Pantheon*, 177–8.

[74] See *Keats and the Mirror of Art*, 232–43; Helen Vendler, *The Odes of John Keats* (Cambridge, Mass., 1983), 233–88; John Creaser, 'From "Autumn" to Autumn in

from his schoolboy reading in Ovid's *Metamorphoses* and (more especially) his classical dictionaries and anthologies of classical literature. Three texts, which Charles Cowden Clarke recalled Keats reading at Enfield, identify the various mythical associations of Ceres. Lemprière's *Bibliotheca Classica; or, A Classical Dictionary*, which Clarke says Keats 'appeared to *learn*', provides the typical image of Ceres, 'goddess of corn and harvests . . . represented with a garland of ears of corn on her head, holding in one hand a lighted torch, and in the other a poppy, which was sacred to her'. Ceres' resemblance to the figure on the banner at St Peter's Fields, with the torch and scales of justice, was not a coincidence—as will shortly appear. Joseph Spence's *Polymetis*, also read at Enfield by Keats, offers an identical image of Ceres 'regarding the laborious husbandman from heaven; and blessing the work of his hands with success'.[75]

That 'To Autumn' was a late harvesting of images and ideas which had been sown in Keats's earliest years at Enfield is suggested by the similarities between the poem and these short extracts from Lemprière and Spence. It is Andrew Tooke's *Pantheon*, however, which elaborates the symbolic roles of Ceres in greatest detail, glossing a passage from the *Metamorphoses* which associates her with fruitfulness, labour on the land, and the origins of justice:

Ovid . . . tells us that *Ceres* was the first that made laws, provided wholesome food, and taught the art of husbandry, of plowing and sowing: for before her time the earth lay rough and uncultivated, covered with briars and unprofitable plants. Where there were no proprietors of land, they neglected to cultivate it; when nobody had any ground of his own, they did not care to fix land-marks; but all things were common to all men, till Ceres, who had invented the art of husbandry, taught men how to exercise it: and then they began to contend and dispute about the limits of those fields from whose culture they reaped so much profit; and from thence it was necessary that laws should be enacted to determine the rights and properties of those who contended. For this reason Ceres was named the *Foundress of laws*.[76]

Keats's Ode', *Essays in Criticism*, 38 (1988), 190–214; Bennett, *Keats, Narrative*, 159–71.

[75] See 'Recollections of Keats', 124; J. Lemprière, *Bibliotheca Classica; or, A Classical Dictionary* (3rd edn., London, 1797), unpaginated; Joseph Spence, *Polymetis; or, An Inquiry Concerning the Agreement between the Works of the Roman Poets, and the Remains of the Ancient Artists* (2nd edn., London, 1755), 103.

[76] *The Pantheon*, 179.

Ceres presides over land originally 'common to all men'; over food, farming, cultivation, and prosperity; and over the laws determining 'rights and properties' among contentious humankind.[77] She represents nature's abundance, and also the rights and laws that determine a just distribution of that plenty. If one glances back at Thelwall's account of the reformists at St Peter's Fields, one might contend that Ceres was the appropriate emblem of those 'labouring classes ... aspiring to ... political rights ... personal liberty and personal consideration'. Certainly, the mythical associations of the goddess, uniting fruitfulness and justice, would have garnered further resonance at a season when killings, trumped-up prosecutions, and rumoured conspiracies seemed likely to provoke a revolution. Perhaps, as Josiah Conder had said, there was 'mischief' indeed at the core of *Lamia, Isabella, The Eve of St Agnes, and Other Poems*. Yet in 'To Autumn' the goddess is a shadowy figure, not explicitly invoked although her presence may be assumed in the question 'Who hath not seen thee oft amid thy store?' The interrogation is knowing and very finely poised, negatively capable in Heaney's sense of being 'affected by all positions'; it addresses the community 'who hath seen' but with a glancing acknowledgement of those who have not, in that they are unjustly excluded from their due share in Ceres's autumnal plenty. That secondary inflection was emphasized in Keats's draft of 'To Autumn', where the question was abbreviated as 'Who hath not seen thee?' And the succeeding lines of the draft fleetingly admit the deprived in search of restitution, 'Sometimes whoever seeks for thee may find thee', subsequently revised to 'Sometimes whoever seeks abroad may find thee'.[78] Perhaps the overt sense of the line suggests that whoever quests widely 'may find', but— just momentarily—the poem quits the shores of Britain for a haven of justice elsewhere.

[77] Andrew Bennett points out that, as a 'pervasive unstated presence' in 'To Autumn' Ceres has a significant relationship to agrarian politics (the Corn Laws of 1815, enclosures, the condition of the rural poor), such that the poem's 'perfected language of pastoral description is invaded by political questions of lawful exchange, agricultural boundaries, private property and labour relations'. Bennett, *Keats, Narrative*, 162–4.

[78] See the draft of 'To Autumn' reproduced in *John Keats: Poetry Manuscripts at Harvard: A Facsimile Edition*, ed. Jack Stillinger (Cambridge, Mass., 1990), 222. For a reading of 'To Autumn' as 'an apotheosis of contemporary Spencean articles of faith about English abundance and fertility', see David Worrall, *Radical Culture: Discourse, Resistance and Surveillance, 1790–1820* (Hemel Hempstead, 1992), 201–2.

Postscript

When in 1821 Leigh Hunt republished his 'Calendar of Nature'
as a volume entitled *The Months,* he prefaced the book with an
advertisement mentioning that 'The good-nature with which
this Calendar was received on its appearance in 1819 . . . has
induced its republication in a separate form, with considerable
additions'. Hunt made no revisions to the text of 'September',
but he did make one notable addition: the second and third
stanzas of 'To Autumn'.[79] 'A living poet has happily personified
autumn in some of the pleasantest shapes under which her
servants appear,' Hunt wrote, and incorporated Keats's poem
within his own celebration of autumnal exuberance. In so doing, however, he explicitly associated 'To Autumn' with the
seasonal 'lesson on justice' that he had drawn from Spenser's
and Shelley's poems, and from Richard Porson's *New Catechism.*
We have seen how in 1819 Hunt's 'Calendar of Nature' might
have offered Keats some images for 'To Autumn'; two years
later, *The Months* gathered 'To Autumn' into a context that
acknowledged the poem's fruitful, negatively capable conspiracy as an expression of Keats's commonwealth, 'a certain
festive abundance for the supply of all creation'.
   Throughout this book I have been concerned to recover
Keats from the contexts of disadvantage in which he has been
fixed by critics from Z to Marjorie Levinson, emphasizing instead the ways in which the circumstances of his life from his
schooldays onwards enabled and enriched his poetry. I have
also sought to show how Keats's poems responded to and nego-
tiated with contemporary history, rather than presenting an
aesthetic resort in which to 'escape' or 'evade' the world. Helen
Vendler has suggested that the music in the third stanza of 'To
Autumn' issues from a 'choir of orphans . . . in mourning for a
dead mother' and that, in the final lines, the poem lifts away
from 'pathos and nostalgia for the past'.[80] Her reading of the
final stanza draws on biography in order to transcend it, although, as we have seen, Keatsian romance never wholly forgets

[79] *The Months Descriptive of the Successive Beauties of the Year* (London, 1821), 5,
102–9.
[80] Vendler, *Odes,* 259–63.

the earth. The mild, autumnal music at the close of 'To Autumn' is a contented valediction,

> Hedge-crickets sing; and now with treble soft
> The red-breast whistles from a garden-croft;
> And gathering swallows twitter in the skies.

—which may hark back to a formative landscape: the 'garden-croft' at Enfield School, scene of Keats's poetic initiation with Charles Cowden Clarke. Here too, in earlier years, John Ryland had set his 'living orrery' in motion, and the whole school had assembled in autumn to watch 'the swallows, which had clustered in surprising numbers on the roof of the building'.[81] Keats was always a 'watcher of the skies', and this most generous of poems concludes with the turning of the season, a gathering for departure, and with one of the 'delighted stares' which Cowden Clarke always associated with Keats's intensity of response.[82] I might have closed here by suggesting that the extraordinary school which shaped Keats's life as a poet had also fostered the delighted welcome for experience which endured almost to the very end of his life. But perhaps that final flourish is better left in silence: a 'wild surmise'.

[81] See Culross, *Three Rylands*, 40.   [82] 'Recollections of Keats', 130.

Appendix:
Correspondence Relating to the 'Cockney School' Essays, from the 'Blackwood Papers' in the National Library of Scotland

The Blackwood Papers at the National Library of Scotland, Edinburgh, contain numerous letters to William Blackwood relating to the publication of the 'Cockney School' essays. The letters are important for what they tell us about contemporary literary culture in Scotland and England, at a period when competition between Edinburgh and London was especially acute. More particularly, the extracts illuminate the publishing background to the essays, in the poems submitted to *Blackwood's* by Cornelius Webb (1*a*) and one of Lockhart's sources of information about Keats (4*a*). Coleridge and John Hamilton Reynolds are shown to have been approached as possible contributors to *Blackwood's Magazine* (3 *a*, *b*, *c*, *e*). The Surrey Institution (targetted by 7. as a Cockney Athenaeum) and its liberal intellectual values are firmly defended (3*d*), and important new Cockney publications such as Hunt's *Literary Pocket Book* and Taylor and Hessey's *London Magazine* are described along with the principal contributors (3*f*, 7*b*). Literary animosities, in which the death of Keats was a focal point, are canvassed in two items (5*b* and 6*a*), and the scandal of Shelley's, Byron's, and Hunt's activities on the Continent is presented in relation to their plan to publish the *Liberal*, and the emergence of John Clare on the literary scene (7*a* and 7*b*). These extracts are reproduced here to give an additional sense of the range and vitality of 'Cockney Culture', and to indicate areas and directions where further research is likely to be rewarding.[1] All quotations are by permission of the Trustees of the National Library of Scotland.

1. From NLS, MS 4002. Blackwood Papers 1817

a. Cornelius Webb to William Blackwood, September 1817. The *Epistle to a Friend* which Webb enclosed (now lost) may have been

---

[1] For the extent of the Cockney community of writers and artists, see in particular Jeffrey Cox, 'John Keats in the Cockney School', *Romanticism*, 2/1 (1996), 27–29.

the source for Z's epigraph to the 'Cockney School' essays. See p.
129n. above.

Mr Editor,

If you can imagine the inclosed *Sonnets* and printed *Epistle to a Friend* have sufficient merit to entitle them to a place in your very excellent Magazine, they are certainly at your service.

Yours, with much esteem, Corns. Webb

Sonnet 1

Hard by there is a secret greenwood nook,
Haply by fairies formed, for the repose
And pleasure of their green;—a silvery brook
Reflecting all that overhangs it—flows
Musically by, with noise of many springs;
The young birds tenant it, and woo and pair,
And silent sit to hear the Thrush, who sings
His frequent song of summer blytheness there.
'Twill soon be reached if we use willing speed;
Then let us hence—making so little stir,
Our light steps shall not rouse the grasshopper.
I have a song to breathe—a book to read,
And we will pass the hours in such employ
As shall to our twin hearts give certain joy.[2]
Pentonville.   Cornelius W-bb

Sonnet 2

I seek not, want not, Peru's buried ore,
Nor any part she has abundantly
Disgorged; nor power, nor state, nor pageantry;
Nor prize the wealth that heaps up Commerce' shore,
Nor that which rides her waves; nor the large store
That Neptune has obtained too frequently
From the sunk travellers of the perilous sea;
Nor all that makes a million misers poor.
Give all those life-bought nothings unto them
By whom they are worshipped; let them have gold
And silver in huge masses, and the gem
That would out-price the richest diadem—
So I but hear sweet Nature's voice—behold
Her cheek—and touch her meanest green robe's hem.[3]
Pentonville.   Cornelius W-bb

---

[2] Published in Webb's *Sonnets, Amatory, Incidental, and Descriptive; with Other Poems.*

[3] Published, with revisions, as 'Love of Nature' in *Sonnets, Amatory, Incidental, and Descriptive; with Other Poems.* Shelley's satire on Wordsworth in *Peter Bell the Third,*

Sonnet 3

Written at the Grave of Dermody the Poet

Tread with the slow, soft step of reverence
Above these still apartments of the dead;
Not that the echo of the heaviest tread
Would break their silence. Here Intemperance
Lies dumbly, soberly; the unreined madness
He revelled and delighted in is spent,
And fallen into this melancholy sadness;—
The glibsome tongue, whose speech was merriment,
And wit, and poetry, and knowledge—moulders
Within the hollow of the unfleshed jaws;—
The ear that drank the praisings of Applause,
Is deaf, though Fame's voice speaks to it. Beholders
Of this youth's grave, it doth become ye sigh
For one who lived so wildly—died so miserably.[4]

Lewisham,   Cornelius W-bb.
Sept. 1817.

b. John Hunt's letter to Robert Baldwin, London publisher and agent
for William Blackwood, requesting to be informed of the identity of Z,
author of 'On the Cockney School of Poetry: No I', which had appeared in *Blackwood's Edinburgh Magazine* the preceding month:

> Mr John Hunt calls upon Mr Baldwin to procure for him the Name
> and Residence of the Writer of an article in Blackwood's Magazine
> for October 1817—signed Z containing the most false, malignant,
> and altogether infamous assertions on the Character of Mr Leigh
> Hunt, the Editor of the Examiner. Nov. 3d. 1817.

c. From Robert Baldwin to William Blackwood, 3 November 1817,
accompanying John Hunt's letter above:

> I know not if *a convicted libeller* can prosecute for a libel; at all events,
> he would not come into court with very clean hands; but if he should
> determine to proceed in the way of indictment instead of action, an
> imprisonment would not be a very welcome visitation to either of us.

d. From Robert Baldwin to William Blackwood, 11 November 1817,
reiterating the Hunts' request:

> He touched the hem of Nature's shift,—
> Felt faint,—and never dared uplift
> The closest all-concealing tunic.

—may have owed something to his recollection of the final lines in Webb's sonnet,
perhaps read on one of those occasions when, as Keats said, Webb had been 'of our
Party occasionally at Hampstead', *Letters,* i. 180.

[4] Published in *Sonnets, Amatory, Incidental, and Descriptive; with Other Poems.*

nothing less than a disclosure of the name of the writer will satisfy them . . . I have reason to believe that they will not attack *us*; (and perhaps certain considerations will prevent them from bringing the matter before a public tribunal at all: but [John Hunt] left me with a very strong insinuation that they would immediately proceed against you, unless they obtain the required satisfaction; and he requested me to say as much in strong terms.

e. From an anonymous letter sent to William Blackwood by 'a gentleman of some consequence', 16 November 1817 (see also the passage from this letter quoted on p. 122):

I am well aware of the bias of political prejudice, and I can make much allowance for a dislike to the politician, influencing our *private* opinion of the man;—but all this is only palliative to a certain extent, and unless the writer and publishers of the article in question are prepared to prove in a most incontrovertible manner that Hunt is in his private life a *notoriously debauched, profligate,* and *licentious* character, there cannot be two opinions on the injustice and wickedness of the charge.

f. John Richardson, solicitor, also protests to William Blackwood, 20 November 1817, although he acknowledges the malign effect of Hunt's *Story of Rimini*:

It seems to me impossible to connect certain parts of the attack with the poet or the poem. The passages beginning 'The very concubine &c.' and 'How such a profligate creature &c.' are personal to the *man* . . . with all his affectation, he is in the domestic relations of life most exemplary . . . a *puritan* in morals . . . I do not however think that a man's pure conduct at home entitles him to spread poison abroad: and I have no doubt that the poem must be regarded as reprehensible—Vice is much more readily insinuated by such books as the new Eloise & Rimini than by coarser works that call such things more plainly by their names: & it is no justification that Dante first told the story.

g. Two days later, Richardson writes again to Blackwood, 22 November 1817, less convinced that a jury would find *The Story of Rimini* 'reprehensible':

There is no doubt, I believe, that Mr L. Hunt can prove himself individually to be almost if not altogether as pure & correct a man as walks the streets of London—& supposing this to be the case—one question which arises is—is the poem of a pure or impure tendency—if a jury will not say that it is impure then you have no case—for if both man & poem be blameless your article is certainly as atrocious a libel as could be penned.

2. From NLS, MS 4003. Blackwood Papers 1818

a. Patrick Tytler remonstrates, with some irony, in a letter to William Blackwood, 24 March 1818:

> to what purpose you have attacked those quiet and inoffensive authors who have no desire to contaminate the public's morals and no ability to vitiate the public taste—but who find an innocent amusement in writing poor works and are already sufficiently unhappy because nobody reads them—I cannot possibly understand.

3. From NLS, MS 4004. Blackwood Papers 1819

a. William Davies (of the London publisher Cadell and Davies, agents for Blackwood in London) reports a conversation with Coleridge about his possible contribution to *Blackwood's Edinburgh Magazine.* To William Blackwood, 6 April 1819:

> as you had stated your wishes as amounting to *scraps,* [Coleridge] was fearful that your views, with regard to him, may not be exactly of the description which he had in his mind, when he previously expressed his readiness to send you articles for the magazine. I, of course, had no hesitation in assuring him that I was persuaded your use of the word *scraps* meant no more than the miscellaneous matter, which constitutes the principal charm of such a mode of publication . . . Mr Coleridge next took occasion to lament that the magazine had acquired so strong a character for personalities and for unjust criticism . . .

b. P. G. Patmore to William Blackwood, 7 April 1819, on John Hamilton Reynolds's regard for *Blackwood's Magazine*:

> I dined with Reynolds a few days ago—& talked to him about writing for you—but, as I expected, from his friendship with Hunt & Hazlitt, he has a feeling about the magazine which prevents him—otherwise I know he would like to do so—for I was pleased to find that he didn't scruple to speak very highly of the general talent with which the work is conducted.

c. William Davies to William Blackwood, 26 April 1819, on Coleridge's further views about *Blackwood's*:

> Mr C. . . . is still clearly of opinion that you should clear [the magazine] of any perceptible bias to either political party, and also from every disposition to indulge in personalities . . . How far, do you think, will he be satisfied with the renewed personality against Mr L. Hunt in your 25th No. just received?

d. J. Millard to William Blackwood, 8 May 1819, responding to the abusive reference to Hazlitt's lectures in the Surrey Institution in the fifth 'Cockney School' essay, April 1819:

> If you happen to know the author of 'The Cockney School of Poetry' p. 97, col. 2 you may tell him that 'The Lecturers of the S.I.' *are* men of genius and are not '*Editors* of *Sunday Newspapers*'—and, that, if he supposes our audience to be composed of '*a*spiring *a*pprentices and *a*ritical *d*erks' (exquisite alliteration)—he must bear to have the words 'stupid and illiberal' sounded in his ears, and the epithet 'idiot' retorted upon him. Nothing can be more injurious to the reputation of a work than false assertions even if said 'smartly'.—Mr Hazlitt may fight his own battles, and is content to do so, but surely the *Surry Institution* might have escaped the flippancy of this concerted anti-cockney. He is travelling out of the Record when he attacks a Literary Institution which broaches no opinions of any sort, but is open to all.

e. William Davies to William Blackwood, 15 June 1819:

> [Coleridge] *must* be much influenced, I think, by what he has discovered of the altered manner in which both he himself and his friend Wordsworth have lately been mentioned in your Magazine.

f. Charles and James Ollier, publishers of Keats's first collection of poems, to William Blackwood, 27 November 1819, announcing the publication of Leigh Hunt's *Literary Pocket Book*:

> we have announced an annual Literary Miscellany. It will be *something* after the manner of those formerly published by Tonson and Lintot.—We expect to be supplied with articles from Mr Shelley, Mr Lamb, Mr C. Lloyd, Mr Procter, Mr T. L. Peacock and other Gentlemen whose names we may not state. These last are, for the most part, *young* writers, but there are among them some minds of originality and power.

4. From NLS, MS 4005. Blackwood Papers 1820

a. John Lockhart to William Blackwood, 1820:

> What I said about Keats was owing to two long and foolish letters from one Aiken of Dunbar whom the Profr. knows—not I.[5]

[5] See W. M. Parker, 'John Aitken and John Keats', *New Alliance and Scots Review* (Oct. 1949), 127, 129. Aitken's letter to Keats, 17 Aug. 1820 (reproduced by Parker), invited him to Scotland 'to renovate [his] weakened frame'. He also told Keats of his 'earnest disapprobation of the treatment you have experienced' from *Blackwood's*: 'some that are connected with it know well how much, by every means

5. *From NLS, MS 4007. Blackwood Papers 1821*

a. Charles Ollier to William Blackwood, 3 January 1821, on Hunt, Byron, Shelley, and the *Liberal*:

> Mr Leigh Hunt, we are told, is gone to Pisa: he and his family are to live with Lord Byron in his Lordship's house, and they (Ld Byron & Hunt) are, with the assistance of Mr Shelley to write a journal to be published here as the neutralizer of the Quarterly Review and, I suppose, of '*Blackwood*'.

b. William Maginn to William Blackwood, 10 October 1821, on literary assassinations:

> Keats too is flung in your face—I wonder how you escape being charged with the murder of Jack Polidori. With respect to Johnny K—it may be said flatly at once that whatever his powers might have been, they were swallowed up by affectation and an aspiring to be Leigh Hunt the second—...I really think you ought on some occasion or the other face the shooting of Scott, and this absurd hubbub about Keats, kept up by the Cockneys once for all—& then be done with it—

6. *From NLS, MS 4008. Blackwood Papers 1822*

a. William Maginn to William Blackwood, 29 April 1822:

> I hope this will find you in London, safe and sound, after escaping all the perils of mailcoaches, drunken drivers, whigs and whiteboys Even if you have, you are not quite out of danger. Taylor and Hessey will make a bold effort to assassinate you—Hazlitt will point his nose at you—the ghost of Jack Keates will come in full figure to disturb your slumbers.

7. *From NLS, MS 4009. Blackwood Papers 1822*

a. Alaric Watts to William Blackwood, 1 September 1822:

> It is a notorious fact and I heard it over and over again at Coligny, near Geneva, that Lord B and Shelley lived together in the same house (an old building looking on the lake of Geneva and the range of the Jura mountains) in promiscuous intercourse with these women; and when Miss Clermont (the sister of Mary Godwin by her father's first wife) added to the family, there was so little certainty as

in my power, I have endeavoured to soften its illiberality.' Lockhart's letter to William Blackwood seems to allude to Aitken's remonstrances with John Wilson ('the Profr.') on Keats's behalf.

to the father of the child that Shelley and his Lordship threw dice for the honor of providing for it . . . It is certain that Hunt has warmly and openly espoused 'promiscuous intercourse'. Indeed in his published work see the Indicator will be found various evidences of the villainous depravity of this creature's mind with respect to women. . . . It is a curious fact that all this class of persons, are entirely without any religious creed whatever. Chas Lamb, Procter, Hazlitt, Hunt, Peacock, Chas Ollier, Talford, Reynolds *cum multis aliis* all boast of their freedom from the shackles of religious sentiment of every kind.

b. Alaric Watts to William Blackwood, 'Memoranda' 1822(?):

Charles Lamb delivers himself with infinite pain and labour of a silly piece of trifling every month in this magazine under the signature Elia. It is the curse of the cockney school that with their desire to appear exceedingly offhand and ready with all they have to say, they are constrained to elaborate every petty sentence as tho' the web were woven from their own bowels. Charles Lamb says he can make no way in an article under at least a week, and poor Mr Reynolds has been spinning a volume of tales for Constable these five years. Then there is John Clare about whom there has been so much twaddle . . .

Bibliography

1. MANUSCRIPTS CITED

Listed by institution and collection

The Brotherton Collection, Leeds University Library:
Novello-Clarke Collection

NCC MS 6: Charles Cowden Clarke's Commonplace book.

NCC MS 7: Notebook kept by Charles Cowden Clarke, dated 'Enfield 1814'.

'Copy of a letter from C C Clarke to Leigh Hunt on the receipt of the accompanying Poem'; dated '67 Frith Street, Novr 14th 1832'. Folded inside a presentation copy of Shelley's *Masque of Anarchy* from Leigh Hunt to Vincent Novello. No shelf mark.

Autograph letter from Richard Monckton Milnes to Charles Cowden Clarke, 15 Dec. 1846, pasted inside a presentation copy of Milnes's *Life, Letters, and Literary Remains, of John Keats* (2 vols., London, 1848) from Milnes to Clarke. No shelf mark.

Autograph letter from Richard Monckton Milnes to Charles Cowden Clarke, 18 Dec. 1846, with Clarke's annotations, pasted into Clarke's copy of *LLL* (see above) with this annotation: 'The figures are in the handwriting of Charles Cowden Clarke. [signed] Mary Cowden Clarke'. No shelf mark.

Houghton Library, Harvard University: Keats Collection

See also *John Keats 1795–1995: With a Catalogue of the Harvard Keats Collection* (Cambridge, Mass., 1995).

MS Keats 3.1: Commonplace book of poems mainly by John Keats, compiled by Richard Woodhouse; summer of 1819.

MS Keats 3.2: Commonplace book of poems etc., mainly by John Keats, compiled by Richard Woodhouse; dated Nov. 1818.

MS Keats 3.13: Commonplace book of verse and prose by various authors, compiled by William Pitter Woodhouse; July–Aug. 1827.

MS Keats 4.4.19: Charles Cowden Clarke, 'Recollections of John Keats'.

MS Keats 4.16.2: Joseph Severn, 'On the Adversities of Keats's Fame', Rome [25 Dec.] 1861.

MS Keats 4.16.3: Joseph Severn, 'Notes on *Adonais*', Rome, 30 Aug. 1873.

MS Keats 4.16.4: Joseph Severn, 'My Tedious Life', Tossa, Sept. 1863.

National Library of Scotland, Edinburgh: Blackwood Papers

MS 4002: Blackwood Papers 1817.
MS 4003: Blackwood Papers 1818.
MS 4004: Blackwood Papers 1819.
MS 4005: Blackwood Papers 1820.
MS 4007: Blackwood Papers 1821.
MS 4008: Blackwood Papers 1822.
MS 4009: Blackwood Papers 1822.

Wills Library, Guy's Hospital, London

MS minutes of the Physical Society at Guy's Hospital.

2. PRINTED SOURCES CITED

ADDISON, JOSEPH, 'Broadsides and "The Two Children in the Wood"', *Spectator* (7 June 1711), in *Selections from the Tatler and the Spectator*, ed. Angus Ross (Harmondsworth, 1982).

AIKIN, JOHN, *Natural History of the Year: Being an Enlargement of Dr Aikin's Calendar of Nature: By Arthur Aikin* (4th edn., London, 1815).

ALEXANDER, J. H., '*Blackwood's*: Magazine as Romantic Form', *Wordsworth Circle*, 15/2 (Spring 1984).

ALTICK, RICHARD D., *The Cowden Clarkes* (London, 1948).

'The Apothecaries' Act of 1815', *Lancet*, 9 (1825–6).

ARNOLD, MATTHEW, *Essays in Criticism: Second Series* (1888), *The Complete Prose Works of Matthew Arnold*, ed. R. H. Super (11 vols., Ann Arbor, 1960–77).

ASKE, MARTIN, *Keats and Hellenism: An Essay* (Cambridge, 1985).

BARBAULD, ANNA LETITIA, *Poems* (London, 1773).

—— *The Works of Anna Letitia Barbauld* (2 vols., London, 1825).

BARNARD, JOHN, *John Keats* (Cambridge, 1987).

—— 'Charles Cowden Clarke's "Cockney" Commonplace Book', in Nicholas Roe (ed.), *Keats and History* (Cambridge, 1995).

—— 'Keats, Reynolds and the "Old Poets"', *Proceedings of the British Academy*, 75 (Oxford, 1990).

BARTON, ANNE, 'Byron and the Mythology of Fact', *The Nottingham Byron Lecture 1968* (Nottingham, 1968).

BATE, JONATHAN, *Shakespeare and the English Romantic Imagination* (Oxford, 1986).

——*Shakespearean Constitutions: Politics, Theatre, Criticism 1730–1830* (Oxford, 1989).

BATE, W. J., *From Classic to Romantic: Premises of Taste in Eighteenth-Century England* (Cambridge, Mass., 1946; rpt. New York, 1961).

——*John Keats* (Cambridge, Mass., 1963).

BAYLEY, JOHN, *The Uses of Division: Unity and Disharmony in Literature* (London, 1976).

BENNETT, ANDREW, *Keats, Narrative, and Audience* (Cambridge, 1994).

BETJEMAN, JOHN, *Summoned by Bells* (London, 1960).

BEWELL, ALAN, 'Keats's "Realm of Flora"', in David L. Clark and Donald C. Goellnicht (eds.), *New Romanticisms: Theory and Critical Practice* (Toronto, 1995).

Bicentenary History of College Street Church, Northampton (Northampton, 1897).

BLACKBURNE, FRANCIS, *Memoirs of Thomas Hollis* (2 vols., London, 1780).

BLOOM, HAROLD, 'Wordsworth and the Scene of Instruction', in *Poetry and Repression: Revisionism from Blake to Stevens* (New Haven, 1976).

BONNYCASTLE, JOHN, *An Introduction to Astronomy: In a Series of Letters from a Preceptor to his Pupil* (4th edn., London, 1803).

BOWEN, JAMES, 'Education, Ideology and the Ruling Class: Hellenism and English Public Schools in the Nineteenth Century', in G. W. Clarke (ed.), *Rediscovering Hellenism: The Hellenic Inheritance and the English Imagination* (Cambridge, 1989).

BRAND, JOHN, *Observations on the Popular Antiquities of Great Britain* (3 vols., London, 1849).

BRIGGS, H. E., 'Two Notes on Hazlitt and Keats', *Publications of the Modern Language Association of America*, 59 (1944).

BROMWICH, DAVID, *Hazlitt: The Mind of a Critic* (Oxford, 1983).

——'Keats's Radicalism', in Susan Wolfson (ed.), 'Keats and Politics: A Forum', *Studies in Romanticism*, 25 (Summer 1986).

BROOKE, STOPFORD A., *Studies in Poetry* (London, 1907).

BROOKS, CLEANTH, *The Well Wrought Urn* (London, 1949).

BROWN, CHARLES ARMITAGE, *Life of John Keats* (London, 1937).

BURKE, EDMUND, *A Philosophical Enquiry into the Origin of our Ideas of the Sublime and the Beautiful*, ed. Adam Phillips (Oxford, 1990).

——*Reflections on the Revolution in France*, ed. C. C. O'Brien (Harmondsworth, 1968).

BUTLER, MARILYN, 'Myth and Mythmaking in the Shelley Circle', *English Literary History*, 49 (1982).

—— *Peacock Displayed: A Satirist in his Context* (London, 1979).

—— *Romantics, Rebels and Reactionaries: English Literature and its Background, 1760–1830* (Oxford, 1981).

BYRON, GEORGE GORDON NOEL, Lord, *Complete Miscellaneous Prose*, ed. Andrew Nicholson (Oxford, 1991).

—— *Complete Poetical Works*, ed. Jerome McGann (7 vols., Oxford, 1980–93).

—— *Letters and Journals*, ed. Leslie A. Marchand (12 vols., London, 1973–82).

—— 'Observations upon "Observations": A Second Letter to John Murray, Esq. on the Rev. W. L. Bowles's Strictures on the Life and Writings of Pope', in *The Works of Lord Byron* (17 vols., London, 1832–3).

CARLYLE, THOMAS, *The French Revolution* (3 vols., London, 1837).

CLARKE, CHARLES COWDEN, *The Riches of Chaucer* (2 vols., London, 1835).

—— and CLARKE, MARY COWDEN, *Recollections of Writers* (London, 1878; Fontwell, 1969).

CLARKE, M. L., *Greek Studies in England, 1700–1830* (Cambridge, 1945).

—— *Richard Porson: A Biographical Essay* (Cambridge, 1937).

COLDWELL, JOAN, 'Charles Cowden Clarke's Commonplace Book and its Relationship to Keats', *Keats–Shelley Journal*, 29 (1980).

COLERIDGE, S. T., 'A Lay Sermon' (1817), in *Lay Sermons*, ed. R. J. White, Bollingen Collected Coleridge Series 6 (Princeton, 1972).

—— *Biographia Literaria*, ed. J. Engell and W. Jackson Bate, Bollingen Collected Coleridge Series 7 (2 vols., London, 1983).

—— *Collected Letters*, ed. E. L. Griggs (6 vols., Oxford, 1956–71).

—— *Fears in Solitude . . . To which are Added, France, an Ode; and Frost at Midnight* (London, 1798).

—— 'Lecture on the Slave-Trade', in *Lectures 1795 on Politics and Religion*, ed. L. Patton and P. Mann, Bollingen Collected Coleridge Series 1 (London, 1971).

—— *Poems on Various Subjects* (Bristol, 1796).

—— 'Reflections on Entering into Active Life: A Poem, which Affects not to be POETRY', *Monthly Magazine* (Oct. 1796).

—— and WORDSWORTH, W., *Lyrical Ballads, with a Few Other Poems* (London, 1798).

Coleridge: The Critical Heritage, ed. J. R. de J. Jackson (New York, 1970).

COLLEY, LINDA, *Britons: Forging the Nation 1707–1837* (London, 1994).

COLVIN, SIDNEY, *John Keats: His Life and Poetry, his Friends, Critics, and After-Fame* (London, 1917).

COOPER, Sir ASTLEY, *The Lectures of Sir Astley Cooper on the Principles and Practise of Surgery* (3 vols., London, 1824–7).

COOPER, BRANSBY BLAKE, *The Life of Sir Astley Cooper* (2 vols., London, 1843).

COOTE, STEPHEN, *John Keats: A Life* (London, 1995).

'Court and Fashionables', *Examiner* (3 May 1818).

COWPER, WILLIAM, *The Works of William Cowper*, ed. Robert Southey (8 vols., London, 1853–4).

COX, JEFFREY, 'John Keats in the Cockney School', *Romanticism*, 2/1 (1996).

CREASER, JOHN, 'From "Autumn" to Autumn in Keats's Ode', *Essays in Criticism*, 38 (1988).

CROWE, WILLIAM, *Lewesdon Hill: A Poem* (Oxford, 1788).

CULROSS, JAMES, *The Three Rylands: A Hundred Years of Various Christian Service* (London, 1897).

DAWSON, PAUL, 'Byron, Shelley, and the "New School"', in Kelvin Everest (ed.), *Shelley Revalued: Essays from the Gregynog Conference* (Leicester, 1983).

DE ALMEIDA, HERMIONE, *Romantic Medicine and John Keats* (Oxford, 1991).

DE MAN, PAUL, 'The Negative Road', in *Selected Poetry of John Keats* (New York, 1966).

DICKSTEIN, MORRIS, *Keats and his Poetry: A Study in Development* (Chicago, 1971).

DILKE, CHARLES WENTWORTH, *The Papers of a Critic Selected from the Writings of the Late Charles Wentworth Dilke* (2 vols., London, 1875).

'Dispersal of the Reform Meeting at Manchester by a Military Force', *The Times* (19 Aug. 1819).

DOBSON, R. B., and TAYLOR, J., *Rymes of Robyn Hood: An Introduction to the English Outlaw* (London, 1976).

DOUBLEDAY, F. N., 'John Keats and the Borough Hospitals', *Keats–Shelley Memorial Bulletin*, 13 (1962).

DRAYTON, MICHAEL, *The Works of Michael Drayton*, ed. J. William Hebel (5 vols., Oxford, 1931–41).

EATON, DANIEL ISAAC, *Politics for the People; or, A Salmagundy for Swine* (9 Sept. 1793–25 Feb. 1795).

EDWARDS, GERALD HAMILTON, 'John Keats and the Hammonds', *Keats–Shelley Memorial Bulletin*, 17 (1966).

ENGELL, JAMES, *The Creative Imagination: Enlightenment to Romanticism* (Cambridge, Mass., 1981).

EVEREST, KELVIN, *Coleridge's Secret Ministry: The Context of the Conversation Poems, 1795–8* (Hassocks, 1979).

FAIRER, DAVID, 'Baby Language and Revolution: The Early Poetry of Charles Lloyd and Charles Lamb', *Charles Lamb Bulletin* (Apr. 1991).

'The Family of Shakespeare', *Examiner* (14 Dec. 1817).

FELTOE, CHARLES, *Memorials of John Flint South* (London, 1884).

'Forged Bank Notes', *Examiner* (8 Feb. 1818),

FRY, PAUL H., 'History, Existence, and "To Autumn"', in Susan Wolfson (ed.), 'Keats and Politics: A Forum', *Studies in Romanticism*, 25 (Summer 1986).

GARROD, H. W., *Keats* (Oxford, 1926).

GITTINGS, ROBERT, *John Keats* (Harmondsworth, 1968).

—— 'John Keats, Physician and Poet', *Journal of the American Medical Association* (2 Apr. 1973).

GODWIN, WILLIAM, *An Enquiry Concerning Political Justice* (2 vols., London, 1793).

—— *Collected Novels and Memoirs*, ed. Mark Philp *et al.* (8 vols., London, 1992).

—— *Political and Philosophical Writings*, ed. Mark Philp *et al.* (7 vols., London, 1993).

GOELLNICHT, DONALD C., 'Keats as a Student at Guy's Hospital', *Canadian Bulletin of Medical History*, 3 (1986).

—— *The Poet-Physician: Keats and Medical Science* (Pittsburgh, 1984).

—— 'The Politics of Reading and Writing: Periodical Reviews of Keats's *Poems* (1817)', in D. L. Clark and D. C. Goellnicht (eds.), *New Romanticisms: Theory and Critical Practice* (Toronto, 1995)

GREEN, D. B., 'Keats, Swift, and Pliny the Elder', *Notes & Queries* (11 Nov. 1950).

GREENE, JOHN, *Reminiscences of the Rev. Robert Hall, A.M.* (London, 1832).

GREGORY, OLINTHUS, *Memoirs of the Life, Writings, and Character of the Late John Mason Good, M.D.* (London, 1828).

HALE-WHITE, Sir WILLIAM, 'Keats as a Medical Student', *Guy's Hospital Reports*, 75 (1925).

HAMILTON-EDWARDS, GERALD, 'John Keats and the Hammonds', *Keats–Shelley Memorial Bulletin*, 17 (1966).

HARRISON, GARY, *Wordsworth's Vagrant Muse: Poetry, Poverty, and Power* (Detroit, 1994).

HARRISON, TONY, *Selected Poems* (2nd edn., London, 1987).

HARTMAN, GEOFFREY, *The Fate of Reading and Other Essays* (Chicago, 1975).

HAYDEN, DONALD O., 'The Cockney School', in *The Romantic Reviewers, 1802–1824* (Chicago, 1968).

HAYDON, BENJAMIN ROBERT, *The Diary of Benjamin Robert Haydon*, ed. W. B. Pope (5 vols., Cambridge, Mass., 1960).

—— *The Life of Benjamin Robert Haydon*, ed. Tom Taylor (2nd edn., 3 vols., London, 1853).

HAZLITT, WILLIAM, *The Complete Works of William Hazlitt*, ed. P. P. Howe (21 vols., London, 1930–4).

—— *The Round Table* (2 vols., Edinburgh, 1817).

HEANEY, SEAMUS, *Place and Displacement: Recent Poetry of Northern Ireland* (Grasmere, 1985).

—— *North* (London, 1975).

HERSCHEL, WILLIAM, 'A Letter from William Herschel, Esq. F.R.S. to Sir Joseph Banks, Bart. P.R.S.', *Philosophical Transactions, of the Royal Society of London. Vol. LXXIII. For the Year 1783. Part I* (London, 1783).

—— 'On the Power of Penetrating into Space by Telescopes', *Philosophical Transactions, of the Royal Society of London. For the Year MDCCC. Part I* (London, 1800).

HILL, CHRISTOPHER, *Collected Essays*, ii: *Religion and Politics in 17th Century England* (Brighton, 1986).

—— *Liberty against the Law: Some Seventeenth-Century Controversies* (London, 1996).

HOLSTEIN, MICHAEL E., 'Keats: The Poet Healer and the Problem of Pain', *Keats–Shelley Journal*, 36 (1987).

HOLT, J. C., *Robin Hood* (London, 1982).

HOMANS, MARGARET, 'Keats Reading Women, Women Reading Keats', *Studies in Romanticism*, 29 (Fall 1990).

HONE, WILLIAM, *The Political House that Jack Built* (47th edn., London, 1820).

HOPKINS, GERARD MANLEY, *G. M. Hopkins, Selected Prose*, ed. G. Roberts (Oxford, 1980).

HUME, DAVID, *The History of England, from the Invasion of Julius Caesar to the Accession of Henry VII* (6 vols., London, 1762).

HUNT, JAMES HENRY LEIGH, 'Apothecaries; and Political Deductions from their Country-Growth', *Examiner* (7 Sept. 1817).

—— 'Attack on the Prince Regent, and a Word or Two of Plain Comment upon it', *Examiner* (2 Feb. 1817).

—— 'Attack on the Prince Regent, and Thanksgiving in the Churches', *Examiner* (16 Feb. 1817).

—— *The Autobiography of Leigh Hunt* (3 vols., London, 1850).

—— 'The Bourbons', *Examiner* (10 Apr. 1814).

—— 'Christmas and Other Old National Merry-Makings Considered', *Examiner* (21 Dec. 1817).

—— *The Descent of Liberty, a Mask* (London, 1815).

—— 'To the English People: Letter II', *Examiner* (9 Mar. 1817).

—— 'To the English People: Letter VI', *Examiner* (27 Apr. 1817).

HUNT, JAMES HENRY LEIGH, *The Feast of the Poets, with Notes, and Other Pieces in Verse, by the Editor of the Examiner* (London, 1814).

——*Foliage; or, Poems Original and Translated* (London, 1818).

——'Harry Brown's Letters to his Friends: No III. To W.H. Esq' *Examiner* (14 July 1816).

——*Indicator*

——'Informers', *Examiner* (6 July 1817).

——'Liberty of the Press', *Examiner* (14 Dec. 1817).

——'Louis XVIII.—The Emperor Napoleon', *Examiner* (1 May 1814).

——*The Months Descriptive of the Successive Beauties of the Year* (London, 1821).

——'Old May-Day', *Examiner* (10 May 1818).

——'On the Proposed Suspension of the Habeas Corpus Act', *Examiner* (2 Mar. 1817).

——'Portrait of Apollo', *Examiner* (13 Mar. 1814)

——*The Story of Rimini: A Poem* (London, 1816).

——'Young Poets', *Examiner* (1 Dec. 1816).

HUNT, LYNN, *Politics, Culture, and Class in the French Revolution* (London, 1984).

——*An Introduction to the Latin Tongue, for the Use of Youth* (Eton, 1768).

JACK, IAN, *Keats and the Mirror of Art* (Oxford, 1967).

JENKYNS, RICHARD, *The Victorians and Ancient Greece* (Oxford, 1980).

JOHNSON, SAMUEL, *A Dictionary of the English Language* (London, 1755).

JONES, CHRIS, *Radical Sensibility: Literature and Ideas in the 1790s* (London, 1993)

JONES, ELIZABETH, 'The Suburban School: Snobbery and Fear in the Attacks on Keats', *Times Literary Supplement* (27 Oct. 1995).

JONES, L. M., *The Life of John Hamilton Reynolds* (Hanover, 1984).

JONSON, BEN, *Ben Jonson*, ed. C. H. Herford and P. and E. M. Simpson (11 vols., Oxford, 1925–52).

KANDL, JOHN, 'Private Lyrics in the Public Sphere: Leigh Hunt's *Examiner* and the Construction of a Public "John Keats"', *Keats–Shelley Journal*, 44 (1995).

KEACH, WILLIAM, 'Cockney Couplets: Keats and the Politics of Style', in Susan Wolfson (ed.), 'Keats and Politics: A Forum', *Studies in Romanticism*, 25 (Summer 1986).

KEATS, JOHN, *John Keats 1795–1995: With a Catalogue of the Harvard Keats Collection* (Cambridge, Mass., 1995).

——*John Keats's Anatomical and Physiological Note Book*, ed. M. B. Forman (Oxford, 1934).

——*John Keats: Poetry Manuscripts at Harvard: A Facsimile Edition*, ed. Jack Stillinger (Cambridge, Mass., 1990).

——*John Keats: The Complete Poems*, ed. John Barnard (Harmondsworth, 1973).

—— *The Keats Circle: Letters and Papers 1816–1878 and More Letters and Poems 1814–1879*, ed. Hyder Edward Rollins (2nd edn., 2 vols., Cambridge, Mass., 1965).

—— *Keats: The Critical Heritage*, ed. Geoffrey Matthews (London, 1971).

—— *The Letters of John Keats, 1814–1821*, ed. Hyder Edward Rollins (2 vols., Cambridge, Mass., 1958).

——*Poems of John Keats*, ed. Miriam Allott (London, 1970).

——*Poems of John Keats*, ed. Jack Stillinger (Cambridge, Mass., 1978).

—— *The Poetical Works of John Keats*, ed. H. W. Garrod (2nd edn., Oxford, 1958).

KERRIGAN, JOHN, 'Wordsworth and the Sonnet: Building, Dwelling, Thinking', *Essays in Criticism*, 35 (1985).

KLANCHER, JON, *The Making of English Reading Audiences, 1790–1832* (Madison, 1987).

KNIGHT, STEPHEN, *Robin Hood: A Complete Study of the English Outlaw* (Oxford, 1994).

KOCH, JUNE Q., 'Politics in Keats's Poetry', *Journal of English and German Philology*, 71 (1972).

KROEBER, KARL, *Ecological Literary Criticism: Romantic Imagining and the Biology of Mind* (New York, 1994).

KUCICH, GREG, 'Keats's Literary Tradition and the Politics of Historiographical Invention', in Nicholas Roe (ed.), *Keats and History* (Cambridge, 1995).

—— *Keats, Shelley, and Romantic Spenserianism* (University Park, Pa., 1991).

LAMB, CHARLES, and LAMB, MARY ANNE, *The Letters of Charles and Mary Anne Lamb*, ed. E. W. Marrs, Jr. (3 vols., Ithaca, NY, 1975–8).

LARKIN, PHILIP, *The Whitsun Weddings* (London, 1964).

LAWRENCE, CHRISTOPHER, *Medicine in the Making of Modern Britain, 1700–1920* (London, 1994).

Laws of the Physical Society Held at Guy's Hospital (London, 1783).

LEMPRIÈRE, J., *Bibliotheca Classica; or, A Classical Dictionary* (3rd edn., London, 1797).

LEVINSON, MARJORIE, *Keats's Life of Allegory: The Origins of a Style* (Oxford, 1988).

'Literary Notices', *Examiner* (14 June 1818).

LOWELL, AMY, *John Keats* (2 vols., London, 1925).

LUCAS, E. V., *The Life of Charles Lamb* (2nd edn., 2 vols., London, 1905).

McFarland, Thomas, *Romantic Cruxes: The English Essayists and the Spirit of the Age* (Oxford, 1987).

McGann, Jerome J., *The Beauty of Inflections: Literary Investigations in Historical Method and Theory* (Oxford, 1985).

—— 'Keats and the Historical Method in Literary Criticism', *Modern Language Notes*, 94 (1979).

—— *The Romantic Ideology: A Critical Investigation* (Chicago, 1983).

Magnuson, Paul, 'The Politics of "Frost at Midnight"', *Wordsworth Circle* (Winter 1991), 6–7.

Mann, Phyllis G., 'John Keats: Further Notes', *Keats–Shelley Memorial Bulletin*, 12 (1961).

Milnes, Richard Monckton, *Life, Letters, and Literary Remains, of John Keats* (2 vols., London, 1848).

Mirror of Literature, Amusement, and Instruction (13 Nov. 1841).

Mitchell, Thomas R., 'Keats's "Outlawry" in "Robin Hood"', *Studies in English Literature*, 34 (1994).

Montagu, Elizabeth, *An Essay on the Writings and Genius of Shakespeare* (3rd edn., London, 1772).

Morris, J. W., *Biographical Recollections of the Rev. Robert Hall, A.M.* (London, 1833).

Morton, Timothy, *Shelley and the Revolution in Taste: The Body and the Natural World* (Cambridge, 1995).

'Mr Hunt's Entry into London', *The Times* (14 Sept. 1819).

Natarajan, Uttara, 'Power and Capability: Hazlitt, Keats and the Discrimination of Poetic Self', *Romanticism*, 2/1 (1996).

Newey, Vincent, ' "Alternate uproar and sad peace": Keats, Politics, and the Idea of Revolution', in J. R. Watson (ed.), *The French Revolution in English Literature and Art*, Modern Humanities Research Association Yearbook of English Studies 19 (London, 1989).

—— 'Keats, History, and the Poets', in Nicholas Roe (ed.), *Keats and History* (Cambridge, 1995).

Newlyn, Lucy, ' "In City Pent": Echo and Allusion in Wordsworth, Coleridge, and Lamb, 1797–1801', *Review of English Studies*, 32 (Nov. 1981).

—— 'Coleridge and the Anxiety of Reception', *Romanticism*, 1/2 (1995).

Newman, William, *Rylandiana: Reminiscences Relating to the Rev. John Ryland, A. M. of Northampton* (London, 1835).

Ozouf, Mona, *Festivals and the French Revolution* (Cambridge, Mass., 1988).

Paine, Thomas, *The Rights of Man*, ed. H. Collins (Harmondsworth, 1969).

Parker, W. M., 'John Aitken and John Keats', *New Alliance and Scots Review* (Oct. 1949).

PAULSON, RONALD, *Representations of Revolution (1789–1820)* (New Haven, 1983).

PAYNE, E. A., 'The Baptist Connections of George Dyer', *Baptist Quarterly*, NS 10 (1940–1).

—— 'The Baptist Connections of George Dyer: A Further Note', *Baptist Quarterly*, NS 11 (1942–5).

—— *College Street Chapel Northampton, 1697–1947* (London, 1947).

PEACOCK, THOMAS LOVE, *Maid Marian* (London, 1822).

PECKHAM, MORSE, *The Romantic Virtuoso* (Hanover, 1995).

PERCY, THOMAS, *Reliques of Ancient English Poetry* (3rd edn., 3 vols., London, 1775).

PERKINS, DAVID, review of Walter Jackson Bate, *John Keats*, *Keats–Shelley Journal*, 13 (Winter 1964).

PIPER, H. W., *The Active Universe* (London, 1962).

PIRIE, DAVID, 'Keats', in D. Pirie (ed.), *The Penguin History of Literature: The Romantic Period* (London, 1994).

Poetry and Reform: Periodical Verse from the English Democratic Press, ed. Michael Scrivener (Detroit, 1992).

The Poetry of the Anti-Jacobin (6th edn., London, 1828).

POPE, ALEXANDER, *Poetical Works*, ed. Herbert Davis (Oxford, 1966).

PORSON, RICHARD, *A New Catechism for the Use of the Natives of Hampshire* (1792), *Examiner* (30 Aug. 1818).

PRICE, RICHARD, *A Discourse on the Love of our Country, Delivered on Nov. 4, 1789, at the Meeting House in the Old Jewry, to the Society for Commemorating the Revolution in Great Britain* (London, 1790).

PRITCHARD, GEORGE, *Memoir of the Rev. William Newman* (London, 1837).

REYNOLDS, JOHN HAMILTON, *The Eden of Imagination* (London, 1814).

—— *Letters from Lambeth: The Correspondence of the Reynolds Family with John Dovaston, 1808–1815*, ed. J. Richardson (Woodbridge, 1981).

—— 'Pulpit Oratory No. 1', *Yellow Dwarf* (7 Feb. 1818).

—— *Selected Prose of John Hamilton Reynolds*, ed. Leonidas M. Jones (Cambridge, Mass., 1966).

RIBEIRO, AILEEN, *Fashion in the French Revolution* (London, 1988).

RICHARDSON, ALAN, *Literature, Education, and Romanticism: Reading as Social Practice 1780–1832* (Cambridge, 1994).

RICHARDSON, B. W., 'An Esculapian Poet—John Keats', *Asclepiad* (1884).

RICHARDSON, WILLIAM, *A Philosophical Analysis* (London, 1780).

RICKS, CHRISTOPHER, *Keats and Embarrassment* (Oxford, 1974).

ROBERTSON, WILLIAM, *The History of the Reign of the Emperor Charles V* (3 vols., London, 1769).

—— *The History of America* (6th edn., 3 vols., London, 1792).

Robin Hood: A Collection of all the Ancient Poems, Songs, and Ballads, now Extant, Relative to that Celebrated English Outlaw, ed. Joseph Ritson (2 vols., London, 1795).

ROE, NICHOLAS, 'The Liberty Man', *Times Literary Supplement* (29 Sept. 1995).

ROE, NICHOLAS, *The Politics of Nature: Wordsworth and Some Contemporaries* (Basingstoke, 1992).

—— *Wordsworth and Coleridge: The Radical Years* (Oxford, 1988).

ROLLINS, HYDER E., 'Benjamin Bailey's Scrapbook', *Keats–Shelley Journal*, 6 (Winter 1957).

ROSSETTI, WILLIAM MICHAEL, *Life of John Keats* (London, 1887).

RYAN, ROBERT M., *Keats: The Religious Sense* (Princeton, 1976).

—— 'The Politics of Greek Religion', in H. de Almeida (ed.), *Critical Essays on John Keats* (Boston, 1990).

RYLAND, JOHN, *The Character of the Rev. James Hervey, M.A.* (London, 1791).

—— *Contemplations on the Beauties of Creation* (3rd edn., 3 vols., London, 1777–82).

—— *An Easy Introduction to Mechanics* (London, 1768).

—— *The Life and Character of Alfred the Great* (London, 1784).

—— *A Tribute of Honour to the Great and Good Men in France* (London, 1790).

SCHAMA, SIMON, *Landscape and Memory* (London, 1995).

SCHLEGEL, A. W. VON, *A Course of Lectures on Dramatic Art and Literature*, trans. John Black (2 vols., London, 1815).

SHELLEY, HENRY C., *Literary By-Paths in Old England* (London, 1909).

SHELLEY, PERCY BYSSHE, *The Letters of Percy Bysshe Shelley*, ed. F. L. Jones (2 vols., Oxford, 1964).

—— *The Masque of Anarchy: A Poem* (London, 1832).

—— *Poetry and Prose*, ed. D. H. Reiman and S. B. Powers (New York, 1977).

—— *The Works of Percy Bysshe Shelley*, ed. R. Ingpen and W. E. Peck (10 vols., London, 1926–30, 1965).

SMITH, HORACE, *Amarynthus, the Nympholept: A Pastoral Drama, in Three Acts: With Other Poems* (London, 1821).

—— *Gaieties and Gravities: A Series of Essays, Comic Tales, and Fugitive Vagaries* (3 vols., London, 1825).

SMITH, OLIVIA, *The Politics of Language 1791–1819* (Oxford, 1984).

SOUTHEY, ROBERT, *The Annual Anthology* (2 vols., Bristol, 1799–1800).

SPENCE, JOSEPH, *Polymetis; or, An Inquiry Concerning the Agreement between the Works of the Roman Poets, and the Remains of the Ancient Artists* (2nd edn., London, 1755).

SPENSER, EDMUND, *Spenser: Poetical Works*, ed. J. C. Smith and E. de Selincourt (Oxford, 1912).

SPERRY, STUART M., *Keats the Poet* (Princeton, 1973).

——'Richard Woodhouse's Interleaved and Annotated Copy of Keats's *Poems* (1817)', in E. Rothstein and T. K. Dunseath (eds.), *Literary Monographs* (Madison, 1967).

STEELE, MABEL A. E., 'The Woodhouse Transcripts of the Poems of Keats', *Harvard Library Bulletin*, 3 (1949).

STEINER, GEORGE, *Language and Silence: Essays 1958–1966* (London, 1985).

STILLINGER, JACK, *The Hoodwinking of Madeline and Other Essays on Keats's Poems* (Urbana, Ill., 1971).

——'John Keats', in Frank Jordan (ed.), *The English Romantic Poets: A Review of Research and Criticism: Fourth Edition* (New York, 1985).

——review of *The Diary of Benjamin Robert Haydon*, ed. W. B. Pope (5 vols., Cambridge, Mass., 1960), *Journal of English and Germanic Philology*, 60 (Apr. 1961).

——review of Robert Gittings, *John Keats*, *Keats–Shelley Journal*, 18 (1969).

——'Wordsworth and Keats', in Kenneth Johnston and Gene Ruoff (eds.), *The Age of William Wordsworth: Critical Essays on the Romantic Tradition* (New Brunswick, 1987).

SWINBURNE, ALGERNON CHARLES, *Miscellanies* (London, 1886).

TATCHELL, MOLLY, 'Byron's *Windsor Poetics*', *Keats–Shelley Memorial Bulletin*, 25 (1974).

THELWALL, JOHN, *An Essay towards a Definition of Animal Vitality* (London, 1793).

——*A Letter to Henry Ccine, Esq.* (London, 1810).

——*The Life of John Thelwall by his Widow* (London, 1837).

——*Peaceful Discussion, and not Tumultuary Violence the Means of Redressing National Grievances* (London, 1795).

——*The Peripatetic* (3 vols., London, 1793).

——*Poems Chiefly Written in Retirement* (Hereford, 1801).

THOMPSON, E. P., 'Disenchantment or Default? A Lay Sermon', in C. C. O'Brien and W. D. Vanech (eds.), *Power and Consciousness* (London, 1969).

——*The Making of the English Working Class* (Harmondsworth, 1968).

——*William Morris: Romantic to Revolutionary* (London, 1955, 1977).

THORPE, CLARENCE De WITT, 'Keats's Interest in Politics and World Affairs', *Publications of the Modern Language Society of America*, 46 (1931).

TOOKE, ANDREW, *The Pantheon* (London, 1783).

VENDLER, HELEN, *The Odes of John Keats* (Cambridge, Mass., 1983).

VINCENT, ESTHER J., 'A Medical Truant', *Surgery, Gynecology & Obstetrics* (Nov. 1955).

WALLACE, JENNIFER, 'The Sociable Revolutionary', *Times Higher Education Supplement* (15 Sept. 1995).

WALMSLEY, ROBERT, *Peterloo: The Case Reopened* (Manchester, 1969).

WARD, AILEEN, *John Keats: The Making of a Poet* (London, 1963).

WARTON, THOMAS, *History of English Poetry, from the Close of the Eleventh to the Commencement of the Eighteenth Century* (3 vols., London, 1774–81).

WATKINS, DANIEL P., *Keats's Poetry and the Politics of the Imagination* (London, 1989).

WEBB, CORNELIUS, *The Man about Town* (2 vols., London, 1838).

——*Sonnets, Amatory, Incidental, and Descriptive; with Other Poems* (London, 1820).

WEBB, TIMOTHY, *Shelley: A Voice not Understood* (Manchester, 1977).

—— *The Violet in the Crucible: Shelley and Translation* (Oxford, 1976).

WHEATLEY, KIM, 'The *Blackwood's* Attacks on Leigh Hunt', *Nineteenth-Century Literature* (June 1992).

White Hat, 1 (16 Oct.–11 Dec. 1819).

WHITLEY, W. T., 'J. C. Ryland as Schoolmaster', *Baptist Quarterly*, NS 5 (1930–1).

WILKS, S., and BETTANY, G. T., *A Biographical History of Guy's Hospital* (London, 1892).

WILLIAMS, HELEN MARIA, *Letters Written in France, in the Summer of 1790* (London, 1790).

WILLIAMS, JOHN, *Wordsworth: Romantic Poetry and Revolution Politics* (Manchester, 1989).

WOLFSON, SUSAN J., 'Feminizing Keats', in Hermione de Almeida (ed.), *Critical Essays on John Keats* (Boston, 1990).

——'Keats Enters History: Autopsy, *Adonais*, and the Fame of Keats', in Nicholas Roe (ed.), *Keats and History* (Cambridge, 1995).

WOLLSTONECRAFT, MARY, *The Works of Mary Wollstonecraft*, ed. Janet Todd and Marilyn Butler (7 vols., London, 1989).

WOOLF, VIRGINIA, *The Moment and Other Essays* (London, 1947).

WORDSWORTH, WILLIAM, *The Prose Works of William Wordsworth*, ed. W. J. B. Owen and J. W. Smyser (3 vols., Oxford, 1974).

—— *William Wordsworth*, ed. Stephen Gill (Oxford, 1984).

—— *Wordsworth Poetical Works*, ed. Thomas Hutchinson, rev. E. de Selincourt (Oxford, 1969).

——and COLERIDGE, SAMUEL TAYLOR, *Wordsworth and Coleridge: Lyrical Ballads*, ed. R. L. Brett and A. R. Jones (2nd edn., London, 1991).

——and WORDSWORTH, DOROTHY, *The Letters of William and Dorothy Wordsworth*, ed. E. de Selincourt, 2nd edn., *The Middle Years Part II, 1812–20*, rev. M. Moorman and A. G. Hill (Oxford, 1970).

The Works of the English Poets from Chaucer to Cowper (21 vols., London, 1810).

WORRALL, DAVID, *Radical Culture: Discourse, Resistance and Surveillance, 1790–1820* (Hemel Hempstead, 1992).

WRIGHT, HERBERT G., 'Keats and Politics', *Essays and Studies*, 18 (1933).

WU, DUNCAN, *Wordsworth's Reading, 1770–1799* (Cambridge, 1993).

WYLIE, IAN, *Young Coleridge and the Philosophers of Nature* (Oxford, 1989).

Yellow Dwarf: A Weekly Miscellany.

Z (i.e. John Lockhart and John Wilson), 'On the Cockney School of Poetry: No I', *Blackwood's Edinburgh Magazine* (Oct. 1817).

——'On the Cockney School of Poetry: No II', *Blackwood's Edinburgh Magazine* (Nov. 1817).

——'The Cockney School of Poetry: No III', *Blackwood's Edinburgh Magazine* (July 1818).

——'Cockney School of Poetry: No IV', *Blackwood's Edinburgh Magazine* (Aug. 1818).

——'On the Cockney School of Poetry: No V', *Blackwood's Edinburgh Magazine* (Apr. 1819).

——'On the Cockney School of Poetry: No VI', *Blackwood's Edinburgh Magazine* (Oct. 1819).

Index

Note: The initial K refers to John Keats

Abbey, Richard 26, 28, 34, 132
Addison, Joseph 137–8 & n., 140
Aeneid 67
Aikin, John, *Natural History of the Year* 260
Aitken, John (of Dunbar) 273–4 n.
Akenside, Mark, *Pleasures of the Imagination* 102 n.
Alexander, J. H. 21 n., 215 n.
Alfred, King 47 n., 108–9 & n., 139, 209
Allen, William 170
Allott, Miriam 108, 198
Althusser, Louis 15 n.
Altick, Richard 8, 26, 28, 50
America 45–6, 54
Analytical Review 223
Annual Anthology 112 n.
Anti-Jacobin 223–5
    'New Morality' (poem) 224–5
    'Ode to Jacobinism' 223–4
Apollo, *see* Keats, John, Imaginative and Intellectual Life
Apothecaries' Act (1815) 90, 162, 180–1
Arabian Nights 193
Arbuckle, James 240
Armstrong, Isobel 42 n.
Arne, Thomas 93
Arnold, Matthew 228–9
Arnold, Thomas 64
Aske, Martin 61 n., 211 n.
astronomy 35–9
    see also Bonnycastle, John; Herschel, William; Keats, John, Imaginative and Intellectual Life
Athens 70
Atlantic Monthly 8

BBC viii & n.
    see also 'Posthumous Life of John Keats'

Babington, William 170, 176, 182, 184
Bacon, Francis 100
Bailey, Benjamin, *see under* Keats, John, Contemporaries and Historical Figures
Balboa 57
Baldwin, Robert 270
Baptists, *see under* dissent
Barbauld, Anna Letitia 96–8 & nn.
    'Sermon for a Fast Day' 96–7 & n.
    Summer Evening's Meditation 97–8
Barnard, John 49–50 n., 94 & n., 99, 100, 155–6, 257 n.
Barton, Anne 250 n.
Bastille, *see* French Revolution
Bate, Jonathan 124 n., 234 n.
Bate, Walter Jackson 3, 7, 14 n., 26 n., 84, 100, 171, 231, 232, 240
Bayley, John 16–17
Beckford, William 193
Beddoes, Thomas 174
Bennett, Andrew vii & n., 249 n., 250 n., 263, 265 n.
Betjeman, John 128, 212
Bewell, Alan 6, 41
Blackburn 211 n.
Blackburne, Francis, *Memoirs of Thomas Hollis* 102 & n.
Blackwood Papers 268–75
Blackwood's Magazine vii, x, 13, 21 n., 24 & n., 63, 161, 203, 205, 212, 215 n., 227–8, 229, 250, 268, 270, 271–5 nn.
Blackwood, William 51, 122, 129 n., 160–1 & n., 162, 202, 215 n., 268–70
Blake, William 45, 46, 113
blasphemy, unitarian charged with 81
Bloom, Harold 68
Boileau, Nicholas 119
Bolingbroke, *see* St John, Henry
Bonnycastle, John, *Introduction to Astronomy* 36–7, 260
Bourdieu, Pierre 15 n.
Bourton-on-the-Water 30

Bowen, James 64
Bowles, William Lisle, *Fourteen Sonnets* 104
Bowyer, James 67
Brand, John 124 n.
Brissot, Jacques-Pierre 175
Bristol 30, 111
Britain:
  fleet 152 n.
  imperial power 153
  invasion of 112–13
  national consciousness 63
  patriotism 66–7 & n.
  repression 179
  shores of 265
British Critic 79 n., 115, 205, 223
British Lady's Magazine 129 n.
Bromwich, David 6, 240, 241 & n., 249 n.
Brooke, Stopford A. 12
Brooks, Cleanth 86 n.
Brown, Charles 166–7, 168, 231
Brutus, Marcus 70–1, 102 n.
Burdett, Sir Francis 73 n.
Burke, Edmund:
  and beauty 11, 114, 225–6
  and K's poetry 11, 20, 226
  and women 11, 225–6
  Philosophical Enquiry into the Origin of our Ideas about the Sublime and Beautiful 11, 225
  Reflections on the Revolution in France 20 & n., 98–9, 156, 261
Burne-Jones, Edward 55
Butler, Charles 174 & n.
Butler, Marilyn viii, 5, 65, 77, 128 n., 145, 146
Butler, Samuel 64
Byron, George Gordon, Lord 15 n., 60, 228, 249–50 & n.
  on Cockney School 215
  and Hunt, J. H. L. 100, 268, 274
  Hyperion, admires 18 n.
  and K 17, 18, 221–2, 226, 242
  K's tribute to 100
  at Lake Geneva 274–5
  and *Liberal* 268, 274
  on the 'new school' 17
  at Pisa 274
  self-recognition in K 18 & n.
  and Shelley 274–5
  suburban school 217
  Beppo 214
  Childe Harold 218
  Don Juan 12, 17
  Letter to John Murray, 'Addenda' to 222
  'Observations upon "Observations"' 17 n., 215
  'Windsor Poetics' 99–100 & n.

Cadell and Davies (publishers) 215 n., 272
Caesar, Julius 102 n.
Cambridge 32
Cambridge University 14, 23, 32, 63
Campbell, John:
  Present State of Britain 48
  Present State of Europe 48
Carlile, Richard 99
  identified with K 14
Carlyle, Thomas 116
Cartwright, Major 27 and K 28
Castlereagh, Robert Stewart, Viscount 210–12 & n., 257 n.
Cato 70
Ceres 263–5
Ceylon 203, 205 n.
Champion x, 183, 207 n., 253, 255–7
Chapman, George 61, 67, 78 n.
Charles I, King 100
chartists 123
Chatterton, Thomas:
  Goddwyn: A Tragedy 95
  'Ode to Freedom' 95
Chaucer, Geoffrey *see under* Keats, John, Contemporaries and Historical Figures
Cheapside 215
Chester Guardian 132 n.
Cholmeley, Henry 170
Chopart, François 175
Christ's Hospital 67
Christie, Jonathan Henry 24 n.
Church of England, *see under* England
Cicero 67
Clairmont, Claire 274–5
Clare, John 23, 268, 275
Clarke, Charles Cowden ix, 23, 25, 26, 28, 173, 174
  ambitious to be poet 103 & n.
  and Barbauld, Anna Letitia 96–7
  and Byron, Lord 99–100
  and Coleridge, S. T. 103
  and Crowe, William 95–6, 103
  education of 28

and Enfield School 8, 27–8, 33, 37,
    41, 46–7, 55, 67, 93, 266–7
and Hunt, J. H. L. 88n., 89, 92 &
    n., 99, 100, 125–6, 257n.
and K ix, 23, 25, 28, 37, 39–40, 41,
    46–7, 49–50, 54, 55, 67, 88–110,
    132, 136–7 & n., 163, 232, 264,
    266–7
on *Masque of Anarchy* 88
memory, weakness of 89–90
and Milnes, R. M. 62–3, 88–90 &
    nn.
music 93
pacifism 95
poetry of 94
and Porson, Richard 98–9
protest literature and 95–8 & nn.
radicalism of 28
reading 93–105
a republican 28, 49, 93, 95, 100–5,
    132
and republicans, English 101–5
and Wordsworth, William 49–50n.,
    95
Commonplace Book 49–50n., 93–
    105, 132
'Four Seasons' 230
'Left on Milton's Tomb' 101
'Memoranda of the early Life of
    John Keats' (1848) 62–3
'The Nightingale' 94
Notebook (1814) 230n.
'Projected Essay on Fame' 108
'Recollections of John Keats' 7–10,
    25–6, 90–1, 93n., 106–7, 163
'Recollections of John Keats',
    manuscript of 9–10 & nn.
Riches of Chaucer 137n.
'Sonnet to Liberty' 102–3
'Sunset' 94
Clarke, Charles and Mary Cowden,
    Recollections of Writers 8, 31–2, 173
Clarke, John 26, 55, 92n.
biblical translation, interest in 27
and Cartwright, Major 27, 28
dissenters, befriends 27–8n., 173
and Dyer, George 27, 28, 31–2, 173
Examiner, subscribes to 28
and Geddes, Alexander 27, 173
and Good, John Mason 173–4
independent-minded 28
K, influence on 28, 33, 46
at Northampton 31–3

and Priestley, Joseph 27, 28, 173
a radical 28
a republican 28, 46, 49
and Ryland, J. C. 27–33, 34, 46
and Wakefield, Gilbert 27, 173
Clarke, Mary Cowden 8, 23
classical culture and literature:
and French Revolution 69–71
and jacobinism 70
and radicalism 69 & n.
and reform movement 71–87
teaching of 63–9
see also Cockney(s); education;
    Enfield School; Eton College;
    Harrow School; Keats, John,
    Education of
Cline, Henry 166, 169, 170, 174–5,
    176, 179
Cobbett, William 60
Cockaigne, Bantam Bards of 51
Cockney(s) 11, 19, 20n., 61–2, 74,
    106, 116, 214
affectation of 110
Athenaum 268, *see also* Surrey
    Institution
baaing vanities of 203
caricatured 20n.
cheerfulness 116
childishness 226–7
classics 60–71
cultural limbo of 214
culture x, 23, 63, 226, 268
curse of 275
and democracy x
disconcerting 22
and dissent x
effeminate 226
as egg, misshapen 226–7
eroticism 16–17
febrile poetry of 22
greenery 125
at Hampstead 214
jargon of 18
Johnson, Samuel, as defined by 226
and London: low citizen of 226;
    native of 226
nature poetry 214–15
north English 22
numerous following of 129–30
Oxford English Dictionary, as defined
    by 226–7
poetic themes of 116, 203, 214–15
rehabilitation of x

Cockney(s) (*cont.*):
 rhymes 19–20
 and romanticism 128n.
 and sociality 109–10, 116–33,
  129n., 130n.
 sublimities of, bogus 215
 and suburban life 214–17
 tea-drinking 116
 vigorous assault of 22
 and Wordsworth, William,
  revaluation of 215–16
 writers x 268n.
Cockney School Essays 10, 11–12,
  122, 129, 217, 226, 268–9
 I (Oct. 1817) 119–20, 127, 203,
  204–5, 214–15, 227, 270
 III (July 1818) 121, 129, 205, 226
 IV (Aug. 1818) 10, 15, 16, 19n.,
  20n., 22, 24n., 61, 161 & n., 202,
  205, 226
 V (Apr. 1819) 129 & n., 273
 VI (Oct. 1819) 60, 216–17
 see also *Blackwood's Magazine*;
  Lockhart, John Gibson; Z
Coldwell, Joan 94
Coleridge, Samuel Taylor 21, 28, 30,
  56, 110, 127–8 & n., 132, 174,
  187, 196, 222, 224
 audience, need for a sympathetic
  113–14
 and *Blackwood's Magazine* 215n.,
  268, 271–3
 and Bowyer, James 67 & n.
 and Burke, Edmund 114
 Christ's Hospital 67 & n.
 clerisy 15
 on contempt for visionaries 114
 contented patriot 115–16
 conversation poems 113
 and Crowe, William 96
 and dissent 114
 on education 14–15, 67
 and Frend, William 32
 and Godwin, William 244, 246
 half knowledge, incapable of
  content with 231
 humane 21
 a jacobin 115–16, 132
 and K, prefigures reception of 116
 at Nether Stowey (1796–8) 111–16,
  127
 Pantisocracy 114–15
 on peace 2

on personal attacks 272
readership, anxiety about 21 & n.
and Shakespeare, William 234–5
social obligations, poetry of 111–12
solitary experience, poetry of 111–
  12
on *'sound book learnedness'* 14–15
and Southey, Robert 114
and Wordsworth, William 215n.,
  268, 273
A Lay Sermon 2 & n., 22
Ancient Mariner 190
Biographia Literaria 25, 235, 242 &
  n.
Conciones ad Populum 115
'Effusion XXXV' 111–12
The Fall of Robespierre 32
'Fears in Solitude' 103, 112–13,
  116
'France; an Ode' 116
The Friend 25
'Frost at Midnight' 113, 115–16,
  126–7 & n.
'Introductory Address' 115
'Lecture on the Slave-Trade' 56
'The Nightingale' 113, 198
Ode to the Departing Year 103
'Reflections on Entering into Active
  Life' 112, 187
Religious Musings 96, 187
'Sonnets on Eminent Characters'
  108
Statesman's Manual 14–15 & n., 21
  & n., 22
'This Lime-Tree Bower' 112–13,
  198
Watchman 96
Coligny 274
Collett, Freelove 30
Colley, Linda 63, 66–7 & n.
Colombo (Ceylon) 203
Columbus, Christopher 58
Colvin, Sidney 3, 4, 164
Conder, Josiah 93n., 132, 251, 265
conspiracies 1, 2, 254–7, 265
Constable (publisher) 275
Cooper, Astley 166, 169–81, 182,
  187n., 192, 193n.
 democratic politics 175–6
 as dresser 166
 French Revolution, partisan of 172
 Guy's Hospital, lectures at 169–70,
  192

and K 166, 169–73, 174–5, 187 n.,
     191–2, 193 n.
  at Paris (1792) 175–6
  and the Physical Society 176, 178
  and Thelwall, John 175–6, 178, 181
Cooper, George 171 & n.
Cooper, Thomas *Reply to Mr. Burke* 97
     & n.
Coote, Stephen 7, 81 n.
Copenhagen Fields 1, 2, 256
Cornwall, Barry, *see* Procter, Bryan
     Waller
Corscombe (Dorset) 102
  see also Hollis, Thomas
Cortez 57, 58
Courier 237–8
Cowper, William 153 n., 157, 196
  'Yardley Oak' 95, 152–3
Cox, Jeffrey 268 n.
Creaser, John 263
Croker, John Wilson 20 n., 79 n.,
     132 n., 205, 221
Cromwell, Oliver 49
Crowe, William:
  Lewesdon Hill 102 & n.
  'Lines at the Installation' 95–6, 103
Cruikshank, George 124 n.
Cruikshank, Robert 124 n.
Cumberland 215
Cunningham, Allan 51
Curry, James 170

Dacre, Charlotte, *Zofloya*, 218
Dante Alighieri 120–1, 271
Danton 175
Darwin, Erasmus 135, 178
Datchet 35
David, Jacques-Louis 69–71, 74–5
  see also French Revolution
Davies, William 215 n., 272–3
Dawson, Paul 18 n.
de Almeida, Hermione 169
de Man, Paul 3 & n.
Demosthenes 67
Desault, Pierre Joseph 175
Dickens, Charles:
  Bleak House 228
  Hard Times 64
Dickstein, Morris 6, 152
Dilke, Charles Wentworth 230–1, 242,
     245–7
Disney, John 174 & n.
dissent 11, 45–50, 91

Baptist 27–33 & nn.
  culture of 15, 27–9
  and educational change 63–5
  K as representative voice of 15 & n.
  Methodists 147 n., 245 n.
  and paganism 81–2
  Quakers 123
  Test Acts 30
  Unitarian 27–9, 30, 81–2
  see also Enfield School; Keats, John,
     Education of
Dobree, Peter Paul 64–5
Dorset 102
Drayton, Michael, *Poly-Olbion* 144 & n.
Dyer, George:
  a Baptist 31
  at Cambridge 32
  and Clarke, John 27, 28, 31–2, 173
  and Coleridge 31, 32
  Enfield School, visits 27, 32, 173
  and Frend, William 32
  and K 28, 31
  and London radicals 32
  at Northampton 31–2 n.
  and reform movement 27–8
  and Robinson, Robert 32
  and Ryland, John Collett 31–2 n.
  teaching of 31–2
Dublin 161
Duffield 211 n.

Eaton, Daniel Isaac, *Politics for the
     People* 98 & n.
Eclectic Review 93 n., 117 n., 129 n.,
     222, 251
ecology 196 n.
Edgeworth, Maria 46, 128 n.
Edinburgh 23, 168, 268
Edinburgh Magazine 93 n., 130, 205,
     219–21, 222
Edinburgh University 174
Edmonton 14, 90, 163
education:
  classical curriculum 63–8
  cockney 60–8
  and cultural change 23
  and dissent 63–5
  and social regulation 23
  and parliamentary reform 65
  patrician 67
  utilitarian 64–5
  see also Enfield School; Eton College;
     Keats, John, Education of

Eldon, John Scott, Earl of 255
electricity 177–9, 180
Elia 275
   see also Lamb, Charles
Elmsley, Peter 64–5
empiricism 182–3
Encyclopaedia Britannica 228
Enfield School 23, 25–6, 27–50, 54,
   56, 64, 90, 132
  benevolent 7
  buildings of 33, 41
  competitive 39–40
  controversial 26
  curriculum, *see under* Keats, John,
    Education of
  dissenting culture of ix, 8, 27–9,
    45–50, 173–4
  eccentric 7
  educational deficits of 14
  enlightened 7, 33
  founded 29, 33
  garden grounds 33, 41, 266–7
  humane 33
  liberal 7, 68
  library at 30, 37–8, 44, 45–50
  living orrery 33–4, 36–9, 267
  modern curriculum 7, 29, 34, 35–6,
    68
  nonconformist 7
  recreative 35–6, 40–1
  political culture of ix, 28, 25, 45–
    50, 54 and n., 170–4
  progressive 7
  republicanism 28, 45–50
  Ryland, J. C. at 29–50, 267
  swallows, departure of 29, 267
  teaching at 35–6, 39–40, 45–50,
    61–4, 68 *see also under* Keats, John,
    Education of
  telescope 37
  utilitarian 7
  unorthodox 15, 23, 26 *see also*
    Keats, John, Education of
Engell, James 234 & nn., 240
England:
  aristocracy 52
  contemporary state of 6–7
  bread shortages in 1
  Church of 23, 30, 78
  commonwealthmen 102 & n.
  constitution 140
  countryside, degradation of 152
  courtly zeal 78

crop failure 1, 6
and dissent 11, 27
economic depression 2, 6, 211 & n.
education 11, 23, 61–9
and famine 2
and feudalism 6
folk culture 124 & n.
foods of 252
and French Revolution 52–3, 223–6
golden age of 151 n.
greenwood 75 n., 136 & n., 140,
  141 & n., 143–4, 152–3, 157–8,
  199
industry 6
inflation 1
invasion of 1, 112–13
jacobins 32, 224–5
landscape 140, 216–17
language 140
Levellers 123
liberties 75 n.
literary culture of 21–2, 268
merry old 151
militarization of 6, 53
Newbury bypass 152 n.
parliamentary reform 1, 2, 27–8,
  53, 65, 71–80, 82–3, 139–40,
  210–12 & nn.
peace 2
popular spirit in 74, 152
public schools 64–8 & nn.
repression 28, 53
republican tradition in 102–5, 109
Revolution 28
riots 1–2
and Scotland 268
sounds 252
suburbs 74, 124–30, 214–17
a tubercular society 22
unemployment 2, 6
venality of 153–4
war 1
woodland, *see* greenwood
English Revolution, *see* England
Environmental movement 123, 196 n.
Enzer, Joseph 73
Epicurus 81–2
Eton College 14, 23, 36 n.
  classical curriculum at 66–8 nn.
  a patriotic standard 66–7
Eton Latin Grammar 66–7 & n.
European Magazine 207 n., 222
Everest, Kelvin 113–14

Every Saturday 8
Examiner ix, x, 8, 9n., 19n., 25, 26,
    28, 38n., 53, 71n., 73n., 81–2,
    99–101, 104–6, 108–9, 111, 116,
    118 & n., 121, 122n., 123, 124n.,
    128, 131, 134, 136–7 & n., 139 &
    n., 140, 141, 151n., 153, 180,
    208, 209–12 & nn., 237–9, 255–
    61, 270
  'Arguments of the Reformers' 53
  'Court and Fashionables' 213n.
  'Family of Shakespeare' 239
  'Forged Bank Notes' 153n.
  'Literary Notices' 213n.
  'Seditious Placards' 259
  'Theatrical Examiner' 238–9
  see also Hunt, James Henry Leigh

Fairer, David, 109n., 114n., 224n.
Fisher, David 238
Floure and the Leafe 136–8, 140
folk-song, Irish 93
Foote, Samuel 160
Franklin, Benjamin 49, 178
French Revolution 2, 20, 22, 28, 46,
    51–3, 84, 87, 115, 174–5, 223,
    225, 227, 237
  Bastille, Fall of 174
  Bourbons 71 & n.
  colour symbolism of 71–5
  and dress 70–1 & n.
  Festivals 70–5, 85–7, 237
  and medical science 173–81
  National Assembly 175
  National Convention 70
  and neoclassicism 69–71
  and sensibility 223–9, 237
  Terror 52–3, 56, 84, 87, 185–6
Frend William 32
Frere, George 91n.
Fry, Paul 6, 247n., 249n., 253n.
Fuseli, Henry 174 & n.

Gagging Acts (1795) 2
Garrod, H. W. 4 & n., 244
Geddes, Alexander 27, 173–4 & n.
Geneva 274–5
Gentleman's Magazine 8, 9n., 58–9
George III, King 236, 249n.
Georgium Sidus *see* Uranus
Gifford, William 21
  The Baviad 20

Gillray, James:
  New Morality 224–5, 227
  Voltaire Instructs the Infant Jacobinism
    223–4
Gittings, Robert 4, 7, 90, 167, 171,
    187n.
Gleig, George, Bishop of Brechin 23–
    4
Godwin, Mary 274
Godwin, William 28, 32, 65–6, 178–9,
    242–7
  on classical education 65–6 & n.
  on translation 66
  Account of the Seminary 65–6, 69
  Caleb Williams 143
  'Of an Early Taste for Reading' 247
  Enquirer 247
  Political Justice 66, 77, 185–6, 242–7
Goellnicht, Donald C., 15n., 168–9,
    170n., 194n.
Good, John Mason 173–4
Greece 65
green, as radical emblem 123–5, 132,
    134–40, 153, 196n.
  see also England, greenwood; Hood,
    Robin
Green, Joseph Henry 171–2
Green Ribbon Club 123
greenery, politics of, *see* green
greenwood, *see under* England
Guy's Hospital 90, 109, 163–81, 187
  see also Physical Society

Habeas Corpus, suspension of (1817)
    109, 139–40, 210–11
Haighton, Dr. 176
Hale-White, William 171
Hall, Robert 39, 45–6
Hammond Thomas 14, 49, 50, 89–90,
    163, 164, 171–2n., 181
Hampden, John 28, 47n., 101–2, 109
Hampstead 126–7, 214, 216–17,
    270n.
Handel, George Fridiric 93
Harrison, Gary 151n.
Harrison, Tony, 'Them and [uz]' 22
Harrow School 14, 15, 23, 67n.
Hartley, David 187, 243
Hartman, Geoffrey 251–2, 261
Harvard Keats Collection, *see*
    Houghton Library
Harvard University, *see* Houghton
    Library

Haydon, Benjamin Robert 51, 84,
  183, 230, 239 n.
  Christ's Entry into Jerusalem viii
Hayley, William, *Life of Milton* 101
Hazlitt, William x & n., 12, 214, 221,
  227, 234 & n., 272–5
  and K 23, 83–4, 183–4, 195–6, 221,
    227, 231–2, 235, 240–2, 247
  *Essay on the Principles of Human
    Action* 240–2 & n.
  'My First Acquaintance with Poets'
    246
  'On Burns, and the Old English
    Ballads' 142–3, 147
  'On Classical Education' 69 n.
  'On Gusto' 231
  'On Manner' 195–6
  'On Poetry in General' 183
  'On Posthumous Fame' 233
  'On Shakespeare and Milton' 241
  'On Mr. Wordsworth's
    "Excursion"' 87
  Round Table 83–4, 195–6, 231, 233
Heaney, Seamus 265
  'Exposure' 237
Henry VIII, King 100
Hermes 187–8
Herschel, William:
  describes Sirius rising 37–8
  discovers 'new planet' (Uranus) 35–
    6, 37, 57–9
  and Ryland, J. C. 35, 37
Highgate, Alps of 215
Hill, Christopher 123, 144 n.
Hispaniola, exploitation of 58
history, *see under* Keats, John,
    Imaginative and Intellectual Life
Hobbes, Thomas 240
Hobhouse, John Cam 60
Holcroft, Thomas 32, 246
Hollis, Thomas 102
Homans, Margaret 16 n.
Homer 58, 61, 65, 67, 78 n., 239 n.
Hone, William, *Political House that Jack
    Built* 227
Hood, Robin 123, 141–55 nn.
  outlaw 143–4, 158
  proto-Jacobin 145–6
  radical hero 145
  republican 146
  vanished idyll of 142–3
  see also England, greenwood;
    Sherwood Forest

Hopkins, Gerard Manley 228
Horace 67
Horne Tooke, John 175
Horsemonger Lane Gaol 92
Houghton Library 8–10 & n., 82 n.,
  100 n., 138 n.
Houghton, Lord, *see* Milnes, Richard
  Monckton
House of Dun 73
Howitt, William 228
Hull 211 n.
Hume, David, *History of England* 53–4
  & n.
Hunt, 'Bristol', *see* Hunt, Henry
  'Orator'
Hunt, Henry 'Orator' 60, 72, 211 n.
  and Byron, Lord 100
  and K 14, 253–7
  at London (Sept. 1819) 72–3, 124
    & n., 134, 253–4
  and Peterloo (Aug. 1819) 72, 254
  white costume of 72–4 & nn.
Hunt, James Henry Leigh viii, x, 3, 9,
  12, 18 & n., 20 n., 23, 24, 25, 28,
  48, 50, 63, 204–5, 228, 272, 275
  affectation of 156
  and Alfred, King 107–8, 109 & n.,
    139, 209
  and Byron, Lord 100, 268, 274
  and Chaucer 199–40 & n., 209 & n.
  at Christ's Hospital 67
  and Clarke, C. C. 88 n., 89, 92 & n.,
    99, 100, 125–6, 257 n.
  and classics 65, 67, 74, 77–8, 81–2
  and Coleridge, S. T., 126–8 & n.,
    222
  a convicted libeller 270
  correct 271
  as created by Z 10 n., 19
  debauched 271
  and *The Examiner* 9 & n., 19 n., 25,
    28, 38 n., 81–2, 99, 100, 104,
    111, 116, 118 & n., 122–4 & n.,
    127 n., 128, 131, 134, 139 & n.,
    140, 141, 151, 180, 209–12 &
    nn., 237–8, 257–61, 270
  on French School 116–17, 119,
    122 n.
  Hampstead, only place for him 127,
    217
  as Harold Skimpole 228
  in jail (1813–15) 91–2 & n., 100
  and K viii, 8, 9, 13 n., 19, 23, 24, 35,

48, 56, 61–2, 63, 74, 76, 78 n.,
  79 n., 81–2, 91–2, 94, 99, 104–5
  & n., 105–10, 116–34 & nn.,
  139–40, 141 & n., 142, 146,
  147 n., 151–2, 156, 167–8, 204–7,
  209–12 & nn., 221, 222, 227–9,
  237–9, 240, 251, 257–61, 266
libels Prince Regent (1812) 25,
  92 n., 100
and *The Liberal* 268, 274
licentious 271
limitations of 127–8
and Marvell, Andrew 209
and Milton, John 209
mock obituary of 216–17
modernity of 216–17
on Mont Blanc 127
nature, unacquainted with 214–15
and Pan, cult of 81–2
and paganism 81–2, 141
at Pisa 274
and Porson, Richard 99
profligate 271
promiscuous intercourse, an
  advocate of 275
pure 271
a puritan 271
and Robin Hood 141–2, 147 n.
a scholar, not 65
at sea 127
and Shakespeare, William 209
and Shelley, Percy Bysshe 77–8,
  85 n., 88 n., 105, 259–60, 268,
  274
sociality 109–10, 117–18, 122 n.,
  125–6, 129–30 nn., 131, 132, 134
and Spenser, Edmund 258, 260
and suburban life 124–5, 126–30,
  214–17
and Sydney, Algernon 209
a tea-drinker 19 n.
villainous depravity of 275
vulgarity 129
and Wordsworth, W. 117–18 n.,
  127–8 & n., 222
'Apothecaries' 160, 163
'Attack on the Prince Regent, and
  Thanksgiving in the Churches'
  211–12 & n.
'Attack on the Prince Regent, and a
  Word or Two of Plain Comment
  upon it' 208–9
Autobiography 25, 56, 67

'The Bourbons' 104 & n.
'Calendar of Nature' 99, 257–61,
  266–7
'Christmas and Other Old National
  Merry-Makings' 122 n., 124 & n.,
  151
Descent of Liberty, a Mask 74, 124–5,
  134
'Description of Hampstead' 126–7,
  134, 212 & n.
Feast of the Poets 109 n., 117
*Foliage; or, Poems Original and
  Translated* 19 & n., 65, 116–
  19 nn., 120 n., 122, 123, 125–6,
  127 n., 132, 140, 141 and n., 142,
  146, 147, 214
'Harry Brown's Letters to his
  Friends' 127 n. *see also* 'To
  William Hazlitt'
The Indicator 141 n., 182, 251, 275
'Informers' 131 & n.
'Liberty of the Press' 237–8
Literary Pocket Book 268, 273
'Louis XVIII.—The Emperor
  Napoleon' 104 & n.
The Months 266
'The Nile' 141 n.
The Nymphs 141 n.
'Old May-Day' 124 n., 141 & n.
'On the Same' 126
'Portrait of Apollo' 38 n.
'Proposed Suspension of the Habeas
  Corpus Act' 210–11
'Songs of Robin Hood' 141 & n.
'Stanzas on the Death of General
  Moreau' 95
The Story of Rimini 20 n., 61 n., 119–
  23 nn., 125, 129 & n., 132, 134,
  141, 207, 226, 271
'To the English People: Letter II'
  139 & n.
'To the English People: Letter VI'
  81–2
'To John Keats' 125–6
'To Kosciusko' 108
'To Percy Shelley' 78 n.
'To Thomas Moore' 215
'To William Hazlitt' 19 n., 122 n.,
  127 & n., 215
'Young Poets' 19 n., 105, 167–8,
  214, 217
Hunt, John 76, 82–3, 85, 270–1
  see also *Yellow Dwarf*

Hunt, Lynn 71 & n.
Hunter, John 174 & n., 177

ideology, Romantic 249–50 & nn.
Indicator, see under Hunt, James Henry
    Leigh
informers 1, 131

jacobin poetry 109n., 223–7
Jack, Ian 260n., 263
Jacobites 73
Jesus College, Cambridge 32
Johnson, Joseph 223
Johnson, Samuel 233
    Dictionary of the English Language
        220–1, 226, 235–6, 255
Jones, Chris 225
Jones, Elizabeth 127n., 214n.
Jones, Thomas 75
Jonson, Ben 142, 154, 241
    'The Forest' 141
    The Sad Shepherd 141–3, 144, 146
    'Under-woods' 141
Joyce, James 68

Kandl, John 57n., 109n.
Keach, William 6, 18n., 19, 61 & n.,
        249n., 257
Kean, Edmund 230, 231, 238–9
Keate, John 66
    see also Eton College
Keate, Thomas 171
Keats, George and Georgiana vii n.,
        49, 50, 132, 151, 206, 253
KEATS, JOHN:
    AND CONTEMPORARIES AND
        HISTORICAL FIGURES:
    Alfred, King 107–9, 110n.
    Bailey, Benjamin 23–5, 26, 80–1,
        147n., 161, 203–5, 240, 244
    Barbauld, Anna Letitia 97–8
    Boileau, Nicholas 119
    Bonnycastle, John 36–7, 260
    Bowles, W. L. 104
    Brawne, Fanny 253
    Brown, Charles 166–7, 168, 231,
        232, 245
    Burke, Edmund 11 & n., 20, 99,
        156, 225–6
    Byron, George Gordon, Lord 100,
        242, 250n.
    Chaucer, Geoffrey 136–40 & nn.,
        154, 209 & n.

Clarke, Charles Cowden ix, 23, 25,
        28, 37, 39–40, 41, 46–7, 49–50,
        54, 55, 67, 88–110, 132, 136–7 &
        n., 163, 232, 264, 266–7
Coleridge, S. T. 108, 110, 187, 190,
        198, 222, 235, 242 & n,
Cooper, Astley 166, 169–73, 174 5,
        187n., 191–2, 193n.
Cortez 57–9
Cowper, William 152–3 & n., 157
David, Jacques Louis 74–5
Dilke, Charles Wentworth 230–2,
        242, 245–7
Godwin, William 69, 186, 242–7
Green, Joseph Henry 171–2
Hammond, Thomas 14, 49, 50, 89–
        90, 163, 164, 171–2n., 181
Hampden, John 102 & n.
Haydon, Benjamin Robert 84, 183,
        230, 232; *see also* Life and Times,
        immortal dinner
Hazlitt, William 23, 83–4, 183–4,
        195–6, 221, 227, 231–2, 235,
        240–2, 247
Herschel, William 36–8, 57, 58–9
Hume, David 53–4
Hunt, Henry 14, 253–7
Hunt, James Henry Leigh viii, 8, 9,
        13n., 19, 23, 24, 35, 48, 56,
        61–2, 63, 74, 76, 78n., 79n.,
        81–2, 91–2, 94, 99, 104–5 & n.,
        105–10, 116–34 & nn., 139–40,
        141 & n., 142, 146, 147n., 151–2,
        156, 167–8, 204–7, 209–12 &
        nn., 221, 222, 227–9, 237–9, 240,
        251, 257–61, 266
Hunt, John 83
Kean, Edmund 230–1, 238–9
Kosciusko, Thaddeus 107–8
Lamb, Charles 183–4, 239n.
Lemprière, John 47, 62, 264
Lucas, Billy 165–6, 193
Mathew, George Felton 48, 107,
        172, 207n.
Milton, John 28, 49, 91, 154, 193,
        196, 198, 231–2 & n., 252
Napoleon 103–4
Ollier, Charles 89, 94
Pope, Alexander 152
Porson, Richard 99
Priestley, Joseph 28
Reynolds, John Hamilton 23, 24n.,
        78n., 84 & n., 105, 138–9, 140,

144, 147–8, 151, 154–8nn., 199,
201, 231, 232–3, 241–2
Robertson, William 54–7 & n., 196
Robin Hood 140–55, 158, 241–2
Ryland, John Collett 30, 35–9, 42–
3, 44, 55
Severn, Joseph 69n., 84–5n.
Shakespeare, William 38, 154, 157,
209, 225, 230–9, 241
Shelley, P. B. 14, 65, 105, 141n.,
162, 167–8, 194n., 228
Smith, Charlotte 104
Smith, Horace 74–5, 80, 94, 135,
230, 232, 245n.
Spence, Joseph 47, 62, 264
Spenser, Edmund 41, 89–91, 209–
10, 241
Stephens, Henry 167–8
Taylor, John 188, 195–6
Thelwall, John 180–1, 189
Tooke, Andrew 47, 62, 263–5
Webb, Cornelius x & n., 129 & n.,
270n.
Woodhouse, Richard 202, 203n.,
246–7, 261–2
Wordsworth, William 49–50, 57n.,
68, 76–7, 83–5n., 118n., 156,
158, 184–7 & n., 190, 210, 217–
18, 222, 230n., 241, 244–5, 246–
7
Z 11, 13 & n., 14, 15, 20n., 22, 23–
5, 60–1, 63, 65, 69, 79, 109–10,
129n., 161–2, 163, 168, 202, 205,
206, 214, 219, 226–7, 250–1, 266
EDUCATION OF:
at Enfield School (1803–11) ix, 2,
7, 8, 10, 14, 15, 23–5, 27–50,
54–7 & n., 59, 62, 65, 67, 88–93,
105, 107, 131, 132–3, 172–3,
232, 260, 264, 267; curriculum
and teaching: astronomy 36–9,
250, classical textbooks 46–47,
62–3, 67–8, 88, competitive
39–45, Greek 40, 60–3, 67, 69,
88, history 47–50, Latin 40,
62–3, living orrery 36–7,
mythology, Greek 47, 63, 67, 69,
Ovid 264, prizes 36–7, 39–40,
260 (see also Bonnycastle, John),
recreative 40–5, telescope 37,
translations 40, 62, 67; K enters
(1803) 14, 33; K leaves (1811)
4, 14 & n., 89, 90, 163–73; K's

reading 8, 25, 30, 36–41, 44,
45–50, 54 & n., 55, 56–7, 62–3,
67, 69, 74, 89–90, 195–6, 255,
264–5; K returns to 90–2; K
transformed by 39–40, 44;
gardens at 41, 90, 92 & n., 266–
7; library, exhausted by K 44, 46;
musical evenings at 93; play, see
curriculum and teaching,
recreative; political culture of:
dissent 1–50, 91, 172–4,
republicanism 28–9, 45–50, 93,
109; Ryland, John Collett,
influence on 33, 36, 41–4, 108–
9; unauthorized 23;
unorthodox 15, 23; see also
Enfield School; Clarke, Charles
Cowden; Clarke, John; Ryland,
John Collett
IDENTITIES OF:
adolescent 221–2
affected 162, 274
aggressive 14
alert 4
alive to life 130
ambitious 4, 10, 14, 40, 44, 48, 55,
59, 105, 132
apathetic sublime 12
apprentice, wavering 10, 15, 19, 20,
22, 24, 161
aspirant 105, 106, 132n., 162, 217,
274
autistic poet 13
bantling 205, 218, 225–6
bastard 205
boy 12, 15
child of 1790s 2
childish 15, 205, 217, 218, 222,
225–6, 227–8
close observer 4
cockney 16–18, 22, 60, 61–2 & n.,
69, 109–10, 206, 214, 226–7
cocky 19
compassionate 59
consistent 48–9
courageous 8
dangerous 7
degenerate 22
delicate and fragile 12, 228
deprived 6
despised in Scotland 24
devotee of beauty 12
disadvantaged 6, 13, 266

KEATS, JOHN (*cont.*):
eager viii
effeminate 11, 16, 62–3 & n., 205, 222, 225–6, 227–9
energetic 39–40
entrepreneur 13n., 14
envious 15n.
escapist 5, 229, 249–50, 266
faultfinder 107
flimsy 10, 18
flippant 251
ghost of 274
home-taught 62
honest 89
humane 4
ignorant 13, 15, 60, 63
ill-read 22
illegitimate 60, 227
immature 217
impatient 251
insolent 13n.
insulated from world 5, 12–13, 196n., 213, 214
intuitive 88
invalid 22
irritable 241, 251
Jack Keates 274
Johnny Keats 15, 19, 23, 129, 162, 274
just of age 217–18
kindly 3
as Leigh Hunt the second 162, 274
as Leigh Hunt's foster-child 225–6
liberty man 8, 10, 25, 130–1
lower-class 10, 15, 60
malcontent 251
mankin 18, 222
marginal 11, 14, 15n.
minimal presence 2, 10
Mr John 161, 168
nurseryman, *see* poet-nurseryman
obscure 14, 213
optimistic 53, 54
outlaw 153, 156, 200
poet: bad 161, 162; of crisis 7; of revolutionary idea 4; pharmacopolitical 162–3, 169, 173, 191, 201; starved 161
poet-nurseryman 41
poet-physician 163, 169, 195
poor devil 162
poor Keats 8, 24, 107, 167
pretender 69
profane 60, 61, 69
profligate 60
proto-capitalist 14
pugnacity viii, 8
pure 88–9
a radical 9, 106
respectable 24
revolutionary 15n.
revolutionary idea, child of 244
ridiculous 160
Sangrado, young 161
shopkeeper 15
sickly 11, 22, 225–7
socially unacceptable 23
son of promise 61
stripling 11, 18, 23
Sweeney-Keats 229
tea-drinker 18
temperate 89
tender 227
thing of beauty vii
uneducated 10–11, 12, 16, 22, 23, 69
unformed 11
ungovernable 8
unrestricted opinion 106, 107
unsettled 18, 19, 69
unweaned 227
victim 8
vigorous 8
vivacity viii
vulgar 60, 61, 69
vulnerable 25, 227
weak 160
young 10, 15, 19, 23, 25, 105, 140, 161, 217–18, 220, 225–6, 227
young Cockney rhymester 13, 15, 61, 206, 226
IMAGINATIVE AND INTELLECTUAL LIFE:
Adam's dream 81
airy citadel 157
alchemy 189
all in a mist 253
America, changing ideas about 49
anatomy 168–9
anti-clerical 78n., 81–2, 203–5 & n.
anti-Newtonian 183–4
Apollo 38–9, 44, 56, 58, 158–9, 184, 194
astronomy and 36–9, 57–9, 98, 260; *see also* Barbauld, Anna Letitia; Bonnycastle, John; Herschel,

William; Uranus; living orrery;
Keats, John, Education of
beauty 29, 81, 88, 225, 229, 230,
  231
belated 61, 68, 211 n.
botany 168–9
camelion poet 246–7 & n.
capitalism, critique of 60, 152–3,
  154 n., 158
character, errors of 204
chemistry 168–9, 182–3, 188–9
classics, knowledge/ignorance of
  46–7, 60–3, 67, 68, 69, 74–87
on Cockney School essays 204–5
commonwealth, ideal 156–9, 186,
  266
community 136
controversial ix, 69, 76, 106, 131,
  257
cultural exclusion 6, 13, 16, 61
Death on the Pale Horse 230
democracy 189
dissenting culture, voice of 15, 28–
  9, 221
divine right, attitude to 102 n.
dogma, unapt for 3
ecological vision 158–9, 196 n.
education, *see* Keats, John,
  Education of
egotistical sublime 246–7
reading, *see* Keats, John, Education
  of
fellowship, individuality and 157,
  189–90 & n.
French Revolution 51–3, 74–87
Greek, knew no 69
green awareness 196 n.
gusto 231–2, 247
health 195–6
heart-vexations 232–3
history: contemporary 51–4;
  theories of 51–60;
  progressive 51–3 n., 187;
  seasonal 252
humanity, prospects for 157–9, 187
individuality, *see* fellowship
imagination 81, 155–9, 183–4, 186,
  187, 189, 194–5, 208, 218–19,
  221–2, 233, 235, 242; *see also*
  poetry
on imperialism 153
and impersonality 232–3, 252–3
intellect, lack of 14, 23

intensity 230–2
joy 60
knowledge, lack of 11, 18–19
knowledge, quest for 29, 39, 42–5
life, dark passages of 156
life of sensations 244
literature, man of achievement in
  238
logic, without 11, 18
love 60
mawkishness 218–19, 221, 224–5,
  228, 235
medicine and 39, 160–81, 184,
  187, 188–91
and Methodists 245 & n.
metromania 20–22
militarism 57–8
mind, thoroughfare for all
  thoughts 245
minds of mortals 157
modern poetry, invents 68–9
negative capability 11, 157–8, 186,
  200, 201, 219, 225, 229, 230–67
neoclassical, *see* classics
and new worlds 57–8
no interest in anything 12
non-egotistic 232
nympholepsy 80
and old poets 154, 156, 241
oppositional 28, 153, 221–9
originality 157
outspoken 106
paganism x, 60, 74–87, 88–9
Pan-worship 74–87, 135–6, 210–12
paranoia 253
passivity 232
patience 158–9; *see also* negative
  capability
philosophy 42, 60, 182–7
and pigs, ethereal 155–9
platonism 188–9
pleasure thermometer 188–91
poetical character 246–7
poetics of dissent 221–9
poetry: abstracted 219; adolescent
  79, 221; aesthetic world of viii, ix;
  agonies and strife in 42, 59, 208;
  amorous 79; arcadian 69;
  archaic 205; as ardent
  listlessness 42, 190; artless 222–3;
  astronomical observations in 38;
  awkward 205; badinage 219;
  bland 110; boldness 220–1;

KEATS, JOHN (*cont.*):

bowers in 41, 206–8; brazen 20; brilliancy 219; changeful 130–2, 220–1, 257; cold pastoral 86–7; colloquial manner 219–20; competitive-recreative patterns in 39–45, 206–7; confused 219; and conspiracy x, 254–7; contented 267; conversational style of 219; couplets *see* loose couplets in; curative power of 194–5; dalliance 79; dangerous 220; decorum, affront to 14; demented 20; detumescent 79; diagnostic voice of 192–3, 194–5, 199; disconcerting 16–17; diseased 20; disoriented 60; disreputable 76; dissenting opinions in 251; effeminate 224–5; elliptical manner of 104 n., 205, 211; eloquent 15, 140; entranced 60; epithets 219; erotic 17 & n., 79–80, 207; escapist 5, 229, 249–50, 253, 266; ethereality of 155–9; exquisite 139; exuberant 205; feverish 219; flashy 220–1; forgetful 59; garden, likened to 40–1; heroic vulgarity of 16; historical change in 5, 51–60, 66–7, 208, humane 4, 42, 92, 251; idealistic 60; imagery: green 123–5, 137, 139, 140; greenwood 136, 140–55, 212; white 74–6, 125; immoral 76; imperious 57–8, 59; impious 76, 78, 79; impotent 17, 18, 221, 222; indecorous 14; indiscriminate 219; indistinct 219; infection of 20; ingenuity of 221; innocent 222; insolent 13 & n.; jacobinical 76, 216, 225–6, 229, 251; jaunty 20; learned 220; licentious 68, 219–21; light, intensities of 38; lisping 202, 205–6, 218, 225, 229; loose couplets in 6, 61; luxuries in 206–7, 208; maggotty 218–20; malady 20; and medical studies 191–3; mine of wealth 69; modish x; myth-making in 65–8; naïve 23, 125;

narrative 41–2, 79, 92; narrative, dilatory 41–2; natural freedom of 207; neologisms in 79 n., 188 n., 221; novelty of 220–1; obscure 205; ominous 83; overwrought 14; perfection of 252 & n.; philosophy, *see* tensions in, as warm philosophy; physiological symptoms in 191–4; plaintive 60; polemic 69, 100, 131; politics, *see* style, politics of; poor sales of 9; post-revolutionary 60; pretty 222; random 20 n., 205–6; raving 16; reactionary 5; realms of gold 57–8; recreative, *see* competitive-recreative; retreats in 41; rhymes of 19–20 n., 221; science 182–7; self-directed 18; sensual 17, 60; shy beginnings 93; sickly 11, 225–6, 251; sidereal vision 37; simple 222–9; slick 69; smart 130, 219, 220; social disease 20 & n.; sparkling 130, 220, 257; speculative 57 n., 81, 157; Spenserian 91–2, 206–7; style, politics of 19, 202–8, 221–9; subjective 59; teaseful 79; tensions in 60; tentative 93; test 40; timid 93, trial 40, 41; truculent 20; underiving 60; undisciplined 61; unillusioned 151; unintelligible 76, 221; unsettling x, 18, 227; unsophisticated 219; versification of 207, 223; vocabulary of 220–2; voices anxiety of his times 6–7; voluble 13 & n.; voyeuristic 17 n.; vulgarity of x, 14, 16, 17, 60, 61, 76, 222; as warm philosophy 184; witty 130, 220, 257

political opinions 6, 25, 28–9, 46–8, 51–4, 74, 75, 83, 91–3, 105–10, 116, 118 n., 119, 123–5, 131, 140, 154 n., 158, 202, 207; liberal 6, 61–2, 65, 69, 136, 206–7; radical 6, 10, 60, 106, 125; republican 4, 46, 48, 54, 107, 172; republican tradition 13 n., 28–9, 45–6, 49, 54, 55, 100–5, 108–9, 172

precocious 103 n.

pretty paganism 83–7; *see also* paganism

reader responses 7, 16–17, 21–2

reading, *see under* Keats, John, Education of

retirement, plan for, *see* study

scepticism 107, 172

scholarship, scanty 62, 69, 88

science 60, 182–7

self-directed 18

sociality 116–33, 221

study 39–40, 42

surgery 163–7, 169–70

sympathetic imagination, capacity for 232

sympathy, philosophic tradition of 233–4

understanding, not capable of 11, 18

uneducated 10–11, 12, 16, 22, 23, 69

well informed 53

wise passiveness 232, 235

LIFE AND TIMES:

affectionate nature of 232

at Ambleside (1818) 118n.

America 49

anti-clerical 78n., 147n.

as apothecary (1811–1815) viii, 14, 24, 89–90, 160–4, 168, 171–2

appearance 171

birth 2, 6, 14, 89–90

boyhood 2

campaign to suppress 7

death vii, 162–3, 268

dissenting culture 1–50, 91, 251

at Edmonton (1811–15) 14, 89–90, 107, 163

Endymion, begins (1817) 81

Enfield, schooldays days at (1803–11), *see* Keats, John, Education of

and the *Examiner* 25–6, 53, 81–2, 104–5, 123, 131, 139, 140, 151, 153n., 167–8, 209–12 & nn., 237–9, 255–6

father, death of 193

financial problems 253

first poems 94, 102, 103–5 108–9

and French Revolution 51–3, 74–87

at Guy's Hospital (1815–17) 90, 109, 163–180nn., 182, 191–2, 193, 194–5; *see also* apothecary; medical career

haemorrhage, first 167

at Hampstead 109–10, 270n.

Harrow School 15

health, fragility of 253

immortal dinner (Dec., 1817) 239n.

lodgings 89, 137n., 171 & n.

at London (Sept. 1819) 253–4

'lost years' (1810–15) 90

medical career (1811–17) ix, 2, 4, 14, 22, 24, 48, 89–90, 160–81nn.; chooses 168n.; conscientious motives 166–7; dresser 164–6, 171–2; examinations 167; lecture courses 169–70nn., 182, 191–2; responsibilities 164–5; return to, contemplates (1819) 168; skills 163–4

mother, death of 167, 193

music 93

new school of poets 105–6

at Oxford (1817) 198, 203

on paper currency 153n.

parliamentary reform, supports 53, 83

and Peterloo Massacre (1819) 53, 83, 253–67

poetic career 2, 4–5, 38–9, 42, 48, 92, 208

poetry, fate sealed for 167–8

reading, *see* Keats, John, Education of

and reform, *see* political opinions

retirement, plan for (1818) 42

social background 4

social status 13–14, 16, 22

sociality 116–33

Swan and Hoop, family home at 172

tragic circumstances of 236

tuberculosis 167

vegetarianism 84–5

and war 96

at Winchester (1819) 184, 252–3

and *Yellow Dwarf* 76, 82–3

see also Keats, John, Education of

POSTHUMOUS RECEPTION:

absurd hubbub about 274

aesthetic view of vii, 196n., 229

among English poets vii, 132

arcadian 69

and the canon ix, 13

KEATS, JOHN (*cont.*):
bicentenary (1995) vii, viii, 6
biological thought 158–9
campaign to suppress 7
deliberately obscures K's relation to
Leigh Hunt 62
doomed 167, 168, 217
as a dreamer 228
feminized 63 & n., 171 n., 228–9
gender 62–3
historical analysis irrelevant to 214
ignorance of classics 62–3
as an invalid 228
as Leigh Hunt the second 162, 274
misleading accounts of 10
modern poetry, influence on 68–9
new historicist criticism 5–6
in nineteenth century 154, 196 n.,
227–9
political life neglected 2–4, 5, 106–
7, 154, 226, 229
posthumous life vii, viii
and Pre-Raphaelites 55
refashioning of 25
romantic 62, 228
sentimental 88–9, 107
youthfulness 154, 228–9
WRITINGS AND PUBLICATIONS:
'Addressed to the Same' 109–10,
131 n.
'La Belle Dame sans Mercy' 182
'Calidore' 206
Endymion: A Poetic Romance x, 10,
17 n., 19–20 & n., 23, 24, 29,
40, 41–2, 61 & n., 65, 68–9,
74–5 & n., 76, 79–87, 92, 104 n.,
123, 132 n., 135–6, 147 n., 161 n.,
162, 163, 188–91 & n., 193–5,
202–5 & nn., 217–18, 219, 221,
235, 248, 251; *see also* 'Hymn to
Pan'
The Eve of St Agnes 93 n., 192
The Fall of Hyperion: A Dream 5, 44,
56, 59, 60, 68, 156, 163, 184,
187, 191, 192, 194, 252
'Hymn to Pan' 29, 74–6, 78, 82–3,
85–7, 92, 135–6; see also
Endymion: A Poetic Romance; *Yellow
Dwarf*
Hyperion: A Fragment 5, 18 n., 34,
38–9, 44, 55, 56, 59, 68, 98, 136
& n., 155, 184, 191–3, 248, 249,
252
'Imitation of Spenser' 91

Isabella; or, the Pot of Basil ix, 250,
251
I stood tip-toe upon a little hill 76, 106,
125, 130 & n., 194–5, 199, 207
'Keen, fitful gusts' 109, 125
Lamia 37 n., 68, 126 n., 183–4,
187–9, 250
*Lamia, Isabella, The Eve of St Agnes
and Other Poems* 154 n., 161 n.,
168, 248–9, 250–1, 252, 265
'Lines on the Mermaid Tavern' 99,
142, 146–7, 148, 150–1, 152
'Lines Written on 29 May, the
Anniversary of Charles's
Restoration, on Hearing the Bells
Ringing' 29, 48, 100
'To Lord Byron' 100
'Mr Kean' 183, 231, 232
'O Solitude!' 91, 105–6, 130
'Ode on a Grecian Urn' x, 55, 62,
85–7 & nn., 249
'Ode to a Nightingale' x, 59–60,
94, 190, 193, 195–201, 208, 249
'Oh! how I love' 207
'On First Looking into Chapman's
Homer' 36–7, 56–9 & n., 61 &
n., 65, 67, 68
'On Leaving some Friends at an
Early Hour' 125, 206
'On Peace' 28–9, 103–4, 105
'On Receiving a Curious Shell' 206
'On Receiving a Laurel Crown from
Leigh Hunt' 126 n.
'On Seeing the Elgin Marbles' 39,
59
Poems, by John Keats ix, x, 9, 10, 22,
23, 89, 92–3, 105–7, 123, 125,
130, 131, 153, 195, 206–8,
209–12 nn., 217, 219, 222, 251,
273
'Robin Hood' x, 99, 142, 146–7 &
n., 148–50, 151–55 & nn., 158,
195, 199–201, 249
Sleep and Poetry 16, 17 & n., 18, 19–
20 & n., 29, 41, 42, 43–4, 59, 92,
106, 107–8, 109, 119, 123, 125,
206–8, 213–14, 225–6
'Specimen of an Induction' 106,
125, 206
'This pleasant tale is like a little
copse' 136–40 & nn.
'To Autumn' x, 5, 6, 29, 94, 99,
186, 229, 236–7, 249 n., 251–3,
254–67

'To Charles Cowden Clarke' 29, 88, 93, 162 n., 105, 106, 130, 131, 219–20
'To a Friend who Sent me some Roses' 131 n.
'To George Felton Mathew' 29, 90 n., 107, 130, 206, 207
'To Hope' 29, 206
'To Kosciusko' 29, 108, 206
'To Leigh Hunt, Esq.' 106, 206, 210–12
'To My Brother George' (epistle) 29, 106, 130–2, 206
'To My Brother George' (sonnet) 131 n.
'To My Brothers' 131 n.
'To one who has been long in city pent' 198
'To Some Ladies' 206
'Written in Disgust of Vulgar Superstition' 78 n., 147 n.
'Written on the Day That Mr Leigh Hunt Left Prison' 9, 29, 91–2, 106, 122 n.

Keats, Tom 151, 167, 171, 195, 198, 236
Kerrigan, John 57 n.
Klancher, Jon 13 n., 21 n.
Knight, Stephen 145 n., 148, 154
Koch, June Q. 4 n.
Kosciusko, Thaddeus 108, 109 n., 173
Kroeber, Karl 68, 158–9, 196 n.
Kucich, Greg 53–4 n., 91 & n.

Lamb, Charles 23, 28, 114 n., 183–4, 196, 224, 227, 246, 275
Lamb, Mary 23
Larkin, Philip 128
laurel, as reformist emblem 73–4
    see also green
Laws of the Physical Society 176 n.
    see also Physical Society
Lemprière, John 62
    Bibliotheca Classica 47, 62, 67–8, 264
Leon, Ponce de 58
Le Sage, Alain René 160, 161 n.
Levinson, Marjorie 6, 13–14, 15, 18, 266
Lewisham 270
Liberal 10, 268, 274
Libra, constellation of 260
Lincoln 204
literary culture, see under England

Literary Journal 218 & n.
Literary Panorama 129 n.
literature, adulteration of 21
Littel's Living Age 8
Little John 146
Liverpool 81
Lloyd, Charles 114 n., 224, 273
    Edmund Oliver 239–40
Locke, John 101
    Letter on Toleration 48
Lockhart, John Gibson 10, 12, 21 n., 23–6 & n., 268, 273–4 and n.
    see also Blackwood's Magazine; Cockney School Essays; Z
London 23, 72, 74, 75, 111, 124, 174, 253–4, 257, 268
London Magazine (Baldwin's) 250
London Magazine (Taylor and Hessey's) 268
London, Tower of 175, 180
London Corresponding Society 146, 175
Lonsdale, William Lowther, Earl of 118
Lowell, Amy 3, 4
Lucas, Billy 164–7, 193
Lucretius 81–2
Ludlow 211 n.
A Lytell Geste of Robyn Hode 144

Magdalen Hall (Oxford) 203
Maginn, William 160–3, 191, 201, 202, 274
Magnuson, Paul 115–16
Manchester 71, 83, 254
Manchester Heroes 260
Manchester Observer 248, 263
'Manchester Politics' 263
Manchester Yeomanry 124 n., 254
'Manchester Y—Y Valour' 248, 262
Marat 175
Marcet, Alexander 170
Marlow 77, 81,
Marseillaise 20
Marvell, Andrew 209
Masson, David 228–9
materialism, philosophical 177–80
Mathew, George Felton 48, 107, 172, 207 n.
Maurice, Thomas 174 & n.
Mayne, Zachary 247
McFarland, Thomas 127–8 n.
McGann, Jerome J. 5–6, 222, 248–50 nn., 252, 257

Medici, Lorenzo de' 141 n.
Methodists, *see under* dissent
metromania 20–2
Middlesex, wilds of 215
Millard, J. 273
Milnes, Richard Monckton 24 n., 203–5
   and Clarke, C. C. 62–3, 88–9 & n.
   on K's ignorance of the classics 62–3
   researches biography of K 88–9, 203–5
   Life, Letters, and Literary Remains, of John Keats 2, 25, 62–3, 88–9
Milton, John 28, 47, 49, 91, 139, 154, 187, 209
   Paradise Lost 120–1, 193, 196, 198, 231–2, 239 n., 247
Mitchell, Thomas R. 147 n., 152 n., 154 n.
Moir, David Macbeth 228
Molière *or* Poqueline, Jean-Baptiste 160
money 153 & n., 154 n., 158
Montagu, Elizabeth 234
Monthly Magazine 112 n., 187 n.
Monthly Review 129 n., 223
Morris, William 55
Morton, Timothy 84 & n., 145 n.
Mozart, Wolfgang Amadeus 93
Murray, John 12
Museum Criticum 65

Napoleon I, Emperor of the French 2, 52–3, 74, 84, 103–4, 106
Natarajan, Uttara 234 n.
National Library of Scotland 268
Nether Stowey 111, 113
New Forest 99, 261
New Historicism viii, 5
new planet, *see* Uranus
New River 215
new school of poetry 105, 110, 223
new world, conquest of 57–9
Newbury bypass *see* England
Newey, Vincent 4 & n., 6 n., 57–8, 75 n., 92 n., 153 n., 206 n., 249 n.
Newlyn, Lucy 21 n., 196–7
Newman, William 27, 46
Newton, Sir Isaac 35 n., 47 n., 187
North, Christopher, *see* Wilson, John
Northampton 30, 35, 45
   Baptist Meeting at 30–1

Ryland, John Collett at 30–3
nympholepsy 80

Ogilvie, John 240
Ollier, Charles 273–5
   'Sonnet on Sunset' 94
Ollier, James 273
O'Neill, Michael vii
'On the Clerical Character' see *Yellow Dwarf*
outlawry 143–59
   see also England, greenwood; Hood, Robin
Ovid 67, 264
   Metamorphoses 16
Oxford 31, 203 & n.
Oxford English Dictionary 16, 20, 35 n., 122 n., 143, 144 n., 153 n., 188 n., 213, 214, 223, 226–7, 232, 254–5
Oxford University 14, 23, 63

Pacific Ocean 58
paganism 63, 74–8, 85
Paine, Thomas 71, 135, 224
   Rights of Man 71, 97, 145, 146
Pan, cult of 74–8 & nn., 82, 85, 135–6
Paris 71, 146, 175, 176
Parker, W. M. 273–4 n.
Paterno, Lodovico 141 n.
Patmore, P. G. 272
Peacock, Thomas Love 63, 128 n., 211 n., 273, 275
   Maid Marian 134, 144–7
   Rhododaphne 78
Peckham, Morse 252 n.
Penn, William 101
Pennsylvania 114
Pentonville 269
Percy, Thomas, Bishop of Dromore, *Reliques of Ancient English Poetry* 143–4
Perkins, David 3 n.
Perth 211 n.
Peterloo Massacre 2, 50, 53, 72, 75–6, 124 n., 227, 249 n., 254–7, 260, 261
Petre, Olinthus, *see* Maginn, William
Physical Society 174–81 & nn., 187
   see also Cooper, Astley; Guy's Hospital; *Laws of the Physical Society*; Thelwall, John
pigs, ethereal, *see under* Keats, John, Imaginative and Intellectual Life

Pirie, David 61–2 n., 75, 130
Plato 70
Poetry of the Anti-Jacobin 224 & n.
Polidori, John ('Jack') 274
Poole, Thomas 113
Pope, Alexander 23, 215
  The Dunciad 16
  Windsor Forest 153
Porson, Richard, *New Catechism* 98–9
  & n., 156, 261, 266
'Posthumous Life of John Keats' viii &
  n.
  see also Bennett, Andrew; Keats,
    John, Identities of; Posthumous
    Reception
Pound, Ezra 68
Price, Richard 46, 118–19 n.
Priestley, Joseph 178, 187
  and Clarke, John 27–8, 173
  intellectual life 27, 35, 54, 174
  and K 28
  and Ryland, J. C. 30, 35–46
Prince Regent 25, 92 & n., 99–100,
  249 n.
Procter, Bryan Waller ('Barry
  Cornwall') 273, 275
protest, literature of 95–9 & nn.
public schools, *see under* England;
  Eton; Harrow; Rugby;
  Shrewsbury; Westminster;
  Winchester

Quakers, *see under* dissent
Quantock Hills 112
Quarterly Review vii, 20 n., 79 n., 132 n.,
  205, 212, 221, 238, 250, 274

Rabelais, François 160
Rees, Abraham 174 & n.
Rees, George 174 & n.
reform movement, *see* classical culture;
  England, parliamentary reform;
  paganism; Pan, cult of
Revelation 262–3
Reynolds, John Hamilton vii, ix, x, 23,
  24 n., 63, 68 n., 78 & n., 105,
  138–9, 147–8 & n., 151, 153–9 &
  nn., 199–201, 207 n., 209 n., 213–
  14, 217, 222–3, 231, 232, 241–2,
  268, 272, 275
  'To E—, with the Foregoing
    Sonnets' 154–5
  Eden of the Imagination 116, 130 n.

'To a Friend: On Robin Hood'
  147–8, 199–200
*The Garden of Florence and Other
  Poems* 147
'Pulpit Oratory' 78 n., 147 n.
A Recollection 130 n.
'Sonnet to Keats' 138 & n.
'To the Same' 148
Rice, James 23
Richardson, Alan 10, 15 n.
Richardson, John 271
Richardson, William 234, 235
Ricks, Christopher 17 n., 261–2
Ritson, Joseph 148
  Robin Hood: A Collection 145–6 nn.
Robertson, William 46, 53–4
  History of America 54, 56–7, 58, 196
  *History of the Reign of the Emperor
    Charles V* 54
  History of Scotland 54
  see also under Keats, John,
    Contemporaries and Historical
    Figures
Robespierre, Maximilien 56, 70, 84,
  115, 116, 175, 185–6
Robinson, Robert 32
Rome 65, 82 n.
Rossetti, William Michael 168, 217
Rousseau, George 20 n.
Rousseau, Jean-Jacques 135, 224, 227
Royal Society 35
Rugby School 64
Russell, William, Lord 47 n., 48, 109
Ryan, Robert 75 n., 204 & n.
Ryland, John Collett 29–50, 54–5
  and America 45–6, 54
  astronomy, interest in 35–6
  a Baptist 29
  birth 30
  books, recommends 47–8
  at Bristol 30
  and Clarke, John 31–3
  classical scholar 30
  death 33, 34
  and Dyer, George 31–2
  educationalist 29, 34
  energy of 29–31
  at Enfield 33–6, 47–50, 267
  Enfield School, founds 29, 33
  French Revolution, welcomes 46
  friend of liberty 29
  and Georgium Sidus 35–6
  and Hall, Robert 39, 45–6

Ryland, John Collett (*cont.*):
  hebraist, a very good 30
  and Herschel, William 35–6n., 37
  humane 29
  intellectual life 30, 34–6
  and K 33–50
  living orrery 33–4, 36–7, 267
  mathematician 30
  at Northampton 30–3 & n., 35, 45–
    6
  and Priestley, Joseph 30, 35, 46
  publishing, active in 29
  religious fervour 29–31, 34
  republican 29, 45–6, 47, 49
  swallows, departure of 29, 267
  teaching methods 34–6n.
  at Warwick 30, 31
  Character of the Revd James Hervey 35,
    43
  Contemplations on the Beauties of
    Creation 34 & n., 35, 37, 43
  An Easy Introduction to
    Mechanics 36n., 47–8
  Life and Character of King Alfred the
    Great 47n., 108–9
  A Tribute of Honour to the Great and
    Good Men in France 46
Ryland, Joseph 30

St Andrews University 20n.
St John, Henry, First Viscount
  Bolingbroke 104–5
  Letters on the Spirit of Patriotism: On
    the Idea of a Patriot King 101, 105
St Peter's Fields (Manchester) 2, 71,
  74, 83, 254, 256, 260, 261, 264,
  265
  see also Peterloo Massacre
St Thomas's Hospital 169, 174, 176,
  180
Salisbury and Winchester Journal 257 &
  n.
Saturn (planet) 33–4
Schama, Simon 134 & n., 136n.,
  152n.
Schlegel, August von 234, 235
Scotland 268
Scott, John 250–1, 274
Selborne 27
Selden, John
  Table-Talk 101, 104–5 & n.
sensibility 223–9
Severn, Joseph:

on K's meeting with Wordsworth
    84–5
  and paganism 82n., 84–5n.
  'My Tedious Life' 84–5n.
  'Notes on *Adonais*' 82n.
  'On the Adversities of Keats's
    Fame' 69 & n.
Shaftesbury, Antony Ashley Cooper,
  Earl of 240
Shakespeare, William 65, 109, 139,
    142, 154, 209, 225, 230–9 & nn.,
    240–2
  As You Like It 142, 143, 146
  Hamlet 233
  King John 142
  King Lear 38, 230–1, 233, 236–7
  Love's Labour's Lost 233
  Macbeth 124 & n.
  Othello 233
  Richard III 124n.
  Sonnets 232, 233
  The Tempest 157, 263
  Venus and Adonis 233
Shelley, Mary Wollstonecraft, *see*
  Godwin, Mary
Shelley, Percy Bysshe 18n., 50, 63,
    64–5, 167, 168, 211n., 228, 249–
    50, 261, 266, 273
  and Byron, Lord 274–5
  on classical education 66n
  and Godwin, William 66 & n.
  and Greece 77–8 & n.
  and Hunt, J. H. L. 77–8, 85n.,
    88n., 105, 259–60, 268, 274,
    275
  and K 14, 65, 105, 141n., 162,
    167–8, 194n., 228
  at Lake Geneva 274–5
  at Marlow 77–8, 81
  vegetarianism 84–5
  and Webb, Cornelius 269–70n.
  Adonais 12, 162, 228
  Alastor, or the Spirit of Solitude 80n.,
    189n., 194n.
  Hellas 65
  Liberal 268, 274
  Masque of Anarchy 88 & n., 257 & n.,
    262
  Peter Bell the Third 269–70n.
  Revolt of Islam 259–60, 261
  Vindication of Natural Diet 84–5 & n.
Sherwood Forest 141, 144, 145, 146,
    148, 152 & n., 155–6, 200–1

Shrewsbury School 64
Sidmouth, Henry Addington,
    Viscount 255
Sirius 37–8
   see also Herschel, William
Six Acts 249 n.
Smith, Adam 240
Smith, Alexander 228
Smith, Charlotte, *Elegiac Sonnets* 104
Smith, Horace x, 23, 63, 67, 74, 80,
    94, 230
   Amarynthus, the Nympholept 71, 74,
    80, 135–6 & n.
   'On a Green-House' 134–5
   'Nehemiah Muggs' 147 n., 245 n.
   'The Poet among the Trees' 67
Smith, Olivia 220
sociality 109–10, 117–18, 122 n., 125–
    6, 129 n., 130 n., 131, 132, 134
   see also Hunt, J. H. L.
Society of Apothecaries 167
Society for Constitutional
    Information 108–9, 175
South, John Flint 165–6, 170, 172,
    195
Southey, Robert 21, 25, 28, 222, 224
Spa Fields 74, 109, 210–11
Spain, conquests in South America
    57–9
Sparta 70
Spence, Joseph, *Polymetis* 47, 62, 67–8,
    264
Spenser, Edmund:
   The Faerie Queene 41, 89–91, 261,
    266
   *Muiopotmos; or, The Fate of the
    Butterfly* 209–10
   Mutabilitie Cantos 258, 260
Sperry, Stuart 80 n., 187–9, 209 n.
spies, *see* informers
Spy Nosy 115
Steiner, George 21
Stephens, Henry 167–8
Stillinger, Jack 4 n., 5, 80 n., 92,
    189 n., 208, 232, 239 n., 248 n.
Stirling 23
Strand 253–4
Stuarton 211 n.
Studies in Romanticism 6
suburbs x, 74, 124–30, 214–17
   see also England
Surrey Gaol 100
Surrey Institution 128, 142, 183, 241,
    268, 273
susceptibility, as Shakespearian
    quality 234–5
Susquehannah River 114
Swift, Jonathan 160
Swinburne, Algernon Charles 122,
    228
Swinburne, Sir John 122
Sydney, Algernon 28, 49, 101, 102 n.,
    209
   Discourses Concerning Government 47
    & n.

Talfourd, Thomas Noon 275
Tatchell, Molly 100 n.
Taylor and Hessey (publishers) 248,
    268
Taylor, John 24, 42, 188, 195–6
tea-drinking 18, 19 n., 116
Tennyson, Alfred 68
Terror, *see* French Revolution
Test Acts 172–3
'Theatrical Examiner', see *Examiner*
Thelwall, John 1 & n., 28, 32, 129,
    175–81, 224, 255
   at Alfoxden House (1797) 75, 115
   arrested (1794) 179
   attends lectures at Guy's Hospital
    176, 180, 187
   and the *Champion* 255–7
   and Cooper, Astley 175–6, 178, 181
   early life 180
   imprisoned (1794) 175, 179–80
   and K 180–1, 189
   lectures on vitality (1793) 176–9,
    187, 189
   materialism 177–9
   and medical science 176–81 & nn.
   optimism 179
   on Peterloo 255–7, 265
   at Physical Society 176–81 & nn.,
    187
   trial (1794) 175, 180
   white hat, wears 75, 115
   'Anarchists in Military Uniform' 255
   Biographical and Imperial Magazine
    180
   Champion 255–7
   'Digression for the Anatomists' 180
   *Essay Towards a Definition of Animal
    Vitality* 176–8 & nn.
   'Origin of Sensation' 179
   Peripatetic 180

Thelwall, John (*cont.*):
  Poems on Various Subjects 180
  Poems Written in a Close Confinement
    180
  'Prefatory Memoir' 176 & n., 179 &
    n.
Thomson, James 196, 247
  The Seasons 257, 260 n.
Thompson, E. P. 14, 19 n., 55, 113,
    211 n., 254
Thorpe, Clarence De Witt 4
The Times 124 n., 255
Times Higher Education Supplement
    128 n.
Times Literary Supplement 127 n.
Tomline, George, Bishop of Lincoln
    204
Tooke, Andrew, *The Pantheon* 47, 62,
    67–8 & n., 263–5
Townsend, H. 1
Trott, Nicola 218 n.
Tyas, John 255
Tytler, Patrick 272
Tyrell, Frederick 171
'To the Memory of John Hampden'
    102 & n.

Unitarians, *see under* dissent
United Irishmen 123
University of Bologna 18 n.
University of London 42 n.
Uranus 95 & n., 37
  see also Herschel, William; Ryland,
    John Collett

Vane, Sir Henry 28, 47 n., 48
vegetarianism 84–5, 119
Vendler, Helen viii, 263, 266–7
Vergniaud 175
Vincent, Esther J. 171
Virgil 67, 239 n.
vitality, animal, debate about 177–9
  see also Thelwall, John
Voltaire (François Marie Arouet) 223
Vox Stellarum 248

Wakefield, Gilbert 27, 28, 173, 174 &
    n.
Walcott, Derek 68
Wallace, Jennifer 128 n.
Walmsley, Robert 254 n.
Ward, Aileen 3, 7, 26, 90, 194 n.
Warton, Thomas 64, 137 n.

Warwick 30, 31
Washington, George 45, 49
Waterloo, Battle of 9, 60, 71, 227
Watkins, Daniel P. 6–7, 57
Watts, Alaric 274–5
Webb, Cornelius x, 129 & n., 214,
    268–70
  Epistle to a Friend 129 n., 268–9
  'Sonnet I' ('Hard by there is a secret
    greenwood nook') 134 & n., 269
  'Sonnet 2' ('I seek not, want not,
    Peru's buried ore') 269
  'Sonnet 3' ('Written at the Grave of
    Dermody the Poet') 270
  Sonnets . . . with Other Poems 129 n.,
    134 n., 269 nn., 270 n.
  'A Walk Near Town' 212
Webb, Timothy 78 n.
Wellington, Arthur Wellesley, Duke
    of 74, 249 n.
West, Benjamin, *Death on the Pale
    Horse* 230–1
Westminster School 67 n.
Wheatley, Kim 10 n., 13 n.
White, Gilbert 27
White, Holt 27
white, as reformist emblem 72–7 &
    nn., 115
  see also Keats, John, Imaginative and
    Intellectual Life; Thelwall, John
White Hat 75–6 & n.
Williams, Helen Maria 56, 236
Williams, Raymond 15 n.
Wilson, John (Christopher North) 1,
    12, 274 n.
Winchester 184, 195, 252–3, 257
Winchester School 67 n.
Wolfson, Susan J. 63 n., 171 n., 229
Wollstonecraft, Mary 11, 28, 32, 56,
    135
  Vindication of the Rights of Woman 11
women 11, 16, 63, 225
Woodhouse, Richard 100 n., 138 n.,
    202, 203 n., 246–7, 261–2
Woodhouse, William Pitter 100 n.
Woolf, Virginia viii & n.
Wordsworth, Dorothy 75, 115
Wordsworth, William 15 n., 21, 23, 28,
    32, 49–50, 56, 57 n., 68, 75, 76–
    7, 95, 127–8 n., 158, 196, 215–16
    & n., 217–18, 222, 228, 237,
    239 n., 269–70 n.
  at Alfoxden 75, 115

an Anglican 77
and Barbauld, Anna Letitia 97
and *Blackwood's Magazine* 215 n.,
    268, 273
a classical poet 77, 227
and Coleridge, S. T. 215 n., 268, 273
egotism of 83–4 n., 156
and French Revolution 185–6
and Godwin, William 185
and Hazlitt, William 83–4 n.
and K 49–50, 57 n., 68, 76–7, 83–
    5 n., 118 n., 156, 158, 184–7 & n.,
    190, 210, 217–18, 222, 239 n.,
    241, 244–5, 246–7
and modern poetry 68, 77
and pagan religion 76–8
on poetry and science 184–7 & n.
at Paris (1792) 176
a Tory 77, 118 & n.
on vegetarianism 84–5
Descriptive Sketches 218
Evening Walk 218
The Excursion 63, 76–7, 83, 118
'Expostulation and Reply' 235, 244
'Goody Blake and Harry Gill' 236
'Great Men' 49, 50 n.
'Immortality' ode 138, 210
'It is not to be thought of' 50 n.
Laodamia 63, 78, 83
'Last of the Flock' 236
'London, 1802' 49, 50 n.
Lyrical Ballads 222, 236, 244–5;
    'Advertisement' to (1798) 21,
    223; 'Preface' to (1802) 117,
    184, 186–7
'A Poet's Epitaph' 184–5
The Prelude 25, 77, 113, 185–6, 192,
    242
Ruined Cottage 97
Salisbury Plain 96
'Simon Lee' 236
'The Tables Turned' 186, 244
'Tintern Abbey' 68, 111, 127, 190,
    196–8
'We are Seven' 223

Worrall, David 265 n.
Wright, Herbert G. 4 n.
Wright, John 81
Wylie, Ian 178 n.

Yeats, W. B. 208
Yellow Dwarf: a Weekly Miscellany ix, 76,
    78 nn., 82–3, 116, 147–8 & n.
Young, Edward 196

Z x, 10 & n., 13–14, 15, 16, 18, 19–
    20, 23, 119, 129–30, 202, 226–7,
    269
    anxiety of 14
    and Burke 20 n.
    caricatures Cockneys 20 n., 214,
        227–8
    cultural agenda of 23
    cultural authority 22
    and Hunt, J. H. L. 119, 121–3,
        127–30, 129 n., 132, 204–5, 206,
        214–17, 226
    identity of 270
    and K, attacks 11, 13 & n., 14, 15,
        20 n., 22, 23–5, 60–1, 63, 65, 69,
        79, 109–10, 129 n., 161–2, 163,
        168, 202, 205, 206, 214, 219,
        226–7, 250–1, 266
    and Lamb, Charles 227
    paranoid 10 n., 13 n.
    pathological 20 n.
    polemic reinforced by Levinson,
        Marjorie 13–14
    scurrilous blaggard 122
    and Surrey Institution 268
    on *The Story of Rimini* 20 n., 119–22,
        132, 134
    on Webb, Cornelius 129 n.
    on Wordsworth, William 127 & n.,
        129 n., 215 n., 227
    see also *Blackwood's Magazine*;
        Cockney School Essays; Keats,
        John, Identities of; Posthumous
        Reception; Lockhart, John
        Gibson